SAGE was founded in 1965 by Sara Miller McCune to support the dissemination of usable knowledge by publishing innovative and high-quality research and teaching content. Today, we publish more than 750 journals, including those of more than 300 learned societies, more than 800 new books per year, and a growing range of library products including archives, data, case studies, reports, conference highlights, and video. SAGE remains majority-owned by our founder, and on her passing will become owned by a charitable trust that secures our continued independence.

Los Angeles | London | Washington DC | New Delhi | Singapore

Cognitive Planning and Executive Functions

Cognitive Planning and Executive Functions
Applications in Management and Education

J.P. Das
Sasi B. Misra

www.sagepublications.com
Los Angeles • London • New Delhi • Singapore • Washington DC

Copyright © J.P. Das and Sasi B. Misra, 2015

All rights reserved. No part of this book may be reproduced or utilized in any form or by any means, electronic or mechanical, including photocopying, recording or by any information storage or retrieval system, without permission in writing from the publisher.

First published in 2015 by

SAGE Publications India Pvt Ltd
B1/I-1 Mohan Cooperative Industrial Area
Mathura Road, New Delhi 110 044, India
www.sagepub.in

SAGE Publications Inc
2455 Teller Road
Thousand Oaks, California 91320, USA

SAGE Publications Ltd
1 Oliver's Yard, 55 City Road
London EC1Y 1SP, United Kingdom

SAGE Publications Asia-Pacific Pte Ltd
3 Church Street
#10-04 Samsung Hub
Singapore 049483

Published by Vivek Mehra for SAGE Publications India Pvt Ltd, typeset in 10/12 pts Adobe Garamond Pro by Diligent Typesetter, Delhi and printed at Saurabh Printers Pvt Ltd, New Delhi.

Library of Congress Cataloging-in-Publication Data

Das, J. P. (Jagannath Prasad)
  Cognitive planning and executive functions : applications in management and education / J.P. Das and Sasi B. Misra.
    pages cm
  Includes bibliographical references and index.
  1. Cognitive psychology. 2. Planning—Psychological aspects. 3. Cognition. 4. Decision making. 5. Management. I. Misra, Sasi B. II. Title.
  BF201.D368   153—dc23   2015   2014034739

ISBN: 978-93-515-0036-0 (HB)

The SAGE Team: Supriya Das, Vandana Gupta, Anju Saxena and Rajinder Kaur

For J.P.'s brothers
Dr Jadunath Prasad Das
Dr Radhanath Prasad Das
And Sasi's wife, Susama and their children
Dr Sarthak Misra
Dr Shalini Misra

Thank you for choosing a SAGE product! If you have any comment, observation or feedback, I would like to personally hear from you. Please write to me at contactceo@sagepub.in

—Vivek Mehra, Managing Director and CEO,
SAGE Publications India Pvt. Ltd, New Delhi

Bulk Sales

SAGE India offers special discounts for purchase of books in bulk. We also make available special imprints and excerpts from our books on demand.

For orders and enquiries, write to us at

Marketing Department
SAGE Publications India Pvt. Ltd
B1/I-1, Mohan Cooperative Industrial Area
Mathura Road, Post Bag 7
New Delhi 110044, India
E-mail us at marketing@sagepub.in

Get to know more about SAGE, be invited to SAGE events, get on our mailing list. Write today to marketing@sagepub.in

This book is also available as an e-book.

Contents

List of Tables ix
List of Figures xi
Preface xiii
Acknowledgments xv
Introduction xvii

Part I
Concepts

1. Cognitive Planning in the Context of PASS Theory   3
2. Models of Planning: Past and Current   19

Part II
Planning and Executive Functions and the Brain

3. Deconstructing Executive Functions   43
4. Executive Functions, Planning, and Intelligence: Can Brain Localization Help?   54

Part III
Attention, Planning, and Executive Functions: Assessment

5. Separating Planning and Attention   71
6. Assessments: History and Selected Studies   96
7. Planning and Executive Function Tests: Ready for Use   116

Part IV
Applications in Management and Education

8. Rational and Irrational in Managerial Behavior   163
9. Cognitive Competence and Managerial Behavior   181
10. The Influence of Emotions and Will   195

Part V
Enhancement of Educational Achievement and Decision Making

11. Planning in Writing: Compositions and Oral Narratives — 211
12. Verbalization Enhances Planning: Application in Education — 224
13. Math Learning — 235
14. Two Programs for Cognitive Strategy Training — 252
15. Planning and Decision Making: Training for Enhancement — 271
16. Revisits and Reprise — 285

Bibliography — 297
Index — 322
About the Authors — 327

List of Tables

6.1	Results of Exploratory Factor Analysis	111
6.2	Do the Three Factors Form One Factor? Yes, They Do, Which Is Planning	112
6.3	Do the Planning Tasks Form One Factor?	113
6.4	Do the Attention Tasks Form One Factor?	113
9.1	Intercorrelations between Essay Ratings	192
11.1	Factor Analysis of Oral and Written Composition Rating Scale Scores	220

List of Figures

1.1	PASS Theory of Intelligence	6
2.1	Plans and Problems	31
2.2	Planning as a Function of the Frontal Lobes	38
2.3	Planning Process Path Diagram	39
A4.1	Hot (Shaded) and Cold (Unshaded) Decision-making Brain Locations	65
A4.2	Prefrontal Cortex Divisions	65
A4.3	(a) Brain Diagram: Limbic System	66
	(b) Brain Diagram: Prefrontal Cortex	66
6.1	The Percentages of Placements Based on Climbing, Combination, and Nonfunctional (Pattern, False Pattern, Trial and Error) Search Methods on Items 5 and 6	105
9.1	Planning Expressed through an Executive's Behavior	191
11.1	Planning and Knowledge Base in Writing	214
11.2	From Cognitive Planning to Quality Narratives	218
13.1	Math Proficiency Model	238
13.2	Attentional Control in Geary's Model	239
13.3	Basic Math Skills	248
13.4	The Five Modules	250

Preface

Cognitive Planning and Executive Functions is a sequel to an earlier book, *Cognitive Planning: The Psychological Basis of Intelligent Behavior,* published in 1996. That book was written at a time when the cognitive revolution was almost over; no longer struggling for recognition, it was a time to enjoy the fruits of the revolution.

A new look at intelligence has emerged since. We are ready to replace "intelligence" by a variety of cognitive processes. Of these, Cognitive Planning is regarded as the major cognitive process, actually a "meta process." It acts on information that has been gathered and synthesized. It is the most important function of the frontal lobes, particularly assigned to problem-solving and decision-making. Two disciplines among several others use cognitive planning and strategies for executing plans—Education whose main concern is Learning and its propagation, and Administrative Behavior, a broad spectrum that includes Management. This book is relevant for both of them.

A further new development is neuroscience. Cognitive neuroscience combines the dual approach to understanding human behavior—Symbolic and Physiological, as Simon (1992) suggested. Both approaches are now accepted as normal and natural ways of understanding underlying cognitive processes in education and administrative behavior. Both disciplines also have developed an interest in cognition and neurological functions; in education for facilitating learning; and in management, decision-making which is "the heart of administration"—Herbert Simon's notable book *Administrative Behavior* has the subtitle *Decision-Making Processes in Administrative Organizations.*

We began writing *Cognitive Planning and Executive Functions* 15 years after the publication of our previous book, *Cognitive Planning.* During that time, neuroscience, especially cognitive neuroscience, influenced almost all important disciplines that study human behavior. Of special relevance for our book's topic are *Educating the Human Brain* by Posner and Rothbart (2007), and propagation of neuroeconomics, and social neuroscience, for example. Our present book, therefore, takes advantage of knowledge available now in cognitive science and neuroscience, particularly neuropsychology. The next generation of books on Executive Function and Planful behavior would emerge from genomics, specially sociogenomics, as we attempt to understand the role that genes play in shaping the evolution of neural circuits in the brain that influence social behavior. This would be a co-evolution of the technological, social, and cultural brain beginning at the molecular level.

Returning to the contents of this book, although much of the material is new, the book does of course contain a significant amount of information from standard sources that have existed prior to the neuroscience revolution. It attempts to be of interest to a wide range of readers.

The result is a book that has three books in one; each is predominantly directed at one of the three groups of readers—those interested in Cognitive Psychology, Education, and Management. Cognitive Psychology and Education are sisters; thus this group of readers will be interested in all of the chapters except three that are mostly about management—the roles of managers, satisficing distinguished from optimization of outcome, training senior executives for decision-making to balance rational and analytical data on the one hand, and affective and predicament situations on the other. Similarly, students in management schools may not be interested in chapters on training for reading and comprehension, and children learning math. However, all readers should have an understanding of the theory and concepts (first two chapters) and the last one that revisits important issues in the book. Education students and those interested in management may skip reading the two chapters on physiological underpinnings of the main concepts in the book—Planning, Inhibition, Shifting, Working Memory, and Intelligence. On the other hand, they may not; we have written this even for the general reader. In fact not for the experts who may find it slightly boring.

"Overview" in Introduction is the best guide for selective reading of the book; we think it is sufficiently detailed for enabling readers for selecting the chapters that would be of interest for them. One other related point: it will be noticed that some information is introduced later in the book rather than in earlier chapters, and some has been repeated. The reason is as follows: Since some readers may not read the entire book, and choose to read only a few chapters instead, important information from previous chapters that are essential for understanding a chapter at hand has been repeated.

J.P. Das
University of Alberta
November 2013

Acknowledgments

I wish to acknowledge the contribution of people who have enabled me to write the book. John Kirby read most of the chapters in an earlier draft of the manuscript. His comments in each chapter made me work hard to revise the book. I found myself cursing him under my breath, although in every page his remarks were extremely helpful.

Rauno Parrila should have been a co-author of the book as we had planned it together some four years back; he was also a co-author with me of the previous book, *Cognitive Planning*. However, his interests had changed—reading and related topics in which he is quite a respected researcher. In addition to assuming other responsibilities of a senior professor, he just could not have enough time to concentrate on writing the new book with me. However, he read each chapter of the book before its final draft was prepared. He said that it was not easy for him to be critical while commenting on the chapters and communicating his remarks to me. I have tried to rewrite some parts of the book in light of his suggestions. However, he rewrote the chapter on Writing and Planning for the book (Chapter 11).

John Kirby, and 20 years later, Rauno Parrila did their PhD with me; often the thought has crossed my mind that they were paying off their debts by working diligently on the manuscript of this book. Whatever flaws you may find in the book are mine in spite of their efforts to revise it.

Sasi B. Misra, the co-author of this book, is also a former student of mine; we worked together on a few chapters on management besides preparing the end part of the book. During my trips to India, we often discussed the contents of the book.

I must also thank Jerry Carlson of University of California, Riverside, and H. Carl Haywood of Vanderbilt University for reading some parts of the book, as well as Professor Zhang Houcan of Beijing Normal University, and several students, including my granddaughter Silpi Das, for helping with editing the manuscript during the long time it has taken to write it.

Sasi Misra wishes to thank Dr Dinesh Awasthi, Director, EDI, for supporting and funding his visit to Bhubaneswar to work with me on the book.

He also wishes to thank Ashok Madnani, EDI, for his invaluable professional services in preparing the end part of the book.

J.P. Das
University of Alberta
November 2013

Introduction

A plan is any hierarchical process in the organism that can control the order in which a sequence of operations is to be performed. A plan is, for an organism, essentially the same as a program for a computer. (Miller, Galanter, & Pribram, 1960)

Almost half a century after the publication of the landmark book we have many more reasons to believe that human plans are not always rationally driven, nor are they impervious to unexpected influences of emotions. Although we know that reason and emotion cannot be regarded as opposites of each other, computer programs are rational. In contrast, emotions have a place in human behavior that unpredictably upsets plans. Additionally, most of our plans are influenced by unexplained inputs from unconscious sources. Finally, we may admit that our free will is not really the *force that causes action*. Can we nevertheless override an action in midstream through contemplation and arduous practice of inhibition and mindfulness? Obviously we can.

We introduce the topics of this book within the broad framework of questions that are asked in regard to explaining human behavior. We have chosen David Brooks, a journalist who is curious about human behavior, to raise the question. Brooks (2011) tells us of a conversation with Walter Mischel, a representative of psychology who made him curious—the conversation provides a broad background for the issues that concern cognitive planning and executive functions (EFs):

1. The power of unconscious processes and the ability to change them.
2. The power of emotion as a central piece in reasoning.
3. The third is the deep interpenetration of people—it simply acknowledges that we are social animals; that our interactions with people, or what others might think of us, penetrate our behavior.
4. The list does not explicitly mention the unmistakable power of context and the environment in which the behavior occurs. None of human prowess, not even intelligence which receives exaggerated respect, flourishes when it is not given a favorable context that includes the social cultural history of the group or community, as well as the biographical history of an individual's life's experience.

5. Given a chance, the veteran psychologist Mischel would like to know more about epigenesis, the most exciting area. This is especially true in the case of changes in expression of genes brought about by environmental handling of the organism. What is activated in the DNA or deactivated in the DNA? How can social events such as licking and grooming turn a rat that has been bred to be hostile into a sweetie pie?—that is important to think about. Brooks even believes that the real reason we succeed is the strength of our unconscious:

> The human brain can take in 11 million pieces of information in a single moment. Yet even by generous estimates, an individual is consciously aware of maybe 40 of them. While the conscious brain is often logical and linear, the unconscious is more sensitive, more judgmental, and more perceptive (Lewis, 2011). One's emotions, intuitions, character traits, genetic inclinations and biases are located in our unconscious inner-mind. (Brooks, 2011)

We will explore the topic of decision making within the context of unconscious and conscious influences on Planning and Executive Functions in our book. We identify four strands or topics: (1) The role of rationality and emotion; (2) the search for evidence of the Planning/Executive Functions in the brain; (3) the origin of Planning/Executive Functions and their operations demonstrated in measurement of these functions; and (4) improvement of Planning/Executive Functions which lead to better performance in both educational achievements and managerial decision making.

Our first topic explains the pull between rationality and affect in decision making. Humans do not make decisions that are purely rational, nor do they make them based solely on emotion. Rather, they make decisions based on both of these factors in differing proportions, based on what is to be decided. Researchers have conducted observational studies which identify that both rationality and affect influence decisions. Therefore, this knowledge does not come solely from first-hand accounts, but is also identified in third-person observation. In the article, "Making Management Decisions: The Role of Intuition and Emotion," Simon (1987) clearly recognized the role of intuition and emotion in making managerial decisions. This interaction between reason and affect is the first major strand that can be detected in several chapters of this book.

Researchers have studied the involvement of these two factors at the cognitive and behavioral levels. Furthermore, they have examined evidence that identifies brain activity associated with reasoning and affect. The evidence is discussed in Part II. Conditions under which failure of logic may occur and intuitions that may misguide planning and decision making are also presented. Managers may be cautioned to examine their decisions when these conditions are detected.

We are, however, aware of the pitfalls of attributing cognitions and behaviors to their neural correlates. New technologies for investigating neural changes may receive unconditional respect. For example, a researcher may consider an anticipated neural change in a narrow area of the brain following cognitive training as an infallible evidence for the efficacy of training, neglecting to gather behavioral and cognitive indices.

Do not try to narrowly localize a psychological function in the brain. Luria (1966) was one of the earliest neuropsychologists to suggest broad functional organizations in the brain. Shimamura (2010) supported this idea by describing narrow localizationists as "naïve." Given below are some tips and cautionary notes:

- Understand that neural events do not *cause* psychological phenomenon. Simon (1992) argued that explanations occur at many levels. The laws of the molecular level do not hold at the level of neural networks, and certainly not at the behavioral level.
- The overarching goal of correlating biology with psychological factors is to identify the mapping between brain function and mental processing (Poldrack, 2010).
- Gonsalves and Cohen (2010) made an important suggestion. They argued that research should show how neuroimaging data have provided unique insights not only into brain organization but also into the organization of the mind (p. 744).

Our third topic in this book is an examination of the origin of the planning and EFs that are engaged in problem solving and how they should be measured. Popper (1972) explained that the origin of these functions comes from three worlds: World 1 is the world of physical objects; World 2 is the world of subjective experiences comprising conscious and unconscious states and psychological dispositions; and World 3 is the world of cultural products, such as language, theories in science, and objects of art, that human beings have created. Cultural predispositions and the individual's own social history impact on decision making. The cultural–historical framework following the overarching approach identified with Vygotsky (1986) is readily apparent throughout this book.

Conceptualization apart, the book presents assessment of Planning and Executive Functions as a pivotal issue. An entire chapter (Chapter 6) is devoted to assessment. In the subsequent chapters, we discuss specific tools that are used in assessment of cognitive competence in various contexts.

Lastly, a serious interest in improvement of planning and EFs that lead to better performance in both educational achievements and managerial decision making is an obvious strand running through the book. The last section of the book specifically discusses it at some length. Rather than didactic teaching of rules, we recommend exploration and discovery as desirable methods for cognitive tutoring.

We will end this introduction by referring to David Brooks' (2011) book, *The Social Animal*, in which he talked about the *importance of brain research*:

> Gordon Brown, when he was Prime Minister of the United Kingdom, was in New York for some United Nations meetings and invited me for coffee at the consulate ... I was describing the brain research and he said, "Well. What are the policy implications?" I really didn't have much of an answer for him so the book flew out of that question. This points out the fact that we are not so much individuals, but we are very deeply interconnected. (as cited in Lewis, 2011, pp. 28–29)

The key concept in management decision making probably is sharing experience, as we are very deeply connected individuals. Our book explores the ways and means of promoting this attitude in its final chapters. At the base of exploration is the role of metacognition in human social interaction:

> Through our willingness to discuss with others the reasons for our actions and perceptions, we overcome our lack of direct access to the underlying cognitive processes. This creates the potential for us to build more accurate accounts of the world and of ourselves. I suggest, therefore, that explicit metacognition is a uniquely human ability that has evolved through its enhancement of collaborative decision-making. (Frith, 2012, p. 2213)

Overview and Summaries

This book is organized into five parts and each part comprises several chapters in order to examine the four major topics of the book, respectively. Part I consists of Chapters 1 and 2. It mainly provides a background for understanding the concepts of Cognitive Processing as it subsumes Planning, Problem-solving, and Executive Functions. Part II has two chapters, Chapters 3 and 4. The neuro-correlates of Planning/Executive Functions are reviewed in this part. The following part, Part III, includes Chapters 5–7, and these three chapters mainly focus on the development, uses, and assessment of Planning/Executive Functions. Part IV consists of Chapters 8–10, which focus on applications in managerial decision making and education. Lastly, Chapters 11–16 form Part V and explore how to boost decision making and planning.

Part I: Concepts

CHAPTER 1. COGNITIVE PLANNING IN THE CONTEXT OF PASS THEORY

In Chapter 1, we describe the Planning, Attention, and Simultaneous and Successive (PASS) processes. We also discuss and describe other theories of intelligence as they relate to the PASS processes. The PASS theory was built on the foundational neuropsychological work of Luria, who in turn studied Pavlov's theories of excitation and inhibition. Pavlov carried out experiments to support that even dogs differ in their predisposition to excitation and inhibition, and their inclination to shift from one to the other when conditions demand it. These are the rudimentary components required in human cognitive planning to which Luria added the important role played by language in higher mental activities, including planning.

In this chapter, we identify how PASS processes, including planning and executive functioning, may be presented in the brain. We use current research in attention deficit disorders and reading acquisition to highlight the localization of PASS functions. Finally, we suggest that a comprehensive theory of cognitive functions should have instruments for assessment. EFs, which are best described as a fusion of planning and attention, are in need of assessment devices. We explore this in subsequent chapters, because we find that in searching for suitable assessment instruments, we examine and clarify the concept of EF.

CHAPTER 2. MODELS OF PLANNING: PAST AND CURRENT

Planning, the first component of the PASS theory, is a broader category than problem-solving. According to Popper (1972), problems may arise from three sources: the physical world, the psychological world, or the cultural world. Human beings are either confronted with problems that they must solve, or they select a problem from their environment. Problems can be broken into two main types: those that require logical deliberations and those that require emotional responses. Yet, categorization of problems is more complex, because all problems require logical and affective responses to some degree. Following selection, we may create a plan for its resolution. The plan is guided by (a) one's goals and objectives and (b) the internal conditions, such as moods, personality, and predispositions, of the individual.

We present a generic analysis of plans for problem solving and suggest a template where the physical, the psychological, and the cultural worlds exist at both the top and bottom of the diagram (Figure 2.1). Sandwiched between these two repeated templates are the selection of a problem (arising out of the problem field), its internal representation, and an action plan for problem resolution. Each person has goals and objectives that are influenced by their internal predispositions. The combination of goals and objectives and internal predispositions leads the person to a plan of action. In this way our goals and objectives shape our actions as much as our urge to act.

Part II: Planning and Executive Functions and the Brain

Chapter 3. Deconstructing Executive Functions

EFs and Planning are separate but dependent functions. Executing a plan and regulating the response thus executed are the general functions of an executive. On the other hand, planning or problem solving involves at least four distinct activities: (a) finding a problem; (b) generating strategies for its solution; (c) selecting an appropriate strategy; and (d) executing the planned action.

EFs have successful outcomes when shifting strategies according to situational demands, and old habits of mind or pre-potent responses that are now maladaptive are inhibited. Is EF distinct from intelligence? The two elements of EF, Shifting and Inhibition, have negligible correlations with intelligence. Is working memory a part of general intelligence? It appears to be so and thus not a core component unique to EF.

The concept that combines both planning and attention is EF. It aspires to organize the constructs of working memory capacity and general fluid intelligence, and relate these to the functions of prefrontal cortex (PFC). The two PASS processes, Planning and Attention, provide measures of EF through the cognitive assessment system (CAS). Luria had observed planning to be located in the prefrontal area of the frontal lobes in the brain. His original observation has been confirmed by brain-imaging studies that continue to focus on this area. In conclusion of this chapter, it is suggested that the search for specific regions of the brain for cognitive functions, such as Intelligence, Working Memory, EF and Executive-Attention, may advance our understanding of their relationships.

Both logical and rational problem solving, and emotional problem solving require the use of planning. EFs are distinct from intelligence measured by standardized IQ-type tests and include some of the following variables: preparation for action, inhibition control, self-monitoring, and flexibility and shifting of mental sets. Although all of these require planning in order to be carried out, brain research has found that EFs do not lie in the frontal lobes where planning resides, but rather in the back of the brain where consciousness is found. Planning and consciousness are two unique human brain functions.

CHAPTER 4. EXECUTIVE FUNCTIONS, PLANNING, AND INTELLIGENCE: CAN BRAIN LOCALIZATION HELP?

The brain region specifically linked to EF is the lateral prefrontal cortex (LPFC) with its two distinct functional blocks: the ventrolateral and the dorsolateral. All decision making and planning involve both of these sites to a greater or lesser extent. Yet each of these blocks is associated with a specific task. The ventral part is generally engaged in retrieval and selection of information in order for it to be used in carrying out a planned sequence of activities. The medial part of the ventrolateral block contains emotions and the so-called social brain. The dorsolateral part, in contrast, is the seat of reasoning. It is linked to higher levels of planning.

Some researchers have suggested that general intelligence is found in both the frontal regions and the posterior regions, such as the parietal area. Thus, executive functioning and general intelligence could have locations in the brain that overlap substantially. However, posterior parts of the brain appear to be involved only when executive demands are minimal. Working memory is not strictly an EF, although it is in specific regions of the PFC. Working memory will be viewed as a part of intelligence, separate from executive functioning.

Part III: Attention, Planning, and Executive Functions: Assessment

CHAPTER 5. SEPARATING PLANNING AND ATTENTION

Planning and attention are separate but interdependent areas of PASS theory. While planning is used in problem solving, among other functions, attention is a mental process by which an individual selectively registers some stimuli while ignoring others. The distinction between planning and attention is supported by the study of atypical cases, which include attention deficit/hyperactivity disorder (ADHD), fetal alcohol syndrome (FAS), and autism.

Individuals with autism perform poorly in tests of executive functioning. This is even true for those with Asperger's syndrome, the least severe form of autism. Individuals with FAS have deficits in planning operations. Yet individuals with attention deficits can be placed into two distinct groups: those who are only inattentive (ADD) and those who are hyperactive and impulsive (ADHD). Although individuals with autism and individuals with ADHD may both be weak in executive functioning, these observations are based on meta-analyses. A closer examination of those with autism may not support executive functioning as the distinct marker for autism. Weaknesses in other cognitive processes may be responsible for autism.

Chapter 6. Assessments: History and Selected Studies

In this chapter we present a variety of tests that are used currently to measure planning and executive functioning. EFs are conceptually presented as processes that require set-shifting and inhibition of a habitual response.

One test that is described at length is the Crack-the-Code test. It measures higher order planning as well as complex problem solving. Crack-the-Code measures deliberate planning as opposed to tests that measure affective planning and decision making. We also describe the Predicament test (Channon & Crawford, 1999, 2004), which consists of several scenarios that involve affective rather than deliberate planning and decision making. Lastly, we include another possible measure of planning, Composition tests for children.

We have described each of these tests in sufficient detail so that this chapter can also be used as an independent testing manual for selected tests of executive functioning.

Chapter 7. Planning and Executive Function Tests: Ready for Use

This chapter provides supplementary documents for the tests in Chapter 6.

Part IV: Applications in Management and Education

Chapter 8. Rational and Irrational in Managerial Behavior

In the business world, top managers must perform a variety of duties that require problem solving, decision making, planning, and goal setting. Yet, managers differ in their abilities to make decisions. The chapter's focus is on cognitive processes that lead some managers to continuously make excellent managerial decisions. Two of the reasons for excellence were that top managers had a superior knowledge base and a superior generic competence for planning. Apart from cognitive factors, motivation plays an important role. However, the motivation behind reasoning may be a liability at times since it can distort rationality. Decision making can be marred by the failure of logic that is forced upon managers because they are required to take decisions under conditions of uncertainty.

In order to improve one's performance in decision making, can strategies be taught? We suggest that teaching strategies through formal instruction will not be effective. The alternative to formal instruction is teaching through experience. While many managers would be able to execute the programs once these are laid out in front of them, only a few would exhibit anticipatory programming, flexible use of information, and consistent changes in their plans as they approached a goal.

We take up the training for enhancement of planning and decision making again in Chapter 12.

CHAPTER 9. COGNITIVE COMPETENCE AND MANAGERIAL BEHAVIOR

Decision making and planning require a rational attitude, which must be objective, but humanistic approaches foster or facilitate innovative and creative solutions rather than rational and objective ones. A good planner is one who can anticipate problems in securing a goal, especially when the goal is beneficial for the whole organization. A good planner also anticipates action.

Empirical studies reported that when studying a group of executives in New York, their supervisors' ratings and their performance in the Crack-the-Code test were predictive of each other. In a different study of executives in eastern India, significant correlation is found between supervisor's ratings and planning component in a composition.

A schematic diagram is presented at the end of the chapter; it shows the following connections: Planning is the common pathway connected to biological and cultural sources. It is expressed through an executive's behavior, supervisor's rating of an executive behavior, and tests of essay composition and the Crack-the-Code test.

CHAPTER 10. THE INFLUENCE OF EMOTIONS AND WILL

This chapter provides a brief introduction on emotions following Herbert Simon's suggestion of the role of synthetic, intuitive thinking. Next, it considers conscious will: Is it a force, or a feeling, or is it an illusion?

Moving on, the chapter briefly examines the complex concept of consciousness and its role in decision making from the Euro-American and the East Indian perspectives. Is there a little man, a homunculus, who makes decisions?

It then considers an existing theory of Planning as a cognitive process. Although planning is already discussed in several previous chapters, the context for discussion is provided by a case history of an entrepreneur. It examines and highlights the infusion of emotional determinants at each step of the decision-making process of the individual.

A special consideration is given to *satisficing*: As you regulate and execute the plan, and anticipate the difficulties that might arise while executing the plan, your representation of the problem keeps on getting adjusted. Given the circumstances, what would be the most satisfying outcome, as opposed to the best one?

The chapter ends as it begins, with a discussion of analytic and synthetic modes. At the end is its beginning, paraphrasing a line from *Four Quartets* by T.S. Eliot. Dual systems variously named as rational and emotional, reason and affect, System 1 and System 2 are essentially alternative names. One of them is deliberate, slow, and rule-bound thinking; the other is an associative, automatic, and fast system. Each has a distinct location in the brain that, if proved beyond doubt, would have significant implications in understanding decision making related to neuroeconomics.

Part V: Enhancement of Educational Achievement and Decision Making

Chapter 11. Planning in Writing: Compositions and Oral Narratives

The first part of the chapter is concerned with writing. Composition of an essay or a narrative requires all the major executive processes. An overall plan needs to be maintained while writing an essay (such as the strategic essay described in Chapter 9) or composing a narrative. Models of writing as these relate to language and planning are presented, including the views of Vygotsky and Luria. Contemporary views of the gap between the intention of a writer and the written product are also discussed. The writer is aware of an unseen audience, and hence creates a mock reader as pen is put on paper.

Speaking and writing are therefore quite different; we speak to listener(s), and have much less time to plan and perform grammatically as there is a demand to continue speaking. This is one of the major differences between speaking and written narratives—speaking allows inadequate time to go back and plan as we do in writing.

As expected, studies reported in the chapter show that good writers are indeed better in tests of Planning than poor ones. However, in regard to children's writing, a certain degree of maturity in writing must develop, as by Grade 6, before the impact of cognitive processes on writing can be discerned.

Differences between oral and written narratives are considered in the last part of the chapter. Both kinds of output by the same participants were judged in terms of quality of composition using five skills: expression, organization, individuality, grammar, and wording. Surprisingly, the two narratives loaded on two different factors. Unplanned oral narratives are spontaneous as in extemporaneous speech. A model for structural equation depicting the relationships among the Planning measures on the one hand and written narrative production on the other was proposed.

Chapter 12. Verbalization Enhances Planning: Application in Education

Verbalization boosts Planning because it allows one to formulate strategies for solving a similar problem and regulates activity through one's own overt or covert speech. Several experiments are presented in support of how verbalization helps poor planners. As a theoretical context for the verbalization procedure, the method of dynamic assessment or interactive assessment is then introduced. Of special interest in these studies is the finding that the positive effect of concurrent, overt verbalization boosts problem solving specifically for poor planners, and not for those who have adequate planning although both groups have low performance prior to verbalization. Overt verbalization also seems to prevent quick deterioration of detailed visual information.

Chapter 13. Math Learning

Planning helps children do mathematics. In order to approach the teaching of mathematics within the framework of Planning, there are some questions we must first ask. For example, what cognitive processes are involved in mathematics? Can the benefits of verbalization be extended to teaching mathematics? Processing strategies are obviously important for competent performance in both reading and math. Specific issues in math performance are discussed, including the foundational concepts of number line, size, and value. Math disability is also reviewed, in conjunction or as separate from reading disability.

Selected experiments on arithmetic improvement through verbalization are summarized in order to facilitate planning. Interactive assessment and cognitive intervention including self-generated verbalization are constructive ways for enhancement of Planning. The studies show how a dynamic approach targets the cognitive processing of the individual learner, as well as the construction of both test material and testing situation.

CHAPTER 14. TWO PROGRAMS FOR COGNITIVE STRATEGY TRAINING

We present two intervention programs in this chapter: PREP for reading and COGENT for getting ready for learning in school. The programs have been used in several experimental and clinical studies and have proved to be effective. Our aim in this chapter is to discuss the essential features of the tasks that are derived from the theoretical base, PASS, and especially, from Vygotsky and Luria as discussed in the two previous chapters on verbalization. An important feature common to both verbalization, PREP and COGENT, is the use of an interactive or dynamic approach that facilitates reflective discussion. Inasmuch as it utilizes dynamic assessment and interactive learning for strategy training, the chapter has a focus relevant to Planning and EF.

Together with the previous chapter on writing and math, the present one on reading and comprehension showcases the application of strategy training in *education*. We then pass on to cognitive training in management in the next chapter.

CHAPTER 15. PLANNING AND DECISION MAKING: TRAINING FOR ENHANCEMENT

This is the last of the group of three chapters, that is then followed by Chapter 16 that presents an overall review of the book. This is especially applicable to management, whereas the two previous chapters have obvious importance for education.

Decision making precedes an impending action, whereas planning is anticipatory decision making. Is ventromedial prefrontal cortex (VMPFC) the location of decision making in the brain? VMPFC is the area mostly associated with risk, fear, and the economic value of decisions. Decision making assumes self-efficacy and conscious choices. The role of an agent as the decision-maker is then examined. However, affect and other unconscious conditions influence even the most rational decision. The chapter discusses Executive Intelligence, and Emotional Intelligence in some detail because of their special relevance for management decision making. Some procedures for improvement of decision making, especially in regard to human relations training, are elaborated. Procedures for coping with affect-laden situations and interactive tutoring in small groups are presented as possibilities for enhancement of decision making that combines feelings and reasoning. Essentially such procedures encourage discovery of the participants' own personalities and the predispositions of others. Finally, compassionate decision making is a new element that is gaining favor as we give importance to affect and not exclusively to rational aspects of decision making. These last three chapters (Chapters 13–15) reaffirm the uses and applications of Planning and Executive functions in education and management.

Chapter 16. Revisits and Reprise

Selected concepts are revisited and some outstanding issues are discussed again at the end of the book. To begin with, Planning and Executive Functions are overlapping concepts, and sometimes used interchangeably. Yet, plans do not have to be executed, and outcomes of execution are not actively evaluated for subsequent action. Executive control is the central characteristic of EF. Control of one's own behavior and the behavior of others whom the senior executive supervises refers to the ability to guide and control; that is to be done according to the goals of the individual or that of an organization. Brain mechanisms engaged in Executive Control are partly common to both Planning and EF, but EF also activates other parts of the brain not shared during Planning. Because of these reasons, *Executive Control*, then, is a better name for Executive Function.

Decisions that need deliberation and reasoning are distinguished from those laden with emotion—this has been a frequent topic discussed in several chapters of this book. The two kinds of decisions are further distinguished by activation of some shared and some unshared parts of the brain. The two kinds are often discussed as the *dual systems*, System 1 and System 2, as though there exist two minds in one brain. The discussion in the chapter then moves on to reconsider intuition and deliberate reasoning. But the two systems influence each other—faulty intuitive decisions, for example, may be inhibited by inputs from deliberate reasoning.

Let us believe that intuition and non-logical thinking need not always be accessible to consciousness. Intuitive thinking, as mentioned earlier, becomes essential when the problem situation is extremely complex and quite novel.

The brain responds positively to experience and instruction. Neuroplasticity is the technical name for this phenomenon, and scientific evidence has begun to support the idea that the brain is made to respond to change by creating new neural pathways throughout life. This is important to know in order to understand how changes in educational achievements or improvements in managerial decision making are brought about by strategy training.

New thinking on training strategies for improvement in reading, comprehension, and learning mathematics involves educational technologies. Changes in executive decision making likewise can be studied by using recently developed technologies, like brain imaging.

Development of human cognition is sensitive to technological, social, and cultural evolution. Clearly, a fusion of rational approach of Western thinking and the necessity for a contemplative approach from the Eastern traditions could be the next step for research on training managers and executives. Co-evolution is a model for changes in human behavior mediated by genes that evolve in interaction with technological, social, and cultural changes. There will be many ways to explain it. Thus the search for explaining human behavior will continue infinitely. Predicting and controlling it is a bonus, as we learn from David Deutsch in *The Beginning of Infinity*.

PART I
Concepts

1

Cognitive Planning in the Context of PASS Theory*

Planning and Executive Functions: New Names for Intelligence?

One of us (JPD) was asked to assess a middle-aged man who had been living in an institution for individuals with mental retardation. In particular, JPD was to investigate the man's use of skills to adjust to a new home, a regular house in a typical community. The main concern of the referral agency that sent him for assessment was to address these questions: How much assistance would he need given that he had limited intelligence? And, did he have enough abilities to plan his daily life and execute those plans?

It turned out that this man was fairly articulate, even a bit garrulous. He brought me a few pages of his writing—almost readable prose with legible handwriting. Given that he had been placed in the institution at the age of 8 or 9 and educated in the institution's school for mentally retarded children, the writing was good indeed.

I asked him, "So, what do you think is your problem?" in order to assess his understanding of the situation. He responded, "I cannot plan my day, I don't know how to organize my time, even when I have been told what I need to do that day."

My assessment of this gentleman's ability to live in an unassisted environment focused on four major processes: his ability to plan, aspects of his attention, his capability to sort out things and events in sequence, and his organization of different things and activities that had a common thread.

The results of his assessment showed that his lowest score was in planning and his highest scores were in remembering and following a sequence. In his strongest area his score almost touched the norm. I did not have to go too far to trace the origin and sustenance of his difficulty in planning. The gist of what he said is as follows:

> You see, in the institution, since childhood we had to follow. When we walked, we would walk in line. We sat at the same place every day in school,

*The authors acknowledge the contribution of Dr Martin Fletcher to this chapter.

and given work we could do easily; I was never challenged. When I grew old enough to work in the garden, we were always supervised, never left to do new things on our own. Even while doing exercise, most frequently walking in the compound of the institution, we followed the same track. On and on ..., following a routine in exactly the same way at the same time.

Planning and executive functions will be discussed throughout this book. These constructs will be examined in relation to other cognitive processes. We favor *cognitive processes* to IQ because we assume that all individuals cannot be judged on a common scale of merit, which is essentially the definition of IQ. In the case of the man with *mental retardation*, he clearly has areas of strengths as well as weaknesses in cognitive processes like all of us. An IQ score would have been utterly uninformative and useless for deciding the areas in which he needs assistance and the kind of support that he would need for community living.

We begin then by placing planning and executive functions in the context of Planning–Attention–Simultaneous–Successive (PASS) processes, and identify assessment tools for each area.

Cognitive Planning in the Context of PASS Theory

A Synopsis of PASS Theory

The PASS theory of intelligence (Das, Naglieri, & Kirby, 1994) proposed that cognition is organized in three systems and four processes. The first system is the Planning system, which involves executive functions (EFs) responsible for controlling and organizing behavior, selecting and constructing strategies, and monitoring performance. The second system is the Attention system, which is responsible for maintaining arousal levels and alertness, and ensuring focus on relevant stimuli. The third system is the Information Processing system, which employs Simultaneous and Successive processing to encode, transform, and retain information. Simultaneous processing is engaged when the relationship between items and their integration into whole units of information is required. Examples include recognizing figures, such as a triangle within a circle versus a circle within a triangle, or recognizing the difference between "he had a shower before breakfast" and "he had breakfast before a shower." Successive processing is required for organizing separate items in a sequence, for example, remembering a sequence of words or actions exactly in the order in which they had just been presented. These four processes are, broadly speaking, functions of four areas of the brain. Planning is located in the front part of our brains, the frontal lobe. Attention and arousal are a function of the frontal lobe and the lower parts of the cortex, although some other parts are also involved in attention. Simultaneous processing and Successive processing occur in the posterior region or the back of the brain. Simultaneous processing is broadly associated with the occipital and the parietal lobes, while Successive processing is associated with the frontal–temporal lobes.

The PASS theory, heavily indebted to both Luria (1966, 1973a, 1973b) and studies in cognitive psychology, promotes a better look at intelligence (Das, 2002).

The four processes can be assessed in a test battery, the Das–Naglieri Cognitive Assessment System (CAS) (Naglieri & Das, 1997a, 1997b). These tests have been used for understanding, assessment, and intervention in regard to educational problems (e.g., mental retardation, reading disability, autism, and attention deficit), cognitive changes in aging, and decision making in management (Das, Kar, & Parrila, 1996).

Core Components of PASS Theory

In this brief review of the PASS theory, the basic division proposed in 1975, Input, Processing, and Output, has been retained (Das, Kirby, & Jarman, 1975). People receive information (i.e., input) from external sources through their senses and internal organs. When that sensory information is sent to the brain for analysis, central processes become active. However, internal cognitive information in the form of images, memory, and thoughts becomes a part of the input as well. The external information may be presented either serially (e.g., listen to these words: cow, hot, wall, man, key, one after another) or concurrently, as in dichotic listening, two different words are presented simultaneously, one to each ear. No such presentation mode can exist for internal input, however. *Automatic*, *learned*, and *effortful* describe the manner in which internal inputs are accessed.

The four components of the central processing mechanisms—Planning (P), Attention-Arousal (A), and Simultaneous (S) and Successive (S) processing—together make up PASS (Figure 1.1). An important addition is knowledge: one's knowledge base is a part of each of the components. The base of past experiences, learning, emotions, and motivations provide the background as well as the source for the information to be processed.

Figure 1.1:
PASS theory of intelligence

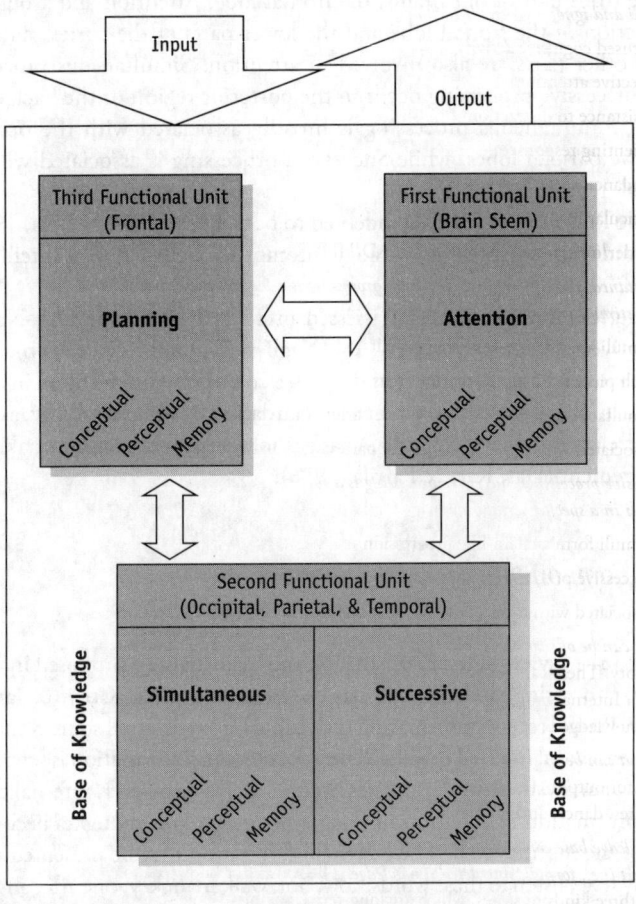

Planning: Planning is a mental process by which the person determines, selects, and uses efficient solutions to problems. It includes:
- Problem solving
- Formal mental representations
- Impulse control
- Retrieval of knowledge

Imaging studies demonstrate selective activation of the prefrontal cortex during planning tasks.

(Table Continued)

(Table Continued)

Attention–arousal: Attention is a mental process by which the person selectively attends to some stimuli and ignores others. It includes:
- Focused cognitive activity
- Selective attention
- Resistance to distraction
- Orienting response
- Vigilance
- Reticular formation as substrate
- Under/over-arousal implicated in AD/HD

Simultaneous processing: Simultaneous processing is a mental process by which the person integrates stimuli into groups.
- Stimuli are seen as a whole or gestalt
- Each piece must be related to others
- Simultaneous processing is not necessarily nonverbal
- Associated with the integrity of the parieto-occipital–temporal regions

Successive processing: Successive processing is a mental process by which the person integrates stimuli in a specific serial order.
- Stimuli form a chain-like progression
- Successive processing is not necessarily verbal
- Associated with the fronto-temporal regions

Input can be of two kinds: external and internal. External input may be, for example, visual or auditory. These can be presented all at once (concurrently) or one after another (sequentially). Internal inputs are images, thoughts, and their emotional contexts as accessed from the knowledge base.

Output can be in two modes as well: concurrent and sequential. An individual may use three tools for output (Donald, 1991). These are: (a) movements, fine, and gross; (b) mimetic, gestures, dance, and music; and (c) language, oral and written, sign language.

Knowledge base comprises implicit (i.e., tacit, experiential, and spontaneous) knowledge, and explicit (i.e., formal, instructed) knowledge. The sources of knowledge are integrated from at least three kinds of stores, which are long-term memory, books and media, and the computer. The vexing questions of "Who knows?" or "Is there a homunculus in the brain-mind?" have not been answered yet.

Thus, the four processes must be active in the context of an individual's knowledge base. It is as if PASS processes were floating on a sea of knowledge; without seawater they would sink. In other words, they cannot operate outside the context of knowledge. "Cognitive processes rely on (and influence) the base of knowledge, which may be temporary (as in working memory) or more long term (i.e., knowledge that is well learned)" (Naglieri & Das, 1997a,

1997b, p. 145). Knowledge can also be tacit (i.e., spontaneous, experiential, or non-conscious) or explicit (i.e., formal or instructed).

The final component of the PASS model is Output—action and behavior. Simply by changing the output demand, a change in performance may become evident. For instance, individuals who may be able to recognize but not recall items from memory can often recall them with a little prompting. In many cases, recognition improves retrieval where recall has failed. Therefore, how we measure output becomes important in measuring performance as an indicator of *intelligence*.

PASS: A Review of Its Background by Luria

Luria (1966, 1973a, 1973b, 1980) theorized that human cognitive functions could be conceptualized in a framework of three functional units. The function of the first unit is to regulate cortical arousal and attention; the second unit codes information using simultaneous and successive processes; and the third unit provides for the planning, self-monitoring, and structuring of cognitive activities. This work of Luria on the functional aspects of brain structures formed the basis of the PASS model (e.g., Das et al., 1994) and was used by Das, Naglieri, and their colleagues and students as a blueprint for defining the important components of human intellectual competence.

According to Luria (1973a, 1973b), the first of these three functional units of the brain, the Attention–Arousal system, is located primarily in the brainstem, the diencephalon, and the medial regions of the cortex. This unit provides the brain with the appropriate level of arousal or cortical tone, and *directive and selective attention*. That is, when a multidimensional stimulus array is presented to a person who is then required to pay attention to only one dimension, the inhibition of responding to other (often more salient) stimuli, and the allocation of attention to the central dimension, depends on the resources of the first functional unit. Luria stated that optimal conditions of arousal are needed before the more complex forms of attention involving "selective recognition of a particular stimulus and inhibition of responses to irrelevant stimuli" (Luria, 1973a, 1973b, p. 271) can occur. Moreover, only when individuals are sufficiently aroused and attention is adequately focused can they utilize processes in the second and third functional units. Luria (1973a, p. 28, 1973b) described function or functional units as opposed to structure as follows: "The presence of a constant (invariant task, performed by variable [variative]) mechanism, bringing the process to a consistent (invariant) result, is one of the basic features distinguishing the work of every functional system". Functional organization is a key concept in understanding the processes that make up cognition. Even noncognitive functions such as respiration and digestion cannot be explained by a simple localization of the function at one region. Each part contributes to the complex of functions—in the case of digestion for example, the esophagus, stomach and gastric secretions, the pancreas, and the small and large intestines are recognized for their contribution to the functional system of digestion; digestion cannot be localized in only one part. By analogy, cognitive functions such as simultaneous processing of information are complex systems that vary according to the contributions of areas in occipital and parietal lobes, their primary projection areas, secondary ones, and the tertiary areas; in other words, these are some of the variable mechanisms identified by Luria. Hence the stimulus (test) and the response (score) may be the same, but the processes, by necessity, are different. Hence a cognitive approach to *mental processes* has a different purpose than a simply psychometric approach to mental abilities.

Pavlov and Luria

Luria's description of the broad functional organization in the brain can be traced to its historical origin by Pavlov. Admittedly, contemporary knowledge about these functions has progressed much since Pavlov and even Luria. Nevertheless, we believe that the historical roots sometimes promote a better understanding of later advances in analyses of cognitive processes.

Pavlov's foundational observations on higher nervous activity (mental processes) provide a background for Luria's neuropsychology of brain functions. Pavlov concluded from his experiments that higher nervous activity can be categorized in terms of (a) strength, (b) balance, and (c) movement (lability).

Building on this categorization, Pavlov further concluded: (a) both excitatory and inhibitory properties vary in strength, with some individuals being strongly excitatory and others highly inhibitory; (b) individuals differ in terms of the extent of the balance between excitation and inhibition; and (c) ease of movement from an excitatory to an inhibitory state, and vice versa can be a source of individual differences as in reversal learning.

Such categorizations are still relevant in contemporary psychology both for understanding special populations and for remedial programs. For example, Luria found it useful to build his studies of special populations, as discussed in the next section.

Luria broadly followed Pavlov's observations, as seen in the following examples from his studies of atypical children including those with mental retardation:

1. Individuals with mental retardation have a weak nervous system in that they require more training to learn and learning is more susceptible to extinction.
2. Children with attention deficit may be predominantly hypoactive or hyperactive.
3. Pathological changes are noticeable in all sensory and motor functions, a disturbance in analysis and synthesis of sensory and motor functions. Specially observed is relative weakness in *speech analyzer*. Knowledge base comprises implicit (i.e., tacit, experiential, and spontaneous) knowledge and explicit (i.e., formal and instructed) knowledge. The sources of knowledge are integrated from at least three kinds of stores, which are long-term memory, books and media, and the computer. The vexing questions of "Who knows?" or "Is there a homunculus in the brain-mind?" have not been answered yet.
4. The presence of functional segmented processes in the brain that could have locations in different anatomical parts of the brain as proposed by Luria (1966) is consistent with Pavlov's basic observation that specific areas of the brain are associated with specific functions; essentially this is in opposition to the earlier view that the brain acts en masse, that loss of brain functions due to lesioning is proportional to the mass of brain tissues lost. Luria's functional organization in the brain that leads PASS theory to segmenting cognitive functions is an affirmation of Pavlov's observation.

Luria's evening lecture on Planning and Consciousness that he gave at the 1969 International Congress in Psychology provides a summary of 50 years of clinical and experimental research on consciousness. The following is a brief outline of the key points in this lecture.

Luria began the talk by referring to the CNS, the Conceptual Nervous System, as dubbed by Hebb and Skinner, two prominent persons in Psychology whom he respected. Luria regarded Hebb especially as a pathbreaker who provided insights into how the mind works in terms of the neural processes by proposing the concept of cell assemblies and phase sequences. Luria specifically identified the frontal lobes as the powerhouse of organizing consciousness. He ended his lecture by declaring the brain as truly an *organ of freedom*, that is, the workings of the brain are characterized by freedom to regulate higher order thinking and freedom to select strategies for action.

Pavlov used language to study conscious processes and the two phases of volition: first arising as an idea in the mind, and subsequently preparing and executing a plan of action. Luria utilized both Pavlov's teachings and Vygotsky's insight to progress even further. He continued to be interested in the conceptualization of consciousness and its underlying neurophysiological structure through his later years of life.

Pavlov and Luria's contributions to brain research can be summed up in the following two sentences:

- The structure of the brain is best described as a complex functional system.
- The brain's initial mechanism is regulation of action by speech.

PASS Theory in the Context of Other Approaches to Intelligence

Contemporary theories about intelligence can be divided into two classes: psychometric and cognitive types. The quantitative approach to intelligence is better reflected in psychometric theories of which Spearman's is an early example. A typical account of the quantitative method used by psychometricians follows Spearman's lead. Tests are constructed sometimes with or without any rationale for selecting each of these; participant is then required to provide an answer or answers. Then, the responses are scored usually by assigning a number in a scale, without any opportunity for the participant to discuss how the test question was solved. The score is then usually normed in percentiles or standard scores. The procedure is more or less universally followed in all psychometric tests of abilities that are looking for *general intelligence*. As is well known, Spearman computed intercorrelations between the test scores and subjected the correlation table to factor analysis. The general factor of overall intelligence was defined as the first unrotated factor (see Jensen, 1981).

In contrast, cognitive theories are both qualitative and quantitative. The *qualitative* aspect regards tests as occasions for observing how the participant approaches the test, and his or her own observations about the process of solution. It allows discussion of the test item before and after the solution in order to get at the processes used by the participant to produce the solution.

Following Spearman, and even his predecessor, Galton, Jensen (2006) is perhaps the chief advocate of general intelligence or *psychometric g* as it is described in the current literature. Another psychometric approach is

Carroll's (1993) theory. It is a proposal for three strata comprising narrow abilities, broad abilities, and a general ability such as Jensen's psychometric g. However, the usefulness of these statistical results within a diverse cultural context has been questioned because the data sets were based only on North American participants. Like all psychometric classification of intelligence, there is a common weakness. "The weakness of psychometric models is related to their strength. They stand on an impressive mathematical model of analysis of a given set of tests, without any clear stance about what the tests should be in the first place" (E. Hunt, personal communication, April 2008).

Intelligence as cognitive processing, in contrast to psychometric approaches, has a common base in cognitive theories of intelligence. Such theories advance the idea that intelligence has multiple expressions based on theories of development and cognition. For example, both Sternberg and Gardner view intelligence as neither a single nor biologically determined factor, but as a number of domains that represent the interaction of the individual's biological predispositions with the environment and cultural context. PASS theory is a further advance in this direction (Das et al., 1994). Its theoretical roots, as discussed later, lie in cognitive theories and the neuropsychology mostly influenced by Luria. Then, it has provided a rational derivation of tests, thus operationalizing the major cognitive processes. PASS theory has a standardized assessment battery for assessment of these processes (as in the Das–Naglieri Cognitive Assessment System). The advantages of having a theoretically motivated assessment battery are discussed later in many places of the book. But first, we present a brief review of the PASS theory.

In the case of reading with the eyes, this would involve the temporal, parietal, and occipital areas. Similarly, in regard to attention, research has shown, for example, that attention is divided into four subprocesses: (a) engagement, (b) maintenance, (c) disengagement, and (d) shifting of attention (Posner, 1993). These functions are spread over several regions of the brain, including at least the posterior parietal cortex, the frontal eye field, the brain stem, the thalamus, and the reticular formation. Posner added the parietal cortex, which regulates spatial processing, to the functional location of attention.

An Experiment on Localizing Simultaneous and Successive Processing

Luria initially located simultaneous processing as a function of the occipital–parietal region, whereas successive processing as a function of a fronto-temporal region. He did not place simultaneous processing in the right hemisphere and successive in the left. Each had a bilateral location. A recent experiment from Japan (Shiho, Shinji, & Hisao, 2009) studied the two processes using electroencephalogram (EEG) coherence. The results surely go beyond Luria, but also confirm the bilateral location of both processes. The researchers investigated EEG coherence patterns during six tasks of the Das–Naglieri Cognitive Assessment System, three from each type of processing. The result revealed two significantly distinguishable coherence patterns corresponding to two different types of information processing. The coherence pattern of the simultaneous processing task was characterized as increased long-range inter-hemispheric connections compared to the median value. In contrast, the pattern of successive tasks was characterized as increased short-range intra-hemispheric connections.

The results of the experiment indicate that simultaneous and successive processing are not simply localized respectively in the right and left hemispheres. Rather, Simultaneous processing is reflected across hemispheres, crossing over the left–right hemisphere division of the brain, whereas Successive processing, in contrast, is associated with an almost identical pattern of coherence in each hemisphere. Both processes are localized in the posterior part of the brain as Luria had suggested. The researchers hope their coherence results may link clinical findings with simultaneous–successive processing in PASS theory.

PASS Theory: An Expansion of Luria's Approach

Psychologists in the mid-twentieth century were aware of the efforts to localize higher mental functions in the brain (Posner & DiGirolamo, 2000). These attempts were met with frustration, and yet, the brain did not operate on the principles of mass action and equipotentiality. This extreme view could not explain how specific regions of the brain were responsible for differences in cognitive functioning. Luria (1973a, 1973b) discussed the problem:

> Whereas the mechanistic view of the direct localization of mental processes in local areas of the brain led the investigation of the cerebral basis of mental activity into a blind alley ... [they] clearly could not provide the necessary basis for further scientific research and ... discovering its material basis. (p. 26)

Luria offered a third alternative to the view that the brain acts as an undifferentiated nervous mass, or that each group of brain tissue is associated with extremely specific mental function, dividing brain into innumerable areas.

He suggested a tripartite concept of brain organization, underscoring the integrated functioning involving distinct areas of the brain (Stuss & Benson, 1990). Simple functions are replaced by *functional systems* (Luria, 1973a, p. 27, 1973b). He explained:

> [M]ental functions, as complex functional systems, cannot be localized in narrow zones of the cortex or in isolated cell groups, but must be organized in systems of concertedly working zones, each of which performs its role in complex functional system [sic], and which may be located in completely different and often far distant areas of the brain. (Luria, 1973a, p. 31)

These functional systems contribute to governing behavior as explained further (Varnhagen & Das, 1986).

We note that Luria's approach accounted for cultural influences on higher cognition as well as biological factors. He stated that "perception and memorizing, gnosis and praxis, speech and thinking, writing, reading and arithmetic, cannot be regarded as isolated or even indivisible 'faculties'" (Luria, 1973a, p. 29, 1973b). We cannot, as phrenologists attempted, identify a *writing* spot in the brain. We must take into account, instead, the notion of functional units along with the influence of culture on the development of these abilities.

Since the brain operates as an integrated functional system, even a small disturbance in an area can cause disorganization in the entire functional system (Varnhagen & Das, 1986). Researchers no longer had to puzzle over the sometimes-paradoxical findings encountered while attempting to locate discrete areas of the brain that could account for specific abilities. Luria (1973a, 1973b) described the advantage of this approach:

> It is accordingly our fundamental task not to "localize" higher human psychological processes in limited areas of the cortex, but to ascertain by careful analysis which groups of concertedly working zones of the brain are responsible for the performance of complex mental activity; when contributions made by each of these zones to the complex functional system; and how the relationship between these concertedly working parts of the brain in the performance of complex mental activity changes in the various stages of its development. (as cited in Christensen, Goldberg, & Bougakov, 2009, p. 34)

Recent research has progressed beyond Luria, but at the same time, finds Luria's division of the activities of the brain into functional blocks useful for theoretical understanding of both typical and atypical mental functions as well as for rehabilitation of neurologically impaired individuals (Christensen et al., 2009).

Luria's relevance in neuropsychology has been affirmed as evidenced in the contributions to special issues of the *Neuropsychology Review* (Das, 1999a, 1999b). The following excerpt from the introduction to that issue summarizes a contemporary assessment.

> Luria's influence on the further development of neuropsychological assessment approaches and methods ... a discussion of neo-Lurian adaptations and extensions of his neuropsychological model is presented ... articles in this issue help to demonstrate the wide influence sustained by Luria's ideas in various regions of the world. (Tupper, 1999, p. 57)

Das (1999a, 1999b) contributed an article on the Neo-Lurian approach in which both the PASS theory and the assessment of the four PASS cognitive functions, as discussed in this chapter, were presented. The four major functionally organized blocks of the brain are dynamic functional units consisting of planning, attention, and simultaneous–successive processing. These cognitive processes, while maintaining a biological correlate, develop in a socio-cultural milieu. In other words, they are in part cultural processes. Luria (1979) noted that "the child learns to organize his memory and to bring it under voluntary control through the use of the mental tools of his culture" (p. 83). This organized conscious activity requires cognitive planning (Das & Naglieri, 1992).

We again encounter the idea that higher cortical processes are shaped by cultural experiences. For example, Kolb and Whishaw (2003) noted that "[a]lthough the brain was once seen as a rather static organ, it is now clear that the organization of brain circuitry is constantly changing as a function of experience" (p. 1). Stuss and Benson (1990) bring together many of the concepts including speech as a regulatory function. Notice Vygotsky's influence in the following quote:

> The adult regulates the child's behavior by command, inhibiting irrelevant responses. His child learns to speak, the spoken instruction shared between the child and adult are taken over by the child, who uses externally stated and often detailed instructions to guide his or her own behavior. By the age of 4 to 4½, a trend towards internal and contract speech (inner speech) gradually appears. The child begins to regulate and subordinate his behavior according to his speech. Speech, in addition to serving communication thought, becomes a major self-regulatory force, creating systems of connections for organizing active behavior inhibiting actions irrelevant to the task at hand. (p. 34)

Luria stressed the role of the frontal lobes in language, organization, and direction of behavior. Speech is a cultural tool that furthers the development of the frontal lobes and self-regulation.

Cultural experiences play a major role. As Luria (1979) pointed out, abstraction and generalizations are themselves products of the cultural environment. Children learn, for example, to selectively attend to objects that are relevant through playful experiences and conversations with adults. Even the coding of information develops through cultural experiences (e.g., learning songs, poems, rules of games).

In summarizing "PASS theory: An expansion of Luria's approach," we offer an alternative to the anachronistic static notion of a general intelligence. Vygotsky (1962) reminded us that "facts are always examined in the light of some theory and therefore cannot be disentangled from philosophy" (p. 15). Das and his colleagues have embraced a scientific epistemology and offer factor analytic support for the PASS theory. This theory of cognitive processing, with its roots in developmental and neuropsychology, gives the investigator an advantage in explanatory power over the static notion of general intelligence (Naglieri & Das, 2002).

As discussed previously, PASS processes have been associated with particular brain structures: "they accommodate a variety of processes underlying different cognitive and motoric behaviors" (Varnhagen & Das, 1986, p. 125).

In that connection, we mention Lidz (1991) who observed a shift in current thinking about psychometrics:

> Authors of psychometric approaches to measurement of intelligence have become increasingly theory conscious, realizing the importance of explicitly stating the basis for derivation of the procedures. Without a theory, it is very difficult to evaluate the relevance and information value of the procedure. (p. 60)

Luria was also critical of the use of standardized IQ tests as indicators of intellectual development, commenting that they were "purely pragmatic" instruments and "hopelessly atheoretical and opaque" (Luria, 1979, p. 82).

As a final note to the present chapter, before we focus on Planning and Problem solving and connection with Attention, we wish to stress the importance of assessment. While other competing theories exist to expand the notion of intelligence as distinct but interdependent cognitive processes such as Sternberg and Gardner's, one may be left to ask, "Where is the test?" (see Das, 2010). PASS theory benefits from the CAS designed to measure PASS processes (Naglieri & Das, 1997a, 1997b). As mentioned in the synopsis, in addition to providing a cognitive theory for intelligence, PASS has the CAS that integrates contemporary cognitive psychological theory with psychometrics (Das & Naglieri, 2001). A brief presentation of the tests in the Das–Naglieri Cognitive Assessment System is provided in the appendix. It will be a useful reference as we discuss the CAS in several chapters of the book.

Appendix: Das–Naglieri Cognitive Assessment System (Naglieri & Das, 1997a, 1997b)

A brief description of 12 tests is given as follows.

Planning Scale. Planning is the cognitive process involved in executive functioning (i.e., determining, selecting, and using efficient solutions). This scale consists of three subtests designed to measure planning: (i) Matching Numbers requires the child to identify two identical numbers in a row of numbers. The numbers increase in length from one to seven digits across four pages. The child must devise a plan of attack to efficiently complete as many rows as possible within the given time limit. (ii) Planned Codes presents two pages with a distinct set of codes shown in a legend at the top of each page. The legend shows how the letters (i.e., A, B, C, and D) correspond to certain codes (i.e., OX, XX, OO, and XO, respectively). Rows and columns of letters above empty boxes fill the rest of each page. The goal is for the child to find an efficient means of placing the appropriate code beneath each letter. (iii) Planned Connections requires the child to develop an efficient strategy to connect numbers in sequence or numbers and letters in an alternating sequential order.

Attention Scale. The subtests comprising the Attention Scale demand that the child resist distraction and maintain appropriately directed attention to the completion of specific tasks. This scale comprises three subtests: (i) For the Expressive Attention subtest, the child must read color words orally, identify the color of a series of rectangles, and name the color of the ink in which words are printed. The distractor is the difference between the word and the color of the ink (e.g., RED printed in green ink). (ii) Number Detection consists of pages of numbers that are printed in various fonts (e.g., outline). Children are given a stimulus (e.g., 1, 2, and 3 in a normal font) and are required to find all numbers that match the number as well as the font. (iii) Receptive Attention involves underlining pairs of matching letters in multiple rows of stimuli. The first item requires that the letters match physical appearances (e.g., R, R), while the subsequent item demands that they have the same name (e.g., r, R).

Simultaneous Scale. Simultaneous processing involves interrelating component parts to arrive at a correct solution. The three tasks designed for the Simultaneous Scale require verbal and nonverbal synthesis of separate components into an organized group. (i) Nonverbal Matrices was designed using the standard progressive matrix format. The child is presented with interrelated geometric shapes, must determine the relationships present, and then choose the multiple choice selection that correctly completes the analogy presented. (ii) Verbal–Spatial Relations requires the individual to answer a question describing the spatial relationships of a specific drawing that has been presented to the child with five distracter drawings. (iii) Figure Memory is the final simultaneous task presented to the child. The examinee is shown a geometric figure for five seconds. From memory, the child is required to find and trace that figure in a more complex drawing.

Successive Scale. The tasks that make up the Successive Scale require the examinee to arrange stimuli into an explicit serial order. The result is a chain-like progression with elements that are only related to the preceding element. This scale also comprises three subtests: (i) For the Word Series subtest, the child is required to repeat a series of words in the same order as presented. (ii) For the Sentence Repetition task, the examinee must repeat sentences, after a single reading, in which the content words are replaced with color words. (iii) The final successive subtest for 8- to 17-year olds is Sentence Questions. Increasingly complex sentences made up of color words are read to the child. The child must answer a question concerning that sentence.

2

Models of Planning: Past and Current

> Human intellectual activity is defined as organized problem solving which relies on logical program of interconnected operations. (Luria & Tsvetkova, 1990)
>
> Human faculties seem to consist not of a solution to one problem, but of knitting together of the solutions to a number of problems. (Premack, 2010)

Premack (2010) describes planning and problem solving as domain-general abilities, a commonly held view. Such a characterization of problem solving is consistent with the proposition that these are based on *logical program of interconnected operations*. Premack goes further as he views problem solving within the broad framework of the question "Why humans are unique?" His answer is a reasonable one: Human intelligence is general whereas animal intelligence is specific (Premack, 2010).

Luria and Tsetkova (1990) would have concurred with Premack's proposition, but do not begin their book *The Neuropsychological Analysis of Problem Solving* with such a broad question. Instead they recognize problem-solving as a central purpose of human intellectual activity. They divide problem solving into distinguishable phases. At the base is "some objective, or the question of the problem which cannot be answered directly. The objective determines the subject's entire intellectual activity ... making it selective in character" (p. 1). First and the primary phase is *orientation* comprising assessment of existing information, distinguishing between what is available and what needs to be obtained in order to solve the problem, and finally a comparison of these data. "The general scheme, or the strategy of problem solving relies on a certain system ... *the verification of the answer, or the comparison of the obtained results with the original problem statement,* is an obligatory essential element of intellectual activity" (p. 1, emphasis added).

As we will present later in this chapter, Stuss and Benson's (1984) scheme of problem solving consisting of representation, anticipation, evaluation, and execution (see Figure 2.2) definitely seems to have its source in Luria's conceptualization of problem solving and EF.

We will also notice essentially the same components in Geary's controlled problem solving, including EFs (2005, Chapter 5), as we present his views later in this chapter. Later in this chapter, while discussing Newell, Shaw, and Simon's (1958) problem-solving scheme, means–ends analysis, we realized how it was anticipated by Luria and Tsetkova regarding the system or phases of problem-solving.

Following these introductory remarks, we begin the next section of this chapter with a somewhat detailed discussion of *plans and structure of behavior* (Miller, Galanter, & Pribram, 1960). It is a historic landmark for our present book on *cognitive planning* and *executive functions*. In the remainder of this chapter, we present some selected models of planning and problem solving following the gist of Miller, Galanter, and Pribram's *plans*. These include opportunistic planning, Newell and Simon's means–ends analysis, Rebok's transactional model of planning, and Gear's controlled problem-solving. Finally, our proposal for a model of planning and problem solving is introduced. The major components of this model include (1) origin of plans and problems in three worlds (see Figure 2.1) (2) and the sequence of problem solving that involves *logical program of interconnected operations* (see Figure 2.3).

Popper and Eccles' (1977) proposal of three worlds essentially states that we have a nonmaterial mind or self which acts upon our material brains; there is a mental world in addition to the physical world. The two worlds may interact using the artifacts of human culture. In Figure 2.1, we connect problem solving and planning with Popper and Eccles' three worlds as we acknowledge that the source of higher mental activities lies in the sociocultural history of the individual. Furthermore, we connect problem solving and planning to the activities of the frontal lobes. In patients with frontal lobe damage, breakdown of preplanned action programs occurs. The link from will to action is broken, as Luria found from clinical studies; strategies fail to develop in such patients because the frontal lobes are crucial for organizing conscious behavior. We take up these connections in the next two chapters as we deal with planning and EFs, and their neurological and psychological bases.

Plans and the Structure of Behavior: Summary and Discussion

The book *The Plans and the Structure of Behavior* had a pervasive influence on the investigation of cognitive processes since its appearance in 1960. This was due mainly to the fact that, as Hebb (1960, p. 206) stated, Miller, Galanter, and Pribram had presented "something worth knowing about human beings." Miller et al. proposed the concept of *plan*, which was analogous to the program for a computer, to fill the theoretical vacuum between cognition and action. Although they regarded computer simulations of human thought processes to be very promising, they acknowledged, "the reduction of Plans to nothing but programs is still a scientific hypothesis and is still in need of further validation" (Miller et al., 1960, p. 16). This brain–computer analogy has since been one of the central problems in artificial intelligence. We will discuss it later in this chapter.

Miller et al. emphasized the description of the structural features of behavior exemplified by ethologists (Thorpe, 1956; Tinbergen, 1951) and linguists (Carroll, 1953; Chomsky, 1957), and asserted that behavior is organized simultaneously at several levels of complexity. With the hierarchical nature of behavior as axiomatic, they defined a plan as "any hierarchical process in the organism that can control the order in which a sequence of operations is to be performed" (Miller et al., 1960, p. 16). A plan could involve anything from a rough sketch of a course of action to a detailed specification of each operation. It is the plan that controls human information processing and supplies patterns for essential connections between knowledge, evaluation, and action.

Miller et al. assumed that all behavior is guided by hierarchically organized plans that may include several subplans and further subplans up to the level of motor action. Thus, they suggested that the Plan is the appropriate unit of analysis for behavior at both the molar and the molecular level. They also offered several examples of such analyses by discussing the crucial role of plans in memorizing, problem solving, and language production, as well as in the formation of automatic skills and habits. Furthermore, they suggested that higher level ability (i.e., the ability to use plans to construct plans) may be the evolutionary breakthrough separating human beings from other animals.

But how do we construct new plans? Miller et al. proposed that most plans are learned either through imitation or through verbal instructions from another person. New plans that are not learned are based either on old plans (i.e., we change old plans to fit new contexts) or on *metaplans* and *heuristic plans*. Metaplans are plans for plan formation that are abstracted from inherited and learned plans in order to lessen the memory requirements for the planner. That is, instead of storing all of the plans that we learn and may need later, we store higher order plans for generating the lower level plans when necessary. Heuristic plans, in turn, are needed when metaplans are unable to produce a solution. Following this line of logic, we would need further plans to form heuristic plans and metaplans, a problem noted by Miller et al. Their solution to this problem involved the idea that heuristic plans are used to produce new heuristic plans and that to construct a general outline of a problem solving, a plausible description of the heuristic process is required. This description, the authors anticipated, would be provided by a growing number of artificial intelligence researchers who were interested in developing heuristic methods for computers. A generally accepted account of human heuristic processes, however, is still lacking; Miller et al.'s description of the planning process may have convinced many researchers to focus their attention on plans and their behavioral results instead of planning activity and its motivational and cognitive determinants.

The second central concept in Miller et al.'s description of cognitive processes is *image*. They defined images as "all the accumulated knowledge the organism has about itself and its world" (1960, p. 17) and maintained that it "includes everything the organism has learned—his values as well as his facts—organized by whatever concepts, images, or relations he has been able to master" (1960, pp. 17–18). Images and plans are, of course, reciprocally related in several ways. A plan can be learned and stored as an image or as a part of it. The accumulated knowledge stored in images is incorporated into plans to provide a basis for guiding behavior; images can therefore form a part of a plan. Changes in an image can be brought about only by executing plans for gathering, storing, or transforming information. Alternatively, changes in plans can be brought about only by information drawn from images. An image, as Miller et al. use it, consists of much more than just imagery. Images are individuals' private representations of the world and of themselves, and they comprise the knowledge base for all cognitive processing.

Miller et al. suggested that *search* is an adequate representation of most of the information processing that takes place during thinking and problem solving. The search that they conceived of was, naturally, planful. They also suggested that we should distinguish between *problems to prove* and *problems to find*.

A problem to find is what we normally have in mind when we refer to searching: How does one find the topic for a term paper? How does one find a friend in a crowded marketplace? We can solve problems to find by forming and implementing a plan that involves searching for different alternative solutions and selecting between them. As Miller et al. note, this type of plan is more often heuristic and based on cues derived from our knowledge base than exhaustive or even strictly systematic; implementing an exhaustive and strictly systematic plan would simply be too laborious for most problems encountered in everyday life. Consider the process of buying a house, for example. How many variables affecting the decision about the type of house to buy and its location can one identify in, say, three minutes? How many different possible combinations can one form from these variables? Clearly, the number of possible combinations is too large for any human being to search through categorically, and the ultimate decision made will be based on limited search or perhaps even on intuition. (Intuition, according to Simon [1992], may be nothing more than the recognition of information already stored in one's knowledge base.) Perhaps the good planners in real-life tasks are those who limit their searchers in the most effective way.

A problem to prove is concerned with evaluating the veracity of a statement that could either be true or false. Examples of such problems can be found, for example, in logic, arithmetic, or in games involving strategies. The problem to prove includes a statement of what is given (A) and a statement of what is to be proven (C), and we need to discover the missing step or sequence of steps (B) that results from (A) to (C). Normally we have to search through a large set of possible B's to find the correct one. If we want this search to be effective, we need a plan to guide it. This plan is often heuristic at the beginning of the task but becomes more systematic toward the end of the task, when the number of viable alternatives has been limited to a more manageable number. Thus, problems to prove are not necessarily different from problems to find; both involve a search that is more effective if it is guided by a functional plan.

Miller et al. proposed *prediction* as an alternative paradigm to explain thinking and problem-solving. For example, we can predict where to find a lost item and then test the prediction by checking if the item is really there. Or we can predict that a certain sequence of steps constitutes B in a problem to prove and then execute them in order to test that prediction. Miller et al. suggest that a prediction paradigm directs our attention more to the image than to the process of planning, mainly because the prediction is based on a hypothetical image. The test, accordingly, either confirms or refutes that image. They make the additional point that evaluations and judgments often involve the construction of a better image, which is not necessarily based on the execution of a plan. But it can be and we should note that when the construction of a better image is planful, this approach is just another way of explaining the process of searching the path from A to C.

Thus, it seems to us that search and planning are largely interrelated, although distinct, concepts. The use of plans and strategies is often a prerequisite for effective search in many experimental (and real-life) tasks. Accordingly, success in these tasks indicates good planning skills as well as good search skills. In Chapter 5, we will introduce a series of studies that have utilized the search paradigm in exploring components of planning.

Linking evaluations and judgments to image (i.e., to a knowledge base) is also an important point. It implies that the basis for good evaluations and judgments depends on enlarging and, perhaps even more importantly, organizing our knowledge base so that it provides the most appropriate image. Older people often make better judgments based on their extensive life experiences. Nevertheless, we all know of at least one person who continuously makes poor judgments and appears unable to learn from negative experiences. Can this be based on poor organization of one's knowledge base? Or is there also, at least in some case, a significant planning component involved in making evaluations and judgments, one that deals mainly with the search for, and the selection of, the most important features of the situation? We believe that these questions may be of significant relevance to career or marriage counseling, or for understanding prevalent adolescent problems such as rising high school dropout rates. Perhaps providing information about different approaches and alternatives (or the lack of them) is insufficient for individuals who lack the essential planning skills to make use of such information. An important implication here is that such individuals may be classified as lacking motivation when, in fact, the problem involves lack of cognitive skills.

Ideas expressed in *Plans and the Structure of Behavior*, though speculative, have proven to be of much heuristic significance for the study of cognitive functions. The book has provided cognitive psychologists with a general frame of reference for investigating strategic behavior and cognitive controls in the deployment of higher mental processes. By introducing the concept of plan, it has revitalized interest in legitimate and significant questions relating to purpose, consciousness, intention, and goal-directed behavior, and has therefore been instrumental in the final split with neo-behaviorism. Also, some of the ideas that Miller et al. put forth tentatively later became central issues in planning research. Two of these are (1) the use of search as a paradigm for planning and (2) the emphasis on the importance of understanding the physiological basis of cognitive processes. Both have been variously discussed in this book.

Although Miller et al.'s book was a compelling attempt to conceptualize planning as a cognitive process, their approach was not free of problems. Their definition of a plan lists *hierarchy* and *sequence* as criteria for plans and thus excludes plans that are not hierarchically structured or that do not include a sequence of operations. Do we have such plans? The answer is: Yes. Sometimes the entire plan consists of one condition that is not necessarily controlled to any extent by the planner and one action is to be taken when that condition is satisfied. Also, as Hayes-Roth and Hayes-Roth (1979) have shown, planning is not necessarily hierarchical in nature. Miller et al.'s definition can also be problematic for developmental psychologists:

If hierarchization and sequencing are used as criteria for establishing the existence of planning, developmentally early planful behavior displayed by infants and toddlers has to be excluded or discussed under some other label (suggested in Chapter 4).

Miller et al. also suggest that all behavior is based on plans. At the same time, they emphasize the role of language in planning. This leads to a disturbing question: Is there, then, no plan (or plans) and accordingly, no behavior, when language is not available (as, for example, in the case of infants)? One can argue that infants do not plan, but one cannot similarly argue that they do not behave. Miller et al. did not discuss the role of language in planning from a developmental perspective, and consequently, they were unaware of the problematic nature of their definition. Moreover, they provided no discussion of the development of planning that could have addressed these questions.

Planning as a Problem Solving Heuristic

Newell et al. (1958a, 1958b, 1959) assumed that intelligent activity is performed by machines and people alike with the help of (a) symbol patterns that represent critical features of the specific problem domain, (b) operations on these representations to generate possible solutions, and (c) searching through these possibilities to select a solution (multiple solutions are not pursued simultaneously). The simplest form of search, referred to as exhaustive search, involves going through all of the possible alternatives. When the number of possible alternatives is large, however, exhaustive search becomes impractical and often impossible. Most often, human beings solve problems on the basis of judgments that guide search to the most relevant and promising aspects of the problem space. This is referred to as heuristic search.

Newell et al. (1959; see also Newell & Simon, 1972) suggested two ubiquitous and powerful heuristic methods: (a) means–end analysis and (b) the planning method. Means–end analysis consists of dividing a problem into a sequence of subproblems that are then solved. That is, given the goal and the situation, the difference between the two is defined and a relevant operator is retrieved from the knowledge base in order to reduce the difference. If necessary, this is done one subproblem at a time.

The planning method, in turn, allows the problem solver to construct a solution in general terms before working out the details. It is used when the problem solver (a) forms an abstract and simpler problem environment by ignoring certain aspects of the original problem; (b) forms a corresponding problem in the abstract task environment and solves it; (c) uses this solution to provide a plan for solving the original problem; and (d) translates this plan back into the original task environment and executes it (Newell & Simon, 1972; Newell et al., 1959).

Newell and Simon's means–end analysis may be a suitable model for problem solving by computers, but not by humans, especially so because the problems are relatively ill-structured, and the end is often unknown. The following critique by Jan-Erik Lane (1986), we think, is a reasonable one:

> The conceptual scheme of means and ends for the analysis of action ... has come under attack from various points and as a result has today lost much of its appeal and status. If some basic distinctions are introduced into the means-end concepts, then it is possible to show that the severe criticism of this conceptual scheme cannot be sustained. (p. 339)

He continues:

> If ends are simply the expression of preferences and if means and ends are difficult to separate, if ends are ambiguous and difficult to pin down, how can there be means-end analysis? Goals are not there to be found; if goals already existed they would not require technology to achieve accomplishment. (p. 339)

One of the earlier models of planning is the opportunistic model (Hayes-Roth & Hayes-Roth, 1979). The two authors proposed an opportunistic model that has a prominent place among models of planning (p. 276).

The Opportunistic Model of Planning

Hayes-Roth and Hayes-Roth (1979) proposed an *Opportunistic Model of Planning* in their influential paper that discussed the structure of planning as a cognitive process. They defined planning as "the predetermination of a course of action aimed at achieving some goal" (pp. 275–276) and like Newell et al., before them, viewed planning as part of the problem-solving process. For Hayes-Roth and Hayes-Roth, planning represented the first stage of a two-stage problem-solving process. *Control*, the second stage, consisted of "monitoring and guiding the execution of the plan to a successful conclusion" (p. 276).

Based on their analysis of the thinking aloud protocols of college students who performed a hypothetical errand planning task and on a computer simulation of the model, Hayes-Roth and Hayes-Roth concluded that the planning process is largely opportunistic and multidirectional in nature. They argued that new decisions and observations made during the planning process suggest different possibilities for plan development and, as a result of the new information, the planner will revise or even abandon the original plan. This is possible because planning comprises the activities of several cognitive *specialists* which operate in a two-dimensional planning space (time and abstraction level defining the dimensions) on the basis of set condition–action rules. Cognitive specialists operate on a *blackboard* that is divided into five conceptual plans, or levels of abstraction, representing different components of the planning process: *plan, plan abstraction, knowledge base, executive*, and *metaplans*. Each planning process proceeds through a series of *cycles* during which different cognitive specialists suggest actions on the blackboard. At the beginning of each cycle, some (or all) specialists have their conditions satisfied and the executive selects one of the invoked specialists to execute its action, that is, to generate a new decision and record it on the blackboard. The new decision invokes additional specialists and the next cycle begins. This process ordinarily continues until: (a) the planner has integrated mutually consistent decisions into a complete plan, and (b) the planner has decided that the existing plan satisfies important evaluation criteria (Hayes-Roth & Hayes-Roth, 1979, p. 291).

In the Opportunistic Model of Planning, a decision made at any level of abstraction can affect subsequent decisions both at higher and lower levels of abstraction. According to Hayes-Roth and Hayes-Roth, this multidirectionality distinguishes the Opportunistic Model from successive refinement models (see, e.g., Sacerdoti, 1977) of planning, which emphasize the hierarchical and sequential special case of opportunistic planning that can manifest under one of the following conditions: (a) the problem exhibits an inherent hierarchical structure; (b) the problem is well defined and familiar to the planner; or (c) the problem can be solved by the planner's habitual method of problem solving.

Although Hayes-Roth and Hayes-Roth (1979) clearly distinguish between plan formation (i.e., planning) and plan execution (i.e., control) at the beginning of their article, their model does not. The task that they used was completely hypothetical and contained no separate execution phase. Thus, for the subjects, the entire problem-solving act consisted of constructing the plan required by the experimenter. From the subject's perspective, they were engaged in planning-in-action and the task contained no distinction between the plan formation and the plan execution phases. In real-life planning tasks, plan formation and plan execution often occur simultaneously—perhaps in a manner that Hayes-Roth and Hayes-Roth suggested—and any definition of planning that claims to be ecologically valid will need to acknowledge this. Our original plans of action are often sketchy at best and are revised and supplemented several times during execution if this process does not proceed as anticipated or if new information suggests better ways of reaching the same goal (or sometimes, better goals).

A further limitation of the model is that Hayes-Roth and Hayes-Roth, like Newell et al., treat planning as a component of problem solving. As we shall see later, this is too narrow a conceptualization of the planning process.

Blueprints for Thinking

Other new ideas and research on planning have been presented recently in a timely and interesting book, *Blueprints for Thinking*. Friedman, Scholnick, and Cocking (Dreher & Oerter, 1987), the editors of the book, present in one volume a number of articles (many of which will be referred to later in this book) from researchers representing a variety of theoretical and practical approaches to the study of planning. In the introductory chapter, Scholnick and Friedman (1987) suggest that the planning process includes at least the following six functions: forming a representation of the problem, choosing a goal, deciding to plan, formulating a plan, executing and monitoring the plan, and learning from the plan. Scholnick and Cocking also suggest that "to plan is to act simultaneously on three levels: in the reality of the problem, in accordance with an imaged scheme, and in the role of mediator between the scheme and the behavior" (p. 3). Relying on these definitions, they offer an integrative review of the current state of planning research. Drawing from a wide range of sources, they identify the following main concerns and sources of confusion in the existing literature on planning:

1. The concepts of plan and planning have been used to explain many different facets of human functioning, with the result that their definitions have become vague. Specifically, two theorists who use the same terms seldom have the same focus. The vagueness of existing definitions may reflect researchers' failure to specify which of the three levels is being referred to and how these levels are integrated. Scholnick and Cocking (1987) further suggest that a theory of planning should be comprehensive enough to encompass every level of cognition. Aside from failing to specify the level being referred to, different analyses of planning tend to emphasize different planning

functions and usually only address one or two at a time. Theories that would adequately describe several functions do not yet exist.
2. Most researchers have treated planning as either a general cognitive skill or as a context-specific activity. Very few have attempted to explain how these different frameworks might be subsumed within one definition. Furthermore, some theorists have regarded planning as a mandatory cognitive activity that we all engage in all of the time, and they have, therefore, concentrated on mechanisms involved in planning. Others, however, have emphasized the voluntary nature of planning and have, accordingly, concentrated on individual differences in whether one decided to plan in the first place. Unfortunately, these two approaches have not yet been merged.
3. Individual differences in planning efficiency have been accounted for either through the number of planning components present and the speed of their execution (i.e., by quantitative differences), or through *stylistic variations* that reflect qualitative differences in the ways that individuals plan.

The above observations by Scholnick and Friedman (1987) summarize several of the central problems that one encounters in the planning literature. Planning is an activity that synthesizes several different components and levels of functioning into one scheme. Researchers have seldom agreed though, about which levels or components should be singled out for discussion. We believe that this state of affairs is a consequence of (a) the lack of a comprehensive theory of planning that would integrate available knowledge from experimental cognitive psychology and allied fields; (b) the prevalent view of planning as equivalent to (or a component of) a problem-solving process; (c) extensive and uncritical reliance on models of computer simulation and artificial intelligence; and (d) the almost total disregard for a neuropsychological basis for planning as a cognitive process. We hope that the remaining chapters in this book will help the vigilant reader to find at least some tentative solutions to the problems identified by Scholnick and Friedman, as well as detect possible new problems.

Planning-on-the-go is an important proposal that has influenced a *transactional model* proposed by George W. Rebok and colleagues. The model is much indebted to the concepts of planning from the writings of Piaget, Flavell, Vygotsky, and Leontiev, as claimed by the author. Transactional models regard plans as "internalized actions which both direct and are derived from problem-solving activities" (Myer & Rebok, as cited in Rebok, 1989). It is based on the early work of Hayes-Roth and Hayes-Roth (1979).

Three major tenets are outlined and presented in Rebok (1989) in regard to opportunistic problem solving. These are as follows:

1. Initial plans are only partially elaborated prior to the execution phase of a problem-solving task, assuming they are elaborated at all.
2. Problem solving has a dynamic, rather than a static, relationship (transaction) between plans and actions.
3. Subsequent plans are dependent on feedback: prior executions and reflections on the relative efficiency of those executions.

The transactional model attempts to determine how plans and goals change as the individual adapts to changing problem and task conditions. Rebok focuses on Action and Operations as the direct connectors to goals and objectives rather than Activity in the three levels of Activity theory of Leontiev. This needs to be examined and elaborated upon. Leontiev's description of feedback and subsequent utilization of information are better explained by referring to Stuss and Benson as given in the diagram shown in Figure 2.2 (Das, Kar, & Parrila, 1996).

Plans and Problems: A Tentative Model

First we offer the following summary to update our information on Planning and to anticipate a detailed discussion of its connection to Neuropsychology, Activity theory, and EFs in subsequent chapters. Then we present the model and explain it. In the next chapter, we update a review of the PASS theory of which Planning is an integral part, before returning to EFs that has become a hot topic for its theoretical relation and its practical application.

Planning and Its Connections: Legacy of Luria

What comprises Planning? Planning is an umbrella. It shelters many kinds of frontal lobe functions. It involves both sensory and motor aspects of cognition. Attention, arousal, memory, language, and visual spatial ability are some of the posterior basal systems that constitute one aspect of planning, as discussed later in Chapter 4 on neuropsychology of planning.

We propose the model shown in Figure 2.1 in an attempt to understand Problem solving and Planning. We suggest that Planning is a broader

Figure 2.1:
Plans and problems

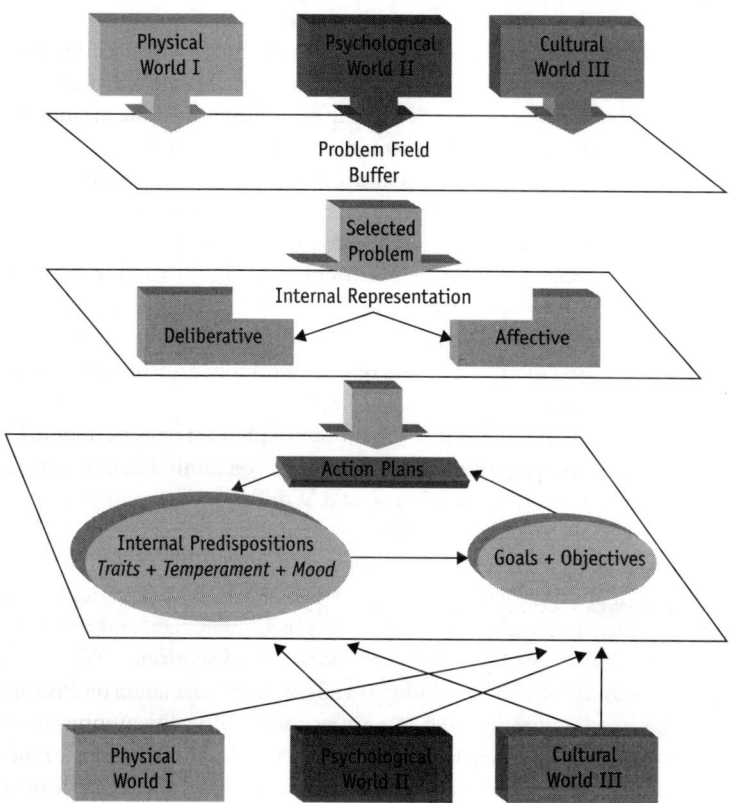

category than Problem solving. Hence the model starts with the source of Plans and the Problem Field. Notes on this figure explain the *boxes* and *plates* in the diagram.

Notes Explaining Figure 2.1

Problem Field

Planning includes problem solving. It involves three hierarchical levels or plates. The first is problem field impacted by problems originating from the three worlds that require plans. One of those problems is then selected; the planning process then moves to the next level, representation of the problem that is recognized as involving reasoning and affect to various degrees. Depending on how it is represented in the mind, appropriate action plans are then worked out influenced jointly by internal predispositions, and goals and objectives in a triarchic loop. All three levels operate within an integrated framework of Worlds 1, 2, and 3. Missing from the figure is the protocol for actual execution of the plan that requires a separate scheme.

Since everything depends upon a constantly changing program, we have conceptualized Problem Field as a buffer in the diagram. It is a buffer because it holds the evaluation of the constantly changing program for a while until a problem is selected. The problem field consists of interactions between the three worlds. Popper and Eccles (1977) attempt to understand the relationship between mind and body in their book *The Self and Its Brain*. We have proposed to use their ideas of three worlds in explaining the origin of problems or plans.

As Popper explains, World 1 is the world of physical objects, World 2 is the world of subjective experiences comprising conscious and unconscious states and psychological dispositions, and World 3 is the world of cultural products such as language, theories in science, and objects of art that we human beings have created. We know something really exists in World 1 through our interactions. What does Popper mean by interactions? One may interpret it to include sensory, perceptual, inferences, and analogies. Obviously, it is the world of our psychological predispositions. We may or may not be aware of all of our thoughts and emotions, and how these interact with objects in nature in order to give us a sense of reality. World 3, our cultural world, may be understood as artifacts of our mental processes, which is obviously so; nevertheless, these are real, and have an effect on World 1. Perhaps some examples are managing our natural resources, concern regarding climate change and greenhouse gas, consequences of war, and famine for human survival. These are perceived as *problems* that demand solutions only through the intervention of World 2, that is, through understanding the importance of the changes in nature. Eccles complements Popper's integration of the three worlds by proposing a self-conscious mind. It is a position that reflects his profound understanding of the brain and the ensuing philosophical discussions.

The Necessity of a Self-conscious Mind

The problem field we have proposed consists of interactions between the three worlds as they are integrated in consciousness or 'The Self-conscious Mind' (Popper & Eccles, 1977):

The hypothesis is that the self-conscious mind is an independent entity that is actively engaged in reading out from the multitude of active centers in the modules of the liaison areas of the dominant cerebral hemisphere. The self-conscious mind selects from these centers in accordance with its attention and its interests and integrates its selection to give the unity of conscious experience from moment to moment. It also acts back on the neural centers. Thus, it is proposed that the self-conscious mind exercises a superior interpretive and controlling role upon the neural events by virtue of a two-way interaction across the interface between World 1 and World 2.

All of our experiences are closely related and integrated, not only with past experiences, but also with our changing programs for action, our expectations, and our theories. This is represented with our models of the physical and cultural environment of the past, present, and future (Popper & Eccles, 1977, pp. 146–147).

Problem Generation

The source of some of the problem may be curiosity, since human beings are genetically programmed to be curious. We create problems, therefore, when the buffer is empty of problems that demand urgent action. Selecting a problem, therefore, is a result of active evaluation.

Internal Representation

Essentially, how we represent the problem guides its solution. Several ways of representing the problem lead to a search for hypotheses and an evaluation of the hypotheses before attempts to solve the problem are made. Problems have different degrees of reasoning and affect. In fact, a selected problem sends out *feelers* to both the reasoning (Deliberative–dorsolateral prefrontal cortex [DLPFC]) and the social–emotional (Affective–Orbitofrontal/ventromedial) regions of the brain. Some problems are obviously biased toward reasoning, such as solving Progressive Matrices, while some are clearly affective, such as predicaments. Examples of the latter can be readily found when we are *between the rock and a hard place*. When you cannot have a good night's sleep because the owners of the apartment above yours, that you have just purchased, have a dog that barks at night—the dog is kept in their kitchen just above your bedroom as there is no other place in their one-bedroom apartment—it is a predicament. What to do in such situations can be a test of Planning (see Chapter 6). Affects can be positive or negative, but may not be so easy to categorize as one or the other: Our sweetest songs are those that tell of saddest thoughts!

ACTION PLANS

A reasonable framework for considering the nature of action plans is provided by Activity theory (Leontjev, 1978, 1979) as given in a previous chapter of this book. Action planning is equivalent to problem solving, whereas activity plans are concerned with realizing or aiming toward life's goals and motives, such as self-fulfillment, self-improvement, and career planning. Activity planning is future-oriented (Das et al., 1996). For example, if an executive's goal is to achieve excellence, rising above the crowd, then the action plan will include choice of the right organization appropriate for his or her career goals and abilities, and internal predispositions, including personality traits.

So as *the model suggests*, action plans are influenced by our internal predispositions. These predispositions may arise out of habits, conditioning, relatively short-lived moods, stable traits, and temperaments. Over-arching goals of life, and immediate goals, both define objectives. The arrow points to Internal Predispositions from Action Plans as well as Goals and Objectives. The arrow from Internal Predispositions points to Goals and Objectives as well. All three are constrained by Worlds 1, 2, and 3. Internal Predispositions may range from well-established attitudes and conditioning (revealed through personality traits) to moods—the former being stable and almost a second nature, whereas the latter are unstable and have a shorter longevity. Means of executing the plan that are available further limit action plans—a World 1 constraint. Finally, a World 3 variable, such as the social desirability of a plan, is a constraint in which a good plan of action is constructed.

Emotions and motivations are World 2 variables like predispositions that integrate one's action plans with socio-cultural as well as physical variables. Some emotions and motivations could be deeply entrenched as a conditioned response, influencing behavior, whereas some others can be present at birth: We notice anxious and non-anxious infant attributed to a genetic or constitutional predisposition. Susceptibility to depression is another example. Others are as transient as moods of elation, sadness, for example. However entrenched some predispositions may be, they are subject to change by either World 1, 2, or 3 events. Sudden changes in climate, political systems, and man-made circumstances (e.g., loss of livelihood, tragedies, and accidents) change internal predispositions, as do religious awakenings and revealed knowledge. The integrative scheme suggests a template of Worlds 1, 2, and 3 at both the top and bottom of the diagram. Sandwiched between the two repeated templates is Selection of a Problem arising out of the Problem Field, its Internal Representation and Action Plans. Action Plans are determined by Internal Predispositions, which in turn shape our Goals and Objectives as much as the demands of the situation urge us to act. We name the model in the figure as an *integrative model* and summarize it below.

INTEGRATIVE MODEL OF PLANNING

Physical Realities, Psychological Processing, and Cultural constructs interact in finding problems. Representing them in the physical mechanisms of brain–mind that include so-called rational thinking that is inextricably intertwined with affect and motivation, then acting on physical reality with an integrated effort utilizing cultural tools. Action Plans are actualized as they are guided by an overarching Activity Plan for general goals of an individual's life with an orientation toward the future.

When ready for execution, Action Plans descend to Operations that must involve strategies and tactics working toward problem solution within the task-imposed constraints (environmental) and societal values. Operations that ignore either one of these constraints, or worse, both of them, end up in failure or maladaptive behavior. A self-conscious mind is absolutely essential for activity and action plans as well as for operations in this three-stratum (term borrowed from Carroll [1993]) model of integrative planning.

Problem Solving: Means–Ends Analysis Revisited

Jan-Erik Lane (1986), as previously discussed, critiqued the means–ends approach, and ended with a positive note: "If some basic distinctions are introduced into the means-end concepts, then it is possible to show that the severe criticism of this conceptual scheme cannot be sustained. In a revised version means-end analysis may be a powerful tool in the hands of the social sciences" (p. 339). We might have just found that revised version in Geary's (2005) model for *controlled problem solving* (Chapter 6).

The type of problem solving (or planning) that we have been discussing up to now can be divided into problem solving in natural environment or in the laboratory situations. Geary includes an extensive and erudite discussion of natural problems in social and ecological contexts, through the labyrinth of evolutionary changes. Laboratory situations, we suggest, include assessments of Planning through tests and constructed scenarios that require decisions. Chapter 7 presents some of these tools for assessment. Geary further introduces two types of problems distinguished as knowledge-lean and knowledge-rich. "These knowledge-lean domains are important because they allow cognitive psychologists to study problem-solving processes that are not influenced by prior knowledge" (p. 183). In contrast, "knowledge-rich problem solving occurs for domains in which individuals have varying degrees of experience and knowledge. Problems in these domains are, in addition, often ill-structured" (p. 186). Nevertheless, Geary following upon *means–ends analysis* writes: "Problem solving in these knowledge-rich domains involves many of the same processes engaged during the solution of knowledge-lean tasks, specifically, a problem-space, operations, representational states, and goals" (p. 186). Then he presents a model of problem solving in knowledge-rich domain.

Knowledge-rich problems are very similar to Cattell's crystallized general intelligence according to Geary, whereas examples of knowledge-lean problems are found in measures of "fluid intelligence." We wish to point out that knowledge-lean and knowledge-rich categories would have a very thin line separating the two. Consider a knowledge-lean task such as Progressive Matrices. This task has been used widely as a nonverbal test of intelligence across cultures. And yet, individuals from oriental cultures (Chinese and Japanese) generally perform better than white Americans—a finding that became a hot topic for intelligence and attracted a great deal of rethinking about American education to mitigate the gap (see Rushton [2006] for a sympathetic review and Mackintosh [2006] for a scathing review of the IQ gap).

A recent study—J.P. Das and colleagues in China and Japan researching PASS—administered PASS tests from the Das–Naglieri CAS (Naglieri & Das, 1997a, 1997b) to Japanese and Chinese children, and compared their normative scores with American norms. They observed a distinctly elevated score for Japanese and Chinese samples, exceeding 1 standard deviation, in Simultaneous Processing tests (includes Matrices and Figure-Copying) that are knowledge-lean measures. In the other PASS process measures, attention, planning, and successive, their normative scores were comparable to American norms. Such superiority in Simultaneous Processing is perhaps not surprising; one has to simply examine their cultural practices, including the learning of ideograms in orthography, and games such as paper folding. The results again remind us of the cultural–historical aspects of intelligence as a higher cognitive activity following Vygotsky and Luria discussed in some detail in Das, Naglieri, and Kirby (1994).

Back to Geary's chapter, specifically to the importance of affect in problem solving, Geary discusses a model that focuses on social or ecological goal achievement. Relevant to our present discussion is the stage or level, *Decision-Making Rules and Mechanisms* that has three components: Affective Responses, Match with Ecological Information Patterns, and Controlled Problem Solving. At the risk of not doing justice to explaining this module fully, we can still approve of the inclusion of affective responses and Controlled Problem Solving in the same module. The role of affect in planning and EFs during problem solving is elaborated in several places of our present book and was introduced as one of the core components of the integrative model in this chapter.

One other component in Geary's model is problem space. How can it be distinguished from *problem field* in our integrative model. Problem solving can work well when important information about the environment is encoded in the problem space. Then the individual can utilize this information to solve problems. The function of the individual problem solver, according to Newell and Simon, is to search within the framework of problem space for solutions that allow changes in the problem space due to experience—social, cognitive, and emotional, as well as through learning (knowledge acquisition). Goal-relevant knowledge influences legal operators that in turn influence schemata. The term *schemata* is described as memory systems of linked operations, and the sequence in which they were executed in previous problem-solving situations.

No doubt, our proposed model in the previous figure is compatible with Geary's in some aspects. However, for a complete picture of problem solving, a comprehensive account must consider several diagrams for social or ecological goals as well as mental models with their link with the brain. Our models then have much in common. In any case, the concept of Problem Field is much broader. In fact, it is an inclusive model that can accommodate both the means–ends analysis and the planning method suggested by Newell and Simon.

The *Planning Method* allows the problem solver to construct a solution in general terms before working out the details. As described in the previous book on cognitive planning (Das et al., 1996), the Planning method is used when the problem solver (a) forms an abstract and simpler problem, (b) forms a corresponding problem in the abstract task environment and solves it, (c) uses this solution to provide a plan for solving the original problem, and (d) translates this plan back into the original task environment and executes it (see Chapter 1 of Das et al. [1996] for a discussion of Newell and Simon's influential proposal on cognitive planning).

We think Stuss and Benson's (1987) diagram of planning as a frontal lobe function outlining the four pivotal activities for carrying out a plan (see Figure 2.2) is quite useful, as we have frequently used it to understand planning and EF. The figure shows the dynamic relation among the four components: representation, anticipation, execution, and regulation, influenced by goals and objectives that are themselves continuously revised by interaction with these cognitive operations. We suggest that the essential

Figure 2.2:
Planning as a function of the frontal lobes

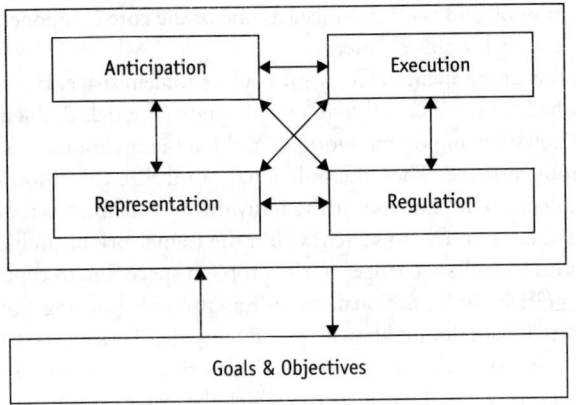

concepts in the figure be harmonious with Geary's, and further extend his model, the *planning method*, to the next stage beyond means–ends analysis. We regard Planning as a function of the frontal lobes.

Note on Figure 2.2 (Stuss & Benson, 1986, 1987)

The figure relates to Luria's conceptualization of planning as an essential function of the frontal lobes. It leads to operationalize planning in terms of the interaction among representation, anticipation, execution, and regulation that depends on the feedback of the planned action. These four operations are guided by the individual's goals and objectives.

At the end of discussing Geary's model, an elaboration of *means–ends analysis*, perhaps like a path diagram as shown in Figure 2.3, charts the sequential steps for carrying out a plan. When originally constructed and presented in Das et al. (1994), it was not constructed as an example of means–ends analysis. We think it presents the simple sequence of activities in executing a plan, and thus links with EFs.

At the level of operations, Figure 2.3 delineates the following steps (Das et al., 1994):

1. The individual asks himself or herself as in the flow chart: Do I need to use a plan?

Figure 2.3:
Planning process path diagram

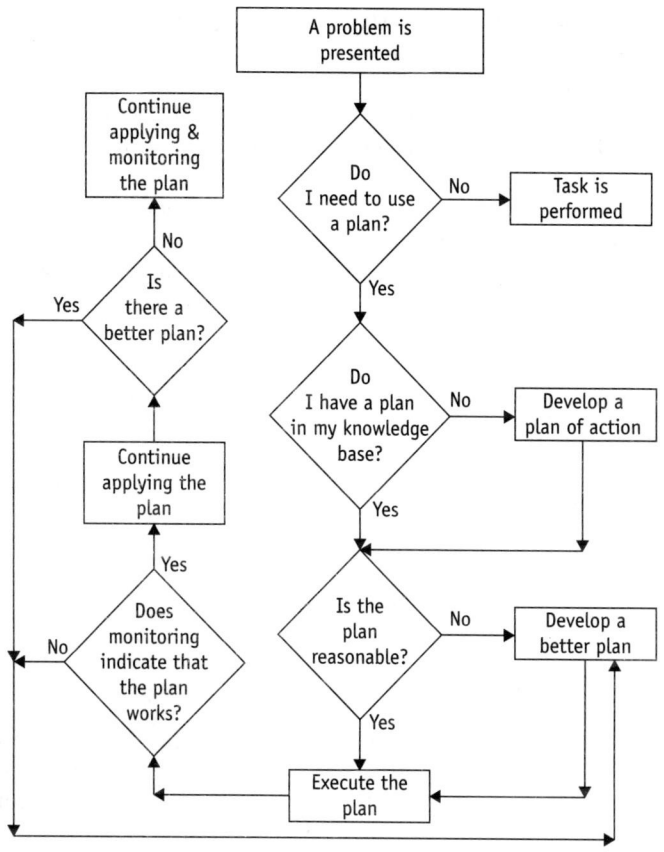

2. If there is no need, then the task is routinely performed.
3. On the other hand, if plans are necessary, the individual asks himself or herself the following question: Do I have a plan in my knowledge base or perhaps in my long-term memory?
4. If the answer is no, then a plan of action has to be followed.
5. If the answer is yes, the individual asks the following question: Is the plan a reasonable one?
6. If no, then the individual has to develop a better plan.
7. If, on the other hand, it is a reasonable plan, the individual executes the plan. This is not where it all ends.

8. In executing the plan, or while executing the plan, one must ask the following question: Is the plan working?
9. If the answer is yes, then continue applying the plan. The individual also wonders if there is a better plan. If there is a better plan, it has to be developed.
10. If a better plan cannot be found, then the planner continues applying and monitoring the plan until the action is completed.

In the next two chapters, we proceed to discuss the anticipated connection between brain functions and Planning/EF. First, the two concepts, Planning and EF are analyzed by selecting appropriate and significant evidence from contemporary research on commonalities and differences between these, and separating them from general intelligence. Then in the next chapter we continue to discuss more about the neuropsychological functions associated with Planning/EF, and attempt to find a place for intelligence in the brain.

PART II

Planning and Executive Functions and the Brain

3

Deconstructing Executive Functions

We propose that Planning and EFs can be regarded as separate but dependent functions. Executing a plan and regulating the response thus executed is closer to the general functions of an executive. Planning or problem solving (used interchangeably) involves at least four distinct activities: finding a problem, generating strategies for its solution, selecting an appropriate strategy, and executing a planned action. During the execution of a planned action, *interferences* that distract the execution have to be resisted, and the execution of the action has to be monitored, responding to feedbacks that necessitate *shifting* strategies. It is not imperative that plans have to be carried out. We are familiar with Friday night gatherings of friends where many problems are jotted down on napkins while having a beer. Brilliant designs for studies, or renovations for an ideal kitchen, are made, but how many of these get to be executed? Those individuals who generate several plans, but may not execute many of these, are neither more nor less intelligent. We mean intelligence as a general ability. The relation between Intelligence and EF/planning, nevertheless, should be understood, which we attempt to do at the end of this chapter before passing on to the next chapter on neuropsychology of EF/Planning.

Planning

According to Luria (1980), the third functional unit of the brain, located in the pre-frontal areas of frontal lobes of the brain, synthesizes information about the outside world and is the means whereby the behavior of the organism is regulated in conformity with the effect produced by its action. Much advance has been made since Luria observed this especially in regard to developmental changes in the pre-frontal area as well as the role of the different areas of pre-frontal cortex in planning and decision making. Thus, the location of planning in the brain has to be updated. However, the main result we will use is that the pre-frontal area is still responsible to a large extent for planning and cognitive decision making.

Executive Functions: From the Executive Brain to Executive Intelligence

The vast panorama of EFs is bounded by two contrasting books, *The Executive Brain: Frontal Lobes and the Civilized Mind* by Goldberg (2001) and *Executive Intelligence—What All Great Leaders Have* by Menkes (2006). Goldberg is a psychologist whose specialty is neuropsychology; Menkes is a psychologist turned a management specialist. EF is at the center of both books.

We begin the discussion in our book by viewing EF from the first boundary post, and end it with the second one in management. All through our book, however, we are focused on cognitive functions, a label that tells us what intelligence is all about. As we proceed reading the chapters, the subtitle of the book, *Applications in Management and Education*, becomes apparent. In some chapters, educational applications are more apparent; in some others, implications for management stand out.

There Are Many Definitions of Executive Functions

EF indeed has several definitions, but we think the core components are remarkably similar.

EF is an umbrella term for functions including initiating, sustaining, shifting, and inhibition/stopping (Rajendran & Mitchell, 2007). The other definitions cited in Rajendran and Mitchell are discussed later.

EF corresponds to planning, decision making, judgment, and self-perception.

Zelazo, Carter, Reznick, and Frye (1997) argue that EFs are behavioral constructs defined by their outcome, and the outcome of the use of executive abilities is rightly defined in terms of problem solving. These authors view EF as an account of problem solving. According to them EF as problem solving comprises four phases: representation, planning, execution, and evaluation. The four components within the framework appear to be extremely close to an earlier designation of Planning suggested by Stuss and Benson in 1986–1987, as discussed in Chapter 1. We mentioned that it is essential to operationalize planning in terms of the interaction between representation, anticipation, execution, and regulation, which depends on the feedback of the planned action. These four operations are guided by the individual's goals and objectives. Problem solving, as an integral part of planning, is a domain-general cognitive process, a view shared by Zelazo et al.

EF Is Like Planning, a Domain-general Ability

An expanded background for considering it as a general process can be traced to Luria (see PASS theory in Chapter 1), specifically, Luria's arrangement of functional organization in the brain as discussed at some length by Goldberg (2001). The idea of a function is embedded in domain-general perspective. In contrast to mapping the brain minutely, to relate each millimeter of brain tissue to a specific behavior, broad blocks of the brain are identified with major cognitive processes. This concept allows flexibility within and between the blocks; for example, when a part of the brain tissue is damaged, other parts can take over. Incidentally, a parallel in functions of organization and regulation within a management unit can be observed. Luria defined function as a dynamic and flexible process that operates between two constants—the cause or antecedent condition may be invariant, and the behavior or response may be invariant, but the processes in between are variable (Luria, 1966).

EFs have successful outcomes only when shifting of strategies as the situation requires it, and these can be carried through to reach their goal. Additionally, EFs are successful when old habits of mind that are now maladaptive can be prevented from influencing behavior (Friedman et al., 2006).

A general acceptance of these two as core characteristics of successful EFs is currently popular as discussed further in the next section.

EF, Planning, and Intelligence: Is EF Distinct from Intelligence?

It appears that we have a consensus of some sort in defining EF. Studies of brain processes generally support that although EF is a heterogeneous function, there is sufficient evidence to support its neural base. Its cognitive and associated neuropsychological characteristics are discussed next, following which we ask an important question: How is it like or unlike intelligence, and is working memory (WM) the link between the two?

We open the discussion with Denckla (1996), follow it with a somewhat detailed consideration of the work of Miyake and colleagues, and complete the presentation by selected studies of intelligence that deal with the commonalities and differences between Intelligence, EF and Planning as Problem Solving.

Denckla, a neurologist (cognitive neurologist), describes EF comprising *interference control*, effortful and *flexible organization*, and *anticipatory* goal-directed preparedness to act. She also includes WM, which involves maintaining internal representations to guide one's actions. But is WM a part of intelligence? If it is a core process common to both EF and Intelligence, how independent is EF in regard to general intelligence?

A convincing answer in support of EF/Intelligence question is given in the study by Miyake and colleagues (Friedman et al., 2006).

Deconstructing EF

We discuss the study of Miyake and colleagues (2006) in some detail because of (1) the evidence for identification of the core characteristics of EF that it provides, and (2) the justification for distinguishing Intelligence and EF.

These researchers identified, from the literature, three different major components of EF, namely inhibiting prepotent responses, shifting mental sets, and updating WM. Then they proceeded to relate these to each other as well as to two kinds of intelligence measures: fluid and crystallized. It is important to note the constituents of these different tests. The fluid intelligence test was solely indexed by Raven's Progressive Matrices and Block Design. In contrast, the crystallized intelligence test comprised vocabulary and general information respectively from a special vocabulary test and the Wechsler Adult Intelligence Information Subtest. The EF tests consisted of measures of inhibition (the Stop-signal task) which is a word categorization response involving a buildup of a prepotent response tendency stopped by instruction, and the familiar Stroop test that involves inhibition of reading the color word, but to read the color of the word (the word "blue," written in yellow ink, must be read as "yellow"). The memory-related task used was Updating, a familiar memory task where the participants were stopped and asked to recall the final three letters in a series of five, seven, or nine letters that occurred unpredictably. That is, they were stopped and asked to recall the last three letters without prior notice. Shifting was measured by the Number–Letter task where the participants had to switch between classifying numbers and classifying letters. Its other test in shifting was a Color–Shape task in which participants switched between classifying shapes and classifying colors.

We wish to comment very briefly on the nature of the tasks so that this information would be critical for discussing not only the results of the Friedman et al. study, but also of EF studies by other investigators. As well, we will consider which of these tasks may be identified with tasks/test used to measure intelligence. The inhibition tasks were related to words—material for both Stop-signal and Stroop tasks. The Memory Update task was a typical example of running memory (Shallice, 1988). The Shifting task could be thought of as similar to the familiar Trail-making task, a widely used test for frontal lobe function and dysfunction (Lezak, 1995). Participants are required to connect numbers and letters in a serial order: 1 to A to 2 to B to 3 to C, and so on, scattered on a page.

Incidentally, we note that some of the tasks except memory updating have close parallel forms in CAS (Appendix to Chapter 1). In regard to inhibiting a response, the Stroop task is very similar to Expressive Attention, and the Trail-making task is almost identical to the Planned Connection task. Continuing with the comparison of CAS with the intelligence tasks, the gf (general fluid intelligence) or fluid intelligence tasks clearly relate to simultaneous processing. In fact, in our past research, it has been shown to be so (Das, Kirby, & Jarman, 1979; Das, Naglieri, & Kirby, 1994). Anticipating the subsequent discussion in regard to Intelligence, EF, and Planning, we state these similarities between CAS simultaneous tests and tests of *fluid intelligence*, Planning and Shifting strategies, and Expressive Attention as it involves inhibition of a prepotent response. The next section continues with the above discussion.

The results of Friedman et al. essentially showed that whereas inhibiting and shifting had minimal and negligible correlations with gf and gc (general crystallized intelligence), the WM task was highly correlated with both measures of intelligence, fluid and crystallized, as mentioned earlier. In fact, their structural equation model left no doubt about these relationships. The values in their structural equation model give path coefficients of .74 and .79 between WM and fluid intelligence on the one hand, and WM and crystallized intelligence on the other. The authors suggest excluding WM if we intend to separate EF from intelligence.

Their suggestion requires the following comment in regard to intelligence—May we propose that the separation of their EF measures from intelligence measures of specially gf could be anticipated from a PASS perspective? The gf tests are indeed tests of simultaneous processing; Raven's Matrices and Block Design load on a simultaneous factor (Das et al., 1979), and Matrices is one of the tests of the CAS simultaneous scale.

The EF tests that purport to measure inhibition and shifting are easily categorized as Attention and Planning in CAS as discussed earlier. Given that in PASS factors, Simultaneous is distinctly different from Planning and Attention, we could anticipate the results obtained by Miyake et al. (2000), that gf is separate from EF and Inhibition (see especially Was, 2007). We will pick up the discussion in regard to the Intelligence–EF relationship in a later section. But for now let us come to a closure regarding the major characteristics of EF before we consider its relation to Intelligence and Planning.

Planning, Shifting, Inhibition, and Monitoring— Do These Concepts Have Construct Validity?

The following is a summary of descriptions of important characteristics of EF, as mentioned in Rabbitt's book, in spite of the questions regarding their empirical validity.

EF Is Contrasted with Nonexecutive Functions

1. EFs are deliberate, not usually automatic. EFs are necessary for suppression, inhibition, and suppression of previously used rules, as well as to respond to feedback, changing plans, and selecting alternatives.
   Non-EF behaviors, in contrast, are automatic, externally driven (e.g., *heat of the moment*, capricious). Executive behaviors are initiated and controlled by goals and objectives.
2. EF behavior involves retrieval of stored information from memory and searching plans in order to actively control the future.
3. EF is necessary for initiating a new sequence of behavior.
4. EF is also necessary to prevent responses that are inappropriate for the context.
5. EF facilitates rapid switching of response.
6. EF entails monitoring performance and correcting error.
7. EF helps prospective memory, that is, to remember to do things at the right time.

According to Rabbitt (1997), EF definition is disturbed by a nagging criticism regarding a lack of validity for the construct. We present a critique most of which comes from Rabbitt's edited book. The book is a long and contentious reply to question: Can we develop useful models and methodologies to study executive behavior?

Is there a single *central executive* that manages EF functions such as those listed above, or are there several independent ones? Additionally, disagreement among researchers exists in regard to EF measures and how verifiable in experimental investigations are the *core* constructs such as *inhibition* or *goal directness*. Brain mapping accuracy is also questioned—the extent to which particular cognitive functions can be mapped on the particular areas of the PFC. If the EF core components cannot be verified empirically to everyone's satisfaction, what kind of methods to study them can be relied upon? How can we locate these core functions unless we are certain of their validity as constructs?

Acknowledging that these doubts have not been completely cleared, research into EF has been thriving well, as evident in the contributions by several investigators to Rabbitt's book. The uncertainty regarding a uniformly agreed upon and commonly accepted definition of EF is a situation not unlike those that prevailed a few years ago in regard to defining Intelligence or Learning Disability. Many serious researchers in those fields think that we have had a very good debate of a theoretical nature; let us now get on with answering some interesting questions that need to be answered for practical applications. There may be some wisdom in taking such a position as the rest of this book discusses EF and Planning.

Intelligence, Working Memory, EF, and Panning

In concluding part of the chapter, we also wish to achieve a closure by briefly examining the relationship among these concepts that have appeared and disappeared at various places in the text.

Is EF Only a Variation of Fluid Intelligence?

Fluid intelligence is frequently assessed by tests such as Matrices and Block Design; these require simultaneous processing. As mentioned earlier, Das et al. (1979) developed a successive–simultaneous battery based on Luria's theory—the two processes became the basis of assessments of children's intelligence, *The Kaufman Assessment Battery for Children* (K-ABC) (Kaufman & Kaufman, 1983; Rabbitt, 1997). However, since intelligence and EF/Planning share the frontal lobe, and yet, intelligence may also be measured by simultaneous processing tasks, reflecting the functions of occipital–parietal regions in the posterior part of the brain, what does research tell us about their independent operations?

A factor-analytic study of a large battery of neuropsychological tests comprising mostly EF tests and fluid intelligence measure provides one of the strategies about how to answer the question. In the study by a British group of investigators (Robbins et al., 1998), a previously known neuropsychological battery was administered to normal adult volunteers. Several tests from this battery, the CANTAB neuropsychological test battery, were previously shown to be sensitive to frontal lobe dysfunction. The major test of EF/Planning was a computerized form of the Tower of London test, a shorter version of Tower of Hanoi. Other tests included were as follows: a self-ordered spatial WM task and a test of attentional set formation and shifting. "Factor analyses showed that performance in the executive tests was not simply related to a measure of fluid intelligence" (p. 474).

Planning and Working Memory

First, a brief discussion regarding the place of *planning* among the above concepts is given. Planning and WM are closely associated as Miller et al. wrote several years ago in their classic book, *Plans and Structure of Behavior* (1960); we discussed this book in some detail in Chapter 2. The authors wrote that we need to posit WM "where Plans can be retained temporarily when they are being formed, or transformed, or executed" (p. 207). Subsequently, a major role for memory in planning was often proposed (e.g., Cohen et al., 1996; Owen et al., 1996), and Cohen argued in particular that WM is important in formulating and revising plans as Gilhooly (cited in Morris and Ward, 2005) discusses the relationship between WM and Planning.

Further discussion of the above relationship leads to considering Simon's model (Newell & Simon, 1972). As Gilhooly explains, the essential element according to this model is proposal of a cognitive system architecture consisting of a vast long-term memory and a small, general purpose WM. However, he suggests that more complex models of WM, going beyond the limited capacity model epitomized in 7 ± 2, will be required. WM as first conceptualized by Baddeley and associates has been revised periodically to accommodate a complex system that can predict complex processes involved in comprehension (Georgiou, Das, & Hayward, 2008).

Does general intelligence depend almost entirely on working memory capacity (WMC)? For if that is so, WM should be a part of intelligence, and not EF.

First, a simple view of the WM concept may be useful for some readers. The concept is defined as the capacity to *store information* for a short period of time and manipulate or *process it* (Baddeley & Hitch, 1974; Gathercole, 2007). Most recently, Baddeley (2012) has offered an integrative overview of WM; his creation, in spite of requiring additional boxes such as the episodic buffer, seems to have grown up well. Briefly described, the *processing* component in WM is prominently identified with a *central executive capacity* within the short period of time that characterizes WM. The *executive* is helped by at least two prominent capacities: a phonological loop that keeps alive the sound-related structure of the input and a visual–spatial sketch pad with its capacity for maintaining nonverbal information. This is the received view of WM, although a recent component, episodic buffer has been added "which is responsible for the integration of cognitive events across different representation domains" (Gathercole, 2007, p. 234; paraphrasing Baddeley, 2000). The *buffer* is a necessary protection against Cowan's (1995) proposal to explain away WM as essentially an attentional process. The distinction between processing and storage originally proposed is maintained, and has propelled several studies as well as generated competing hypotheses. One of the serious ones is to equate WM with intelligence.

In regard to the connection between Intelligence on the one hand and WM on the other, we begin the discussion of a recent study that has been cited by several sources; its authors (Ackerman et al., 2005) report the results of a meta-analysis seeking to answer if Intelligence and WM were the same or different. They found a correlation between intelligence, gf, and WM to be .36.

However, WMC is not claimed to be identical to gf or to reasoning ability. Ackerman's paper invited several critiques, some elaborating the relationship further. For example, the results of a study by Ackerman et al. (2005) showed that WMC and gf/reasoning constructs are more strongly associated than Ackerman et al. indicate after reanalyzing the data—a strong correlation between WMC and gf reasoning factors (median $r = .72$) was obtained. There have also been other critiques that estimate the correlation to be much higher, and indeed go a step further in suggesting that an explanation for general intelligence may be found in WM.

In an independent study following the paper by Ackerman et al., Colom et al. (2004) observed a high correlation between short-term memory (STM) and WM. However, in regard to general intelligence, g, the correlation between WM and g disappeared when STM was partialled out. The study suggests that it is the *storage component of STM in WM that was contributing to the correlation between g and WM.*

Perhaps the argument about the place of WM in Intelligence, and further, the definition of intelligence in terms of WM, has been more or less resolved.

An alternative view of Intelligence as cognitive processes comprising three factors, Planning, Simultaneous and Successive (Das, Kirby, & Jarman, 1975)—was reinforced. Since then, the model of cognitive processes has been gathering evidence (Das, Naglieri, & Kirby, 1994; Das et al., 1979) and various research reports as reviewed in the previous chapter of this book. Even before PASS theory was operationalized in tests of CAS (Naglieri & Das, 1997a, 1997b), K-ABC (Kaufman & Kaufman, 1983) used the simultaneous–successive processes; perhaps the first standardized psychometric test theta promoted the alternative view. When Planning tests were combined with the original edition of K-ABC (Kaufman & Kaufman, 1983), it emerged as a distinct factor in addition to simultaneous and successive (see Das, Mensink, & Misra, 1990). In regard to WM, we seem to have some evidence now to suspect its close connection with intelligence rather than with STM as reviewed earlier—the correlation between intelligence measure and WM seems to disappear when STM is partialled out. Essentially, then, the low correlation between gf and WM is supported. At the same time, in regard to WM and EF, perhaps it is difficult to disagree with the proposal by Miyake et al. (2000) that WM is closer to general intelligence than it is to the core components of EF, Inhibition and Shifting.

How should one regard WM in relation to Intelligence and EF/Planning? No doubt, WM is used in solving intelligence tests and performing EF tasks. Rethinking WM and its connection with not only EF, but also Intelligence in general, Kane and Engle (2002) have proposed an *executive-attention* framework that aspires to organize the constructs of WMC, gf, and relate these to the functions of PFC. Specifically, they suggested that the dorsolateral PFC has a critical role to play in executive-attention functions.

In concluding this part of the chapter, we are still not convinced that the concept of g, general intelligence, can contribute anything useful for understanding EF/Planning and WM. Consider Colom et al.'s (2005) results—the correlation between WM and fluid intelligence disappeared when STM was partialled out. So is STM the critical individual difference variable that determines a relationship between WM and general intelligence? Is it really so because tests of general intelligence such as Wechsler are a theoretically constructed, and by and large, represent an eclectic combination of various tasks that range from tests of school achievement (e.g., arithmetic, vocabulary), general knowledge, and nonverbal tasks such as Progressive Matrices and Block Design? Unless we provide a theoretical context for general intelligence, such as the PASS comprising measures of Simultaneous (gf), successive (STM, WM), Planning (Tower of Hanoi type, Trail-making), and attention (e.g., Stroop test), we would not progress in understanding EF as a process in the context of *g*. Incidentally, the last two PASS processes, that is, Planning and Attention, provide measures of EF (shifting and inhibition of prepotent response). Even one could suggest that *executive attention* can be housed among them. We propose this as an idea that invites further consideration. We believe that searching and locating a place in the brain for Intelligence, WM, EF, and Planning may advance our understanding of these pivotal concepts. In the next chapter, we attempt to do this for the above concepts except not so much for Planning as that has been included in the previous chapters.

Connection to the Next Chapter

The next chapter gives more information on brain mechanisms. Its objective is not to go deeply into neuroscience. Rather it is limited to provide a better understanding of Planning, EF, and Intelligence. For example, the difference between the two components of EF—inhibition of a prepotent response and shifting; whether these two are represented in different regions of the brain; whether it is more informative to consider intelligence not as a whole, but to separate its various aspects to *fractionate* intelligence, and then show where in the brain they can be located.

4

Executive Functions, Planning, and Intelligence: Can Brain Localization Help?

There is considerable evidence by now that the prefrontal cortex plays a major role in high-order control processes that exercise a top-down regulation of cognition and behaviour. (Petrides, 2005)

As interest in EF has been growing rapidly, the concept has been expanded so much that it threatens to replace *intelligence* and *thinking*. As a consequence of broadening the concept, EF may not be specific enough for explanation of circumscribed cognitive functions and operations. Its underlying brain structure and functions will then be difficult to determine. We discuss a few specific studies relating EF to brain functions that may argue in favor of using EF as a relevant explanation of cognitive processing and exploring its link to the broader concept of intelligence.

Revisiting the scope of the concept of EF, the citation from Gailliot (2008) is a concise statement of its broad functions of what he termed the *central executive*: "The central executive can be defined as a cognitive system that allows for self-control or self-regulation (i.e., overriding habitual patterns of behavior; persisting at mental or physical tasks; coping with stress; and controlling emotions, thoughts, and urges), and higher ... executive functioning allows for effortful, complex cognition" (p. 245). Poor EF, on the other hand, is suggested to lead to a wide variety of failure of social intelligence, including criminal behavior, increased aggression, impulsivity, poor control of attention, and diminished self-control (Gailliot, 2008). Unfortunately, neuroimaging cannot provide localization of neural activation to represent such general behavior, and personality characteristics. It can be informative only under certain conditions: Both the cognitive process and its coincidence in performance under study must be isolated, and precisely specified so that activation of the region of interest in the brain may be analyzed. The behavioral response such as reaction time is a popular measure, as are the well-defined parameters of imaging in magnetic resonance imaging (MRI)/positron emission tomography (PET) scan. While obtaining data from the behavioral and imaging studies following traumatic brain injury, chronic epilepsy, and stroke for example, an exact location of the lesion is essential. This is not always possible. A constraint for reaction time measure is task simplicity and automaticity (Kadosh & Walsh, 2009). Stroop task is a prototypical one, instantiating the conflict in incongruent conditions (name the color, not the word). A response that is automatic has a better chance of yielding reliable data about a specific process under study. With these cautionary notes in mind, we present a few selected studies.

We have isolated two components of EF for further analyses both in terms of brain imaging and behavioral performance. We have selected a few tasks to review that satisfy the above criteria to a significant degree. At the end of the chapter, we focus again on brain and intelligence, and consider if there is a place for general intelligence in the brain.

Relevant Brain Functions for EF

The brain region specifically linked to EF is the LPFC.

A brief introduction to the areas of the PFC, especially involved with EF/Planning, is provided below. Explanations of the different regions of the frontal lobe associated with EF are given in the appendix at the end of this chapter, which may also be helpful to follow the discussion in papers we review.

The PFC represents regions in the front section of the frontal lobes, as its name suggests. The PFC is often divided into several regions, such as the ventrolateral, dorsolateral, orbitofrontal, ventromedial, basal, orbital, and frontopolar areas. The ventrolateral and dorsolateral regions are located on the side of these frontal lobes. The ventrolateral prefrontal cortex (VLPFC) is sometimes called the *inferior frontal cortex*.

How are these different? Let us get to the basics—the difference between the VLPFC and dorsolateral prefrontal cortex (DLPFC) roughly corresponds to the difference between the ventral and dorsal pathways of the cortex.

These two regions of the frontal lobes have generally distinct functions that relate to EF/Planning. Whereas the VLPFC is involved in promoting those aspects of the environmental stimuli that are consistent with the goals of an individual, the DLPFC is mostly attentive to rules and reasoning as in problem solving. The first is also named as the Ventral Affective System, in contrast to Dorsal Executive System. Put another way, the two sub-serve the general function of the PFC:

> The PFC is critical in situations when the mappings between sensory inputs, thoughts, and actions either are weakly established relative to other existing

ones or are rapidly changing. This is when we need to use the "rules of the game," internal representations of goals and the means to achieve them. (Miller & Cohen, 2001, p. 167)

Miller and Cohen, in fact, mention the two EF tests typically used for EF— The Stroop test and Wisconsin Card Sorting are given as examples of *rules of the game*. PFC is a *functional block*, remembering Luria.

The different regions of the PFC may also be carrying out qualitatively different operations required in EF/Planning. However, Miller and Cohen propose an alternative theory that we need not discuss here. Suffice it to suggest that the various regions of the PFC that are mentioned in the discussion later regarding Planning/EF carry out distinguishably different functions. A useful paper by Tanji and Hoshi (2008) provides a general view of current research on executive control.

Executive control, synonymous with EF, refers to those mechanisms by which behavioral performance is optimized in cognitive processing (Tanji & Hoshi, 2008). LPFC has two distinct functional blocks—ventrolateral and dorsolateral—as mentioned earlier. The ventral part is generally engaged in retrieval and selection of information in order to be used in carrying out a planned sequence of activities. The dorsal part is linked with higher levels of behavior planning that comprise putting together multiple pieces of information such as planning, manipulating, and integrating information from many sources. In fact, as mentioned several times in previous chapters, the entire frontal cortex has the broad function of planning and decision-making. This has been observed by Luria and supported by later neuropsychologists as we have discussed in PASS theory. However, the brain region is further specified in the study; its focus is LPFC.

The LPFC has been known to have an important role in regulating aspects of volitional acts by not only humans but also in other primates; see Tanji and Hoshi's review for details. In fact, that review is an excellent source to understand and appreciate the anatomical as well as the functional divisions of the LPFC and their relation to specific types of EF. To elaborate further, "the dorsal part of LPFC receives inputs from areas in the medial PFC, whereas the ventral LPFC receives afferents mostly from areas in the orbitofrontal cortex" (Tanji & Hoshi, 2007, p. 4). Further, the orbitofrontal cortex sorts through and manages inputs from several sensory areas including visual and auditory; it then retrieves and integrates the necessary information. In contrast, the dorsal LPFC works on signals that have been already processed and are multimodal in nature (see the appendix for relevant brain areas).

Inhibition and Shifting

Is it possible to assign specific processes including inhibition and shifting to distinct parts of the brain, particularly to its prefrontal region, continuing with our effort to understanding EF? A recent study provides the requisite evidence (Aron, Fletcher, Bullmore, Sahakian, & Robbins, 2003). The study focused on the activity of right lateralized *inferior frontal gyrus* (IFG). Patients diagnosed to have impairment in this brain region were administered a *Stop task*, recognized as a measure of suppression or inhibition of response (see Chapter 3). Patients showed a greater variability in reaction time for stopping the response; that is an indication of difficulty in response inhibition. The right IFG activation is suggested to have an important role in other tasks requiring inhibition or suppression of response. The investigation provides evidence that specific functions within EF can be localized. Furthermore, response inhibition measured by other tasks that require it, such as the Stroop task, activates the same region of the PFC.

The next study we present is an inquiry, broader in scope, into the functions of the PFC and its relation to Planning and EF (Huey, Krueger, & Grafman, 2006). Both left and right PFC are specifically involved in determining the features and meaning of individual events, whereas the right PFC integrates all of the relevant information, making sense of the plan as a whole. The ventral PFC that is concerned with emotions and the so-called *social brain* is engaged in plans that have a social–emotional significance.

Much has been written about DLPFC, as a "seat of reasoning" in matters that do not concern affect.

EF/Planning is not strictly confined to one region. At the center of the brain function of PFC "are representations composed of goal-oriented sequences of events that are involved in planning and monitoring complex behavior" (Huey et al., 2006, p. 169).

We recall here Luria's classic observation that the frontal lobes process inputs at the tertiary level, where the inputs have lost their specific modality. What makes that possible? The two divisions of lateral PFC, dorsal and ventral, make the loss of modality characteristic possible as the two divisions have extensive interconnections and perform integration of information from multimodal sources on a large scale.

The above statement in Huey et al. (2006) appears to support a general purpose view of EF, in apparent contradiction to the view that specific functions of EF are localizable, as shown in the study by Aron et al. (2003). The contradiction is only an apparent one, and can be reconciled by referring again to Luria. Although the brain can be divided into three main functional blocks, nevertheless, specific regions of the cortex within each block, and even across the blocks, are recognized to exist. Therefore, investigation into the contribution of the specific regions is useful both for theoretical understanding and for their clinical applications as in lesions of the right frontal lobe (Aron et al., 2003).

More on Shifting and Inhibition

Evidence for supporting a general purpose view or a modular view continues to be of interest. Is there a single executive process or are there multiple executive processes that work together toward the same goal in some task? Aron et al. provided evidence for response inhibition as measured by the Stop task, but speculated that the same area of the PFC would be involved in *response switching* as well. We have referred to Trail-making test (part of the CAS Planning Scale; Naglieri & Das, 1997 a, 1997b) in Chapter 1 as an example of shifting. The cost of *shifting* from one cognitive set to another (Trail-making Part 2, joining number 1 to letter A, then to 2 to letter B, and so on) in terms of response time is an accepted measure of shift. One method of computing the cost of switching cognitive sets, or shifting, can be estimated by dividing the *time* required for Part 2 by the *time* for Part 1 (Arbuthnott & Frank, 2000).

Is there a single executive process or are there multiple executive processes—the question was asked again by a group of researchers (Sylvester et al., 2003) using fMRI. In their experiments, they focused on the two major components of EF that have been previously identified: response switching (shifting) and response inhibition tasks. The objective was to examine the neural underpinnings of these two cognitive processes—specifically, the switching of attention between tasks and the resolution of interference between competing responses. What was their finding? Common neural areas across both tasks were found. However, the two cognitive processes could be further distinguished. The study identified special areas involved in the *shifting* of attention and the *inhibition* of a prepotent motor response as in Stroop. In conclusion, their study provides evidence for the separability of Shifting and Inhibition—the two cognitive processes of executive control or function. This result certainly supports statistical separation of the unified factor of EF shown in the Miyake and Friedman (2012) study.

Shifting and inhibition are distinguished by the type of tasks and the variables common to EF. It is important to understand the basic difference in paradigms or procedure apart from the contents of the task. Switching between cognitive sets has as its core the pre-requisite that a set has been established (joining numbers in order from 1 to 25 as in Trail-making Part 1). However, the set is not established by presenting the Trail-making Part 1 several times prior to the switch in instruction to join letters to numbers. Although one may argue that the number to number joining set has been established as a familiar and overlearned skill acquired by the participant, *switching* from a set established during the experiment by requiring the participant to follow a rule by repeatedly presenting the several prior sessions is typical in set-switching paradigm (see Crone, Bunge, Latenstein, & van der Molen, 2005), which is not a normal procedure in administering Trail-making.

To what extent does it involve inhibition of a prepotent response as in a typical Stroop interference task? We submit that the answer to this will determine the extent of overlap between shifting and inhibition, that is, the distinction between Trail-making and the Stroop test. Crone et al. (2005), however, did not pursue to answer in their study the difference between inhibition and shifting, but provided a valuable experiment on shifting or set switching for locating the regions of the brain most closely involved using fMRI.

The study is significant for two reasons relevant for the discussion of shifting: (1) in demonstrating the importance of delineating the specific cognitive processes involved in shifting, that is, representation and reconfiguration and (2) brain imaging resulting from cognitive processes must have a design in which each process studied has a simple and precise response (Press the left or the right key) so that the process is isolated from variables of task demand. Inasmuch as these two conditions exist in the experiment, imaging and performance data can be integrated for a better conceptualization of the cognitive process.

Concluding the Above Discussion

The various brain-imaging studies should answer the big question: Is there one unitary mechanism responsible for allocating attentional resources, such as a supervisory attentional system (Shallice, 1988) or a central executive proposed by Baddeley? The general conclusion appears to be *no*. Focusing on response switching or shifting, and on inhibition, there is a common mechanism that involves the parietal cortex and PFC. However, further separation of the two core EF activities has been made and cannot be overlooked (Sylvester et al., 2003; MacDonald, Cohen, Stenger, & Carter, 2000). There is reasonable evidence in regard to cognitive control in order to distinguish between two components—one to implement control and another to monitor performance.

The above studies are just a few examples of several others that relate brain imaging to EF and Planning operations. They also lead us to conclude that specific roles of DLPFC and anterior cingulate cortex exist in both allocation of attention and conflict resolution that feature prominently in research on EF. The scope of such investigations has expanded tremendously since the EFs for emotional (e.g., conflict resolution) and economic behavior, such as risk taking, have been added to contemporary research. Some discussion of emotion and its role in decision making is presented in a later chapter (Chapter 10).

A Location in the Brain for Intelligence

The best approach to gain knowledge about the place of intelligence in the brain is not by regarding intelligence as a global function, consisting of a conglomeration of albeit an eclectic collection of *intelligence abilities* (IQ), and the tests purported to assess each of those abilities. In fact, a global and general function is not amenable to localization in the brain as we have mentioned in the beginning of this chapter. Instead, a better approach is to study the various ways in which small parts of the brain are associated with specific cognitive functions attributed to each one, and explained in the several experiments reviewed in this chapter. We agree with Chris Frith on this matter:

> The brain consists of a great many that process information more or less independently of each other. It seems likely that it will be easier to discover how one of these modules works than to explaining the functioning of the brain as a whole. (Frith, 1997, p. 5)

Going along with fractionating brain functions, EF and general intelligence could have locations in the brain that overlap substantially. EF is broadly located in the LPFC, as Tanji and Hoshi (2008) concluded in their review. The functions of the LPFC include attention for action, retrieval, and manipulation of relevant information, behavioral planning, and goal selection. The LPFC even participates "in formulating concepts that enable subjects to effectively deal with complex behavioral demands" (p. 23). So is there a possibility of finding a place for *intelligence* in the brain? Consider a neural basis for general intelligence resembling Spearman's g. Given a *spatial task* to do that has a high g-loading in a brain imaging study by Duncan et al. (2000), "the strongest high-g activations occurred bilaterally in the lateral prefrontal cortex" (p. 455). The research report continued:

> In a recent analysis of imaging findings, indeed, we have shown that diverse forms of demand, including task novelty, response competition, working memory load, and perceptual difficulty, produce broadly similar lateral frontal activity ... all these demands are also associated with specific recruitment of the dorsal part of the anterior cingulate, close to the medial frontal activity seen here only for the spatial problem-solving task. (p. 8)

The spatial tasks such as Matrices and Block Design load on a *simultaneous* factor as discussed in PASS theory (see earlier sections of this chapter and Chapter 1). Recalling Shiho Tanaka's EEG coherence pattern in Chapter 1, each of the simultaneous tests crisscrossed the hemispheric boundary and showed a very similar pattern. Tanaka's pattern justifies Luria's unwillingness to localize visual–spatial processing in the right hemisphere. Duncan did not localize spatial problem solving to only one hemisphere of the brain either. The role played by anterior cingulate, a part of the cortex activated during conflict resolution, is again highlighted as part of the general intelligence. As we have discussed in the previous section, in making intelligent decisions, the necessity of conflict resolution is obvious, and affect cannot be dissociated from making important decisions.

Of course, research by Duncan et al. (2000) has not gone without challenge, but we believe that it is not wrong-headed. The research has been criticized in regard to locating general intelligence so narrowly in the brain (Jung & Haier, 2007). The authors proposed to broaden the location, to an integration of parietal and frontal activities (P-FIT). That view itself has had several critics. But essentially, research reported by Duncan et al. (2000) has brought EF and general intelligence closer. As one of the critical replies to Jung and Haier's main article suggests, posterior regions are involved only when executive demands are minimal and domain general functions, such as working memory, can be mapped on to specific regions of the PFC (Prabhakaran & Rypma, 2007). General intelligence is still mediated mostly through the PFC. Involvement of parietal lobe in an EF task, cognitive set switching, seems to be well accepted any way (Crone et al., 2005) as discussed in this chapter. According to the results of Crone et al.'s (2005) fMRI study, the medial PFC, including supplementary motor area and cingulated motor area, is consistently engaged during task switching along with the superior parietal cortex.

A final thought about EF and intelligence: Why are psychologists so very interested in EF? Precisely because as Banich wrote, psychologists are interested in expanding the understanding of EF; for it is thought to be a key process in intelligent behavior (Banich, 2009).

Overall Conclusions

In concluding this chapter, do we agree that EF and Planning overlap, but can be distinguished? Yes, at least in two important aspects. First, we think that Planning may not always necessarily lead to execution of the plan. It arises as an idea, but the mechanisms of execution require a different protocol. Second, Planning is much broader than the two components of EF, inhibition and shifting. Plans for the future, sensitivity to cultural milieu with its customs and traditions, and an ability to engage in domain-general problem solving (Premack, 2010) are some of the hallmarks of human planning.

This chapter presented more information on brain mechanisms; its objective was to have a better understanding of Planning/EF and general intelligence that could not have been accomplished by consideration of behavioral performance alone. We think the chapter clarified certain refractory issues. Planning and attention at the neurological level still remain to be distinguished. The issue is further complicated by extending the term attention to the domain of planning. Executive attention, supervisory attentional system, and controlled attention in problem solving (see Chapter 2) are frequently used as variations of *attention*. Brain-imaging methods need simple isolated behaviors that can best be measured by reaction time, as we suggested in the beginning of this chapter. The few studies of this type are given in this chapter that fractionate even the shifting or task switching, and question the generality of the core components of EF. *Single case studies* of neurological impairment need to support the results of imaging studies with *normal controls*. We end the chapter by citing the following review of studies as an example of data based on both kinds of participants on control of goal-directed attention.

> We review evidence for partially segregated networks of brain areas that carry out different attentional functions. One system, ... is involved in preparing and applying goal-directed (top-down) selection for stimuli and responses ... The other system, ... is not involved in top-down selection. Instead, this system

is specialized for the detection of behaviourally relevant stimuli, particularly when they are salient or unexpected ... Both attentional systems interact during normal vision, and both are disrupted in unilateral spatial neglect. (Corbetta & Shulman, 2002, p. 201)

More such studies on specific types of attention, planning, and EF are required for future research.

Neural Correlates of Executive Functions/Planning: Summary

It is time to gather together the discussion on the neural correlates of EF and by default the planning process. Banich (2009) has made this task easier.

1. EFs comprise a group of cognitive, affective, and conative processes. As Banich suggests, there is a general agreement with the idea that EF is a multidimensional function, a process used to guide behavior toward a goal especially in nonroutine situations.
2. Assessment of EF is difficult. As we review in Chapters 6 and 7, different conceptual models of EF provide justification for specific assessment measures.
3. There appears to be broad agreement in regard to a few assessment measures, notably Wisconsin Card sorting, Stroop test, Trails, Tower of Hanoi (London), and WM. These are conceptually grouped as measures of Inhibition, Shifting, and Memory updates.
4. The frontal lobes are the primary organs for EF and Planning. However, there is little agreement in regard to a manner in which the frontal lobes may support specific executive/planning functions. Our review in this chapter up to now is useful but leaves several open questions. However, the DLPFC and its associated regions, such as anterior cingulate, ventrolateral, and ventromedial regions, appear to be helped by posterior regions of the cortex.

   It is clear that neuroimaging cannot provide localization of neural activation to represent such general functions as *central executive*. As we mentioned earlier in this chapter, especially the central EFs are expressed in general behavior and personality characteristics.
5. However, agreement seems to exist in regard to the association of the three main types of EF (Inhibition, Shifting, and Memory updates),

each with a different part of the frontal cortex. Evidence from studies of patients with focal frontal lesions supports that "initiating and sustaining a response rely on medial frontal regions, task setting relies on left lateral regions, and monitoring involved in checking and adjusting task performance over time relies on right lateral regions" (Stuss & Alexander, 2007). The reference to Stuss and Alexander is especially welcome for linking Luria's frontal lobe functions to Planning as Stuss and Benson do; we reviewed their model in the beginning of this book and return to it in the last chapter as we revisit decision making.

6. In sum, the above conclusion is in agreement with the findings of Aron et al., Huey et al., and Tanji and Hoshi's reviews in this chapter.
7. Lastly, we agree with Banich in regard to the implications of understanding EF/Planning, of presenting an integrated view for training and treatment of deficiencies in EF. For us, the deficiencies in various forms exist in general populations. As we progress through subsequent chapters of the book, we discuss attentional deficits, failures of logic, emotion and will, and soiled mind-wares that distract us from decision making. In the final chapters, we present proposals for training.

In the next chapter, we return to Planning and Attention, distinguishing them primarily at the behavioral level, and secondarily at the level of their neural correlates.

Appendix

Brain Maps

Neural Systems Involved in Deliberative Decisions (Dorsal) vs. Affect-Laden Decisions (Ventral) in EF/Planning

The dorsal system includes brain regions typically associated with *cold* EFs, such as the DLPFC and the lateral parietal cortex (LPC), which are critical to the active maintenance of goal-relevant information. The ventral system includes brain regions involved in *hot* emotional decision processing, such as the amygdala (AMY), the VLPFC, and the medial PFC. See the research article in Iordan, Dolcos, and Dolcos (2013).

Figures A4.1-A4.3 show the basic areas of the brain, simply demarcating them.

Figure A4.1:
Hot (shaded) and cold (unshaded) decision-making brain locations

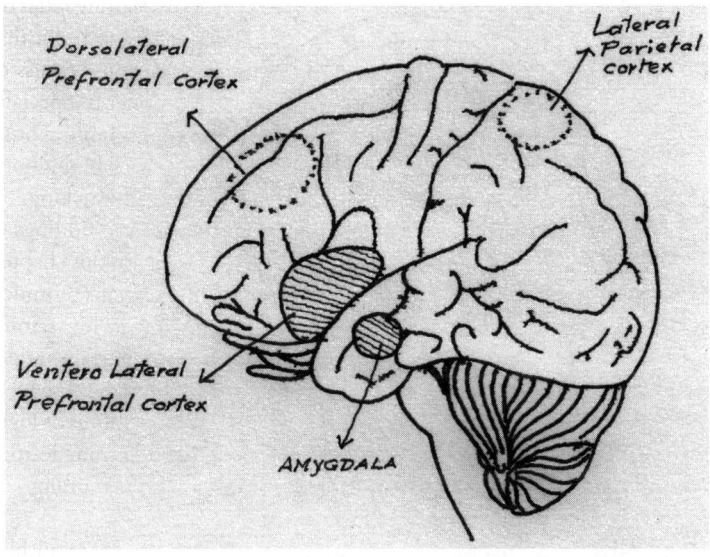

Figure A4.2:
Prefrontal cortex divisions

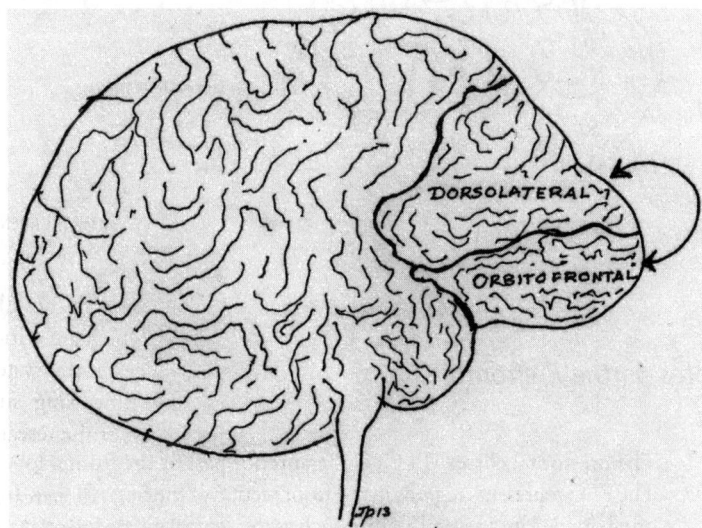

Figure A4.3:
(a) Brain Diagram: Limbic System (b) Brain Diagram: Prefrontal Cortex

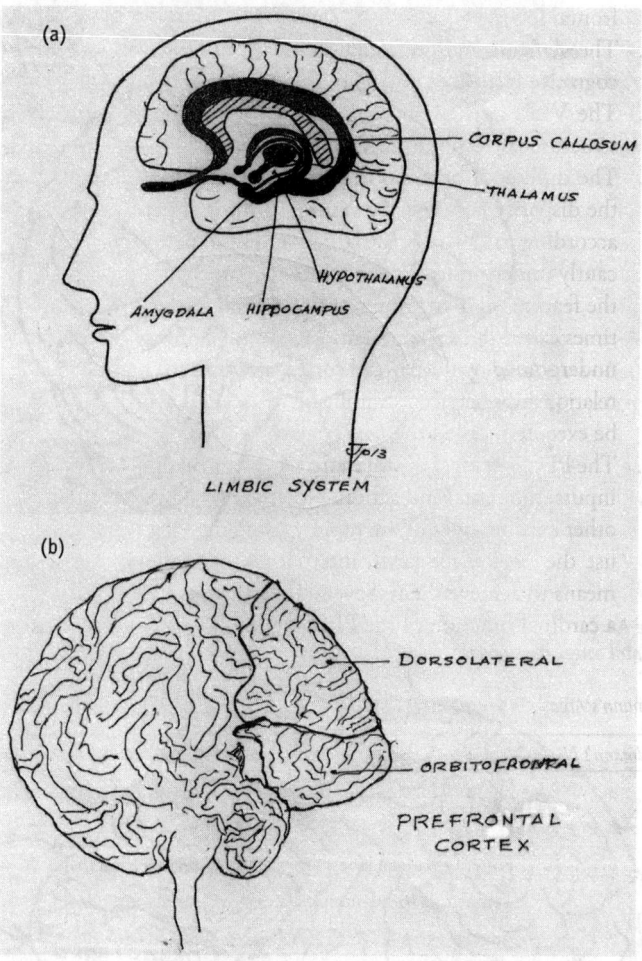

Notes on the Prefrontal Cortex

1. The prefrontal cortex (PFC) is the anterior part of the frontal lobes.
2. The PFC represents regions in the front section of the frontal lobes. It is often divided into several regions such as the ventrolateral, dorsolateral,

orbitofrontal, ventromedial, basal, orbital, and frontopolar areas. The ventrolateral and dorsolateral regions are located on the side of these frontal lobes.

3. The ventrolateral prefrontal cortex (VLPFC) mediates some of the cognitive responses to negative emotions.
4. The VLPFC is sometimes called the inferior frontal cortex. This structure corresponds to Brodmann's areas 44, 45, and 47.
5. The difference between the VLPFC and DLPFC roughly aligns to the disparity between the ventral and dorsal pathways of the cortex, according to O'Reilly (2010). The ventral pathway, which is significantly underpinned by the temporal cortex, attempts to characterize the features and attributes of the stimuli in the environment, sometimes called the *what* system. The dorsal pathway, which is primarily underpinned by the parietal cortex, attempts to characterize the spatial relationships between stimuli and to ascertain which responses should be executed, called the *how* system.
6. The PFC is critical in situations when the mappings between sensory inputs, thoughts, and actions either are weakly established relative to other existing ones or are rapidly changing. This is when we need to use the *rules of the game*, internal representations of goals, and the means to achieve them. Several investigators have argued that this is a cardinal function of the PFC.

Brodmann's Areas

Broadmann's No.	Name	Function
17	Occipital lobe	Visual projection cortex
18		Visual association cortex
19	Posterior parietal lobe	Visual association cortex
37	Tempero–parietal–occipital area	General sensory association cortex
39	Angular gyrus	Word recognition
40	Supramarginal lobe	Somatosensory association cortex
1, 2, 3	Postcentral gyrus	Somatosensory projection cortex
5, 7	Superior parietal lobule	General sensory association cortex
41, 42	Middle 1/3 of superior temporal cortex	Auditory projection cortex
22	Superior temporal gyrus	Auditory association cortex
21, 20, 38	Inferior temporal cortex	General sensory association cortex

(Table Continued)

(Table Continued)

Broadmann's No.	Name	Function
4	Precentral gyrus	Primary motor cortex
1, 2, 3	Postcentral gyrus	Somatosensory projection cortex
6, 8, 9	Premotor cortex	Motor association cortex
41, 42	Middle 1/3 of superior temporal cortex	Auditory projection cortex
44, 45, 46	Broca's area	Motor association cortex—specific to speech
10	Preftontal cortex	General motor association cortex
11	Orbital gyri	General motor association cortex

Notes: Anterior cingulate: also known as area 24 of Brodmann. The anterior cingulate is a defined area of the cerebral cortex including parts of both the cingulate gyrus and the frontal lobe. Numerous studies have implicated both anterior cingulate and PFC in attentional control and conflict resolution.

Area 11: Orbitofrontal area (orbital and rectus gyri, plus part of the rostral part of the superior frontal gyrus).

Area 12: Orbitofrontal area (used to be part of Brodmann's area 11) refers to the area between the superior frontal gyrus and the inferior rostral sulcus.

PART III

Attention, Planning, and Executive Functions: Assessment

5

Separating Planning and Attention

Executive Attention

> Steadiness of attention which makes us aware of much that our ordinary vision is not able to observe. Its power is proportional to our detachment from regrets over the past and anxieties for the future.
> The unwavering steadiness by which, through concentration, one controls the activities of the mind, the life breaths and the senses—that steadiness of attention is of the nature of sattvik (goodness). Radhakrishnan (1948, Chapter 18, verse 33, p. 362)

Attention is a mental process by which a person selectively registers some stimuli and ignores others. Attention has at least two primary aspects: It can be focused and it can be selective. In both focusing attention and selecting relevant information from irrelevant information, an individual must resist distraction. Posner and Boies' (1971) classic paper identified three major components of attention: alertness, selectivity, and processing capacity. A modification to these components (Posner, 1980) introduced two fundamental aspects of attention—Orienting and Detection. Let us explain the various components suggested thus far.

Orienting response is an older concept, traced to Pavlov (1928), and later elaborated by Sokolov (1963). Pavlov named it the "what is it" reflex. It is easily observed in animals as well as humans, externally in movements and postural changes in the body, as well as internal changes, such as autonomic heart rate and electrical changes in the skin, and in the central nervous system. It is essentially understood as *arousal* that remains a viable physiological response in contemporary research on attention. In humans, it is modified by instructions and other semantic stimuli, by ideas and imaginations. It can be conditioned, although unconditioned orienting responses occur to suddenly presented stimuli, such as a startled response to loud noise, a defensive response, a pinprick in the finger. Even a defensive response can be conditioned and evoked by semantic stimuli (Luria & Vinogradova, 1959). These have been discussed in detail in the chapter on Attention in Das, Naglieri, and Kirby (1994). Orienting response as a measure of Arousal is a cognitive component of attention. Justification is provided later.

Orienting Response Is Basic to Attention

Posner and colleagues have used visual locations as a model for studying orienting response, and have made significant contributions to understanding visual attention. An additional component to orienting response is suggested by Posner (1980), that is, "detection." A person may orient, but not detect. Perhaps, a banal example is found when your student may look at you while you lecture, but fails to detect the critical part of your speech. In any case, a third component that Posner suggested is "alerting"; the individual prepares to receive a significant stimulus or event. Actually, Pavlov and Luria, and other Soviet researchers incorporate it in orienting response; the anticipated visual event increases the sensitivity of the specific visual perceptual mechanisms including the projection areas in the brain (Das et al., 1994).

A basic component of attention is orienting response; it cannot be easily categorized as a planning behavior. Orienting response is a simple response to novelty. It habituates when the stimulus is presented repeatedly. Therefore, a mismatch between existing models and the new stimulus evokes an orienting response. The general "what is it response" can be specifically aroused by semantic stimuli as in an early experiment by Luria and Vinogradova (1959). Blood flow to fingertips and to the forehead, first of all, was altered depending on the nature of the stimulus—for example, a defensive response to a pinprick in the finger can be aroused through conditioning through a simple non-semantic stimulus such as a sound; blood flow at the fingertip and forehead was comparable. However, when a semantic stimulus (word "doctor") is presented, doctors give you injections and break your skin; it is painful, and blood vessels in the fingertip constrict; in contrast, blood vessels in the forehead dilate apparently suggesting "thinking." Orienting response is a cognitive response. It can be altered by instruction, as in evoked potential (electroencephalography [EEG]) recordings: When asked to attend to light flashes, and not clicks, evoked potentials are appropriately observed to light, and vice versa when the instruction changes, to respond to click, not lights. (See Das et al. [1994] for a discussion of some of the earlier studies on attention and orienting response.) The question then concerns categorizing such responses as Planning. As orienting response tasks become cognitively loaded, the involvement of frontal lobes becomes apparent. Following the aforementioned conceptual treatment of orienting response, its measurement as a component of attention is considered next.

How to Measure Planning and Attention?

We come to a practical question: How to measure attention and planning in a psychometric test, CAS? Wherever selective attention is required for doing a task, such as physical versus name identity (modification of Posner's task—detect two letters of the alphabet that are in an identical pair of uppercase versus two letters that have the same name, one in uppercase and the other in lowercase), the latter demands greater discrimination. Most probably the latter involves greater input from the frontal lobes, to simplify the argument, and is therefore closer to Planning. Furthermore, inhibiting a response, not only focusing attention on a relevant one, adds to selectivity, and as in the Stroop test for resolution of conflict. We should reflect then on the unique characteristic of attention compared to planning. Attention by definition is attending to the salient stimulus, and it resists distraction. However, in atypical individuals, such as ADHD, control and regulation of behavior is the primary concern—the distinct functions of dorsolateral prefrontal cortex and ventromedial prefrontal cortex.

The selectivity aspect of attention relates to intentional discrimination between stimuli. Visual searching of a target, a number embedded among other numbers, for example, requires selection. However, a number embedded among pictures may require less effort, and a number in red ink in a field of other numbers in black will be automatically detected. These are well-known concepts that have been used in tests of visual search. Auditory vigilance provides another widely used test of selective attention. The Attention tests in the Das–Naglieri Cognitive Assessment System (CAS) are discussed at several places of the present book. Lastly, processing capacity obviously assumes that it is limited. The concept is not unique to attention; memory, especially working memory, assumes a limited capacity that is influenced by attention. Indeed, it is a critical component of Planning and general intelligence as discussed in the previous chapters.

Working Memory, Attention, and Planning

The connection between working memory and attention is suggested clearly by Baddeley (1986, also see Baddeley, 2012). It has been further elaborated by Cowan (2001). Working memory, according to Cowan, plays a pivotal role in directing and sustaining attention. In fact, in remembering a series of digits such as a seven-digit telephone number, chunking the numbers into smaller units should improve recall. However, Cowan focused on many situations in which people presumably could not carry out chunking because attention was diverted away from the stimuli until after they were presented. The presentation is serial as usual. The point of this discussion is to understand that attention is very much similar to an "executive" process. It directs selective perception. There is thus a blurring of the distinction between planning and attention. Like planning, the region of the brain associated with executive attention is the prefrontal cortex, as we have discussed in the preceding chapters.

The distinction between attention as part of executive processes and attention as arousal, orienting response, and automatic filtering mechanism in perception (as in visual search) can be a matter of degrees. It may be argued that since attention is essentially a cognitive process, automatic responses can begin as deliberate and effortful responses, but become automatic habits through numerous practice sessions. And even automatic response, as in the Stroop test that compels the individual to read the word rather than the color of the ink automatically, may be manipulated. In any case, words take precedence over color as a result of intense familiarity with reading words.

Working memory according to some authors is a component of EF, whereas others doubt that it should be so because it aligns itself more with general intelligence (see discussion in Chapters 2–4). EF and by default Planning are then drawn into this conceptual debate. When working memory overlaps with attention and core components in working memory now accommodate the role of attention by adding "episodic buffer," how should we view the relation between Attention and Planning?

Revisiting Attention–Planning Disconnection

Tests of attention such as the Stroop test and Vigilance in contrast to Planning tests, such as Trail Making and Crack the Code (see the next chapter for a discussion of tests) have been found useful in diagnosis of special populations, such as individuals with attention deficits and fetal alcohol syndrome (FAS), which we will discuss next. We will present these in a subsequent section, and conclude that by maintaining a distinction between Planning and Attention, we can achieve conceptual clarity as well as better understand the special populations. In other words, we will establish their construct validity and pragmatic validity.

Their brain localizations or neural networks of planning and attention can further separate the two constructs. Early on, Luria (1966) suggested that planning and the basic attention processes are separable at the level of both cognition and the brain. Current research agrees with this. For instance, consider that Executive Attention that is characterized as maintaining focus and direction and reflects intention is closer to Planning. Planning includes executive functions (EFs), judgments, decision making, and evaluations, as we have discussed in the previous chapters. To recap, Luria listed three characteristics of Planning as a goal-directed activity in contrast to attention: (1) recoding of information, (2) the formation of action programs that select appropriate responses, and inhibition of interfering ones, and (3) a comparison of the effect of action with the original intention. These are the three characteristic features of conscious activity. The intentional activities are carried out with the intimate participation of speech processes (Das et al., 1994, Chapter 5). Executive control fits the description of planning better than EF. Perhaps, it is hard see how Attention will subsume Planning.

In contrast, planning with automatic attention and selective attention filters information even before it is perceived. These are controlled by the posterior attentional network based primarily in the parietal cortex. Executive attention, on the other hand, depends on the anterior attentional network located in the prefrontal cortex (Dietrich, 2007, p. 201). Further discussions of the neural basis of EFs, in general, have been presented in the previous chapters of this book.

In the following section, we discuss some empirical studies adding evidence to establish the relative independence of Planning and Attention constructs.

Relative Independence of Planning and Attention: The Case of ADHD

The key difficulty of a child with ADHD is not inattention or poor attention; rather, it is the failure to stop, look, listen, and feel. A deficiency in the child's ability to inhibit behavior is implicated, characterizing a failure of EFs—or Planning as in the PASS theory. Consistent with this line of conceptualization of ADHD are Barkley's (1997) attempts at solidifying ADHD explanations in terms of dysfunction of the frontal lobe. It has for its centerpiece the concept of behavioral inhibition, of which children with ADHD seem to have an extremely low level.

We suggest that if behavioral inhibition of children with ADHD is explained as a cognitive deficit, it is a variant of Planning processes (Das et al., 1994). Planning function is organized in the frontal lobe, the same major brain area that differentiates between ADHD and "normal" children. The frontal lobe's size is smaller, and its activities are decreased in children with ADHD (Panksepp, 1998). Cortical under arousal or diminished activation of the front part of the brain has been suspected in children with ADHD, who are found to have low metabolic activity in frontal lobes.

Before we follow the suggestion that ADHD is a Planning deficit that assumes a weakness in frontal lobe functions, we wish to step backwards and consider the arousal level as a primary component of attention. The reason is simple—hyperactivity may indeed be characterized by hyperarousal, and contrasted to states of hypoactivity (apathy, slow to be excited) or low arousal. Neither of these states can be regarded as components of Planning.

Attention and Arousal: Hyperactive and Hypoactive Children

Luria (1963) was one of the first researchers to observe three types of children in terms of arousal: the hypoactive, the hyperactive, and the normal (normoactive). As the names suggest, hypoactive types are underaroused and the hyperactive are overaroused, whereas the normoactive maintain a balance between excitation and inhibition. The descriptive terms imply Pavlov's assumption that we differ in the types of nervous systems that are easily prone to excitation or inhibition and the balanced type. Hyperactive make many errors of commission in a typical vigilance task ("tap the table when you hear the number 3 spoken" within a continuous stream of single digits is an example of a simple vigilance task). In contrast, hypoactives miss out tapping for the target number. Such types of children may be found among those with learning disability. When the cognitive load in the attention task is high (tap for number 3 only when it is spoken immediately following number 1), it is possible to observe the three types; however, if it is low (tap for 3), differences disappear. Das (1970) and Williams and Das (1979) were able to identify the three types of participants among normal, learning disabled, and children with mental retardation. Research has not been plentiful in this area. However, an interesting study that is not so strongly associated with Luria's theoretical notion of excitatory and inhibitory nervous system demonstrated the difference between the vigilance performance of two groups of children with learning disability. The study by Ozolins and Anderson (1980), who used feedback or knowledge of results (KR) in a vigilance study, has suggested that hyperactive and hypoactive children with learning disabilities might respond differently to KR. Having identified the two types among children with learning disability, the author found that the respective arousal levels of hypoactive and hyperactive children with learning disabilities can be used for producing improved level of vigilance. It is possible to change a child's arousal level by the manner through which knowledge of performance was given. Specifically, this was observed in hyperactive children by strengthening their level of inhibition.

Poor Planning in Children with Attention Deficit

If we accept the explanation that the location of the cognitive difficulties of ADHD is likely in the frontal cortex rather than in the limbic system, and temporal, occipital, parietal (TOP) areas of the cortex, the logical next step is to present some empirical results using the CAS with the intention to single out Planning measures as particularly relevant.

A study by Naglieri et al. (2003) is mentioned as an example of evidential validity. The part of the study that is relevant here concerns the comparison between a sample of 25 children with ADHD and a normative group on two tests, the CAS and the WISC-III. The purpose was to examine the assumption that the PASS theory and its derivative, CAS, may be particularly sensitive to the cognitive difficulties of children with ADHD, whereas the general intelligence test, WISC-III, is inadequate for diagnosis of ADHD. Specifically, a low Planning score was expected for the ADHD sample. The results showed a large difference in scores on Planning between the ADHD and the standardization samples. However, in regard to the Attention scales, a smaller difference was observed. The differences between the two samples in Simultaneous and Successive scales were not significant at all.

The next study we examine is closer to an attention deficit (Papadopoulos et al., 2005) and reinforces a connection between planning and attention deficit. We think its merit to be special attention because, first, it included EF tests in addition to the Planning and Attention tests in CAS tests, and, second, the low and high attention groups that were compared had been selected on the basis of teachers' rating of inattention in the class as well as the criteria for hyperactivity from *Diagnostic and Statistical Manual of Mental Disorders*, Fourth Edition (DSM-IV). Incidentally, all children who were in Cyprus spoke Greek, and were tested with Greek translation of EF tests and the CAS. The participants were 98 children (Grades 4 and 6), 49 in each group, with a low attention group and a control group of children who were judged to be normal in attention. The star EF/Planning task was the Crack-the-Code (CTC) test that has been previously used in several studies (Das, Kar, & Parrila, 1996). To briefly explain, participants in this test are shown two to five information lines that contain two to five colored disks in a particular order followed by labels, indicating how many of the disks are in the correct place. Participants must integrate information from all the lines and work out on which colored disk should go to which place on the response line. Because we will describe the test in detail in the next chapter of the book; the above description will suffice for now. The CTC, in some versions, has six problems, and in other versions, there are additional three or six problems that vary in levels of difficulty. Each problem was scored for a correct/incorrect answer, the time taken to think before the participant made the first move for placing the disk on the answer line, the time to evaluate the answer after completing all the moves, and the total time for solving the problem.

Which of these will reflect EF/Planning? Without the benefit of the results of the study, we would expect that the control children would be superior to the attention-deficit children in every measure. Actually, the total time taken for solution was not significantly different, that is, speed of solution did not distinguish between the groups. The number of correct solutions was greater for the controls, as expected. These children also took longer to think before they made any moves at all; they were working out their strategies. However, once they had arrived at the solution, they were sure of their answers and spent less time evaluating it. We cite the results of CTC in some detail because the task allows us to analyze the process of planning and decision making, the key activities of EF. We regard CTC as Planning, rather than a measure of attention.

Planning Deficit Predominant in Fetal Alcohol Syndrome

The difference between Planning and Attention is again found to be meaningful in the research on FAS, as suggested in a recently completed study (Mackey, English, Bisanz, & Kulak, 2003) which is briefly reported. Its purpose was to determine whether Planning (the authors use Executive Function, or EF, as equivalent to Planning) was a relative weakness in the FAS population. The participants included 7 children (5 boys and 2 girls) diagnosed with FAS and 11 children (7 boys and 4 girls) with confirmed prenatal exposure to alcohol, who did not have the physical characteristics required for an FAS diagnosis. The mean age of the FAS group (years:months) was 10:7 (R = 7:9 to 13:4). The mean age of the group with alcohol-related effects other than FAS was 9:4 months (R = 6:1 to 12:8). The mean full scale standard score of the sample was 84.6 (SD = 13.2).

To determine whether the four PASS scores differed, a repeated measure, ANOVA was performed. The analysis indicated an effect of PASS components, $F(3, 57) = 11.12$, $p < .001$. Importantly, tests of simple effects showed that the mean planning score was lower than the mean for the other components ($p < .001$). Further, the mean Simultaneous processing score was higher than the mean of the Attention and Successive processing scores ($p < .005$), and the latter two did not differ. As predicted, the sample of children with alcohol-related effects scored lower on the measures of Planning than on measures of other cognitive processes. Effect of medication (Ritalin) revealed no differences between the children who were medicated and non-medicated, and the interaction between PASS component scores and medication was not significant. In sum, children with FAS and children with other alcohol-related effects performed equally poorly on the Planning component. In contrast, both the groups performed normatively in Simultaneous processing. In sum, a relative weakness in Planning appears to be the critical variable.

Fetal Alcohol Spectrum Disorder (FASD) and Planning

If we combine the two samples in the previous study (Mackey et al., 2003) of the 7 FAS children and the 11 children with confirmed prenatal exposure to alcohol, who did not have the physical characteristics required for an FAS diagnosis, all the 18 children would fit the FASD diagnosis. Therefore, the findings of the second study and the first one could be compared.

By the time a second study was carried out to examine the link between FASD and Planning processes as measured by CAS (Odishaw, 2007), a proposal to describe EFs comprising the three components (working memory, inhibition of a prepotent response, and set shifting) had gained prominence (Miyake et al., 2000). In that proposal, EF was characterized as a unitary construct with the three aforementioned partially dissociable components.

Odishaw (2007) took note of Miyake's (2000) proposal in choosing appropriate tests from Delis and Kaplan (Delis, Kaplan, & Kramer, 2001).

She selected two tests to assess set shifting and two tests for assessing inhibition. The Verbal-Fluency Category Switching test and the Design-Fluency Switching test do not have a parallel measure among the eight CAS tests selected for the present study. On the other hand, one of the two tests that assessed inhibition did have a similar match in CAS; the Color–Word Interference test is similar to Expressive Attention, and both are variants of the Stroop test.

The other test for planning and EF assessment is the Tower of Hanoi (TOH) (see Lezak, 2004). The TOH puzzle has proved to be a suitable task for studying a variety of executive processes. Like other tests of EF, described in the next chapter, the task has demonstrated sensitivity to prefrontal lobe dysfunction (Miyake et al., 2000) and taps processes, such as planning, working memory, updating, and inhibition (Gwenny et al., 2010). Simon suggested that the constraints of this task encourage spontaneous generation of several problem-solving strategies. These differ in their effectiveness. That may explain normal individual differences in performance (cited in Gwenny et al., 2010).

Performances of these EF tests were compared to CAS test scores. It should be noted at this point that EF tests from Delis and Kaplan include attention, a Stroop-like test. As a whole, Delis and Kaplan do not separate attention from planning, unlike PASS theory and CAS.

A sample of 38 boys and girls who had been clinically diagnosed as FASD cases was selected from specialized clinics. The mean age was 12 years, ranging from 8 to 16 years. Tests included the Delis–Kaplan Executive Function System (Delis et al., 2001). Results were compared with the normative scores for the specific tests. CAS standard scores for the four scales are reported below:

	Mean	Median
Planning	85.63	85
Simultaneous	94.39	94
Attention	92	94
Successive	87.66	89

As all tests were not normally distributed, mean and median scores were different for some tests reported. Planning, rather than Attention, appears to have the lowest score for the sample, especially if median scores are considered. This is consistent for the results of the previous study on FAS. However, a simple repeated measure, ANOVA, used mean scores, and the results $F = 7.29$ were significant ($p < .05$). Follow-up tests revealed differences between pairs of CAS scales as follows: Planning–Attention significant at the $p < .01$ level as also Planning–Simultaneous, Simultaneous–Successive, Attention–Successive ($p = .03$). But differences between Planning and Successive as well as Simultaneous and Attention were not significant ($p > .05$). The results of interest concern the relatively lowest mean score in Planning and the relatively high mean score for the Simultaneous scale in the FASD sample. In sum, low Planning and relatively high Simultaneous processing appear to characterize the FASD samples in both the studies. The studies generally support a ground for viewing Planning and Attention separately.

Planning Deficiency in Autism

Autism, as diagnosed today, comprises three kinds of impairment: social interaction; verbal and nonverbal communication; and restricted, repetitive, and stereotyped interests and activities (Grossberg & Seidman, 2006). The term that has replaced autism is *Autistic Spectrum Disorder* (ASD). The three diagnostic criteria for ASD seem to be generally acceptable now as they were in 1989, the year Frith's comprehensive and influential book, *Autism*, was published (Frith, 1989).

Core Components of Autism

Frith's (1989) book contains graphic case histories, including those concerning Asperger's syndrome—a group of individuals with normal or superior IQ, but sharing the core components of autism. It is generally accepted that an individual with autism has a deficient Theory of Mind; he or she cannot anticipate the intentions and motivations of others, at least not always and not in unfamiliar surroundings such as in a party or gathering of other individuals. However, when we examine the cognitive profile of individuals with Asperger's syndrome, or within the broad category of ASD, it will be apparent that there is a great variation in cognitive and social abilities.

It is difficult to propose an integral core of disorder for diagnosis and treatment of autism. Autism refers to a heterogeneous diagnostic group: "Extreme unevenness in cognitive skills is a common feature of autism"

(Grossberg & Seidman, 2006, p. 485). Happé, Ronald, and Plomin (2006) seem to have the last word on acknowledging the heterogeneity in autism at not only the cognitive and behavioral levels, but also at the genetic level. Especially at the cognitive level, they conclude that half a century of research has failed to find a single explanation for autism. Their article recommends that one way out of this impossible problem of defining autistic characteristics comprising social, communicative, and rigid/repetitive behavior is to study the relationship among these three traits in the general population. Such an orientation sits well with PASS theory—it is a theory of major cognitive processes that are "fractionated" and applied to normal variations in general populations, and at the same time useful for identifying specific cognitive weakness in atypical samples. An integral picture of the three traits defining autistic-like behavior cannot be obtained, as Happé et al. (2006) insist that we abandon such efforts and focus on fractionable traits. In their review, two of the traits—social and communicative difficulties—appear to exist together in 32 per cent of children. Is there then a hope that both difficulties are linked to the broad category of cognitive processes we have named "Planning"? Happé and Ronald (2008) in their review mention evidence for weakness in planning—Planning tasks such as TOH activate a broad area consisting of fronto–parietal–thalamic connection. Such connection is weak in ASD among adult volunteers.

Do autistic individuals perform poorly in tests of EF excluding attention? The rationale for *studying atypical cognition in order to gain further knowledge about cognition in general* and vice versa has been accepted for some time, and in agreement with Happé et al. (2006). We have tacitly accepted it as well—the concepts of PASS as general cognitive processes have been nourished by the *clinical observations* of Luria. The practice continues in contemporary studies using brain imaging. A recent study on executive dysfunction in autism (Hill, 2004) is selected as an example.

Hill (2004) restated the functions that define EF: planning, working memory, impulse control, inhibition and shifting, and the initiation and monitoring of action. The list of functions overlaps with the one provided by Friedman (Friedman et al., 2006). Deficits in planning (as exemplified by the TOH task) and flexibility (as in strategy change and reversal shifts in learning tasks) have been frequently noticed, according to Hill's (2004) review of the autistic cognitive profile. Hill's review, however, does not affirm that individuals will show deficient performance with all tests of inhibition or shifting; she is more certain of planning tasks, such as the TOH. An equivalent task is CTC, which we will review in detail in a separate chapter. Finally, Planning and Set-shifting as two processes that were commonly found to be weak among a sample of autistic children (Pelicano, 2010) encourage us to assume a Planning/EF weakness, but not attention.

Admittedly, the aforementioned discussion is more about autism than about the distinction between Attention and Planning. However, autism is used as an example of a syndrome that is better understood as a dysfunction in Planning/EF than in attention. For now, we return to the theme of this chapter, that is, to determine how separate Attention and Planning are in the CAS, as instantiated by the performance of a university student with Asperger's.

The Case Study

The participant was L, a 20-year-old university student. She took the CAS twice, separated by nearly 3 weeks. We asked her the following: L, please write a short history of your experience in school and college. What are some of the difficult situations—social planning, attention, visual–spatial and short-term memory? Describe your experience of first testing on CAS and second testing on CAS. What was different for you? What did you do differently?

Since she was a university student, we did not expect her to have generally poor cognitive performance in CAS. We were curious, however, to learn of her processing strengths. She was given eight CAS tasks, two from each of the four scales (Planning, Attention, Simultaneous, and Successive). The standard administration procedure was followed as prescribed in the CAS administration manual (Naglieri & Das, 1997a, 1997b); additionally, she would talk to herself as she was completing the test. The first administration showed the following standard scores ($M = 100$, $SD = 15$): Planning = 82, Attention = 88, Simultaneous = 123, Successive = 128, and Full Scale = 108. Note that Full Scale is usually not informative if the subtest scale scores are quite diverse, as it is in this case. The norm tables given in CAS for 17–18-year-olds were the basis for calculating the standard scores. In the second administration of CAS, L was also allowed to talk to herself as she was doing a test. The second administration showed the following standard scores: Planning = 77, Attention = 94, Simultaneous = 132 and Successive = 137, and Full Scale = 114.

First, we will discuss the scores and then, briefly, relevant excerpts from her verbal protocol during test taking. The profile shows superior cognitive processing in Simultaneous and Successive processing. She is clearly above the norm in both the processes, even above two standard deviations on second administration. Her Planning remains the weakest point in her profile, and did not seem to benefit from her first experience with the test. In contrast, her Attention score increases sufficiently to include her performance in the normal range.

At this point, her verbal protocol could be very helpful in describing her thinking through the task, her executive processing. She was doing the Matching Number task; the task is to find two numbers in the same row that are identical to each other and underline the pair of numbers. An example is given below:

L: 914. Okay, unless something matches with the 9, 4, 1. 884. 824, does anything match with it?

Dr Das: Now that was matching numbers, tell me how you did it.

L: I'm trying a new strategy, so I got a bit confused using it. What I did was I started with the two outer numbers, right and see if anything matched with them, then I went into these two, does anything match with these two, and then I finally go to the two ones in the middle.

She was clearly using strategies, but realized that she needed to change when the numbers got larger.

Dr Das: Oh good. Now the next one we are going to show, are you going to use the same strategy?

L: I think so.

Dr Das: Now let's do the next one.

L: 6962 and 9682. Okay 6982, 6982. I noticed right there I didn't have to go. I was still comparing it with the first two in the middle.

Dr Das: Go ahead.

L: 7136 okay, 7316. 9153, 9513 (*mumbles numbers, inaudible*)

Dr Das: Now tell me how you did it.

L: Okay, I tried to continue with the strategy but they were too big and I was getting confused and then all mixed up and reversing them. So what I eventually did was I went back to the thing of taking the first one, memorizing the first one and going along, and then going with the second one. I'm trying to find a good strategy for this; I don't really see any good strategies.

Dr Das: Do you think it works or you could change the strategy?

L: I could change the strategy but I'm not sure what to change it to.

Her thinking is clearly focused on the task; she is aware that a change in strategy is necessary, but cannot find the right one. This gives us an example of the inner speech regulating EF.

Spontaneous verbal responses while working on Matching Numbers task:

L: I'm going to move it to the middle. Does it match with these two? No. Does anything match with these two? Okay. I spaced out. This was stupid. Does anything match with any of these ones? Yep. Okay 438, does anything match with 438? No. 348, yes. Okay! (see the appendix).

Summing Up the Case Histories

Our interest in this chapter is in regard to separating attention and Planning/EF.

A typical cognitive profile for Autism, including Asperger's, may reveal that some individuals could be deficient in shifting, whereas others in inhibiting a prepotent response. Alternatively, some groups of individuals with autism may have attentional deficit, rather than a Planning/EF deficit. In either case, it is useful to review the relationship between Attention on the one hand and Planning on the other, within the broader concept of EF. The construct of EF has been discussed in the previous chapters. One of the major problems is with the tests we use to assess EF, specifically in CAS, as this is the primary battery of tests for assessment in all the three diagnostic categories. Given that one of the two major components that define EF is inhibition of a prepotent response (the other is response shift) that is typically assessed by the Stroop test (Expressive Attention test in CAS), we may have to consider an attentional measure as a diagnostic test for ADHD, FASD, and Autism. On the other hand, should EF be narrowly assessed by tests of "inhibition of a prepotent response" and shifting? For several researchers cited in Rajendran and Mitchell's (2007) review, it should not. For example, Tranel, Anderson, and Benton (1994) define it as planning, decision making, judgment, and self-perception; none of these is a part of the definition of Attention in PASS theory, and all of them are elements of construct of Planning. In our particular case of Asperger's, planning deficit was clearly present. Planning, and not attention deficit, emerged as the important variable as we have suggested in examining the cognitive deficit associated with ADHD, fetal alcohol syndrome/effects (FAS/E), and Autism. These issues will be resolved to some extent in the subsequent section and epilogue.

Commonality between the Clinical Groups: Another Look at PASS Framework and Executive Functions

Outside our own research, there is ample evidence that all the three clinical groups, ADHD, FAS, and autism, do manifest some degree of weakness in EF. Working memory has been accepted as a part of EF. In the chapters on Planning and EF (Chapters 2 and 3), we argued that EF is a fairly unique process, distinguished from general IQ, inasmuch as IQ is significantly related to working memory. Indeed, the so-called fluid intelligence and working memory capacity taken together make up general intelligence, according to several authors (e.g., Geary [2005] for a recent review, in addition to Chapter 2 in this book). We sided with the proposal of Miyake et al. (2000) in favor of maintaining the distinction between IQ and EF. Not only is this a theoretically significant proposal, but also it informs the practitioner for rehabilitation and treatment of the three clinical groups discussed earlier.

Another Look at ADHD

ADHD is a more pervasive disorder than either Autism or FAS. A recent paper (Nigg, 2010) provides a comprehensive review of ADHD; the markers for identifying ADHD are personality and cognitive measures. The cognitive measures include EFs and vigilance. Rather than referring to a large battery of EF measures, Nigg specifies *response suppression and shifting* that are broadly accepted as core components of EF, as we have discussed in previous chapters. Vigilance is known to be a core test of attention (Das et al., 1994), whereas the measures of response suppression (Stroop-like test) and shifting (Trails) are parts of Attention and Planning tests, respectively, in CAS (Chapter 1). It appears that EF includes CAS tests of attention and planning scales.

Inhibition and ADHD

We had begun to discuss the historical roots of inhibition as a major component of EFs in a previous chapter. To recap, inhibition has been recognized as a fundamental property of an organism's neural function by Pavlov (1928).

He recognized excitation and inhibition as the two basic characteristics of the nervous system. The importance of inhibition has continued to be recognized in contemporary psychology, especially in regard to EF. Which one of the three EF components—Inhibition, Shifting, and Memory updating—has the highest loading on the common heritable factor? It is inhibition (one of the star measures is the Stroop-like test)! This elevates inhibition to the most heritable and a defining function of EF, accounting for its unity (Miyake & Friedman, 2012).

Inhibition is also at the center of explanation for ADHD. It is a key concept for diagnosis of attention deficit and hyperactivity. The problem is in distinguishing between at least two major concepts of inhibition—behavioral inhibition and inhibition that has Pavlovian roots. We should examine each one of them in relation to ADHD. In fact, we have briefly summarized an attempt to do so in a previous paper (Das & Papadopoulos, 2003).

Barkley has continued to present "behavioral inhibition" as the major explanation for diagnosis of ADHD (Barkley, 1997) and the focus of treatment (Barkley, 1997). The children with ADHD do not have a problem with attention. Rather, it is their failure to stop, look, listen, and feel. In a nutshell, it is a failure of executive control. Here then is a strong link to EF; it is a deficit in behavioral inhibition. Consistent with the location of EF, as we have discussed in the two previous chapters, we will side with Barkley as he associates the failure with the activities of the frontal lobes. The disagreement lies in accepting ADHD as a label for hyperactivity; a less stringent definition includes a combination of inattention and hyperactivity. Additionally, we propose a deconstruction of behavioral *inhibition to comprise internal and external inhibition, and disinhibition.* To elaborate, ADHD children have a special difficulty in maintaining attention, especially when the teacher is working out the answer to a simple multiplication because there is a delay between different steps of solving the problem. This is analogous to a gap before the solution arrives. During this delay, however, the students are expected to maintain attention, a set, without getting distracted.

They have to *actively* inhibit attending to interrupting events around them and block mind-wandering as well. Active blocking is an instance of internal inhibition; in contrast, sudden disturbances in the environment are sources of external inhibition that interrupt the students' attentional set—an instance of disinhibition. In both cases, *control of behavior* is in operation, that is, the essence of EFs.

We conclude that an inclusive category of ADHD should include inattention, hyperactivity, impulsiveness, and conduct disorder. ADHD is an atypical condition associated with EF dysfunction. It is broad enough to include both cognitive deficiency as well as dysfunction in social–emotional behavior. ADHD may be thus associated with both a dysfunction of the dorsolateral prefrontal cortex as well as with a deficit in the orbitofrontal region.

What is new in the integrative paper by Nigg is a proposal to separate ADHD behavior, first into two theoretical categories—*controlled responding* and *reactive responding*. To elaborate, controlled responding is represented by conscientiousness (a personality variable) and resiliency (a temperamental variable), as well as the two cognitive processes—response inhibition (Stroop/stop task) and set shifting (Trails). Reactive responding means responsible behavior, that is, not an emotional reaction. However, Nigg does not believe that there is firm evidence of the relation between ADHD and shifting.

Elaborating Nigg's hypothesis in regard to psychological processes that influence ADHD, his evidence is based on mothers' rating of their children as *conscientious and resilient*, and on lab tasks that provide objective measures of the two cognitive processes, *inhibition and shifting*. The first three measures (two personality and temperamental, and response inhibition) are lower in inattentive children as rated by teachers. In addition to this, such children rated as having attention problems are also found to be poor in a sustained attention task—*vigilance*. Clearly then, this group of simple *inattentive* children, who are not hyperactive, are distinguished from those with Hyperactivity–Impulsivity group, rated by teachers. The author's conclusion from his review is as follows: It is now apparent that whereas some forms of attention are normal in ADHD, cognitive control and vigilance are impaired (pp. 28–29).

A separation between simply inattentive and hyperactivity types was supported in our previous work on a teacher's rating (Das & Melnyk, 1989; Papadopoulos, Das, Kodero, & Solomon, 2002) discussed in the next paragraph. However, we agree with Nigg's conclusion that ADHD is a heterogeneous syndrome; perhaps, there are multiple routes to this syndrome and their corresponding neural routes.

What does it all mean? Why give so much space to Nigg's review? Harking back to the previous work on attention and ADHD reported that (in an earlier section of this chapter) there was an apparent contradiction. Whereas ADHD appeared to be associated with a Planning deficit, Nigg's review and proposal suggest that inattentiveness, as distinguished from hyperactivity–impulsivity, is characterized by the cognitive deficit in response suppression. In the framework of CAS, Stroop test (Expressive Attention), and Vigilance are measures of attention. Can teachers rate their students as inattentive, different from hyperactive and impulsive? Indeed, they can (Das & Abbott, 1995; Das, Snyder, & Mishra, 1992; Papadopoulos et al., 2002).

These studies were based on regular class students, not specially selected for ADHD. There was little overlap in teachers' rating between the Attention scale and Connor's Hyperactivity-Impulsive scale when the two scales were given to teachers for rating their students' behavior as revealed by factor analysis. Objective tests of attention included the Stroop Expressive Attention and two tests of vigilance. Results showed that the low-attentive group was significantly lower than the high-attentive group in their test performance.

Thus, the aforementioned studies offer support to Nigg's distinction, using teachers' ratings as well as objective tests of attention. It is important to note that the studies were carried out, as Nigg noted. In a general population of classroom students, separating the simply inattentive children from the hyperactive–impulsive children has practical benefits as well, apart from clarification of the construct of ADHD.

Such a neat separation would reduce heterogeneity of ADHD. This was not done in the meta-analysis reported in an important paper by Pennington and Ozonoff (1996) that we have selected to discuss next. The paper is relevant for this chapter as it covers both ADHD and Autism.

ADHD and Autism: Reducing Heterogeneity (Pennington & Ozonoff, 1996)

In regard to ADHD, admittedly, a heterogeneous population was included in the studies for meta-analysis; the authors concluded that EF deficit was associated with ADHD. The major tests in those studies consisted of a mixture of both attention and planning, as well as impulsivity—Stroop, Trails, Kagan's Matching Familiar Figures, and measures of motor inhibition. It is worth noting, as the authors point out, that the performance of ADHD groups is compared in some of the studies with that of Learning Disabled groups—groups that include some participants who are also diagnosed of ADHD. Pennington and Ozonoff recommend further research and specific experiments to examine the conclusions of meta-analysis.

The Pennington and Ozonoff review presents important conclusions regarding EF deficits among individuals with autism. "With a very few exceptions, investigations that have explored executive functions abilities in individuals with autism have found them deficient ... 13 out of 14 studies found significant difference between autistic and control subjects on at least one EF measure" (p. 75). This was the TOH task that was frequently used as a test of EF, but could be characterized as a planning task similar to CTC used in Papadopoulous et al. (2002), as reported earlier in this chapter (also see Chapter 6). The next citation from Pennington and Ozonoff firmly suggests that EF may be the most significant deficiency in autism: "deficits on EF tasks have been consistently found in autistic samples across many studies, using a wide variety of measures" (p. 76). These measures are Wisconsin Card Sorting, Trails (Planned Connections in CAS Planning scale), and TOH. Returning then to a distinction between planning and attention, these tasks are closer to planning.

In regard to ADHD, we recommend that attention deficit should be separated from hyperactivity and conduct disorder. We suggest that in order to reduce conceptual confusion, *attention as arousal and orienting response* should be distinguished from *attention as an executive response, as in the Supervisory Attentional System* (Shallice, 1988). The latter is central to controlled problem solving (Geary, 2005). This will reduce heterogeneity in classification, and consequently will result in a better understanding of the psychopathology of ADHD, Autism and FAS, and aid rehabilitation as well. Overall conclusion in regard to Autism and FAS is that the major cognitive deficit in both is in Planning (EF), not attention. Concerning autism, we are reminded of a Planning deficit in the case study of the college student with Asperger's syndrome. In regard to FAS, the most frequently cited deficit is in Planning (EF) tasks (Connor et al., 2000; Matson & Riley, 1998).

Epilogue: Concluding Remarks for This Chapter—When Attention Is Stretched, It Looks like Planning and EF

We conclude this chapter by a few general observations. In retrospect, we have written in the introduction to this chapter: "Perhaps, we need to expand the boundaries of attention itself to interface with Executive Functions and self-regulation." We now discuss this in the concluding part of the chapter because of two reasons: (a) Given that this book aims to be useful for the two disciplines of education and management, the contents of this chapter will be relevant to management by stretching the boundaries of attention to accommodate executive attention, or directed attention, a concept that is logically connected with the Supervisory Attentional System (Shallice, 1988), (b) We acknowledge that EFs are heterogeneous, and in assessing them, one of the star tests is the Stroop test, arguably a test of attention. The Stroop test, like Visual Search (see the next chapter), is often used to predict ability related to planning, and planning dysfunctions associated with frontal lobe impairment (Teuber, 2009; also see Das et al. [1996] for an extensive discussion). So, we shall focus on two recent studies that have an explicit implication for executive decision making; when attention is stretched, it looks like planning and EF!

EFs are effortful. Attention can vary from effortful and deliberate to effortless and automatic. This is nothing new in the literature on attention. In controlled problem solving, as we have discussed in previous chapters, attention is directed and requires mobilization of attentional resources. Directed attention and effortful EFs are the topics of the two recent papers that we will discuss in the following paragraphs.

Effort must have a physical aspect, that is, energy consumption. Gailliot (2008) explores this as he presents a case linking depletion of energy to use of glucose in blood stream, and glucose stored in the brain during decision making that is hard and stressful. Referring to a central executive as discussed in the previous chapters of our book, Gailliot defines it as "a cognitive system that allows for self-control or self-regulation (i.e., overriding habitual patterns of behavior ... and controlling emotions, thoughts, and urges) and higher-order cognition ... Executive functioning allows for effortful, complex cognition." (p. 245) Mark the words self-control and self-regulation—these are the central themes in the next article (Kaplan & Berman, 2010) that we consider, entitled "Directed Attention as a Common Resource for Executive Functioning and Self-regulation."

EFs rely on a limited energy source; glucose is at least one of the energy sources. Building this case, Gailliot reviews evidence from studies on working memory, problems associated with depleted glucose such as aggressive and impulsive acts, and fluctuations in self-control with daily fluctuations in efficiency of glucose transport and storage. He proposes that capacity for executive functioning is reduced when brain glycogen is low, especially in the evening after a hard day's work at executive decision making. Self-control or self-regulation, especially its failure, is associated with energy depletion; however, he acknowledges that it is only a part of the explanation. To conclude, executive functioning, involving inhibition and self-control, is metabolically expensive: glycogen being one source of metabolic energy.

Directed attention uses our capacity for inhibition to resist not only distractions, but also emotionally charged impulses and temptations, as advocated by Kaplan and Berman (2010); the argument draws upon a widely noticed book by Kaplan and Kaplan (1989). The concepts of Attention and Planning, as used in assessment in some studies, are overlapping cognitive processes. In regard to EF, neurological locations suggest that it is a heterogeneous ability (see Chapters 3 and 4). Firm conclusions await further research to understand the complex relationship between Planning and Attention. One of these is awareness and attention, and the place of mindfulness in decision making. We have virtually arrived at the end of this chapter on Attention and Planning.

Attention, Awareness, and Mindfulness: A New Direction

Must we be conscious and fully aware when we are attending? Or do we attend sometimes without being consciously aware of the object or the event?

Awareness varies all the way from a minimal state, as in a coma to higher states of concentration as in meditation. To answer the first question, we do attend without being fully aware or conscious. Simple examples are found in common perceptual phenomena described in elementary textbooks of psychology (e.g., Shift in attention: now I see a face, now a vase; binocular rivalry)—the object remains the same, but inadvertently we attend to one or the other aspect of the object. Awareness is consciousness, and consciousness can direct attention as in meditation (Dietrich, 2007). However, we do attend without being conscious of what we are attending to; in this sense, attention may appear to be independent of consciousness.

Two kinds of meditative procedures are recognized— concentrative and insightful meditation. Both require some degrees of "executive attention." Concentrative meditation is used interchangeably with focused attention. It is sustained attention on a selected object, such as breathing, sensations of the body, or a mental image of sight or sound. Attention is focused and awareness is narrow.

On the other hand, mindfulness meditation practices, also called "open monitoring" or "insight" meditation, requires expanding of awareness with no explicit focus (except awareness itself). In mindfulness, practitioners are instructed to allow any thought, feeling, or sensation to arise in consciousness while maintaining a nonreactive awareness to what is being experienced (Cahn & Polich, 2006). In either kind of meditation practitioners, definitive changes in the frontal lobe function occur. Meditation also results in enhanced perceptual and pre-attentive processing. We will discuss in later chapters of this book the benefits of mindfulness arising out of Buddhist meditational practices in decision making. However, as far as the present chapter is concerned, awareness or consciousness and its relation to attention add another level of complexity that must enter into the question: "Can Attention be separated from Planning?" Certainly, the answer to the question is not a simple yes or no.

Appendix

Diagnostic Criteria for the Three Subtypes of Attention-Deficit/Hyperactivity Disorder According to DSM-IV

A. "Persistent pattern of inattention and/or hyperactivity-impulsivity that is more frequently displayed and is more severe than is typically observed in individuals at comparable level of development." Individual must meet criteria for either (1) or (2): (1) Six or more of the following symptoms of *inattention* have persisted for at least six months to a degree that is maladaptive and inconsistent with the developmental level:

Inattention

- Often fails to give close attention to details or makes careless mistakes in schoolwork, work, or other activities
- Often has difficulty sustaining attention in tasks or play activities
- Often does not seem to listen when spoken to directly
- Often does not follow through on instructions and fails to finish schoolwork, chores, or duties in the workplace (not due to oppositional behavior or failure of comprehension)
- Often has difficulty organizing tasks and activities
- Often avoids, dislikes, or is reluctant to engage in tasks that require sustained mental effort (such as schoolwork or homework)
- Often loses things necessary for tasks or activities at school or at home (e.g., toys, pencils, books, assignments)
- Often easily distracted by extraneous stimuli
- Often forgetful in daily activities

(2) Six or more of the following symptoms of *hyperactivity–impulsivity* have persisted for at least six months to a degree that is maladaptive and inconsistent with the developmental level:

Hyperactivity

- Often fidgets with hands or feet or squirms in seat
- Often leaves seat in classroom or in other situations in which remaining seated is expected
- Often runs about or climbs excessively in situations in which it is inappropriate (in adolescents or adults, may be limited to subjective feelings of restlessness)
- Often has difficulty playing or engaging in leisure activities quietly
- Often talks excessively
- Is often "on the go" or often acts as if "driven by a motor"

Impulsivity

- Often has difficulty awaiting turn in games or group situations
- Often blurts out answers to questions before they have been completed
- Often interrupts or intrudes on others, for example, butts in other children's games
    - A. Some hyperactivity–impulsive or inattentive symptoms that cause impairment were present before the age of seven years.
    - B. Some impairment from the symptoms is present in two or more settings (e.g., at school, or work, or at home)
    - C. There must be evidence of clinically significant impairment in social, academic, or occupational functioning.
    - D. The symptoms do not occur exclusively during the course of a Pervasive Developmental Disorder, Schizophrenia, or other Psychotic Disorder, and are not better accounted for by another mental disorder (e.g., Mood Disorder, Anxiety Disorder, Dissociative Disorder, or Personality Disorder).

Based on these criteria, three types of ADHD are identified:

ADHD, Combined Type: If both criteria 1A and 1B are met for the past six months.
ADHD, Predominantly Inattentive Type: If criterion 1A is met but criterion 1B is not met for the past six months.
ADHD, Predominantly Hyperactive–Impulsive Type: If criterion 1B is met but Criterion 1A is not met for the past six months.

Source: American Psychiatric Association (2000).

(I) A total of six (or more) items from (A), (B), and (C), with at least two from (A), and one each from (B) and (C)

(A) Qualitative impairment in social interaction, as manifested by at least two of the following:
1. marked impairments in the use of multiple nonverbal behaviors, such as eye-to-eye gaze, facial expression, body posture, and gestures to regulate social interaction
2. failure to develop peer relationships appropriate to developmental level
3. a lack of spontaneous seeking to share enjoyment, interests, or achievements with other people (e.g., by a lack of showing, bringing, or pointing out objects of interest to other people)

4. lack of social or emotional reciprocity (note: in the description, it gives the following as examples: not actively participating in simple social play or games, preferring solitary activities, or involving others in activities only as tools or "mechanical" aids)

(B) Qualitative impairments in communication as manifested by at least one of the following:

1. delay in, or total lack of the development of spoken language (not accompanied by an attempt to compensate through alternative modes of communication, such as gesture or mime)
2. in individuals with adequate speech, marked impairment in the ability to initiate or sustain a conversation with others
3. stereotyped and repetitive use of language or idiosyncratic language
4. lack of varied, spontaneous make-belief play or social imitative play appropriate to developmental level

(C) restricted repetitive and stereotyped patterns of behavior, interests and activities, as manifested by at least two of the following:

1. encompassing preoccupation with one or more stereotyped and restricted patterns of interest that is abnormal either in intensity or focus
2. apparently inflexible adherence to specific, nonfunctional routines or rituals
3. stereotyped and repetitive motor mannerisms (e.g. hand or finger flapping or twisting, or complex whole-body movements)
4. persistent preoccupation with parts of objects

(II) Delays or abnormal functioning in at least one of the following areas, with onset prior to age 3 years:

(A) social interaction
(B) language as used in social communication
(C) symbolic or imaginative play

(III) The disturbance is not better accounted for by Rett's Disorder or Childhood Disintegrative Disorder.

Source: American Psychiatric Association (2000).

# 6

Assessments: History and Selected Studies

Part I: History of Constructs and Tests

In one of the earliest papers on planning in PASS theory, Das and Heemsbergen (1983) defined planning as follows: "Planful behavior is a broad category of responses including decision-making, judgments, and evaluation of one's own activity as well as those of others" (p. 1). More recently, a similar view of executive functions (EFs) was found in Tranel, Anderson, and Benton (1994). The authors define EF as planning, decision making, judgment, and self-perception, as already mentioned in the previous chapter. All of these characteristics of EF are also elements of the construct of Planning in PASS theory. These definitions will fit EFs also in the context of more recent conceptualizations, such as in Lezak (2004), and some others given in Chapter 3.

Attention, on the other hand, in PASS theory is assessed by tests that include the Stroop test (Expressive Attention), as well as search tasks, two other tests that require visual search of targets embedded among distractors. These are not as strategic as the CAS Planning tasks (described later in this chapter). Neither are they as effortful as the Planning tasks that exist in CAS, nor are they absolutely automatic (e.g., target does not pop out from the background of distractors, as a red letter in a field of black letters). While maintaining the relative difference between Attention and Planning, consistent with PASS theory, we present measures of both. However, the two CAS scales—Planning and Attention—cannot be simply combined and renamed as an EF measure.

To rename the Planning scale as EF or simply suggesting renaming Planning tests in CAS as EF tests would not be satisfactory. The latter has been advocated by Best, Miller, and Naglieri (2011). The logic for renaming CAS Planning tests as EF tests appears to be unspecified. The stated reason given by the authors is that the Planning subtests in CAS are "complex" compared to Attention subtests, they measure EF. However, the explanation does not have a theoretical support within the definition of EF; especially, the Stroop Color–Word test is left behind in the Attention tests in spite of being counted as one of the three major components of EF in contemporary research (Miyake & Friedman, 2012).

We have added to the Planning tasks in CAS some new tasks that explicitly require response shift and decision making. In a later section of this chapter, we report the results of such a study.

Thus, much more research on EFs has been carried out since our early paper (Das & Heemsbergen, 1983). Previous chapters in the present book attest to this. Ideally, EF measures need to be derived from basic theories. However, this is not always so. We also note that EF tests have been used for diagnosis of clinical cases, such as frontal lobe impairment and early dementia. There are new efforts aimed at utilizing the tests as models for constructing rehabilitation programs for neurological impairment. An excellent review of measures of EF and the challenge of application in rehab has been provided by Chan et al. (2008).

EF is admittedly a heterogeneous construct at present, so it is perhaps best to select tests from both Attention and Planning tasks and add to them in order to make an EF assessment battery, staying with CAS tests for now, in a proposed assessment. The test in CAS, Expressive Attention, is a transparent adaptation of the Stroop test. This is also one of the two core measures of EF interpreted as inhibition of a prepotent response. We have added another Attention task similar to Stroop, an Arithmetic Stroop task, in order to strengthen the bridge from Attention to EF. This additional test is presented later in the chapter together with the new tests of Planning.

In the remaining parts of this chapter, we will begin with a reminder of existing tests of Planning and Attention, and then present the additional tests for both.

Part II A: CAS Tests of Planning and Attention

Summary of Tests/CAS Tasks

An example of each task is given in *CAS Interpretive Handbook* by Naglieri and Das (1997a, 1997b).

A description of the CAS is already presented at the end of Chapter 1. The goal of the present section is to recap the gist of the tests so that it would be easier to discuss them in studies in which the tests are used.

Planning Tasks

1. *Matching Numbers:* The child's task is to find and underline the two numbers that are the same in each row. Each item has eight rows of numbers, and each row contains six numbers.
2. *Planned Codes:* The child's task is to write letters into specific codes. Each page contains one item, which consists of boxes marked with the letters A, B, C, and D. The code system of Xs and Os (e.g., A = OX, B = XX) appears at the top of each page. For each item there is a different set of codes and a different arrangement of response locations.
3. *Planned Connections:* The child's task is to connect a series of boxes containing numbers or letters in the correct sequence. Items 1–6 involve a sequence of numbers only; items 7 and 8 involve a sequence of numbers and letters (e.g., 1-A-2-B-3-C, etc.).

Attention Tasks

1. *Expressive Attention:* Expressive Attention is composed of two sets of items. The first set administers children aged 5–7. The child's task is to identify the stimulus pictures as either large or small animals, regardless of the relative sizes of the pictures on the page. The three items depict the animals in the same size (Item 1), in a size relative to the actual size (Item 2), and in a size opposite usual actual size (Item 3). Only Item 3 is used for scoring purposes. The second set of items is administered to children aged 8–17. The child's tasks are to read words such as "blue" and "yellow" (Item 4), to identify the colors of a series of rectangles (Item 5), and to identify the color ink in which color words are printed rather than to read the words (Item 6). Only Item 6 is used for scoring purposes.
2. *Number Detection:* The child's task is to underline numbers on a page that match stimuli at the top of the page. Each item consists of rows of numbers, which contain both targets (numbers that match the stimuli) and distracters (numbers that do not match the stimuli).
3. *Receptive Attention:* The child's task is to find and underline pairs of pictures or pairs of letters that are the same. Each item consists

of rows of pictures or letters, which contain both targets (pairs that match) and distracters (pairs that do not match). For ages 5–7, the child must underline picture pairs that match either on the basis of physical appearance or on the basis of category (name). For ages 8–17, the child must underline pairs of letters that are physically the same or have the same name.

Part II B: Details of Other Tests as Measures of Inhibition, Shifting, and Working Memory

The subtest Expressive Attention in the CAS is a good example of a measure of *inhibition* in a battery of EF tests. The central requirement in the Stroop test is to inhibit responding to the word (the word "red") written in a contrary color (in blue color). Participants are required to read the color of the ink in which the word is written and to inhibit reading the word. Reading the word is a primary response, that is, the most habitual response among people who have a fair skill in reading simple words, such as "red," "green," "yellow," and "blue." Only following suppression they can respond to the color in which the word is printed. This kind of inhibition is aptly described as inhibition of a preponent response, the inhibition of a habitual response, and facilitating the other. In the CAS, inhibition is placed within the Attention scale. However, it is a favorite choice for measurement of EF (Miyake et al., 2012). It is also a test for "executive attention."

Another component of EF is *shifting*. Shifting can be shown in various tests, such as in the CAS planned connection and the old Trails test. In these tests, the participant is not only drawing a line from one digit to its adjacent digit (such as 1 to 2 to 3 to 4, and so on until 15, which might be the goal or the finish line) in one part of the Trails, but also shifts and keeps shifting the strategy of response in the second part of the test, which requires alternating between joining numbers and letters of the alphabet sequentially—1 joined to A joined to 2 joined to 3, and so on). The letters, like the numbers, are scattered randomly all over the page; thus, there is a fair amount of search involved in this task. Neuropsychology textbooks and psychologists like us have been discussing the task for many years, not so much as a clinical test, but rather as a test of planning ability in the general population.

Other Tests of Executive Function and Planning Not Included in CAS

Patterns and Reversals: Z and N Test

EF/PLANNING TESTS

1. *A test of Shifting or Set Switching: Patterns and Reversal—Z and N Test. (J.A. Naglieri assisted in constructing an earlier version of the test—Planned Pattern.)* One of the three components of EF is the ability for *shifting*. This ability is measured in a new task, Pattern Recognition, that requires the participant to join four numbers in a square array arranged from the smallest number to the largest, so that the line between the numbers creates either a "Z" pattern or an "N" pattern. Shifting is required not only in proceeding from the smallest number to the largest, but also, importantly, by introducing a reversal shift design. For further explanation, see the example below. In a typical page, there appear several relatively big and small numbers within a square frame. There are only four numbers in any frame. The first few patterns may reinforce a stereotyped Z or N pattern; then suddenly the pattern changes to the opposite, that is, if the first several patterns are Z, then without notice, the pattern of arrangement changes to N. This is an instance of a reversal shift and even of an extra dimensional reversal shift, which is harder and requires better appreciation of shifting ability.

    This test may be used as an alternative to the Wisconsin Card Sorting test, including some of the main features, such as category shifts, perseveration, and cost of set switching. It is also appropriate for children of age 4 and above. It can be administered by a computer; this will make it easier to collect both accuracy and reaction time (RT) responses, and to compute the cost of switching at the point of shifting from one set to another.

2. *An additional test item for Inhibition and Reversal Shift.* Using a one-digit frame of an item, the participant is required to say N when the pattern is Z, and to say Z when the pattern is N. Shifting occurs as in regular Planned Pattern items. The test is similar to Luria's reciprocal motor or semantic response: "When I tap once, you tap twice, and

when I tap twice, you tap once." Inhibition of a prepotent response is, thus, an additional requirement.

Since it includes items suitable for adults, the test can be used to collect normative data for ages 4–55.

See Chapter 7 for Pattern Recognition (Planned Pattern) Test Material.

PART III: Selected Studies

Crack-the-Code Test: A Test of Planning Strategies

The Crack-the-Code test (CTC) is the best test of planning we have used in our previous research, as presented in our book *Cognitive Planning* (Das, Kar, & Parrila, 1996). Within the framework of the concept of EF, we discuss how CTC fits in with general tests of EFs. Following a review of CTC, we present results of some selected empirical research.

HISTORY AND STRUCTURE OF CRACK THE CODE

The CTC is based on a game called Mastermind. In the earliest paper on CTC, we actually used Mastermind as a planning test (Das & Heemsbergen, 1983). In that early research, the following results were noteworthy: A planning factor emerged based on tests that tapped into perceptual and mnestic (memory) cognitive domains. We are using Luria's terminology in characterizing these tasks. Perception, memory, and conceptualization are the three mental functions usually considered in psychology. Functions, however, need to be further analyzed in terms of mental processes for understanding them. In this case, we use it for the Planning process. That translates to understanding a host of useful skills, such as reading and comprehension to EFs related to management (Das et al., 1996). In fact, Luria's ideas shaped the model of mental processes proposed earlier (Das, Kirby, & Jarman, 1975), which was offered as an alternative to abilities as in an IQ test. In a subsequent section, we cast the Planning tasks within an EF framework.

We find an example of a perceptual planning task in *Visual Search* (*Planned Search*). This is already described in the book on cognitive planning (Das et al., 1996). The objective of visual search is to find either a target embedded among distracter items that are member of a very different category of stimuli (a digit as a target embedded among pictures) or a target embedded in a field of items from the same category (digit is the target in a field of other digits). The first kind is often an automatic search because the incongruous target stands out of the field, whereas for the second kind, where a target is embedded among items from the same category (picture in picture, number in number), one has to go about finding the target in a deliberate manner (i.e., it is not an automatic search). Whereas automatic search may be deemed as an instance of pure attentional response (the odd one pops out), deliberate search requires strategies; inasmuch as it does so, it moves closer to planning (Das, Naglieri, & Kirby, 1994; Das et al., 1996).

Examples of (a) automatic search and (b) deliberate search are created in several ways. One of the automatic search items used earlier in our Visual Search research (Das et al., 1996) is a search of a picture in a field of numbers (automatic, pop-up). A deliberate search is necessary in search field of numbers, when one of the numbers is a target as designated by the examiner.

An example of the mnestic planning task would be found in Matching Numbers, which is a CAS task for Cognitive Planning. It shares prominent aspects with Visual Search as well as making minor demands on working memory. Minor rather than major, as all the six numbers in a row given in the test are visually surveyable, and the demand is reduced significantly by adopting appropriate strategies (e.g., in the series of numbers that have five or more digits, compare the first two or last two digits in the items, eliminate others that are not identical, and then limit search to those thus identified).

The other tasks presented later have been grouped under conceptual planning.

Planned Connection, an adaptation of Trail Making (Lezak, 2004), is most probably a "conceptual" task with a significant input from memory, or mnestic to follow Luria's terminology. Both in Form A, which requires joining numbers serially, and in Form B, the combination of numbers and letters of the alphabet that require to be joined alternately in a serial order, knowledge retrieved from long-term memory is used.

The best example of the "conceptual" Planning task is CTC. It is undoubtedly a complex task of strategies that nevertheless involves perceptual and mnestic abilities. As far as it does that, CTC is a pre-eminent example of Planning as a metacognitive process.

CTC has been much researched by our colleagues. It is important to note that in its earliest use in planning research, we found (Das & Heemsbergen, 1983) that efficiency in solving CTC problems can be predicted by efficiency in Visual Search, a test that is best categorized as perceptual planning, whereas CTC is predominantly a conceptual test. The three categories, Perceptual, Mnestic, and Conceptual, may be separate, as proposed in the PASS theory; however, the processes within each are interdependent (Das et al., 1996).

CTC as a complex planning task may stand apart from other planning tasks, as we have observed earlier (Das et al.,1994). Evidence in support of including CTC as one of the key planning tests has been reviewed in the same book (Das et al., 1994). Early research reports factor analyses in which the "Planning factor" consisted of a cluster of tests comprising CTC, Planned composition, and Visual Search in one study, and a cluster comprising CTC, visual search, and Trails in another study. None of the studies had used any other "planning" tests. So, in a sense, the Planning factor was defined by these aforementioned tests.

Selected Studies Relating to CTC

We now present brief summaries of some studies carried out by J.P. Das and his associates. In doing so, we have two objectives. The first is to place CTC in the context of ongoing research on planning. The second is to guide us toward further research in CTC.

THE DEVELOPMENT OF PLANNING SKILLS IN CHILDREN

The study by Parrila (1996) concerned the development of planning from students in Grades 3–11. The data was obtained from schools in Bhubaneswar, India, under the supervision of J.P. Das, and published in a research article (Parrila, Das, & Dash, 1996).

Fifty participants in each of Grades 3, 5, 7, 9, and 11 were administered an earlier version of CAS (Naglieri & Das, 1988). CTC, Matching Numbers, and Visual Search were used as representatives of planning.

Without going into detail, what the factor analysis showed was that CTC was somewhat distant from other planning tasks. This was clearly supported by a cluster analysis; CTC was significantly distant from the two other Planning tasks, Matching numbers and Planned Search (Visual Search). In other words, this conceptual planning task was different from the perceptual and mnestic tasks. However, in line with other planning tasks,

CTC showed a developmental increment from Grade 3 through to Grade 11 (Das et al., 1996).

Strategies Used by Participants in Solving CTC (Parrila, 1996)

Since CTC is conceptualized as a game of strategies, what are the major strategies that are used by the participants? Parrila (1996) and Das et al. (1996) advanced the following four hypothetical solution models or search strategies that could be used for solving CTC problems:

(1) *Random Search*, which is essentially the same as a trial and error method.
(2) *Climbing*, in which the subject attempts to place one color at a time in its position or proceeds with one position at a time trying to find the correct color for the position.
(3) *Pattern*, in which the subject builds the solution as a response to one instruction line.
(4) *Combination*, in which the subject integrates information from two or three instruction lines when building hypotheses about the correct answer (e.g., comparing line 1 with line 2).

Random search and pattern were the least efficient strategies. Thus the two have been combined in reporting the results of strategies used by participants (see Figure 6.1).

Combination is the most advanced method, as Parrila observed. It demands a heavy use of working memory. The easier problems used two color disks and two lines of instruction (zero, or 1 correct), whereas the harder problems used four color disks, and four lines of information (e.g., zero correct, 1 correct, 2 correct, zero correct). The excessive load on working memory makes it difficult for younger children to solve the problem. Parrila reported that only more Grade 8 children could use the Combination strategy; all Grade 4, 6, 7, and 8 children used the Climbing strategy; and Grade 6 and 8 children used the Climbing strategy more frequently than the younger children.

These hypothetical solution models were all represented in subjects' performance. Several protocols included statements indicating more than one solution model since the subject changed the search strategy used during the task. However, from their verbal online report, only the Grade 8 children were able to use the combination strategy well. They were clearly more advanced in their planning.

Figure 6.1:
The percentages of placements based on climbing, combination, and nonfunctional (Pattern, False Pattern, Trial and Error) search methods on items 5 and 6

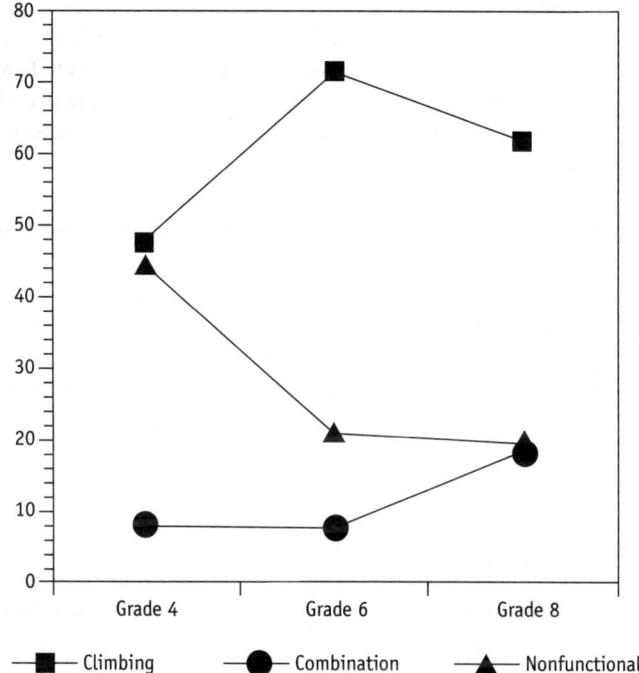

We suggest that CTC is a test that is appropriate for participants in Grade 6 (about 12-year-old) and above.

Working Memory and Speed: Contribution to CTC Performance

The next fairly intensive study was conducted by Misra and is already reported in the cognitive planning book in the chapter "Conceptual Planning" (Das et al.,1996). Briefly, the purpose of the research study was to examine the relative contribution of working memory and speed to both CTC outcomes—total solution time and accuracy of performance.

College students were recruited in an eastern state of India. Apart from CTC, they were given other tests of CAS as well; however, we will consider only the working memory and speed components. In order to produce a working memory score, two successive processing tests, Sentence Repetition score and the serial memory in Word Series, were combined. The range of scores on both variables was then divided at the median. The High Working Memory group consisted of students who scored above the median on both variables and the Low Working Memory group consisted of those who scored below the median in both tests.

In terms of the relationship between working memory and speed or accuracy of solving CTC problems, results showed that those with high-accuracy scores on CTC also tended to have high scores on working memory. Working memory scores were significantly correlated with both speed and accuracy of solving CTC items. This may imply that working memory scores reflected a general cognitive competence. Thus, the most meaningful finding was that the ability to *solve CTC problems, especially at medium difficulty levels, was positively related to working memory capacity as derived from Sentence Repetition and Word Series tests.*

In regard to speed score, Misra's research showed that the total solution time of a problem in CTC does not really predict how accurately that problem would be solved—speed of solving the item (total time) and the number of problems solved correctly (accuracy score). All of our CTC investigations also demonstrated a certain relationship between first movement time and the difficulty level of the problem—harder problems required longer time to think before the first move was made.

A Study on the Usefulness of CTC in Attention Deficit

We end this section of the research summary on CTC by briefly discussing a study on planning in children with attention deficits. The study by Papadopoulos, Panayiotou, Spanoudis, and Nastapoulos (2005) administered CTC along with other tests to groups of attention-deficit children and a control group. Their results were quite interesting in that the attention-deficit children were indeed poorer on CTC compared to the control; again, however, the middle level difficulty items were the most sensitive as it was in Mishra's study. The task was presented on a computer, so that the time taken to make the first move as well as the total time taken to solve each of the problems could be accurately recorded. Results showed that control children took longer to make the first move in solving the item in front of them accurately. Obviously, they took time to think of the best strategy to solve the problem.

In conclusion of this presentation on CTC, the test has continued to be a complex Planning task mainly because it demands the ability to use higher level problem-solving strategies. Although it is clearly a Planning task, it may stand apart from relatively simpler ones included in CAS.

A New Study of Executive Function

Two objectives of the study correspond to (1) confirmation of a unified EF and (2) viability of planning and attention measures.

1. We test whether or not a common EF factor can emerge by adding new measures of Shifting and Inhibition to selected tests from CAS Planning and Attention scales.
2. Secondly, the study was designed to *examine if Planning and Attention will be retained as two viable factors in CAS*. This is important in regard to separation of Planning and Attention (see Chapter 5). If indeed Planning and Attention emerged as two interdependent if not independent factors, we would have succeeded in answering the question raised in the previous chapter—Are Planning and Attention the same or different? Addition of set shifting to inhibition of prepotent response together should increase the unity of EF.

Preliminary results of a study are presented below.

1. Among the existing tests of CAS, Inhibition and Shifting measures can be identified. Expressive Attention (Stroop) subtest, as mentioned earlier, provides a measure of inhibition. However, it is only *one* subtest; others need to be included which we did in this study as described below.

    Similarly, within the CAS tests, "shifting" is measured by Planned Connection, a transparent adaptation of Trail Making. The test has a page of joining numbers to number, and in another page numbers to letters.

The third component of EF is memory updating; this was most closely linked to general intelligence in a study by Miyake et al. (2000). Hence, in order to distinguish EF from measures of intelligence, they preferred to exclude this component, thus defining the core components of EF to be inhibition and shifting. We accept that as a reasonable approach to operationalizing EF in the present study.

Up to this point, in regard to *inhibition* measures, CAS has only one good test, Expressive Attention (Stroop). We should then add other tests of inhibition in order to increase the strength of this component of EF.

Likewise, in regard to the other component, *shifting*, additional tests will be required besides Planned Connection (Trail Making), thus extending the CAS structure.

2. *Planning and Attention Processes*: Extending the CAS to establish the two as separate measures in adults is the other objective.

   However, no one to our knowledge has refurbished the Attention and Planning scales by (1) eliminating obviously similar contents among some of the tests and (2) introducing tasks of attention and planning that raise the complexity of the test and increase their cognitive load. The latter is essential for adult participants who may find the existing Planning subtests that do not involve demanding strategies for task solution.

We have introduced new tests that increase, and, thereby, strengthen the important aspects of each construct in this preliminary investigation. The tests are Planned Recognition and Number Stroop constructed by J.P. Das. It is an analogue of the traditional word Stroop. The results may show promise of obtaining a common EF construct, our first objective. A second objective of the study was to examine if Planning and Attention could be sustained as separate factors by the modification of CAS tests suitable for adults; the study was carried out on a young adult sample. To restate, the results may be encouraging to proceed with the extension of Planning and Attention scales within the CAS structure. Then following this preliminary investigation, a more comprehensive investigation, specially focusing on EF, could be designed. That will include additional tasks that purportedly assess each of the *three* components of EF according to Miyake et al. (2000): updating, shifting, and inhibition, rather than only the last two as in the present study we report in the next section.

Hypotheses of the Study

There is a unified factor named "Executive Functions," which can emerge by adding new tests that fit the constructs of inhibition and shifting to the existing structure of PASS tasks.

Secondly, in spite of its overlap with EF, Planning will be retained as a PASS cognitive process by selecting tasks that require the use of strategies for efficient performance in solving simple and complex problems.

Attention will be retained as a separate measure as well, even though previously, Planning and Attention have not always emerged as separate factors as strongly as the two other factors—Simultaneous and Successive—in CAS (see *CAS Interpretive Handbook*, Naglieri & Das, 1997a, 1997b).

Method

The 100 participants were undergraduate students who chose to be subjects for this research project as part of their class requirement. English was their primary language.

The following tasks were used for *EF assessment*; all of them have been described earlier in this chapter.

1. *Planned Patterns and Reversal*: Restating in brief the Planned Pattern test, the following administration instructions were given.
    (a) *Planned Patterns*: Look at each frame, and draw an imaginary line from the smallest to the next bigger, next bigger, and the biggest digit. It will either be a "Z" or an "N." Then *you must say* "Z" or "N" as fast as you can without mistakes. We note that in this version of the test, drawing lines to make a "Z" or an "N" has been replaced by speech. Another change is that the *Planned Pattern*, as administered in this investigation, uses *only* two of the pages, 7 and 8.
    (b) *Reverse Planned Patterns*: Look at each frame as before. You will see either a "Z" or an "N" pattern. This time when you see a "Z," say "N." When you see an "N", say "Z." Say it as fast as you can without mistakes.
2. *Planned Connections (Trails)*: The participant's task is to connect a series of boxes containing numbers or letters in a correct sequence.
    (a) *Number to number connection*: Items 5 and 6 were administered first. The items involve a sequence of numbers only.

(b) *Number to letter connection*: Items 7 and 8 involve a sequence of numbers and letters (i.e., 1-A-2-B-3-C, etc.).

3. *Stroop Color–Word and Arithmetic Stroop*
   (a) *Stroop Color–Word*: This is the familiar Stroop test, adapted in CAS as "Expressive Attention." It consists of three conditions: reading the words red, green, blue, and yellow, followed by naming color strips of red, green, blue, and yellow color, and finally the interference condition which requires the participant to identify the color of the ink in which color words are printed rather than to read the words, a measure of prepotent inhibition. Only the last condition is used for scoring purpose.
   (b) *The Arithmetic Stroop:* Arithmetic Stroop was designed by creating a Size versus Value conflict. On incongruent trials, 7 and 6 were printed in smaller fonts, whereas 4 and 3 were in larger fonts, as described in the next chapter. We expect the two Stroop tests, Numbers and Words, to share the same construct of inhibiting a prepotent response.

Each of the three tests, thus, has two subtests. In the event of deriving a common EF factor, we expect to have three separate factors, each representing the three tests. If indeed a common EF factor is found, the three should load on one factor.

The second goal of our investigation was to determine the retention of separate Planning and Attention factors. Planning will be retained as a PASS cognitive process by selecting tasks that require the use of strategies for efficient performance in solving simple and complex problems (e.g., CTC). Similarly, Attention will be retained as a separate factor.

TESTS OF PLANNING

The following three tests were selected for inclusion in the modified battery of Planning in CAS. Among them, Planned Connections (Trail Making) and CTC were those that had been used in very early studies on planning. *Planned Connection* (Trails) was retained as in CAS.

Planned Patterns (Recognition of Patterns), as described earlier, and Planned Pattern Reversal were not a part of the test used as a measure of Planning. Time for solution for each of the two pages was recorded as the only score. Errors were immediately corrected by the participant.

CTC was the third test of Planning. The test had eight items in total. We used only the number of problems correctly solved as the score for the first six items as the last two had only around 30 percent or less participants who could solve the items.

TESTS OF ATTENTION

Number Detection from CAS was retained as a test of attention. This is a vigilance-type test, except that stimulus presentation is controlled by the participant rather than by a predetermined presentation rate. The participant is instructed to underline numbers on a page (1–9 printed in a predetermined random order) that match target numbers at the top of the page.

Expressive Attention (Word Stroop) from CAS, and a new test, *Arithmetic (Number) Stroop*, are the two other attention tests.

Results and Discussion

Executive Function—Exploratory Analyses: Is There a Unified Factor Named Executive Function?

A summary of the analyses is presented in Tables 6.1 and 6.2. Using exploratory factor analyses, the first step was to find the correlation between the two forms of each of the three major tests. The correlations were found to

Table 6.1:
Results of exploratory factor analysis

	Factor Loadings		
Variables	1	2	3
1 Planned Connections 1 and 2			.905
2 Planned Connections 3			.712
3 Planned Patterns 1 and 2		.869	
4 Planned Patterns Reverse		.852	
5 Color Stroop	.809		
6 Math Stroop	.700		
7 Math Stroop Reverse	.714		

Note: Method of extraction was principal components analysis with varimax rotation. All three factors explained 70 percent of the variance.

Table 6.2:
Do the three factors form one factor? Yes, they do, which is planning

Variables	Factor Loadings
	1
1 Factor 1	.738
2 Factor 2	–.748
3 Factor 3	.717

Note: The factor accounted for 54 percent of the variance.

be high, and, as a result, three factors were obtained. As shown in Table 6.1, each of the three tests formed recognizable clusters: Planned Connections, Planned Patterns, and Inhibition of prepotent response.

The next step was to obtain a factor score for each of them. That enabled the exploratory analysis to progress and examine if the three-factor scores would share a common factor.

Table 6.2 shows the result of this analysis—all of the three loaded on the same factor. Some loadings were smaller than the others, but probably the differences were not large enough to be statistically significant.

The first hypothesis is clearly supported. We should have a reasonable ground then for building a structural equation model from this preliminary data analysis.

PLANNING AND ATTENTION FACTORS

We had two goals in the present investigation, each identified by a hypothesis. The second goal was simply to test if Planning will be retained as a PASS cognitive process by selecting tasks that enhance the use of strategies for efficient performance in solving simple and complex problems.

Attention will be retained as a separate measure as well, even though, previously, Planning and Attention have not emerged as separate factors as strongly as the two other factors—Simultaneous and Successive. The determined exploratory factor analyses in Tables 6.3 and 6.4 are in accordance with the second objective of the study.

Table 6.3 presents the factor loadings of three *Planning tasks*: Planned Connection (Trails), Planned Pattern (excluded the Reverse condition as that was not a core component of the Planning factor), and CTC. The last task demands strategy use, complex reasoning, and monitoring and evaluating feedback; all of these are some of the distinct components of planning.

Table 6.3:
Do the planning tasks form one factor?

Variables	Factor Loadings 1
1 Planned Connections 1, 2, and 3	.720
2 Planned Patterns 1 and 2	.762
3 CTC Accuracy	−.643

Note: The factor accounted for 50 percent of the variance.

Table 6.4:
Do the attention tasks form one factor?

Variables	Factor Loadings 1
1 Number Detection	.626
2 Color Stroop	.757
3 Math Stroop	.623

Note: The factor accounted for 45 percent of the variance.

The results reveal a common factor on which each of the tests had acceptable loadings; CTC held its position as a test of Planning. Presumably, this complex task is anticipated to have larger amount of unique variance compared to the other two tests with which it shares the same common factor.

Table 6.4 reports the same kind of exploratory analysis for the three attention tasks. Number Detection and Expressive Attention (Stroop Color–Word) as in CAS, together with the added Arithmetic Stroop test, define this factor.

Tables 6.1–6.4 satisfy the requirement of testing the hypotheses of the present investigation.

A supplementary question that was raised essentially tested whether or not the Planning and the Attention scales can be combined and renamed as EF as suggested by Best et al. (2011). We had resented such simple amalgamation of the two types of subtests in CAS. However, our present data are collected from undergraduates rather than samples of school students; CAS norms are available only up to the age of 17. So whatever the results of the analysis that we present, it is not a strong refutation of the Best et al. paper.

Nevertheless, our question then requires us to force the six tests of Planning and Attention to confirm to a single common factor. That calls for deploying a confirmatory factor analysis/Structural Equation Modeling (SEM) as a parsimonious statistical procedure.

What did we find? SEM, thus, derived could not fit a unitary factor. The result would be uninterpretable by forcing the tests to be consistent with one common factor solution.

Concluding Notes

Several tests of EFs have been presented in this chapter. In this preliminary study, we concluded that we could arrive at a unified construct of EF comprising the two core components of EF—Shifting and Inhibition—even by selecting a limited set of tests. Some of these had not been used in previous research reported by Miyake et al. (2000). Nevertheless, the new tests followed the basic elements of EF construct—inhibition and shifting; excluded were tests of working memory.

We suggest that number Stroop as used in this study should be easily accepted as with Executive Attention, and by default as one of the basic components of EF.

EF is very closely aligned with executive attention (Smith & Koslyn, 2007). It seems to be a construct well represented by Stroop and its variations.

What is the purpose of this chapter?

Is it to present tools to use for the assessment of planning/EF? Is it to provide support for earlier conceptual distinctions?

It is both. We cannot assess the constructs without clarifying the conceptual distinctions which, in turn, depend on specific tools for operationalizing the constructs.

Understanding the theoretical likeness of the constructs of Executive Attention, Inhibition of prepotent response still needs clarification. An unresolved issue concerns the necessity of including working memory as a core component of EF, if we aim at distancing EF from a general measure of IQ, for that may prove to be difficult as discussed in the previous chapters of this book.

Beginning to understand the origin of EF, we presented two competing sources, Luria's seminal clinical research and Baddeley's (1986) Central Executive. The first has been substantially elaborated in a recent work of

Goldberg (2001), to which PASS theory has added Planning as a domain-general cognitive process much in keeping with Luria's proposal of assigning it the status of a major function, if not the sole function of frontal lobe. An operational tool for assessing planning was provided earlier (CAS, Naglieri & Das [1997a, 1997b]), which has been extended by new tests not included previously in CAS; some of those which are necessary are specially challenging for testing older adolescents and young adults (CTC).

However, could these be viable indices of the broad concept of EF as Diamond (2013) construes in a recent review? This is an active area for contemporary research.

In other chapters of this book concerning EF, we will return to further discussion of EF, as appropriate for the themes of the chapter. More discussion of other concepts that are frequently bracketed with EF will be presented. These comprise Executive Attention, Attentional control, and areas of overlap between EF and Planning, including Metacognition.

In the next chapter, a description for the administration of CTC and other EF/Planning tests is given in detail. The next chapter in combination with the present one can be used for further research by those who are interested in the investigation of Planning/EF as applied to Psychological and Educational studies and applied studies in Management, especially regarding organizational behavior.

7

Planning and Executive Function Tests: Ready for Use

A Planning Test for Executives

Executive functions have been divided into "cold" and "hot" (Grafman & Litvan, 1999). The first label is applied to relatively cognitive tasks, and the second, to cognitive tasks that have a fair amount of affect or arousal. All of the three planning tasks in CAS are "cold" according to this division. However, the next test described clearly contains an affective component.

Predicament Test: A Test That Embodies Social as well as Cognitive Decision-making

TASKS FOR EVERYDAY PLANNING

In an article by Channon (2004), it is suggested that practical everyday planning does not correlate with tests of planning or executive function given in neuropsychology. Her predicament test, described later, however, may be an exception.

Channon (2004) has described a predicament test where the participants read a short episode and then are asked to generate as many solutions as possible to the problem, and then finally choose the best solution from among those they have offered. They evaluate the final solution in terms of three criteria: (a) Have all the pertinent facts been taken into account? (b) Is the solution socially appropriate? and (c) Is the solution effective from a practical viewpoint? According to Channon, it is the social appropriateness criterion that distinguishes between patients with Asperger's syndrome and control participants, as well as some brain-damaged patients. In contrast to the first and third criteria, the second criterion would discriminate between brain-damaged patients and normal controls, especially those with the left frontal lobe damaged in the dLPFC region.

Scenario 1: Dog in the Kitchen (Channon, 2004)

You have an apartment; a family that rents the apartment above yours has a dog. The dog is housed in their kitchen at night. Their kitchen is above your bedroom. The dog barks at night. You cannot have a good night's rest. You complain to the renter. He says that is the only place they have for the dog as they live in a one-bedroom apartment. What can you do?

Participants are asked to write as many solutions as they can within two minutes—short solutions. Next, they are asked to choose one of the solutions that they can justify best and give the reasons for justifying it. The answer is given to three judges who rate how appropriate is the solution. The Predicament test has two scores—a *fluency score* (number of solutions generated) and a *socially appropriate judgment score* (as rated by independent raters). The latter is the more important among the three ways of rating the participant's answer: (a) Have all the pertinent facts been taken into account? (b) Is the solution socially appropriate? and (c) Is the solution effective from a practical viewpoint?

PREDICAMENT TEST—NEW SCENARIOS

We provide the following scenarios similar to Channon's. These are ready to be used for future investigations.

Scenario 1: Navy Ship

Twenty cadets are placed in a training ship with an officer and his young wife, who is the only woman on the ship. The officer's quarters are directly above the cadets' dormitory. Naturally, at night the officer and his wife play music and break into a dance or two, the sound of which can easily be heard in the cadets' dormitory since there is no soundproofing in the floor. The cadets cannot sleep at night and are usually tired in the morning, especially on the nights when the dance and music go past midnight, which happens quite frequently. What can the cadets do?

Question for the participant: Write down as many solutions as possible for the problem, and then choose the best one and give some reasons for choosing it. Judge the solutions first on the criterion of fluency, that is, how many solutions were generated by the participant that took into account all the important aspects of the problem. The best solution is rated in terms of social appropriateness and practical effectiveness.

A twist: Channon did not consider what we are proposing as an extension. On the next page of the problem solution, ask the participant if he or she were the officer with a young spouse, how would he or she solve the problem? The participant will be asked what do you think the officer should do. Thus, in the same problem-solving situation we get the participant to assume the role of the officer as well as the cadet.

Scenario 2: Stranded Soldiers
Five soldiers walk into a hotel in a mountainous area. This is the only hotel that exists within a 40 km radius, so the soldiers have to stay the night in that hotel. They come in with their guns. The hotel manager has 20 civilian guests that night, including some children. They watch the soldiers come in and become quite anxious at the sight of the guns. The hotel manager shows the soldiers the house rules of the hotel, chief of which is that no firearms are allowed in the guests' rooms. The soldiers insist that they usually sleep with their firearms and this is their custom. The hotel manager is polite but insists that firearms should not be taken into their rooms. What would you do if you were one of the soldiers?

After the participants have given as many solutions as possible, they are asked to choose the best one and write a couple of lines justifying their choice. In the next phase they are asked to put themselves in the position of the hotel manager and to write as many solutions as they can come up with and select the one that the participant thinks will work. Rating proceeds as before.

Scenario 3: Fanatics
Some Hindu extremists have occupied a temple city because their leader has urged them to declare it for Hindus only and therefore throw out all non-Hindus from the small city of about 500 people. The government calls for military reinforcement. The military convoys surround the city. There are about 50 Hindu extremists holed up in the temple in the city. The military has come with 500 soldiers. There is going to be a showdown. The commander of the military unit first wants to try a diplomatic procedure. He befriends a moderate group of Hindu priests from outside the city and sends them as emissaries for negotiating with the Hindu extremist leader to surrender. The participant in this scenario is asked what arguments they would use if they were one of the moderate Hindu priests trying to persuade the extremists to give up their siege of the city. Again, the participant is asked to write a short paragraph justifying the best solution. In the next phase of the task the participant is put in the position of the leader of the extremist group. What kind of solutions would he offer? Write a justification in one paragraph of the best solution.

Planned Composition: Narratives

Composition of an essay or narrative requires all the major executive processes. An overall plan needs to be maintained while writing an essay (strategic essay as described in Chapter 9) or composing a narrative. By asking subjects to write a story from a picture, we require them to use all five of the skills listed in the rating scale given below. Of these, Planning is indexed by the quality of organization, the individuality in writing, and to a certain extent by the choice of written expression. Several studies on Planning have been carried out using narratives or essays as measures. These are discussed in Chapter 11. Here, we show how written narrative may be used as a tool for measuring EF/Planning.

To obtain written composition, any picture that can tell a story is used. Subjects individually or in groups are given blank sheets of ruled paper and asked to write a one-page story about the picture. Raters are asked to read each story and then assess the essay according to the perceived quality of the underlying plan and logistical sequence. The rating of planned composition is carried out employing a Likert-type 7-point scale. The stories rated for expression, organization, wording, mechanics (sentence structure, spelling, and punctuation), and individuality (uniqueness and originality). The rating of interest is organization. Following are two stories written by subjects from Grade 8 along with the ratings received (1, 3). Each story has a title and text which are reproduced (including errors).

Instructions for the Planned Composition

Composition requires writing. Thus an entire chapter on Panning and Writing discusses it as a measure of composition (Chapter 11). However, a planned composition test is presented along with other tests of Planning/EF in the appendix.

Planned Composition for Children

NARRATIVES

Young children below age 8 may not be able to write a composition that would allow us to isolate the Planning process from the demand of writing skills or transcription skills (letter and word formation, spelling, and syntax). Narration of stories can be an appropriate method of measuring their planning. Narrative composition task can be given at an easy, medium, or difficult level. In the *easiest level* as described below, a short six to eight line story is read to the child; he/she is required to listen to it, and then given a group of pictures that must be placed in the sequence described in the story. At a *medium level of difficulty*, these pictures are interleaved with distracting pictures that do not correspond to the story. At the higher level of difficulty, only the story's sentences are given in an interleaved passage; the child is required to arrange the sentences to construct the story. The test can be made more complex at each level by adding new details to the story. Addition of new episodes would be another device for increasing the difficulty of the test.

Two stories are given later; the first is shorter than the other, hence easier.

In the first part of the test, children are asked to separate words in a sentence. This tests their ability to identify words. Also it requires some effort. Therefore, they pay attention to the content and meaning of the sentences. The sentences are interleaved. The children are asked to arrange them in the right sequence to make a story. Thus, they are asked to compose a narrative using the sentences. These tests require comprehension as well as a coherent composition. Writing a composition requires planning. This is discussed at length in Chapter 11.

Two Stories: Tiger and Cake Story, and Deer Story

PRACTICE EXAMPLE
Separate the words. Place a slash between the words
Like this: *separate/the/wordsplaceaslashbetweenthewords*
NOW do it:
Atigerlivedintheforest
Hecamelookingformeat
Sohekilledthegoatandateit
Onenightthetigerwashungry

Now slash slash to separate the sentences. Like this: //. Then give a number to each sentence (1, 2, 3, ...) like this

Atigerlivedintheforest 1
Cut up the paper into strips; each sentence is in a strip.
NOW
Arrange the strips of the sentences to make a story.
THEN, write the number of the sentence after you have made the story.

Test 1. Separate the words. Place a slash between the words
Like this: *separate/the/wordsplaceaslashbetweenthewords*
Start!
Onceuponatimetherewasabrotherandsister
theylivedinahouse
thebearsateatingit
thehousewasnearatree
whenhewasfinishedhewentaway
onenightabearcametothehouse
theythrewapieceofthecake throughthewindow
thebearknockedonthedoorbecausehecouldsmellacake
Now slash slash to separate the sentences. Like this: //. Then give a number to each sentence (1, 2, 3, ...) like this
Onceuponatimetherewasabrotherandsister 1
Theylivedinahouse 2
Cut up the paper into strips; each sentence is in a strip.
NOW
Arrange the strips of the sentences to make a story.
THEN, write the number of the sentence after you have made the story.

Test 2. Separate the words. Place a slash between the words
Like this: *separate/the/wordsplaceaslashbetweenthewords*
onceuponatimetherewasadeer
thedeerhadbighornswhichheliked
hehadlonglegswhichhedidnotlike
hishornsgotcaughtinabush
hewassafelyawayfromthehunter
somehowhepulledthemoutofthebush
hestartedrunningasfastashecould
onedaythedeerwasrunningawayfromthehunter
everytimehelookedathislegshedidnotlikethem
hewasveryhappytoseehislegs
Now slash slash to separate the sentences. Like this: //. Write the sentences and number them (1, 2, 3).

Appendix: Administration Manual for Number Stroop, Pattern Recognition, CTC, and Planned Composition: Story and Strategic Essay

Addition to Attention Tests: Number Stroop

NUMBER STROOP TEST

As in the Stroop test, the task presents two simultaneously competing responses for selective attention.

We designed the Number Stroop by creating a Size versus Value conflict. On incongruent trials, 7 and 6 were printed in smaller fonts whereas 4 and 3 were in larger fonts. Participants were required to respond "big" to 7 and 6 and "small" to 4 and 3 irrespective of the size of the print.

Look at this page. It has the same numbers—7, 6, 4, and 3 on it. Tell me if each number is big or small. Remember, a big number is bigger than 5 and a small number is smaller than 5. Do it as fast as you can.

The test page contained 40 digits, divided into six rows of six digits and a row of four digits. In order to discourage response based on reversing the size of the print rather than attending to the value <"I simply say big if the print is small; and small if the print is big">, 15 percent of the stimuli were congruent in size and value.

Three conditions were included as in Stroop: a neutral condition, a congruent, and an incongruent.

AN EXAMPLE FOR THE PRACTICE TEST IN THE NEUTRAL CONDITION

Example

7	4	3	6	3	4
4	3	6	7	3	6

Example Incongruent

7	4	3	6	3	4

Example Congruent

7	4	3	6	3	4

NUMBER STROOP TASKS

Demonstration

Expose Items 1-1 and 1-3 and say:
> Look at these numbers.

Point to the first number on Item 1-1 at the top left-hand corner and say:
> What is this number?

If the response if correct, say:
> Yes, that is number seven.

If incorrect, say:
> That is number seven.

If the response is correct, say:
> Yes, that is number six.

If incorrect, say:
> That is number six.

Then say (point to the number seven):
> Is this number a big number or a small number? In this case, a big number is bigger than five. A small number is smaller than five.

If the response if correct, say:
> Yes, that is a big number.

If incorrect, say:
> That is a big number.

Point to the third number on Item 1-1 and say:
> What is this number?

If the response is correct, say:
> Yes, that is number three.

If incorrect, say:
> That is number three.

If the response is correct, say:
> Yes, that is number four.

If incorrect, say:
> That is number four.

Then say (point to the number three):
> Is this number a big number or a small number? In this case, a big a number is bigger than five. A small number is smaller than five.

If the response is correct, say:
> Yes, that is a small number.

If incorrect, say:
> That is a small number.

Then say (point to the number four):
> Is this number a big number or a small number? In this case, a big a number is bigger than five. A small number is smaller than five.

Repeat the directions for the remaining numbers on Item 1-3:

> four (small)
> six (big)

Example A

7	4	3	6	3	4
4	3	6	7	3	7

Expose Example A and say:
> Look at this. It has the same numbers on it. Tell me if each number is big or small. Remember, a big number is bigger than five and a small number is smaller than five. Do it as fast as you can. Begin here (point to the first number) and go this way (point to the first row in a sweeping motion from the examinee's left to right). When you finish these (point to the first row), do these (point to the second row in a sweeping motion).

> Ready? (Provide a brief explanation if necessary.)
> Begin. (Correct the examinee immediately as necessary.)

Discontinue testing if the examinee makes more than five errors.

With Example A still exposed, say:
> I'll show you another page with many numbers to look at. Tell me if each number is big or small. Begin as soon as I turn the page, and do it as fast as you can.

> Ready? (Provide a brief explanation if necessary.)

Item set 1-1
Expose Item Set 1-1 and say:

> Begin. (Start timing when the examinee says the first word.)

Record the examinee's responses and the time to completion.

Planning and Executive Function Tests: Ready for Use 125

If the examinee is still working after 180 seconds (3:00 minutes), say:

Stop. (Record 181 seconds [3:01 minutes].)

Item set 1-2
Follow directions for Item Set 1-1

Example B

7	**4**	**3**	6	**3**	**4**

4	**3**	6	7	**3**	6

I'll show you another page with many numbers to look at. Tell me if the value of each number is big or small. Begin as soon as I turn the page, and do it as fast as you can.

Ready? (Provide a brief explanation if necessary.)
Stop. (Record 181 seconds [3:01 minutes].)

Examiner Record Form/Answer Sheet

Example A

Big	Small	Small	big	small	small
Small	Small	Big	big	small	big

Example B

Big	Small	Small	big	small	small
small	Small	Big	big	small	big

Item sets 1-1, 1-2, 1-3, and 1-4

Big	Big	Small	Big	big	small
small	Big	Big	Small	small	big
small	Small	Big	Big	small	small
Big	Big	Small	Big	big	small
Big	Small	Small	Big	small	small
small	Big	Small	Big	small	big
Big	Small	Big	Small		

Item sets 2-1 and 2-2

small	Big	Big	Small	big	small
small	Small	Big	Big	small	big
Big	Small	Big	Small	big	small
Big	Big	Small	Big	small	small
small	Big	Small	Big	big	small
Big	Small	Small	Small	big	big
small	Big	Small	Big		

Item sets 3-1 and 3-2

small	Small	Big	Small	big	Big
Big	Small	Big	Small	big	Small
small	Big	Small	Small	big	Big
small	Small	Big	Big	small	Big
small	Big	Big	Small	big	Small
small	Small	Small	Big	small	Big
small	Big	Big	Small		

Time Sheet

Item Set	Time Limit
1-1	180" (3:00 min)
1-2	180" (3:00 min)
1-3	180" (3:00 min)
1-4	180" (3:00 min)
2-1	180" (3:00 min)
2-2	180" (3:00 min)
3-1	180" (3:00 min)
3-2	180" (3:00 min)

CONGRUENT STROOP

3	6	7	4	7	3
4	4	6	6	3	7
6	4	7	4	7	3
7	7	3	6	4	4

3	7	4	6	6	3
6	4	3	3	6	7
3	7	4	6		

INCONGRUENT

4	4	7	3	6	7
6	3	6	3	7	4
4	7	3	4	6	6
3	4	7	6	3	7
4	6	7	3	7	4
3	4	6	6	3	7
3	6	7	4		

NEUTRAL NUMBER STROOP

6	7	4	7	6	3
3	6	7	4	4	6
3	4	6	7	3	3
7	7	4	7	6	3
7	4	3	6	3	4
3	6	4	7	4	6
6	3	7	4		

REVERSE STROOP: INSTRUCTIONS

When you see 7, SAY THREE. When you see 3, SAY SEVEN.
  Let's practice.

Example A

7	3	3	7	3	3
3	3	7	7	3	7

When you see 6, SAY FOUR. When you see 4, SAY SIX.
  Let's practice.

Example B

6	4	4	6	4	4
4	4	6	6	4	6

Use Neutral Stroop page for the Reverse Stroop test.

NUMBER STROOP FOR YOUNGER CHILDREN: KINDERGARTEN TO GRADE 2

Administration of the same test, but separate form for 7 and 3, and a parallel form for 6 and 4 is recommended. The obvious reason is to reduce the demand on number comparisons, two at a time, for children rather than comparison requiring four numbers.

A second reason for making the parallel forms is in anticipation of the shorter response time for the distant number pair, 7 and 3, compared to 6 and 4; the latter is closer in number line location. In fact, the developmental study of interference or inhibition could use the separate forms, and determine at what age the gap in response time is reduced to insignificance.

A third use would be to test the child's proficiency in development of number concept.

Can Number Stroop be a tool for anticipating arithmetic competence in preschool to early school years?

Finally, it will be an age-appropriate measure of EF development in young children in addition to a few other construct-driven tests in EF, an active field of research.

Pattern Recognition

(An earlier draft of the test, Planned Patterns, was constructed with assistance from Professor Jack N. Naglieri.)

Item No.	Configuration	N of Points and Items Given	Ages 5–7	Ages 8–21
	Demonstration A and Samples A, B, and C			
1	Child connects little to big shapes making a Z or an N			
2	Child connects little to big shapes making a Z or an N			
	Demonstration B and Sample D			
3	Child connects a number that is sized little to big making a Z or an N			
4	Child connects a number that is sized little to big making a Z or an N			
	Demonstration C and Sample E			
5	Child connects single digit numbers in order making a Z or an N		16	16
6	Child connects single and double digit numbers making a Z or an N		16	16
7	Child connects two-digit numbers in numerical order making a Z or an N		16	16
8	Child connects three-digit numbers in numerical order making a Z or an N		16	16
9	Child connects four-digit numbers in order making a Z or an N			16
10	Child connects four-digit numbers in order making a Z or an N			16
	n of frames	64	64	96
	n of items	4	4	6

Administration Directions

Description

The participant's task is to connect a series of shapes or numbers within a box from the smallest to the largest in the correct sequence. Each item is comprised of a square with a shape or number in each of the four corners. The child's task is to draw a line from the smallest to the largest. Items 1 and 2 involve geometric shapes of different sizes, Items 3 and 4 involve a number presented in increasing size, and the remaining items involve one- to four-digit numbers. There are 16 squares per page with items arranged in a pattern. Children who approach the task strategically recognize the pattern and the shifting patterns and complete the task more accurately. This subtest is included in the children's Battery only.

Materials	Record Form, page ...
	Response Book for Ages 4–7, page ...
	Response Book for Ages 8–17, page ...
	Red pencil
	Stopwatch
Administer	Age 4: Demonstrations A and B and Samples A, B, C, and D, Items 1–4
	Ages 5–7: Demonstration C and Sample E, Items 5–8
	Ages 8–17: Demonstration C and Sample E, Items 5–10
Time Limits	All Items: Record time to completion
Record	Time in seconds
	Number Correct
	Strategy Assessment

Administration Comments

1. This subtest is comprised of 16 items per page. Each item requires the child to draw a line from the smallest to the largest shape or number contained within a square. Begin timing when the item is exposed, and stop timing when the child completes the item.
2. If the child stops before reaching the last shape or number, immediately say: Keep going.
3. Complete the Strategy Assessment Checklist on the Record Form.

Scoring

1. Record the number correct and the time taken to complete each item.
2. The item is scored correct if the child connects all four shapes or numbers in the correct sequence (there is no partial credit).

DIRECTIONS   AGE 4

Observed Strategies

During the administration of this subtest, observe the strategy or strategies the child appears to be using. Record these observations on the Record Form in the Observed (Obs) column of the Strategy Assessment Checklist.

Demonstration A

Demo A items 1 and 2

Expose the Demonstration A and Samples A, B, and C page in the Response Book and say:

Look here (point to Demonstration item 1), I'm going to draw a line from the small shape to the big one, watch me. I draw a line from here, to here, to here, and then to here. I do this one the same way (point to Demonstration item 2). I draw a line from here, to here, to here, and then to here.

Demo A item 3

Give the child the red pencil and say: Now you do this one (point to Demonstration item 3). Start here (point to the second box). Draw a line from here to here (point to the next larger circle and correct the child as needed). Now draw a line from here to here (point to the next larger circle and correct the child as needed), and now from here to here (the biggest circle). We go from the smallest to the biggest. Ready? (Provide a brief explanation if necessary.) Begin

If the response is correct, say: Good.
If the response is incorrect say: Let's do this one together. Start here. Draw a line from here to here (point to the next larger shape and correct the child as needed). Now draw a line from here to here (point to the next larger shape and correct the child as needed), and now from here to here (the biggest shape). Begin. Examiner immediately corrects all errors. Provide additional help as needed.

Demo A item 4
Say: Now do this one (point to Demonstration item 4). Start here (point to Item 4).

If the response is correct, say: Good.
If the response is incorrect say: Let's do this one together. Start here. Draw a line from here to here (point to the next larger shape and correct the child as needed). Now draw a line from here to here (point to the next larger shape and correct the child as needed), and now from here to here (the biggest shape). Ready? (Provide a brief explanation if necessary.) Begin. Examiner immediately corrects all errors. Provide additional help as needed.

Sample A
Now you do these (point to the second row Sample A in a sweeping motion from the child's left to right). Draw a line from here (point to the smallest shape) to here (point to the next larger shape), then to here (point to the next larger shape), and then to here (point to the largest shape). Go from the smallest to the biggest. Ready? (Provide additional help as needed.) Do all of these (Examiner points in a sweeping motion from left to right at the remaining Sample A items). Ready? (Provide a brief explanation if necessary.) Begin. If any errors are made, immediately correct them and provide further explanation as needed.

Sample B
Now you do these (point to Sample B in a sweeping motion from the child's left to right). Start here (Examiner points to the smallest shape). Draw a line from here to here (point to the smallest shape), from here to here, from here to here, and from here to here. Go from the smallest to the biggest. Do all of these (Examiner points in a sweeping motion from left to right at the remaining Sample A items). Ready? (Provide additional help as needed.) Begin. If any errors are made, immediately correct them and provide further explanation as needed.

Sample C
Now do these (point to Sample C in a sweeping motion from the child's left to right). Start here (Examiner points to the smallest shape in the first item). Go from the smallest to the biggest. Do all of these (Examiner points in a sweeping motion from left to right at the remaining Sample A items).

Ready? (Provide a brief explanation if necessary.) Begin. If any errors are made, immediately correct them and provide further explanation as needed.

Page 1
Expose Page 1 and say: Look at this page. There are more of these for you to do. Do these (point to the first row in a sweeping motion from the child's left to right), then these (point to the second row in a sweeping motion from the child's left to right), and so on without skipping any. Work as quickly as you can. If you make a mistake, cross it out and keep going. Remember go from the smallest to the biggest. Ready? Provide a brief explanation if necessary. Begin. Examiner begins timing. Record the time to completion and strategy use.

Page 2
Expose Page 2 and say: Now do these (point to the four rows from left to right and top to bottom in a sweeping motion). Examiner begins timing. Record the time to completion and strategy use.

Demonstration B

Demo B items 1 and 2
Expose the Demonstration B and sample page in the Response Book and say:
  Look here (point to the Demonstration B Item 1). I'm going to draw a line from the small number to the big one, watch me. I draw a line from here to here, to here, and then to here. I do this one the same way (point to Demonstration item 2). I draw a line from here, to here, to here, and then here.

Demo B item 3
Give the child the red pencil and say: Now you do this one (point to Demonstration B item 3). Start here. Draw a line from here to here (point to the next larger number and correct the child as needed). Now draw a line from here to here (point to the next larger number and correct the child as needed). Now draw a line from here to here (point to the largest number and correct the child as needed). We go from the smallest to the biggest.

If the response is correct, say: Good.
If the response is incorrect say: Let's do this one together. Start here. Draw a line from here to here (point to the next larger number and correct the

child as needed). Now draw a line from here to here (point to the next larger number and correct the child as needed), and now from here to here (the biggest number). Begin. Examiner immediately corrects all errors. Provide additional help as needed.

Demo B item 4
Say: Now do this one (point to Demonstration item 4). Start here (point to second box).

If the response is correct, say: Good.
If the response is incorrect say: Let's do this one together. Start here. Draw a line from here to here (point to the next larger shape and correct the child as needed). Now draw a line from here to here (point to the next larger shape and correct the child as needed), and now from here to here (the biggest shape). Begin. Examiner immediately corrects all errors. Provide additional help as needed.

Sample D
Now you do these (point to the second row Sample A in a sweeping motion from the child's left to right). Draw a line from here (point to the smallest number in Item 1) to here (point to the next largest number) to here (point to the next largest number) and then to here (point to the largest number). Go from the smallest to the biggest. Do all of these (Examiner points in a sweeping motion from left to right at the remaining Sample D items). Ready? (Provide a brief explanation if necessary.) If any errors are made, immediately correct them and provide further explanation as needed.

Item 3
Expose Item 3.
Look at this page. There are more of these for you to do. Do these (point to the first row in a sweeping motion from the child's left to right), then these (point to the second row in a sweeping motion from the child's left to right), and so on without skipping any. Work as quickly as you can. If you make a mistake, cross it out and keep going. Remember go from the smallest to the biggest. Ready? Provide a brief explanation if necessary. Begin.
Expose Item 3 and record the time to completion.

Item 4
Expose Item 4 and say:
  Now do these. Begin. Record the time to completion.

Reported Strategies
With the last Item still exposed, say:

> Tell me how you did these. (Indicate the pages in the Response Book just completed by the child.)

If necessary, say:

> How did you complete the page? (You may briefly clarify the question provided that you give no examples.)

Record the child's reported strategies on the Record Form in the Reported (Rep) column of the Strategy Assessment Checklist.

AGES 8 TO ADULT

Observed Strategies
During the administration of this subtest, observe the strategy or strategies the child appears to be using. Record your observations on the Record Form in the Observed (Obs) column of the Strategy Assessment Checklist.

Demo C items 1 and 2
Expose the Demonstration C and Sample E page in the Response Book and say: Look here (point to Demonstration Item 1) I'm going to draw a line from the small number to the big one, watch me. I draw a line from here to here, to here, to here, and then here to here. I do this one the same way (point to Demonstration C Item 2). I draw a line from here, to here, to here, and then to here.

Demo C item 3
Give the child the red pencil and say: Now you do this one (point to Demonstration C Item 3). Start here (point to the second box). Draw a line from here to here (point to the next larger number and correct the child as needed). Now draw a line from here to here (point to the next larger number and correct the child as needed), and now from here to here (the biggest number). We go from the smallest to the biggest.

Sample E
Now you do these (point to the second row Sample A in a sweeping motion from the child's left to right). Draw a line from here (point to the smallest number), to here (point to the next larger number), to here (point to the

next larger number), and then to here (point to the largest number). Go from the smallest to the biggest. Ready? (Provide a brief explanation if necessary.) Begin. If any errors are made, immediately correct them and provide further explanation as needed.

Page 5

Expose Page 5 and say: Look at this page. There are more of these for you to do. Do these (point to the first row in a sweeping motion from the child's left to right), then these (point to the second row in a sweeping motion from the child's left to right) and so on without skipping any. Work as quickly as you can. If you make a mistake, cross it out and keep going. Remember go from the smallest to the biggest number. Ready? Provide a brief explanation if necessary. Begin. Examiner begins timing. Record the time to completion and strategy use.

Items 6–8

Expose the page and say: Now do these (point to the page). Examiner begins timing. Record the time to completion and strategy use.

Items 9 and 10

In the next two items, you will notice that some boxes have a dark shade and some are light.

Hint: It is for you to discover if that information may help you to do the tasks faster. DO NOT ASK ME HOW?

Reported Strategies

With Item 10 still exposed, say:

Tell me how you did these. (Indicate the pages in the Response Book just completed by the child.)
If necessary, say:

How did you complete the page? (You may briefly clarify the question provided that you give no examples.)
Record the child's reported strategies on the Record Form in the Reported (Rep) column of the Strategy Assessment Checklist.

Planning and Executive Function Tests: Ready for Use 137

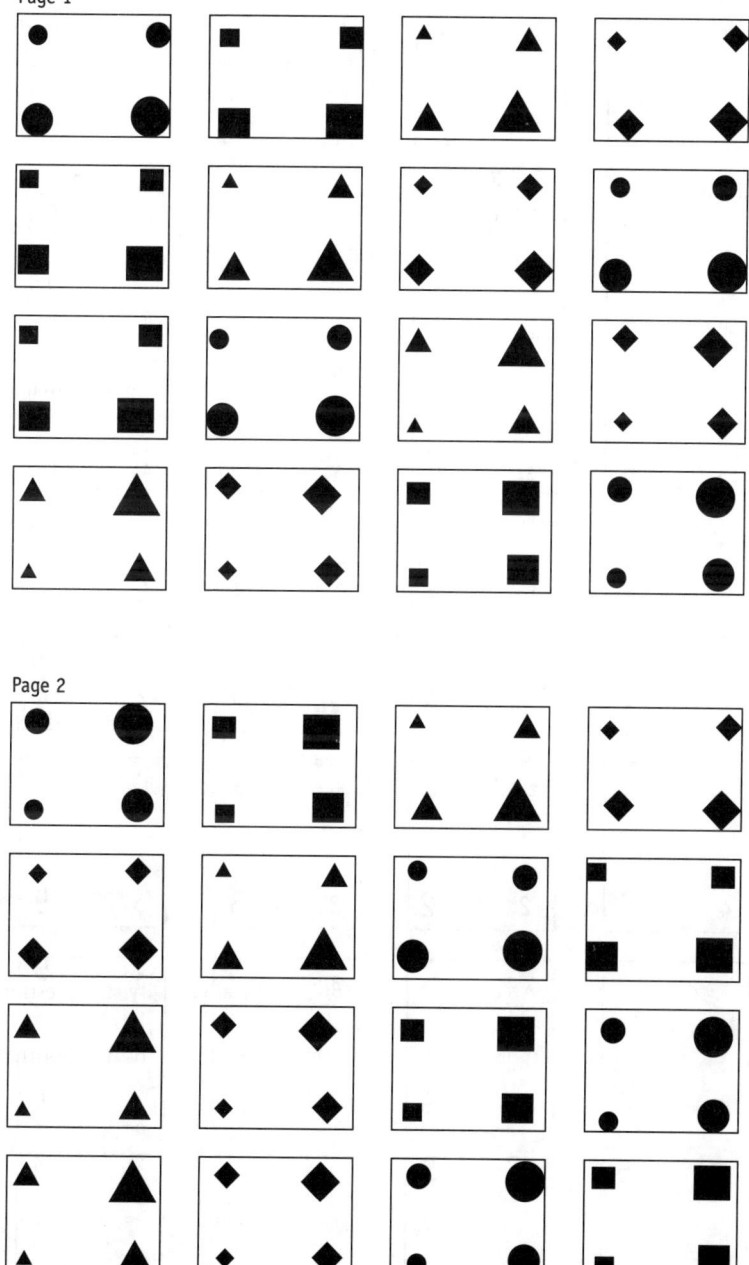

138 Cognitive Planning and Executive Functions

Demo C

| 1 4 / 6 8 | 2 4 / 5 9 | 8 5 / 3 2 | 9 7 / 3 1 |

Sample E

| 1 4 / 6 7 | 1 3 / 6 9 | 2 3 / 5 7 | 2 4 / 6 9 |
| 1 3 / 5 8 | 7 5 / 3 1 | 8 6 / 3 2 | 9 5 / 4 1 |

Page 3

3 3 / 3 3	5 5 / 5 5	2 2 / 2 2	4 4 / 4 4
4 4 / 4 4	2 2 / 2 2	3 3 / 3 3	5 5 / 5 5
2 2 / 2 2	4 4 / 4 4	3 3 / 3 3	5 5 / 5 5
5 5 / 5 5	3 3 / 3 3	2 2 / 2 2	4 4 / 4 4

Page 4

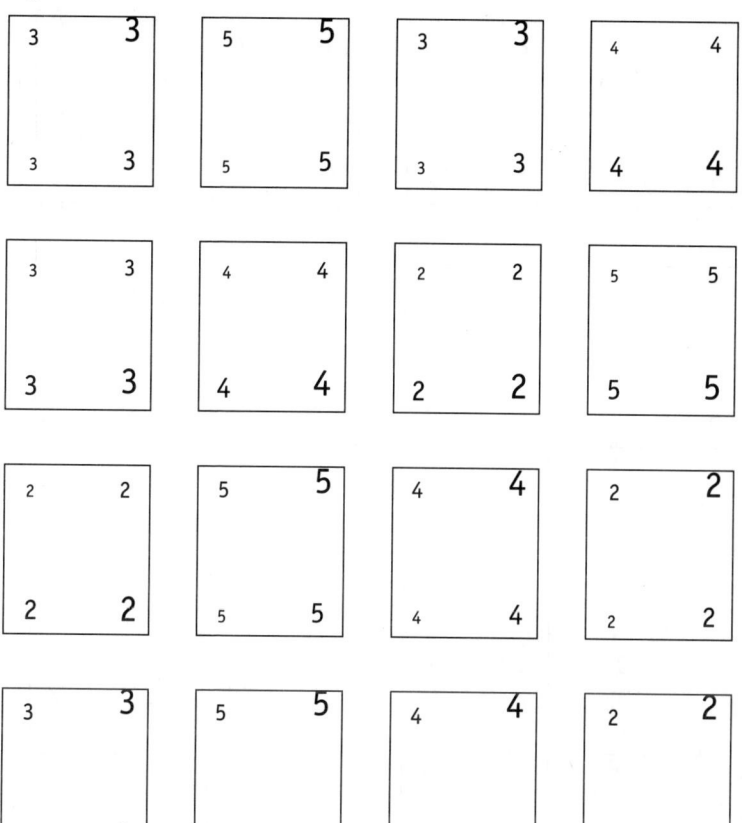

Page 5

1 3 5 7	2 3 6 9	1 4 5 9	2 3 6 9
1 3 6 8	1 3 6 7	1 4 5 8	1 4 5 7
2 3 5 9	1 4 6 9	4 9 2 5	3 8 1 5
4 8 2 5	4 9 1 6	3 9 2 5	4 9 2 6

Page 6

6	16
4	11

9	18
5	11

5	9
12	19

3	8
14	17

4	8
15	17

2	6
13	17

5	7
11	18

5	8
13	19

3	9
11	17

2	7
10	18

3	7
10	16

5	7
13	17

6	19
3	12

8	19
3	13

9	18
3	12

9	17
4	11

Page 7

| 22 24 | 21 24 | 21 23 | 21 24 |
| 25 28 | 25 27 | 25 28 | 25 27 |

| 20 23 | 21 23 | 20 23 | 20 24 |
| 25 28 | 26 29 | 26 28 | 25 27 |

| 22 24 | 22 24 | 24 28 | 24 28 |
| 26 28 | 26 29 | 21 26 | 20 25 |

| 23 27 | 24 27 | 24 27 | 23 29 |
| 22 26 | 20 26 | 22 25 | 21 25 |

Page 8

235	421
143	305

233	420
162	327

235	403
150	368

224	457
106	382

241	437
125	364

277	487
161	364

238	474
109	388

202	494
170	389

297	442
129	331

229	439
101	374

177	292
311	462

180	207
354	459

130	258
364	429

121	244
314	486

190	231
336	488

128	214
353	498

144 *Cognitive Planning and Executive Functions*

Page 9

| 1297 1831 | 1216 1266 | 1451 1986 | 1041 1301 |
| 1158 1674 | 1510 1890 | 1175 1523 | 1512 1830 |

| 1001 1480 | 1215 1289 | 1495 1839 | 1365 1873 |
| 1517 1910 | 1678 1854 | 1076 1713 | 1113 1626 |

| 1446 1874 | 1298 1993 | 1025 1435 | 1098 1366 |
| 1048 1582 | 1152 1701 | 1719 1967 | 1577 1859 |

| 1128 1417 | 1453 1880 | 1064 1430 | 1435 1894 |
| 1766 1907 | 1013 1704 | 1583 1931 | 1018 1585 |

Page 10

1424 1924 1100 1585	1381 1938 1094 1761	1142 1415 1737 1970	1193 1330 1681 1991
1061 1252 1637 1916	1217 1254 1613 1992	1287 1975 1170 1531	1287 1856 1044 1580
1088 1447 1577 1926	1492 1867 1000 1782	1071 1329 1581 1866	1467 1952 1010 1754
1258 1947 1091 1709	1046 1350 1580 1838	1488 1897 1203 1739	1210 1489 1554 1994

Administration Manual for CTC

In this planning subtest, the participant's task is to determine what the correct sequence of colored chips is when given a limited amount of information. The participant is given one trial to figure out the correct order of chips for each item. The subtest is organized into four sets of problems, three items in each set. The items are numbered continuously from 1 (sample) to 13. A 3-minute time limit per item is given except 5 minutes for Items 10, 11, and 12. Do not administer to grades K-2.

Materials

Materials include a response booklet, record form, stopwatch, and five round chips (black, blue, yellow, white, orange) or cut-outs with the words black, blue, yellow, white, orange.

Sample

Say: Look at this page. You see there is a black circle here and a blue circle here, but these colors are not in the correct places (point to the statement "none correct"). Put these (provide blue and black chips to the subject) here (point to the last row) in the correct order. Provide a brief explanation if necessary. Start timing. If correct say, good, and proceed to Item 1. If incorrect say, if we put the blue one here (point to the circle under the black) and the black one here (point to the circle under the blue) then they are both correct.

ITEM 1

Now look here (point to the top row). One of these is in the correct place (point to the first row and read the statement "1 correct"), but none of these is in the correct place (point to the second row and read the statement "none correct"). Then say: put these (point to the chips) here (point to the last row) in the correct order. Start timing and allow 3 minutes to complete.

Time Limit

Time limit is 3 minutes for each item for all subjects except Items 10, 11, and 12, which is given for 5 minutes. However, allow 5 minutes for older subjects (65 years and older for Items 1–9). Older subjects are not expected to succeed doing Items 10–12. Record the actual time taken by the participant for each item.

Failures

If Item 1 is failed, give a clue. The single clue is one of the colors from the row that says "1 correct." For items that have 2 correct, a single clue is given for one of those items. For items that have 3 correct, a single clue is given for the three correct items. Then following the trial, re-administer the item and start timing again. Record the time in the appropriate column. If the subject failed the item or could not give the correct answer within the time limit, continue to give the next item. If failed again, stop. But, if passed, go on to the next set (Items 4, 5, and 6). If those are passed, go to Items 7, 8, and 9. If those are passed, go to Items 10, 11, and 12.

Scoring

For each item the subject finds the correct solution with no mistakes, score = 2. If the subject fails to find the correct solution for the first item, a clue is given. If the correct solution follows the clue, score = 1. If the subject fails the item even after the clue, show the correct solution. Re-administer the item. If the subject does not pass, score = 0. Then, proceed to the next item. If the score = 0 on two consecutive items, STOP the test.

Scoring Time

First move latency: Time is recorded for making the first move after an item is presented.

148 *Cognitive Planning and Executive Functions*

Total time taken: Time is recorded as soon as participant says, "I have finished" or gives up.

Record both First move latency and Total time taken for incorrect solution. (See CTC sample figures below.)

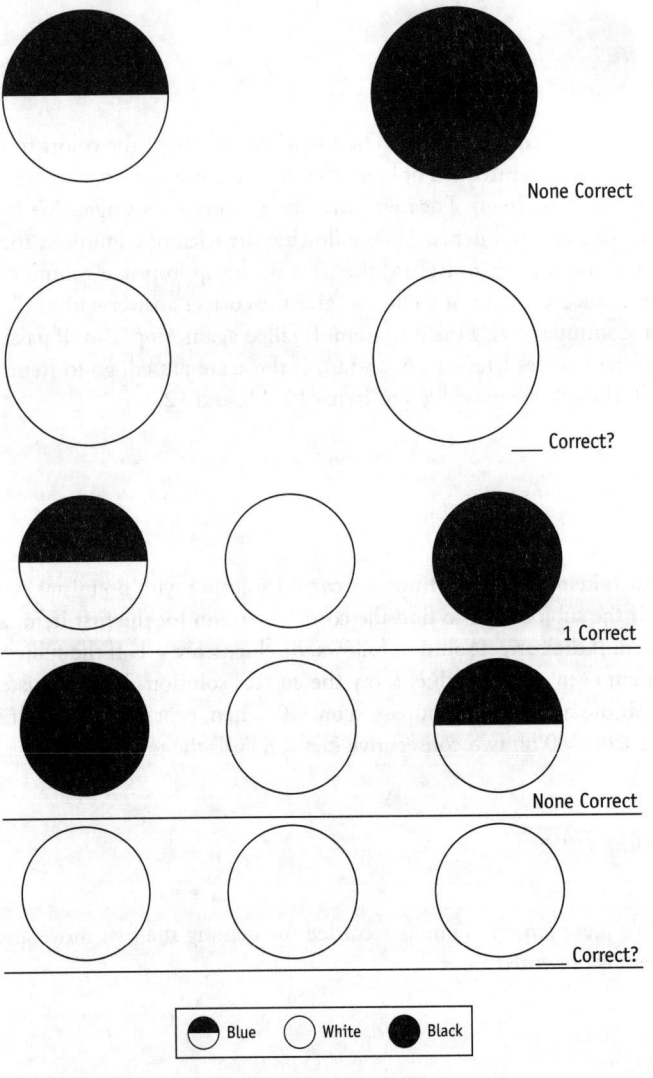

Planning and Executive Function Tests: Ready for Use 149

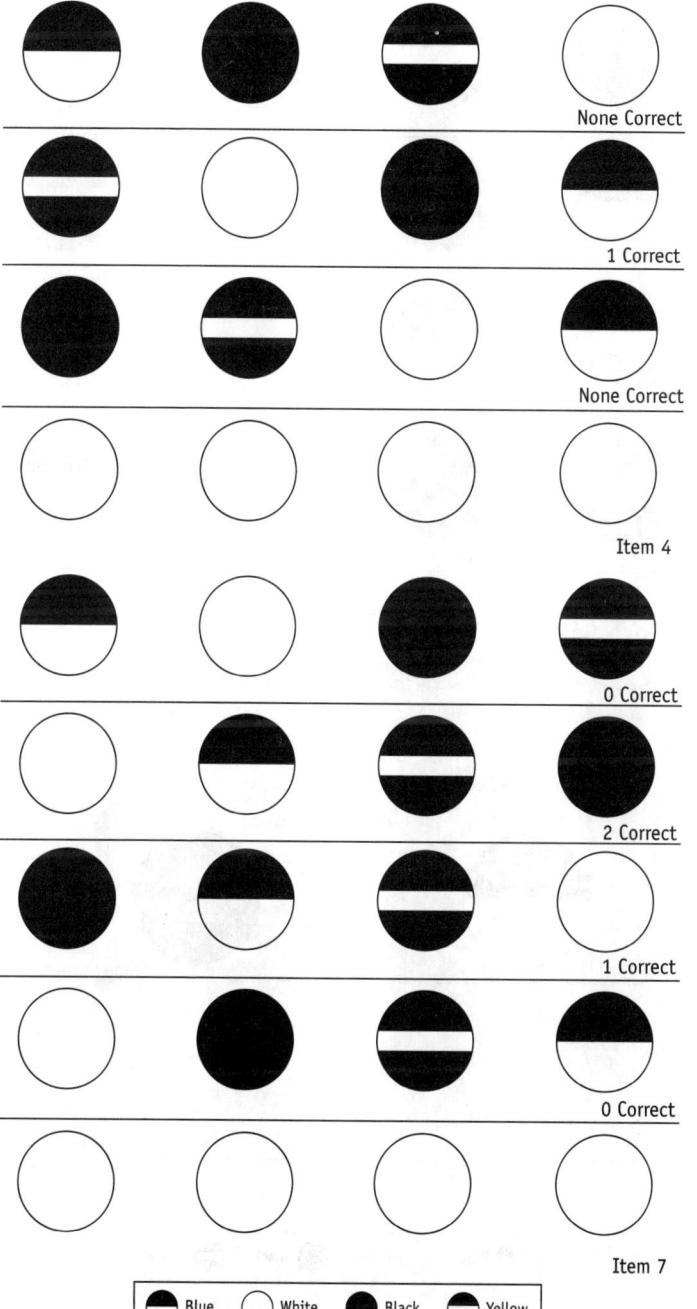

150 *Cognitive Planning and Executive Functions*

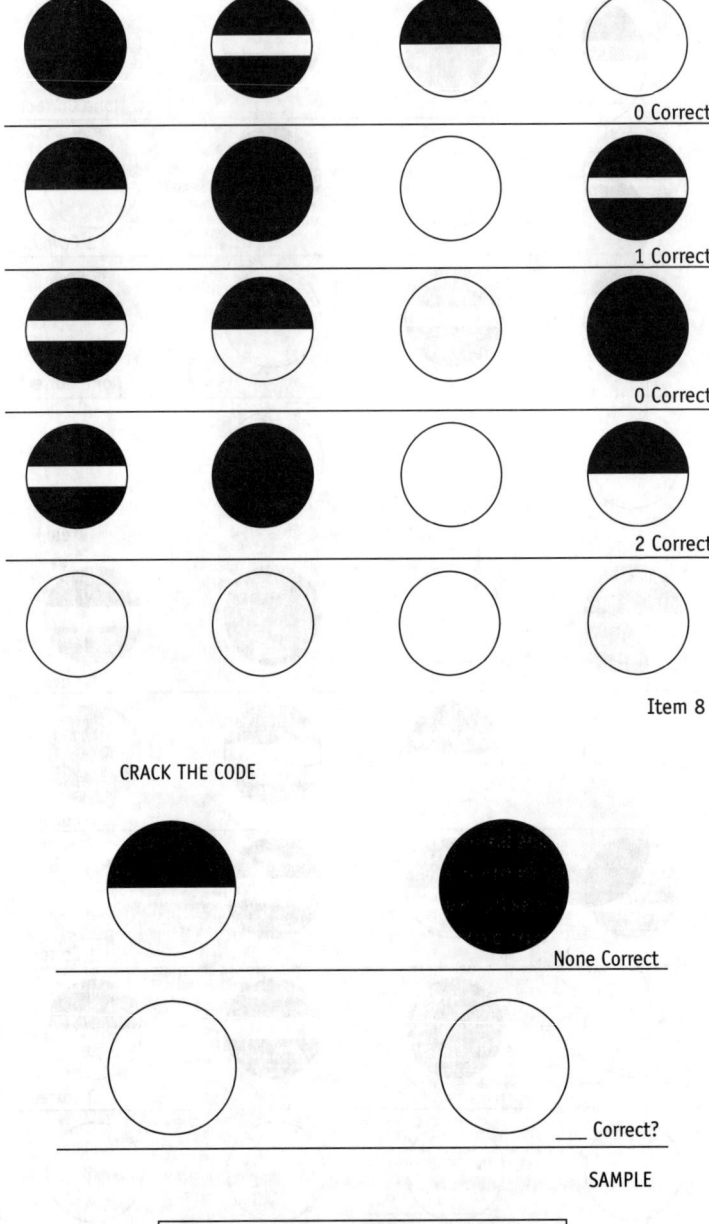

Planning and Executive Function Tests: Ready for Use

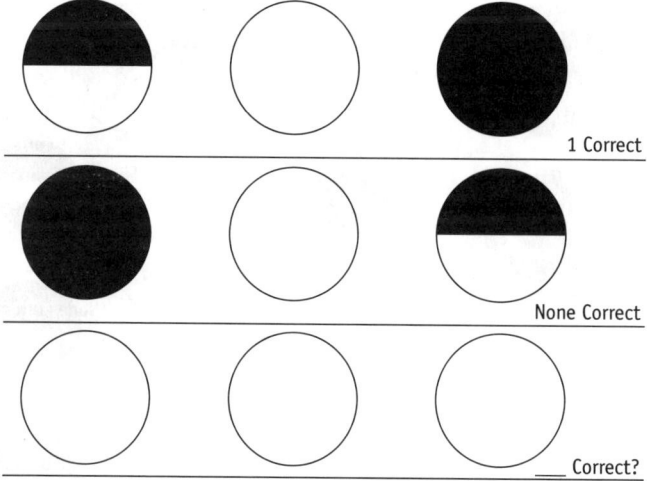

1 Correct

None Correct

___ Correct?

Item 1

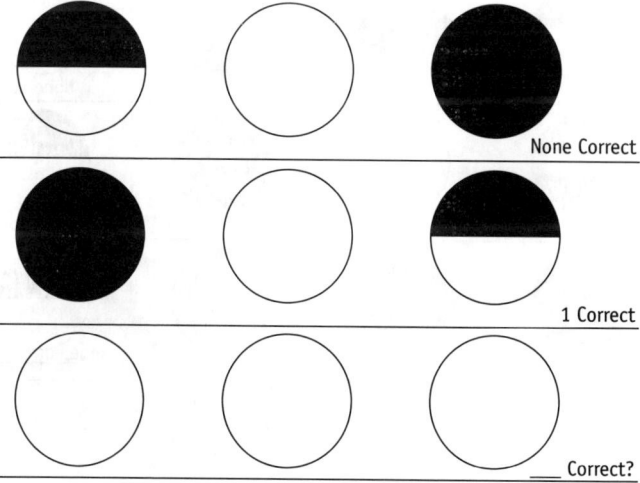

None Correct

1 Correct

___ Correct?

Item 2

Blue White Black

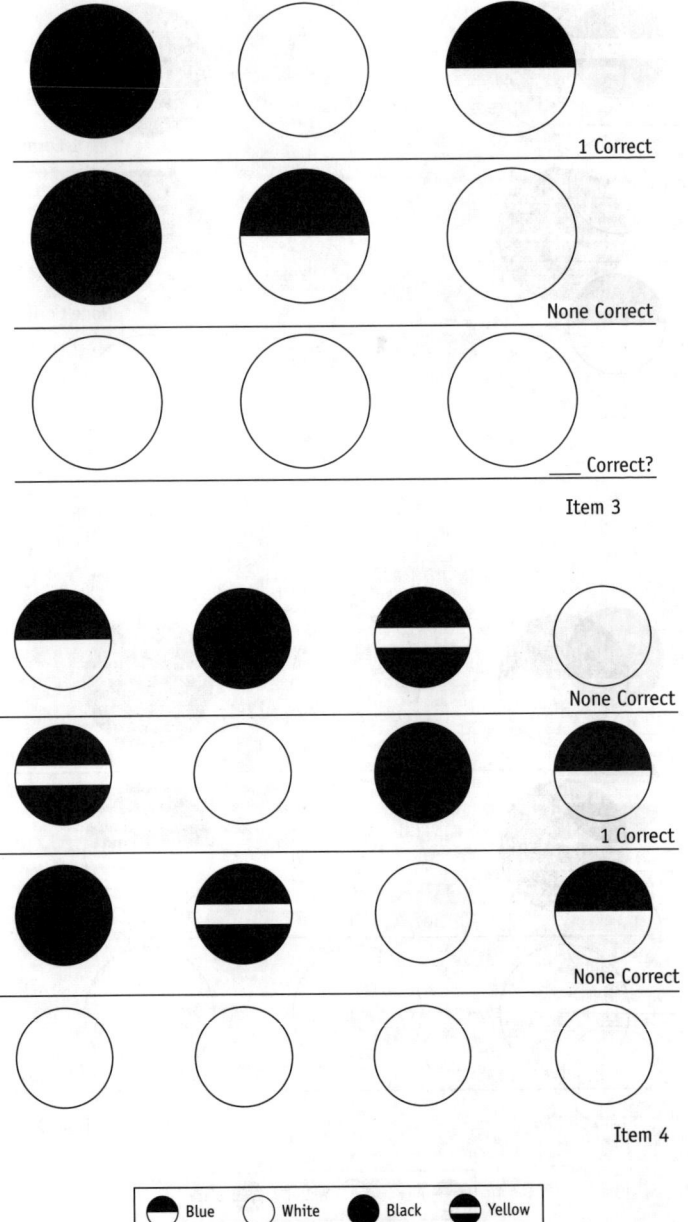

Planning and Executive Function Tests: Ready for Use 153

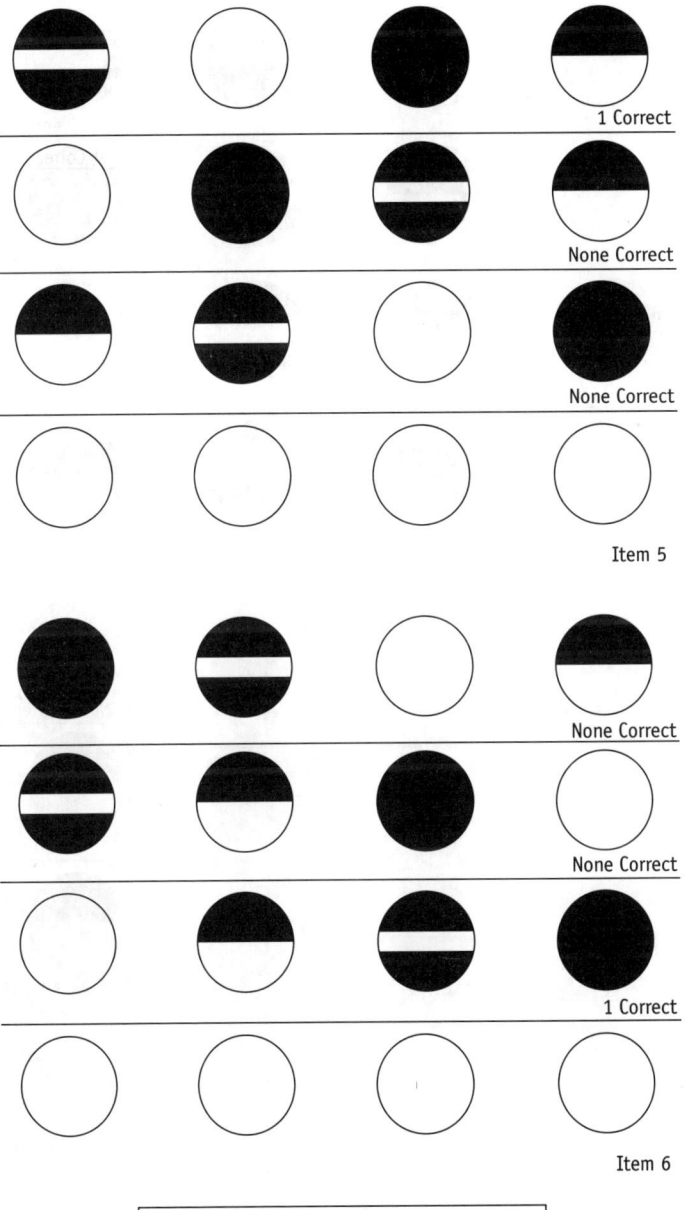

154 Cognitive Planning and Executive Functions

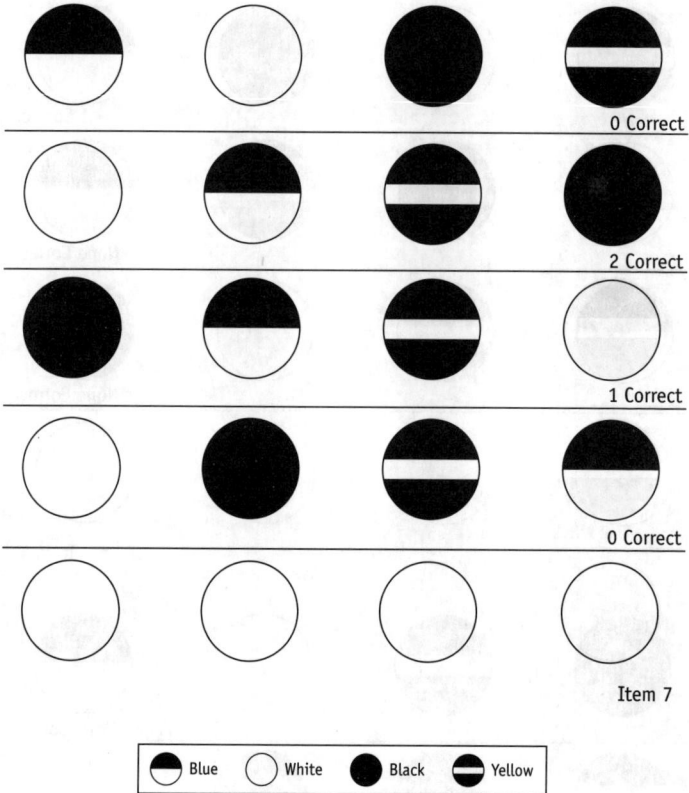

Item 7

Planning and Executive Function Tests: Ready for Use 155

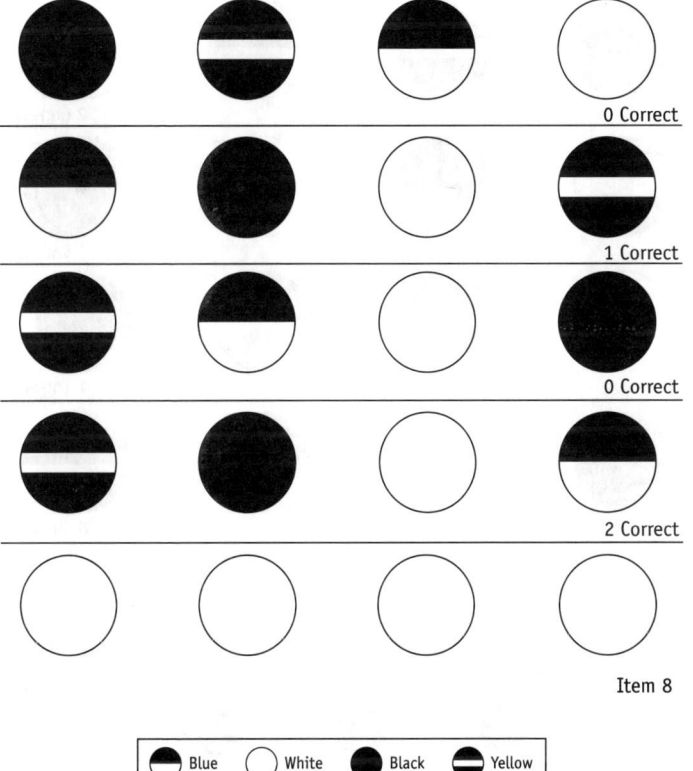

Item 8

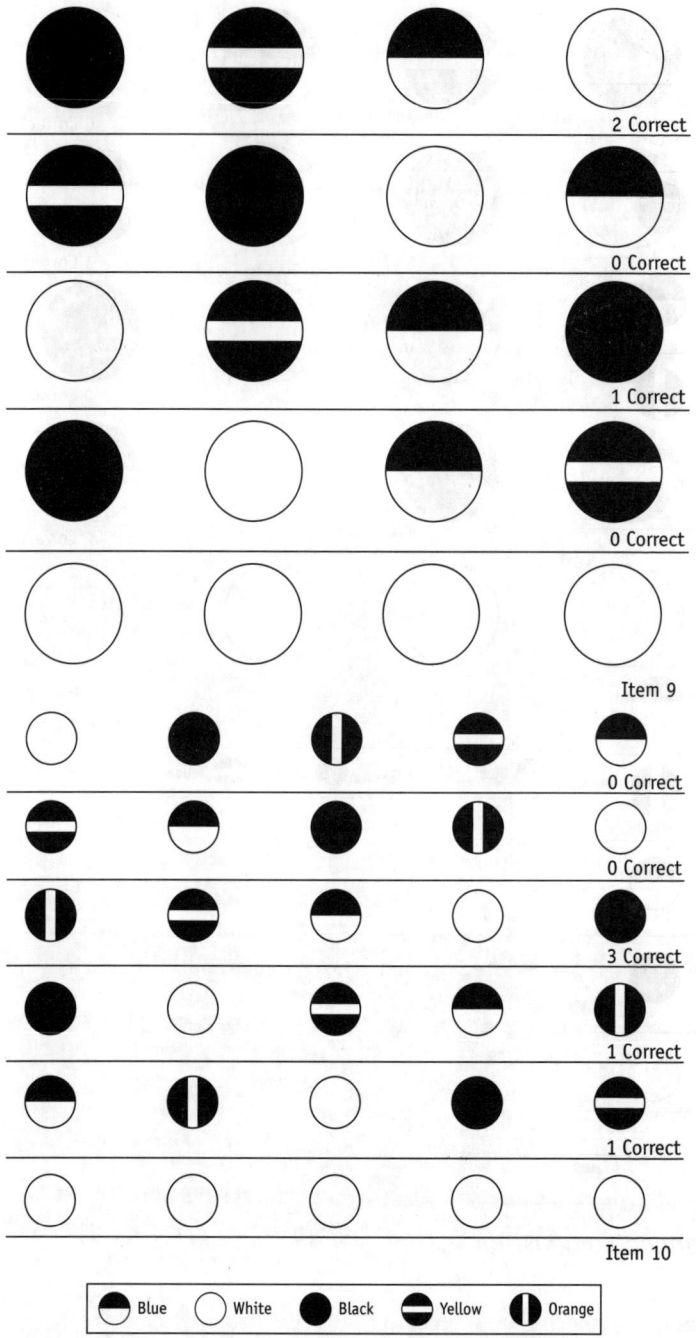

Planning and Executive Function Tests: Ready for Use 157

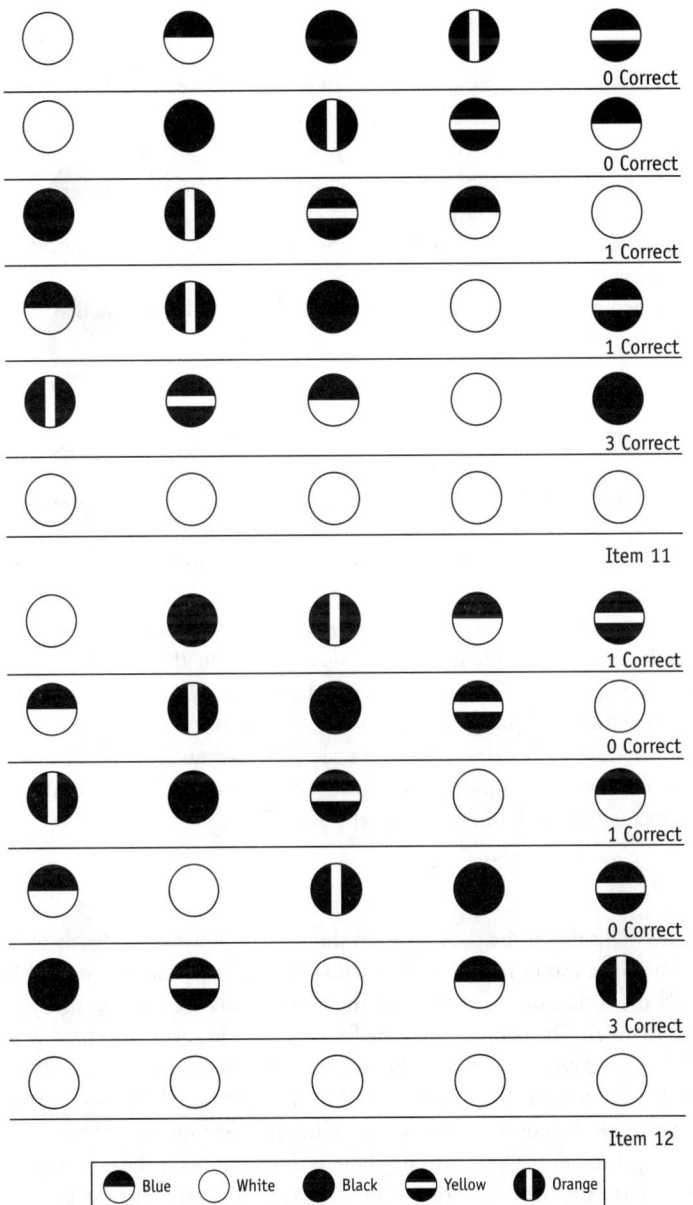

Planned Composition: Story

Picture 2 from Thematic Apperception Test (Murray, 1943).

Instructions given to subjects:

"This is a test to see how well you can write a short essay. All you have to do is think up and write a story that would go with this picture. You will have ten minutes to write your story, and from experience we know that most people your age should be able to fill one page in that time. Please use the lined sheet you have been given."

"You can make up any kind of story you wish; it could be happy, sad, exciting or dull."

"Remember, you have ten minutes. I will let you know when you only have five minutes left to write."

"Are there any questions?"

Instructions given to the essay raters:

"We have attempted to make the rating of essays as easy as possible by typing the children's essays right onto the rating form, thereby removing the hazard of illegible handwriting and the trouble of using more than one sheet for each essay."

"All compositions are to be written by adolescents (Grade 8 and upwards), adults and older individuals, and were based on the stimulus picture which is enclosed. The essays are reproduced exactly as written—spelling, punctuation and paragraphing have not been changed."

"Please rate each story using the scale provided at the bottom of each sheet. Draw a circle around the number rating which best represents your assessment of each dimension of the essay."

REMEMBERING

As Jane walks down the country road she realizes how she really misses the city where she was born. All of her friends she grew up with the crowds. She missed the sound of the traffic and the children playing. The country was quiet, to quiet. The people here were friendly and they were also hard workers. They worked on what they thought was the best was of living. But Jane felt different. She just could not bring herself to see herself as some farmer's wife living in the country for the rest of her life. She dreaded the thought. She longed to get back to the city. Jane walked on down the country road to school (trying to) wondering if she would ever get back to the place she loved so well.

Organization

- 1–2: Good starting point; has a sense of directed movement in the story; appears to have an underlying plan; seems logically arranged.
- 3–4–5: Organization is standard and conventional; some trivial points given more importance than deserved; logic in progression not always clear.
- 6–7: Starts anywhere and never gets anywhere; ideas are presented randomly with no apparent forethought.

THE FARMER AND HIS FAMILY

The farmer and his wife were in the field when his sister from Boston came to visit. The farmer's wife was pregnant. One day the farmer's wife had the child with his sister's help. Five years later the boy and his father went to the lake which was only a short walk from the house. That day was when the farmer drowned and the child became the man of the house. As the child grew he became stronger and was soon able to cultivate. Twenty years after the farmer died the boy decided to leave the farm, but his mother tried to beg to stay.

Organization

- 1–2: Good starting point; has a sense of directed movement in the story; appears to have an underlying plan; seems logically arranged.
- 3–4–5: Organization is standard and conventional; some trivial points given more importance than deserved; logic in progression not always clear.
- 6–7: Starts anywhere and never gets anywhere; ideas are presented randomly with no apparent forethought.

Planned Composition (Strategic Essay Writing)

Note: Empirical research is reviewed in the Management section of this book.
Phase I: Suppose, in a pharmaceutical company, you are the Chief Executive Officer. The company can have the following overall strategies in order to prosper:

* A Be innovative.
* B Achieve a good share of the market.
* C Be known for its economical price—low cost of products.
* D Produce high-quality goods.

Cautionary Notes for Each Strategy

"A" requires an outlay of capital in research and development. But the world record shows that in the last five years, research and development money has increased five-fold, but the number of new products launched has remained the same. "B" requires aggressive advertisement, but the company's star product is about to be replaced by a new break-through medication for fever. "C" requires getting the components of the products from manufacturing to packaging from developing countries where labor is cheap. But this has a disastrous effect on employment at home. "D" may cost so much more that it would make the product uneconomical.

In the 30-year past history of the company, the following weight had been given to the strategies with results indicated. Your job is to achieve a 100 per cent growth by rearranging the strategies, but you must take into account the information from the past results: In the past, one manager gave 1st place to C, 2nd place to D, 3rd place to A, and 4th place to B. None of CDAB was in the correct position. The profit dropped to 0 percent because not even one of the strategies was in the correct place. The choice of C in the first place, D next, A, and then B in order of importance resulted in zero profit. This is expressed as CDAB = zero.

Another manager gave 1st place to C, 2nd place to A, 3rd place to B, and 4th place to C. Two of DABC were in the correct position. The profit was 50 per cent because only two of the strategies were in the correct place. You do not know which two. DABC = 2.

Another manager gave 1st place to B, 2nd place to C, 3rd place to D, and 4th place to A. Of these, two choices were in the correct place. Again, we do not know which ones these were. The profit again was 50 per cent because like the previous choice, only two of the strategies were in the correct place. BCDA = 2.

Your task is to assign the priorities so that the right strategy will have the right place to give a 100 per cent profit.

Phase II: Write an essay of about one page justifying how the plan produces the best results when the solution is DCBA (or BADC).

PART IV

Applications in Management and Education

8

Rational and Irrational in Managerial Behavior

This is the first of the three chapters that have significant implications for management and organizational behavior. It sets the stage for discussion by first defining the specific competencies that managers and senior executives need, and then a broad range of issues that include the issues related to Reasoning, Intuition, and Intelligence that blend in with the specifics of management and administrative behavior.

Roles and Activities of Top Managers

Top-level executive functions (EFs) include a variety of activities described as problem solving, decision making, planning, and goal setting. Runaway successes and spectacular turnarounds of mammoth corporations, in retrospect, have largely been attributed to the competencies of their senior personnel, particularly the "masterminds" of the chief executive officers. The questions then arise are: (a) What characterizes outstanding managers? (b) Are there some generic or generalizable competencies that determine managerial success?

Generic competencies refer to intellectual or cognitive processes. It is argued here that these processes play a significant role in nonroutine and loosely structured managerial problem-solving and decision-making situations. Such problems and situations require qualitative judgments, intuition, and creativity, all of which are antithetical to quantitative, analytical, and logical thinking. Yet, it is not unscientific to accept qualitative judgments.

Another question is, what could these cognitive processes be? More than 50 years ago, Barnard (1938) referred to them as some unarticulated non-logical mental processes that lead a decision-maker to a particular judgment or action in the face of novel and unprogrammed situations. Barnard mentioned intuition, judgment, as well as illogical processes that respond to emotions. Since then, non-logical thinking, or synthetic thinking, has been recognized as a necessity for decision making in novel and complex situations (Simon, 1987). However, the problem now is that researchers and thinkers in the field of management have swung the pendulum to an extreme because of their growing disenchantment with logical and analytical thinking. For example, Leavitt (1975) tried to find solutions in eastern mysticism such as Zen or transcendental meditation. In fact, his search was for a different philosophy which will be an alternative to empirical analysis and logical thinking. Many management writers, notably Mintzberg (1976), have also considered physiological bases for their philosophy. They have looked for alternatives in the spectacular outcomes of the dissociation between the left and right hemispheres of the brain. The research on split brains, however, is irrelevant for a new philosophy in management because it has been typically taken out of context and interpreted as supporting holistic and non-sequential thinking (right-brain activity) in contrast to rational and logical routines of thought (left-brain activity).

Taking split-brain research findings at their face value results in encouraging a myth (Corballis, 1980). As Corballis explains, the specialized centers on the left and right sides of the brain have to do with how the normal brain processes the world, and not with how people differ from each other. He continues to say that the fact that the two hemispheres have somewhat different functions is not a myth. But it is wrong to say that one or the other side is universally dominant. Dominance is task related, not person related.

An example of misplaced enthusiasm for cultivating non-analytical thinking is a book by Agor (1984). He advocates the use of right brain and integrated brain thinking for managers. In contemporary perspectives of neuropsychology, however, such dichotomies in thinking are nearly mythical and are not supported by research. In fact, both analytical and synthetic approaches are considered characteristic of top-level managers because they are adept at making balanced decisions. This point is further elaborated in the next chapter, a sequel to the present one.

Cognitive Processes in Managerial Decision Making

A manager may make an outstanding decision, thereby achieving significant success in advancing the aims of the organization. He may not be equally successful in future. However, the wise thing to do is to focus on the processes that led to such excellent outcomes. Process analysis can proceed by using two metaphors. The first metaphor originates from cognitive science, which has made great strides through the seminal work of Simon (1978) in relation to management. It regards an individual as a mental symbol system or as an information-processing system. The second metaphor is derived from neuropsychology, which can be traced to the original work of Luria (1966) and several others (see Denes & Pizzamiglio, 1999; Gazzaniga, 1979).

Luria's neuropsychological framework has been advanced by the cumulative research of Das, Kirby, and Jarman (1979) and Das, Naglieri, and Kirby (1994). The metaphor holds that mental functions of individuals are to be determined by the interaction between their neuromechanism and their life's experience. These two approaches—the information-processing model of human intelligence and the neuropsychological accounts of cognitive functions—are by no means unrelated to each other. The distinction merely serves to focus on the unique features of the two approaches and does not deny their commonalities.

As mentioned earlier, the work of Simon and his colleagues in cognitive science has been applied to managerial planning and decision making. German psychologist Dietrich Doerner (1985), in the course of his pathbreaking research on human thinking and the problem-solving processes of an individual faced with complex, poorly-structured, and fast-changing situations, has developed sophisticated computer simulations which provide valuable data with regard to the course of decision making in management. Simon (1967) has also reported specific studies on managerial decision making that show how intuitive thinking can be embodied in computer programs. However, the computer simulation obviously cannot accommodate non-conscious processes that affect decision making (subsequently discussed in this and other chapters).

Let us believe that intuition and non-logical thinking need not always be accessible to consciousness. Intuitive thinking, as mentioned earlier, becomes essential when the problem situation is extremely complex and quite novel. The conditions under which intuitive, or non-conscious, thinking arises will be discussed later in this chapter and a subsequent one in some detail. But let us here identify at least two essential conditions that favor intuitive thinking: (a) the large number of contingencies that are associated with the problem and (b) the interactions between the different facets of the problem situation that are expected to be complex. Intuitive thinking is used well by competent executives; one of the major factors that makes managers excellent decision makers is their openness to consider intuition, and the decisions informed by intuition as credible and legitimate, just like analytical knowledge.

Why Individuals Differ in Their Ability to Make Decisions?

There are many reasons as to why individuals differ in their ability to make decisions, but one can divide them basically into two—cognitive competence and motivational orientations. Both are deeply influenced by beliefs and the accessible knowledge base of the individual. First, we shall describe the bases of individual differences in cognitive competence in relation to the PASS model outlined earlier in Chapter 1.

There are three components in the model, each of which may cause better or worse performance in a manager. Let us first consider the *mode of input*. Some managers or executives may be so brilliant that they sit down in a meeting, hear and see the information given, and arrive at an efficient solution to the problem or make a very appropriate decision after only listening to the other participants. Others need to look at a script of the arguments. Most individuals, however, may not have a strong preference for processing information gained through one modality to another.

Some psychologists and neuroscientists have questioned the scientific basis for the theories on which individual differences in regard to *inherent preference* for a selected modality are based (Pritchard, 2009).

Although cognitive style differences are not to influence instruction in the classroom, it remains a fact that some of us gain information easily from a visual presentation, whereas others are more comfortable with auditory presentations. We suspect, of course, that most of us are in between. There are individuals who must take notes and actively summarize while listening to a presentation in order to use that information later for decision making. These are people who have less facility with auditory presentations. Similarly, there may be people who are poor information gatherers when information is presented visually in the form of graphs, charts, and flow diagrams. This example may indicate a minor source of individual differences, but recognizing what his or her preferred mode of receiving information as perceived by the individual, and then taking steps that will facilitate the gathering of information is necessary for every manager.

Next we consider *processing* and *knowledge base*. Methods of processing information, such as sorting information, categorizing it, putting it into files of the mind which can be cross-referenced—and thus can be easily retrieved—are familiar coding mechanisms. Two aspects of knowledge base are important enough to be singled out. The first is Long-term Memory that includes storage and retrieval. This is just not a simple storage bin. Your identity, a sense of continuing self, has its origin here. Afflictive emotions and trauma, both physical and mental, can cloud it, or even eliminate it. Thus, it is much more than the type of filing system that was alluded to. The other aspect concerns how helpful or pernicious the knowledge is that is stored and retrieved. Everyone has sometimes wished to forget an unpleasant memory that evokes a conditioned emotional response.

We have added to these two other information-processing preferences: simultaneous processing and successive processing. Adults as well as children may have a higher score on tasks that require one kind of processing than on tasks that require the other. For example, a weakness in simultaneous processing usually accompanies poor reading ability for maps, rotating a figure or diagram in the head to look at it from another angle, or comprehending a written discourse or narrative. Comprehension requires separating the text into a hierarchy of themes, main and secondary ideas, and understanding the sentences that make up the passage. In contrast, adults, including executives, may have a relative weakness in understanding syntax, remembering the sequence of events or actions. At the basic level, they may hate to learn by rote.

Notwithstanding the manner in which information has been gathered and coded, gathering of information (i.e., the sorting and analysis of information) itself needs direction, purpose, and a goal. This makes the *role of planning* quite important in coding processes. Without plans, coding of information is blind, and without coded information, plans and decisions are empty. Thus, the apparent synergistic relationship between planning, attention, and coding processes creates further sources of individual differences in decision-making competence.

Finally, there is the *output*. The manner in which a response is required determines how competent an individual will be in that specific output mode. For example, if a manager needs to program the steps of action, which are consequent to having taken a decision, the procedure would depend very much on the mode of output. Is it a procedure that the manager has to lay out for the action to be executed? Then the infrastructure necessary for the actual carrying out of the decision also needs to be there. Thus, an effective action depends only partially on efficient decision making; the other part is concerned with the mechanics of carrying out the decision. We started by asking questions with regard to the action—whether it is a procedure that has to be laid out as a consequence of a decision, or alternatively, whether the manager has to present an analysis of the solution to the problem and thus make the decision available to others for execution. The latter would be an output involving declarative knowledge. Communication of the plan then becomes the salient problem in the output mode rather than the actual carrying out of the plan. However, a ubiquitous knowledge base is constantly required and is consistently relevant to any kind of intellectual activity comprising the receiving of information, processing it, and determining an output.

For many managers, a good knowledge base of the system in which they work and for processing the information that they have to deal with may account for 100 percent of the variance in competencies, that is how effective the managers are.

However, we argue that although a knowledge base does seem to distinguish between expert and novice managers, and to a lesser extent between successful and unsuccessful decision makers, the managers may significantly differ from each other in their generic competencies. In other words, some managers may have a superior generic competence for planning. Included within planning are the abilities to pose the right sort of problems, to formulate plans, and to select between different plans. These abilities enable the manager to successfully execute the plans that have been made. A good manager may be able to gather diagnostic information about the problem in such a way that it is both broad and specific for solving the problem at hand. In other words, a manager builds a broad base of knowledge, at its apex is the final decision made by him or her. Therefore, we feel that there may be as much variance contributed to successful or unsuccessful management by the generic processes outlined in the PASS mode as is contributed by the knowledge base.

Dual Processes of Reasoning

Intuitions and Reasoning have been distinguished for a long time in the history of human thought. For example, the main sources of knowledge have been identified in Indian philosophy as: (1) perception, (2) inference and analogical reasoning, and (3) testimony, that is, knowledge from books and authorities. One could add knowledge stored in a database in computers! Knowledge base has been discussed earlier as a part of the model of cognition in PASS theory of intelligence (see Chapters 1 and 2, and the current chapter). Outside the domain of scientific knowledge, we could add knowledge directly obtained or even revealed to a person without the use of sensory and motor organs, or mental mechanisms posited above as reasoning and intuition. Leaving aside the last kind of knowledge, we could say that rational knowledge is based on reasoning, as the term suggests, and is contrasted with intuition. Managers use both kinds, and the interaction between the two has been discussed at length because human beings in general and managers in particular may not reason properly (Evans, 2003).

Rationality and Reasoning, and a Place for Arguments

The failure of logic or rationality has been discussed in several contexts, including in this chapter in which the context is decision making. For example, an entire conference on "dual process" recently drew selected scholars, who worry about the issues and implications related to reasoning and intuition, as presented in Evans and Frankish (2008). Introductory statement describing the objective of the conference gives a clear picture of the issues involved.

There has been growing interest recently in the so-called "dual-process" theories of reasoning and rationality. Such theories postulate two distinct systems (or sets of systems) underlying human reasoning—typically distinguishing an evolutionarily old system (System 1) that is associative, automatic, unconscious, parallel, and fast, and a more recent, distinctively human system (System 2) that is rule-based, controlled, conscious, serial, and slow.

The two systems—affect and reason—are named as an affective associative affect-based mode of decision making (A) and a deliberative rule-based mode of decision making (D), by Mukherjee (2010) in an important review article. Affective and deliberative problem solving are discussed at length in the present and previous chapters (Chapters 2 and 6) of this book. The special contribution of Mukherjee (2010) is in building models—mathematical—which is too complicated to explain here, in order to support the general notion that human behavior can be explained by a dual-processing mode rather than a unified mode. As he explains, the dual-processing mode is especially useful for explaining decision making under conditions of ambiguity, in which precise information about probabilities is not available.

In a slightly different context, without the brain location, the dual system has been discussed in Chapter 8. So, the readers at this point assume that System 1 is best described as intuitive knowledge, and System 2 as rational knowledge (see note 1 in Mukherjee, 2010).

Sanfey (2007) and references in this article have reviewed neurological locations for the two modes or systems. System 1 is affective/automatic. It engages structures, such as the amygdala, insular cortex, orbitofrontal cortex, anterior cingulate cortex, and nucleus accumbens. In contrast, System 2 is deliberative/controlled and broadly involves structures, such as dorsolateral and anterior prefrontal cortex, and posterior parietal regions. We have also mentioned these regions as possible locations for affective and deliberative Planning/EF in Chapters 3 and 4.

So, the readers at this point assume that System 1 is best described as intuitive knowledge, and System 2 as rational knowledge as Evans (2003), one of the early writers on the dual system uses. However, Intuition and Reasoning are revisited in the last chapter of the book, best described as a reflective summary.

Now, turning back to Evans' paper, it is best to cite his concluding observations on Systems 1 and 2 discussion within the broad framework of Reasoning in cognitive psychology:

> Theoretical and experimental psychologists need to focus on the interaction of the two systems and the extent to which volitional process in System 2 can be used to inhibit the strong pragmatic tendencies to response in inference and judgment that come from System 1, especially where the latter are known to result in cognitive biases. (Evans, 2003, p. 457)

Reasoning and argument, the two related concepts, have been discussed further by Mercier and Sperber (2011). In their argumentative paper, they argue that reasoning and intuition, both, need to be supported by arguments. They define *argument* as a mechanism for establishing the truth or the fallacy of *reasoning*. Reasoning is a potential source of new mistakes, as Mercier and Sperber agree with Evans. Reasoning can be used to accurately evaluate arguments. While the focus of reasoning is inference, as in syllogisms to arrive at correct conclusions, the purpose of arguments is to evaluate the conclusions themselves in order to persuade people to accept or reject the conclusion. Motivated reasoning is familiar to all of us when we see how people use reasons for accepting a pre-existing belief. Arguments can be constructed to justify a bias or a belief from intuitions or even syllogistic reasoning.

One of the major reasons for the failure of logic may indeed be the individual's use of persuasive arguments for convincing himself/herself, as much as other members of a management board that makes decisions. In the subsequent sections, we discuss how inferences can be false, arguments may be motivated, and the entire outcome of making a rational decision is admittedly influenced by affect, that is, by a powerful irrational component in decision making.

The Concern: Rational Decisions—A Sign of Intelligence

Are we missing something by encapsulating the cognitive process just discussed within the old box of intelligence as its sole occupant? Specifically, rationality? Stanovich, Toplak, and West (2008) have argued it to be the essential core of intelligence, and that it has not been accorded an important place in education.

In our first year book in a course of logic, we read that "man is a rational animal," a statement that had been attributed to Aristotle. But even then, man was also a political animal. It is then doubtful that man did not have expediency and diplomacy sway his decisions, and egotism and emotions as well, as we will see later in this chapter.

Stanovich et al. do recognize the role of emotions, and confusions that affect rational thinking. However, for the time being, let us consider rationality. To begin with, they distinguish between two kinds of concepts within rationality—what is true, and what to do. Critical thinking is a subspecies of rational thought, and that educators should be more concerned with the superordinate concept—rationality. It is a concept that encompasses both epistemic (what is true) and instrumental (what to do) thinking. Then they elaborate. For our beliefs to be rational, they must correspond to the way the world is—they must be true. For our actions to be rational, they must be the best means toward our goals—they must be the best things to do.

As many readers may argue that this is a very complex assumption, as it alludes to truth and means of achieving one's goals—what is true? Isn't it conditional? Does the ethics of adopting means to reach one's goals be considered by third parties?

However, rationality can be obstructed by "faulty mind-ware," a concept they forcefully introduce. Of course, irrationality in practical applications can encompass a variety of sources. Problems with rational thinking in the domain of mindware come in two types—mindware gaps and contaminated mindware (Stanovich, 2009). Mindware gaps occur because people lack declarative knowledge that can facilitate rational thought. Examples are the knowledge of probabilistic reasoning rules, the knowledge of scientific reasoning, and rules of logical consistency and validity.

Many readers would like to add a caveat at this point. Knowledge, be it declarative or procedural (Toplak, West, & Stanovich, 2012), does not seem to emphasize action, or "what to do." It is only effective when the individual has a motivation to act based on the knowledge. Many good instances can be found in the public domain—the evidence of smoking causes lung cancer printed on a cigarette packet, or heavy drinking must be avoided because it is associated with a number of physical and mental illnesses; such shocking information only works when the individual is motivated. We consider the role of motivation later in this chapter.

Continuing with contaminated mindwares, the following are listed in Toplak et al.:

> People display confirmation bias, they test hypotheses inefficiently, they display preference inconsistencies, they do not properly calibrate degrees of belief, they overproject their own opinions onto others, they combine probabilities incoherently, and they allow prior knowledge to become implicated in deductive reasoning. (See Stanovich, 1999, 2004, 2009 among the references in their article.)

The fact that man is really not a rational animal, his reasoning being invariably impacted by affect and intuitions, has been discussed at length in this and the subsequent chapters. How do we cleanse the so-called contaminated mindwares by training has been suggested by Toplak et al. But they acknowledge that these procedures are still tentative in the present time. We postpone this discussion and resume it when reviewing Doerner's suggestions for avoiding the failures of logic, and further on the procedure that Buddhists recommend for cleansing the mind.

Beyond Cognition: Motivation for Reasoning and Motivated Reasoning

Simon, like several thinkers before him from ancient times to the modern age, considered motivation and emotion to be major influences on cognitive activities. Motivation and emotions not only work toward good and efficient cognitive processing, but they also act as detractors of good cognitive processing. In other words, they influence the manner in which we process information and execute it. More recently, Kunda (1990) underscored the importance of motivation for reasoning which, we think, in managerial situations can determine decisions. Reasoning, being an activity of an individual from the broadest perspective, must have a motivation, and at the same time motivated reasoning could work to improve the quality of cognitive processes, especially the decisions that we make. However, motivated reasoning could be the grime and grease that covers the mirror of clear rationality. Reasoning may be a rationalization. We agree with Kunda, that when someone wishes to draw a specific conclusion, he or she usually tries to justify that conclusion which would appear to be plausible to a dispassionate observer.

We now specify when and why motivation, such as preserving self-esteem, especially a very high self-esteem, can prevent rational decisions. Managers who are egotistic are not very effective in following an orderly sequence of actions when their high self-esteem is punctured!

Failure of Logic in Planning and Decision Making

Doerner (1985) outlined an orderly sequence of planful behavior which, however, may not be followed in the practice of planning. The orderly sequence of behavior starts with goal specifications followed by seeking and attaining information; evaluating the prognosis or the possibility of the course of action within the plan and its outcome; planning the evaluation of action and the consequences of these actions; and finally, self-reflective analysis of the action. Doerner does not believe that action planning passes through this orderly sequence. However, he shares with many others before him the following basic steps that are followed in any kind of planning, including decision making in managerial situations: information seeking, forming hypotheses, and action planning. According to Doerner, information seeking is concerned with knowing what kind and how much information should be sought. This is followed by hypothesis formation, and subsequently, action planning.

All three activities that determine efficient decision making can be marred by the failure of logic that is forced upon managers because they are required to take decisions under conditions of uncertainty. Under certainty, probabilities of future events can be estimated, but there are several known fallacies that occur. Some of these fallacies include the manager's insensitivity to the probabilities, such as the belief that what is valid for large samples is also valid for small samples, or the simple fact of regression to the mean that should warn him or her that a spectacular performance of an executive is most unlikely to be repeated, and the occurrence of "gambler's fallacy" (i.e., if the choice is between hypothesizing the occurrence of the event a or b, and event a has occurred successively four or five times, making a decision that event b is likely to occur next). These examples of irrational decisions are so common that our faith in analytical thinking is weakened. However, there is logic as to why and when rationality fails.

In his papers, Doerner (1985) discusses the anatomy of the failure of logic. Managerial decisions are sometimes so far beyond logic that the only way we can describe them is irrational. However, in spite of the apparent failure of analytical thinking for solving some managerial problems, there is no mystery as to why managers use non-rational methods of thinking.

Simon's (1967) advocacy of the use of intuition and creativity was based on some compelling reasons. These reasons, in a nutshell, consist of the indetermination of the antecedents and consequence of managerial problems as realized, and the inability of the human mind to hold together the myriad of components interacting with each other in a complex manner. The other reasons why logic fails are clearly demonstrated in computer-simulated games that Doerner used. He designed a game: a famine in a small country in West Africa and a simulation called *Moro*. The game had the usual real-life complex variables: population, birth and mortality rates, cattle stock, groundwater level, vegetation area, precipitation area, areas of farmland, the harvesting of different crops, and so on. All these variables are closely linked with each other and obviously result in a network of interdependencies. The system is also dynamic, and like real-life conditions develops and changes even when there is no intervention. The object of the game designer is to obtain instances of behavior in the face of formidable conditions and inability to predict the action that may be required. Thus, following a certain decision made by a player, feedback is given which changes his decision and compels him to gather relevant data and make a decision that would be compatible with the changed conditions.

In any case, Doerner observed that in solving complex problems while making a series of online decisions, the following errors detract from staying on course and making appropriate decisions. An error in goal formation is one of the first mistakes observed in a frustrated player when faced with complexity. The player decomposes the comprehensive goals of the game into partial goals and tries to achieve these partial goals. However, these partial solutions conflict with the objectives of the overarching goals, such as the control of famine.

So, the first error is *an insufficient goal elaboration*. Secondly, there may also be *errors in information seeking* in many of the players. The players dogmatically follow a particular solution using the wrong statistics, while trying to reduce everything to one cause. They engage in superstitious behavior. The *third error is in planning*. The players ignore the long-term effects and side effects of their actions and do not work out proper procedures for goals that are set. The next major error is in *deciding and evaluating the effect of their actions*. Once a step is taken, the players assume that it will succeed. They start doing things without planning; they act without checking the current relevance of the steps they are about to take; when a certain hypothesis does not work, they keep adjusting the hypothesis rather than discarding it. There is a marked decrement in self-checking and self-reflection. To add to this, there is a typical *emotional reaction*, which Simon might have anticipated:

the desire to maintain high self-esteem and the feeling of confidence at any cost. This leads to a tendency to over-generalize. It can be labeled as over-inclusive thinking.

The desire to maintain high self-esteem and a feeling of confidence, together with a limited capacity to hold information in the mind while solving a complex and dynamic problem, are perhaps the major sources of the failure of logic. None of these, however, can be easily corrected. Human information processing capacity is limited, although no one can exactly describe the limits. Similarly, the desire to maintain high self-esteem and a feeling of confidence in the face of an apparently hopeless situation is ingrained in human character. The question then is, do we have to tolerate the failure of logic and accept the consequences of faulty managerial decisions even when these have disastrous effects? Can we really teach potential managers and working managers how to avoid these failures?

Can We Teach Strategies?

Strategy training has become a popular subject, and many authors have published several books and manuals on this subject. Some of these are serious books that focus on how one can improve one's thinking. The *pundits* of managerial science, such as Leavitt and Mintzberg, have suggested the adoption of strategies that are consistent with right-brain thinking (i.e., holistic and synthetic decision-making strategies), rather than quantitative and analytic ones. Others are more concerned with spectacular improvements in critical thinking, although the exhortations for engaging right-brain rather than left-brain thinking are now regarded as wrong-headed (Corballis, 1980).

de Bono is an influential author on critical thinking. He has written copiously on promoting different kinds of thinking that are novel. de Bono's (2009) book, *Simplicity*, paid direct attention to the value of the concept. When discussing the unnecessary complexity of many things, he suggested that some people are afraid of simplicity—something simple cannot be of high quality—craving complexity instead, as the logical alternative.

If something is simple, there must be deficiencies. Give me something complex—even if I can't guarantee, I will understand it. This sums up de Bono's position.

For example, building logical structures is the usual procedure adopted when thinking of a solution to a problem. This is labeled *vertical* thinking in contrast to *lateral* thinking. de Bono suggested that we step aside and engage in lateral thinking, that we abandon thinking in terms of "either/or," and that we give up going around the loop of considering the positive and the negative. Instead, we should think laterally in terms of the aspects of a problem situation that we may not have considered before. For example, a young boy asked to explain the meaning of the proverb "the early bird catches the worm" replied: "I understand it may be good for the bird to catch the worm early, but what good does it do to the worm?" de Bono would perhaps label this as an *interesting* aspect of the problem—an example of lateral thinking distinctly different from the positive and the negative. So, how can we teach strategies: the positive, the negative, and the interesting dimensions of the problem? How can we teach strategies in order to avoid the failure of logic? In *Simplicity*, he gives the following suggestions that may be particularly relevant for our discussion on improving managerial competence:

1. You need to understand the matter very well.
2. You need to design alternatives and possibilities.
3. You need to challenge and discard existing elements.
4. You need to be prepared to start over again.

These are surely simple steps to avoid failure of logic. Later in Chapter 14, we have discussed some other specific issues and procedures in regard to strategy training. The following sections anticipate some of that discussion.

Return to Managers' Problems

Let us return to the original problem of managers. Their problems are characterized by multiple contingencies and complex interactions. We suggest that teaching strategies through formal instruction will not be effective, as the contingencies and the interactions that provide the specific context for the problem cannot always be anticipated. So, rules and procedures need to be flexible and adapt to the demand of the situation. These cannot be learned by rote, or by posing a major and minor premise that leads inexorably to a conclusion.

The alternative to formal instruction is teaching through experience, using inductive rather than a deductive approach. This would allow the individual to learn when provided with a program of structured experiences. The structure instantiates a principle without directly teaching it. The method here is inductive, not deductive. The common principle of inductive inferences is generalizations based upon experiencing particular principles a number of times. Such generalized inferences need not be totally conscious, nor do they have to be articulated clearly. In other words, acquiring knowledge is inductive; it is often insidiously acquired without the conscious effort of the individual. The situation then is very similar to the acquisition of concepts.

Concepts can be acquired in two ways: spontaneously through experience and through formal instruction. According to Russian psychologist Vygotsky (1962), scientific concepts are learned through formal instruction. A child, however, does not really know the concept unless it can be internalized. The process of internalization is mediated through experience. In managerial decision making, many a case is novel. The problem is, therefore, indeterminate; the system that produces the problem is dynamic and continuously developing. As mentioned before, novelty and complexity are the central characteristics of the problems of a top-level manager. The process of internalization must take place through experience. Only then will a person, who has to solve a problem, be able to transfer the knowledge and the strategies to a similar but new situation. The purpose of any learning is transfer. If a learned skill is so specific that it cannot be transferred, then it is practically useless. So the question boils down to transferring strategies. How can strategies be transferred? Obviously, it presupposes that strategies are amenable to training for transfer to specific situations concerned with management and organizational behavior. How to structure such training?

We have presented the topic of strategy training in some detail in an entire chapter (Chapter 14), the last of the three that have practical implications for management.

Dissociation

An important note for strategy training: Since we acknowledge the importance of intuitive knowledge in making decisions, explicit reasons for those decisions cannot be given. There is thus a disconnect between reasoning that is verbal, propositional, and deductive—the characteristics of the rational decision-making process and implicit grounds for intuitive decisions. Dissociation is noticed in many instances between explicit reasoning and intuitive judgments.

The dissociation is between what an individual says and what the individual does while solving the problem under uncertainty. The following is an excellent example from the computer simulation of problem solving that makes the point.

Broadbent, Fitzgerald, and Broadbent (1986), like Doerner, studied individuals' behavior in computer-simulated problem-solving context. Their purpose was to delineate the conditions under which dissociation develops between the ability of a person to carry out an apparently successful action responding to a situation, and the ability of the same person to answer questions about that very same situation. The complex problem-solving situations that Broadbent and his associates presented to the problem solver had two common conditions. First, there were so many interrelationships among the different elements of the problem that the person could not possibly see or describe how the elements in the situation interacted with each other. As we mentioned before, these interactions are just too numerous to hold in the mind at the time of questioning and answering. Second, there were so many conditions guiding the action that the person simply did not know which was the critical condition. Both conditions characterize the situations in which managers have to solve problems. So, there existed two separate realities: one for the verbal knowledge of what the problem solvers were doing in the complex situation, and the other the action itself. Broadbent et al.'s simulated games showed that improvement in action can occur without improvement in the database which the action shares with verbal knowledge. The manager can make decisions on past exemplars. The present problem may have an analogue in the manager's past experience. The method that works could be an inductive learning procedure, as Vygotsky recommended. Doerner's recommendations for acquiring strategies also favor the process of induction, rather than learning general rules.

According to Doerner, it is not a matter of learning a few readily grasped principles, but of learning a lot of small, "local" rules, each of which is applicable in a limited area.

We conclude this section on strategy training with the statement made by Broadbent et al. that we paraphrase. According to them, it would be unwise to assume that verbal knowledge is the ideal toward which the less explicit intuitive decision making is developing.

When all is said and done in favor of inductive learning, one recognizes a certain place, a specific need for deduction and rule learning. We remind ourselves of Vygotsky's (1962) intuitive and insightful dictum regarding formal instruction and spontaneously acquired knowledge; formal concepts (such as democracy) should come down to the level of experience, and at the same time, spontaneously acquired ones (such as friendship) must rise to the level of formal definitions.

Concluding Remarks: The Central Role of Planning

We suggest then that there should be at least two distinct categories of planful behavior—routine and novel—that could be used when observing the managers. While many of them would be able to execute the programs once they were clearly given or laid out in front of them, only a few would exhibit anticipatory programming, flexible use of information, and consistent changes in their plans as they approached a goal. The observers of these "managers in action" are then likely to discover the motivations of the managers' reasoning and anticipation, the situations in which motivated reasoning may act as an impediment, as well as where and when reasoning and logic failed to influence the managers' decision making. We expect that from such biographical observations, we will also obtain information that will help improve the teaching of strategy.

Finally, for strategies to be taught through structured experiences (i.e., inductively rather than deductively), we have made three sets of suggestions which will be helpful in designing a group of experiences (see the appendix). Our suggestions have been distilled from several sources and convergent strands of research. Details of the relevant studies of Doerner presented in Set I list several "do's and don'ts" of strategic behavior. Set II is from Klemp and McClelland (1986). In this set, we have included three different categories of generic competencies that are needed for senior managers. Each one of these can be incorporated in the group of structured experiences for teaching management strategies. Set III is taken from social psychologist Janis' (1989) research on decision making. We have constructed a brief questionnaire (Brief Evaluation Activity Form), which embodies the strategies that are recommended by Janis for a "vigilant problem-solving approach to decision making." The questionnaire can be used by supervisors, both before and after strategy training, for the purpose of evaluating the competence of their managers. The reader will find that some questions are positive (where one indicates "competent") and some are negative (where one indicates "incompetent").

Appendix

Set I: This set is derived from Doerner's work: (a) Do not lose sight of the overall goal, complex as it is, by decomposing it into partial goals. (b) Do not try to reduce everything to one cause. When facts disprove your hypothesis, abandon the hypothesis; do not merely adjust it. (c) Be less concerned about your self-esteem (losing face) when changing your hypothesis and decision.

Set II: This set is from Klemp and McClelland (1986; see note 34, p. 41). We have given here eight generic competencies put into three different categories, such as intelligence, influence, and self-confidence that are needed for senior managers.

The eight senior manager competencies

Competency	Competency Indicators
The intellectual competencies	
Planning/casual thinking	Sees implications, consequences, alternatives, or if–then relationships
	Analyzes relationships
	Makes strategies, plans steps to reach a goal
Diagnostic information seeking	Pushes for concrete information in an ambiguous situation
	Seeks information for multiple sources to clarify a situation
Conceptualization	Understands how different parts, needs, or functions of the synthetic thinking organization fit together
	Identifies patterns, interprets a series of events
	Identifies the most important issues in a complex situation
	Uses unusual analogies to understand or explain the essence of a situation
Concern for influence (the need for power)	States a desire to persuade people
	Anticipates the impact of actions on people
Directive influence (personalized power)	Confronts people directly when problems occur
	Tells people to do things the way he/she wants them done
Collaborative influence (socialized power)	Operates effectively with groups to influence outcomes and get cooperation
	Builds "ownership" of controversial decisions among key subordinates by involving them in decision making
Symbolic influence	Sets a personal example for an intended impact
	Uses symbols of group identity
Self-confidence	Sees self as the prime mover, leader, or energizer of the organization
	Mentions being stimulated by crises and other difficult problems
	Sees self as the most capable person to get the job done

9

Cognitive Competence and Managerial Behavior

Successful managers are successful at decision making and planning. The orientation to management has been split into analytic and humanistic approaches, each of which uses decision making and planning to determine managerial qualities. Decision making and planning require a rational attitude, which must be objective, but humanistic approaches foster or facilitate innovative and creative solutions rather than rational and objective ones. Therefore, the importance of decision making and planning in organizational behavior has been reestablished in the recent literature. Planning and decision making have been considered in mainstream psychology for some time now; one notable example is the work of Simon (1987), perhaps the most important authority in information processing. Simon and his colleagues in cognitive science have applied their knowledge to planning and decision making as used by managers. Since Simon related these two cognitive sciences, the information-processing model of human intelligence became immediately relevant for organizational behavior. This line of thinking has been followed up later by several workers in the field (Das, Kar, & Parrila, 1996).

Cognitive planning/executive functions (EFs) occupy a unique position at the center of human activity, as evident in the classic book by Miller, Gallanter, and Pribram (1960). These authors for the first time considered planning in detail, which has led to obvious connections to organizational behavior. No matter how badly or well structured the plan is, it may change many times during the process of planning. Even when the goal is not readily apparent, he/she continues with planning as a subconscious cognitive process. The Test–Operate–Test–Exit model that these authors have developed is discussed again at the end of this chapter.

Managers and their subordinate employees, who might be at the beginning management stage, differ in the nature of plans and decisions they make when they are allowed to do so. Change is the specialty of a good planner in an organization. A good planner is one who can anticipate *problems* in securing a goal, especially when the goal is beneficial for the whole organization. A good planner also anticipates *action*. In this sense, a distinction must be made between problem solving and planning even of a routine nature.

A further discussion of the attributes of a good planner is appropriate at this point as these relate to problem solving.

Anticipation: At the conceptual level, a good planner selects and manipulates the environment to anticipate the most appropriate problem that is required to be solved. A good manager can think of sequences of steps that are consistent with the anticipated problems that will be faced and have to be solved. A good manager is a good planner because he or she is flexible in nature; therefore, the plans change according to the feedback that is received while approaching the goal. Anticipation and flexibility go hand in hand for good planning.

The other components of planning include representation, execution, and regulation, influenced by goals and objectives that are themselves continuously revised by interaction with these cognitive operations. A dynamic relation among the four components exists. This has been discussed earlier in Chapter 2.

Managerial Decision Making and Measures of Planning: Four Studies Using Strategic Essay Writing and a Higher Order Planning Task, Crack the Code

Simon's (1987) point is that planning and decision making are not entirely rational activities; it is not only the excellence in intelligence that makes a good manager a good planner, but also emotional, motivational, and personality predispositions play a part in planning. Much has been written since on the role of affect and its cortical basis in the orbitofrontal region accompanying emotion. These are discussed in detail in a subsequent chapter (Chapter 10). Instead, within this chapter, we report two empirical studies that are worlds apart on managerial decision making and objective measures of Planning. The first test links the performance of subordinate executives to the rating of their supervising managers. It uses Crack-the-Code Test (CTC) as a measure of Planning. The second, a sequel, uses the same instrument for rating of the executives, but as an objective measure, composing an essay that must justify a given set of decisions (Samantaray, 2005). At the end, we propose a path diagram, a picture of the relationship between Planning/EF and the tests of Planning/EF. Both components are placed within a basic model of cognitive functions, the PASS theory (see the appendix). Some of the connections between the paths have empirical support, whereas others invite fresh studies to fill in the gaps. Our hope is that readers will take away with them a theoretical framework and tools to measure Planning/EF when examining managerial behavior.

Job Performance of Management Executives Is Predicted from CTC

In the first study, we report executives' performance in an investment company. Das, Naglieri, and Murphy (1995) explored the relationship between planning and job performance within the investment banking sector. They focused on one position—quantitative analyst—within the research area of a major investment bank. The person in this position is required to analyze the portfolios of a bank's financial holdings to assess the quality of the investments, predict the rate of return over various time intervals, and recommend alternative investment configurations to obtain the desired level of return. This job requires various attributes such as motivation, organization, analytical thinking, and good interpersonal skills. According to the supervisors of these quantitative analysts, the following are seen as particularly important: (a) the ability to define and analyze a problem, (b) pooling knowledge to solve problems, (c) the ability to understand their assigned work, (d) persistence when performing a difficult task, (e) good organization and planning skills, (f) knowing what decisions can be made independently, (g) knowing when to seek information or the help of others, (h) flexibility and receptiveness to other ideas, and (i) adaptability to the ambiguities of the task.

The activities described above certainly involve planning. Both planning and the task of the quantitative analyst require organization, hypothesis generation, problem solving, self-monitoring, and completing tasks efficiently. Because the intellectual requirements of the quantitative analyst's job are consistent with the construct of planning as described in this book, a complex planning test for adults like Crack the Code (CTC) should be effective in predicting high or low job performance.

To examine the extent to which CTC would be effective in identifying individuals whose job performance would be highly or poorly rated by their supervisors, 30 subjects (16 males and 14 females) were used. These individuals were the current employees of one of the largest investment banks in the world, located on Wall Street. Managers selected subjects so that a range of competence on the job would be represented. All the subjects had been working as quantitative analysts for at least one year. Supervisors rated subjects' job performance using a brief rating scale developed from job descriptors. The Brief Evaluation of Activity Form (BEAF) was created to provide a rating of activities considered important by upper management (e.g., understanding a problem, being aware of the goals to be attained, selecting the best approach, seeing alternatives, minimizing risks, and thinking critically). See the appendix for the items included in this form.

The CTC task was administered in groups, and each subject's score was the number of items answered correctly within a 45-minute time limit. Upper managers responsible for supervising the quantitative analysts completed the BEAF for each individual they supervised. Each subject's item scores were summarized to yield a total raw score, which was then transformed into a standard score.

Internal reliability was .981 for the BEAF and .895 for CTC, using the split-half method (corrected using the Spearman–Brown formula). The relationships between the planning test, CTC, and the evaluation of actual job performance as determined by the BEAF were examined in several ways. First, the rankings of individuals on the basis of their BEAF and CTC scores were correlated. The coefficient (Spearman Rho = .553) was significant. Next, the average BEAF rating scores were compared for subjects who scored highest and lowest on the CTC task. The group with the lowest CTC scores earned a mean BEAF score of 89.1, and those with the highest CTC scores earned a mean BEAF score of 111.8. The difference between these means was significant indicating that CTC was effective in identifying those who were rated as strong and those who were rated as poor in job performance on the basis of the BEAF rating scales.

The results of this study suggest that planning, a construct not measured by traditional IQ tests, is related to job performance in a demanding employment setting. More specifically, planning as a process appears to be related to complex job performance involving organization, defining a problem, independent functioning, flexibility, and adaptation.

The Connection between Crack the Code and Strategic Essay Composition

Is there a common planning component for both CTC and Strategic Planned Composition? As mentioned in earlier studies, beginning with Ashman and Das (1980), it has been shown that lack of planning in written compositions can be related to deficiencies in simple planning tasks involving visual search (Das et al., 1996). This is also consistent with Olson (1994), who demonstrated that writing requires strategies and planning, particularly in imagining what the reader might understand from the written text, in other words, a "meta-knowledge." We will discuss the connection between narrative writing and planning in a special chapter (Chapter 11).

We wish to briefly report a different kind of writing, *strategic essays*, which is closer to management skills in the next three studies. Specifically, we will discuss in some detail how predictive is performance in the planning task. CTC could be of proficiency in strategic essay writing.

The test has been previously described in Das et al. (1996) as well as in this book in Chapter 7 as a composition test that is derived from CTC—the test follows the logic and procedure of CTC for the assessment of Planning and EF. How closely is it related to CTC, especially in a sample of undergraduate students? We present a study by Mathur and Das (1997) to answer the question.

It is a test that was administered to a group of engineering college students who are most likely to need management skills in their jobs. Incidentally, these students gained admission to the engineering institute in India on the basis of exceptional academic record. Since the sample did not represent normal distribution of intelligence, rather was likely to be at the high end, the correlations between CTC and Strategic Essay scores were likely to be smaller or attenuated. In spite of this, if these are found to be reasonably strong, one of the explanations would be that general intelligence differences among the individuals in the sample are not reflected in performance of the two tests. Planning strategies is a major characteristic of EF. At the relatively high end of intelligence, it should not influence competence in generating and executing strategies.

The strategic essay-writing task is repeated here for ease of discussion of the results of the study on engineering students.

Recap of Strategic Essay Writing

Instructions for participants are as follows. Suppose in a pharmaceutical company, you are the chief executive officer. The company can have the following overall strategies in order to prosper:

1. Be innovative
2. Achieve a good share of the market
3. Be known for its economical price—low cost of products
4. Produce high-quality goods

Cautionary Notes for Each Strategy

"A" requires an outlay of capital in research and development. But the world record shows that in the last five years, research and development money has increased fivefold, but the number of new products launched has remained the same. "B" requires aggressive advertisement, but the company's star product (i.e., Bayer Aspirin) is about to be replaced by a new breakthrough medication for fever. "C" requires getting the components of the products from manufacturing to packaging from developing countries where labor is cheap. But this has a disastrous effect on employment at home. For "D" it may cost so much more that it would make the product uneconomical.

In the past 30-year history of the company, the following weight had been given to the strategies with results indicated. Your job is to achieve a 100 percent growth by rearranging the strategies, but you must take into account the information from the past results. In the past, one manager gave first place to "C," second place to "D," third place to "A," and fourth place to "B." The profit again was 50 percent because, like the previous choice, only two of the strategies were in the correct place. None of "C," "D," "A," and "B" was in the correct position. Your task is to assign the priorities so that the right strategy will have the right place to give a 100 percent profit. Actually, the manager who places "D" first, "C" next, "B" next, and "A" in the last position of priorities got 100 percent profit.

Write an essay of about one page justifying how the plan produces the best results when the solution is DCBA.

How Were the Essays Rated?

The Essay (Planned Composition) Rating Scale (Das et al., 1996): A total score will indicate a general level of proficiency. However, the essence of planning could be the sum of only organization and individuality, and, to a certain extent, expression as well.

EXPRESSION   1   2   3   4   5   6   7

Rating of 1 = Appears that thought has been given to the story; the writer says what is meant; points related to the topic; no padding.

Rating of 4 = Impression has been given that the writer does not fully understand what is meant; does not related clearly; some padding and irrelevant material.
Rating of 7 = Hard to tell what the writer is saying; makes little sense; gives the impression of trying to get something on paper.

ORGANIZATION 1 2 3 4 5 6 7

Good starting point; has a sense of directed movement in the story; appears to have an underlying plan; seems logically arranged.
Organization is standard and conventional; some trivial points given more importance than deserved; logic in progression is not always clear.
Starts anywhere and never gets anywhere; ideas are presented randomly with no apparent forethought.

WORDING 1 2 3 4 5 6 7

Use of uncommon words or words in unusual combinations, which shows imagination; word experiments need not be successful 100 percent of time.
Uses common phrases or expressions; no apparent concern with the use of words.
Uses words carelessly; many mistakes in usage; unclear wording or childish vocabulary.

MECHANICS 1 2 3 4 5 6 7

No serious errors in sentence structure; punctuation correct; spelling consistent and appropriate for grade.
Some errors in structure but do not obscure meaning; violations in punctuation and spelling.
Serious errors in sentence structure making the story difficult to understand; many punctuation errors make the story fragmented; many spelling mistakes.

INDIVIDUALITY 1 2 3 4 5 6 7

Unique or creative approach to material; unusual or original ideas; gives the story a "twist."
Some originality shown; few interesting or unique aspects.
Not original at all; ideas are mundane, not creative and uninteresting.

Modification for Strategic Essay Writing

The above scale is a generic one used for rating compositions, usually, narratives. However, these criteria were elaborated further to make up a special scale for rating strategic essays. The extended scale had 10 items. Two major factors emerged in an exploratory factor analysis. These were internal organization and external organization, besides a composite score for all the 10 items (Das et al., 1993).

Briefly, the *internal organization factor* included rating on the following criteria:

> Have all the strategic choices been mentioned in the essay? Has justification been given for the relative position of the strategies? Have conjunctives, qualifiers, conditionals, and causality been used appropriately? Do sentences follow each other logically and meaningfully?

In contrast, the *external organization factor* included the following:

> Is there evidence of external knowledge (that is, use of information not included in the description of the task)? Is the composition unique and original (that is, unique and creative approach to material, unusual or original ideas)? These make up 9 out of the 10 item scales that had clear loading on one or the other factor. The only item that had a split loading was: "Have all the cautionary notes been used directly or indirectly?" So that was not clearly loading on primarily one of the two factors. The total score however included ratings on all 10 items.

Between the internal and external organization factors, it would be the internal organization that incorporates the important aspects of Planning and decision making.

Results revealed a moderately strong association between CTC and Strategic Essay writing scores. CTC problems that were within the medium range of difficulty in solution could predict the students' performance in Strategic Essay writing. In fact, we divided the students into two groups on the basis of their performance on CTC, and then checked to see if the groups of high and low performers in CTC were comparatively so in Strategic Essay writing; indeed, they maintained the same position. High performers in CTC were high on essays and so on.

In sum, it is remarkable that accuracy in performance on a complex planning task, Crack the Code, "can predict the ... ability to write coherent, integrated essays" (Mathur & Das, 1997, p. 490). However, the findings were not entirely unexpected, considering the fact that the essays were rated by using criteria that are common to strategies in problem solving as in CTC. The criteria for rating an essay that the raters were urged to use, for example, were: Have all the strategic choices been mentioned in the essay? Has justification been given for the relative position of the strategies? Do sentences follow each other logically and meaningfully?

The first two instances of the criteria are similar to even the BEAF questions for rating competence among managers/senior supervisors. The next sections discuss supervisors' ratings of their subordinate executives: Do the ratings at all correspond to the proficiency of the junior executives in strategic tasks such as the composition of strategic essays?

Supervisors' Rating of Executive Function May Predict the Quality of Essay Composition

The research is similar to a study reported earlier in this chapter on a group of supervisors and their subordinate executives in an investment company. Although the two studies were located worlds apart—in New York and Orissa—both asked the question: Does supervisors' rating predict excellence in use of strategies as measured by Planning tests? The research was carried out in Orissa state, India, by Samantaray (2006) as a thesis requirement. As it has not been published, it is discussed here in some detail. However, the Das, Naglieri, and Murphy research explored the link between BEAF and CTC, whereas the one in Orissa used strategic essay writing. We believe this test is a better reflection of decision making in composing arguments instantiated by real-life problems for executives.

Samantaray (2006) selected two cognitive tasks for planning as well as the BEAF rating scale, as described in earlier pages for the use of supervisors to rate the planning/EF efficiency of their employees in terms of decision-making behavior. So a questionnaire, BEAF, was used as before, which contains discreet questions regarding the evaluation of the subordinate's executive behavior to be answered by the supervisor. Samantaray used two tests of planning. One of the tests is Matching Numbers (as in Das–Naglieri CAS), a basic test of planning behavior that is a combination of visual search, and, to a lesser extent, working memory. It does not require language or very complex strategies. Both have been implicated in planning function (Das et al., 1996).

In several previous studies, Matching Numbers has a significant correlation with other tests of planning (see Das, Naglieri, & Kirby, 1994). Performance on this relatively simple Planning test may then be compared with more complex levels of planning that are required in composing an essay. The essay writing has been described as "a test of strategic planning" (Das et al., 1996, pp. 155–158). The essays were rated using "the planned composition rating scale" (Das et al., 1996, pp. 144–145). Previous research encouraged us (see Das et al., 1996; Mathur & Das,1997) to combine three of the five scales (Expression, Organization, Individuality [EOI]) as the most salient rating for judging the planning component of the essay and the other two scales (Wording and Mechanics, and WM) together to indicate writing and language skills.

Objectives and Hypotheses

This short project had the following major objectives:

1. *Brief evaluation of the employee's activity (BEAF):* To use an objective outline for evaluating employee's activities by the supervisor. In an organization, there are hierarchies in terms of responsibilities assigned to an employee. The employee reports to a "boss" who must, in turn, report to a higher supervisor. Sometimes the evaluator is not given clear guidelines. Even when the guidelines are provided, these are not concrete enough for application. Therefore, one of the main objectives of using BEAF is to find out how the supervisor applies the specific criteria to evaluate the employee. What is the range of evaluations, from excellent to poor? Is there a spread or are the evaluations bunched up either at one extreme or in the other? A hypothesis may be derived and stated as follows: Supervisors will be sensitive to the variety of criteria contained in the questions so that the competence of employees can be differentiated.
2. *Essay writing:* The main point in writing an essay or composition is to express how one arrives at composing and representing knowledge. The essay in this project provided an occasion for expressing the writer's knowledge and implicit reasoning. The main criterion for evaluating the essay is not the quality of the writer's language, but how original and well organized the essay is. The hypothesis, therefore, is as follows: A good management employee, who is a good decision maker, will get high ratings on individuality and originality as well as in organization in the essay.

3. *Planning test:* Samantaray (2006) selected Matching Numbers from a battery of Planning tests in the Das–Naglieri Cognitive Assessment System, as described in a previous chapter on assessment of EF/Planning (Chapter 6). The test is accepted as a reliable test of basic planning ability, not a complex planning ability, such as CTC or planning and composing the strategic essay. It is acknowledged that the relationship between the supervisor's rating (BEAF) and the employee's ability for writing a strategic essay or doing well in a baseline test of planful behavior is quite tenuous. An empirical study is therefore necessary to sort out the relationships between BEAF ratings and an employee's performance in two Planning tests—a simple (Matching Numbers) and a complex one. The study was really based on the assumption that the rating given by a supervisor for one employee and the employee's actual ability as an executive or planner is fairly accurate. Furthermore, this ability can be captured by the two EF/Planning tests. The employee's EF will remain a latent variable expressed about his/her behavior toward the job. But what the supervisor is rating is his/her own perception of the employee's behavior. We repeat that BEAF remains a subjective evaluation; it is expected to predict the other two objective measures of an employee's EF/Planning. A schematic diagram of the assumptions, interactions, and empirically confirmed interrelationships is given at the end of this chapter (see Figure 9.1).

Figure 9.1:
Planning expressed through an executive's behavior

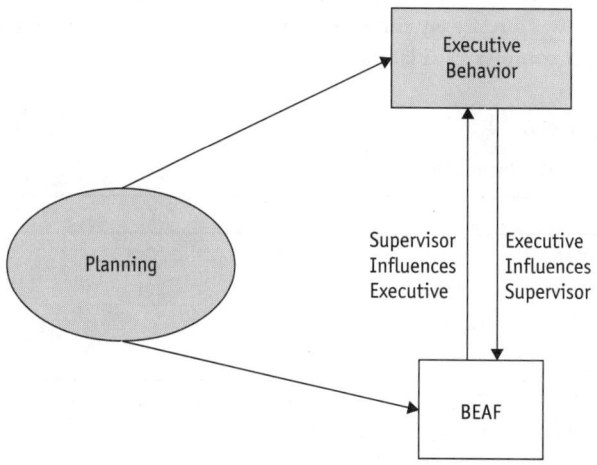

Participants were 28 senior-level employees at the office of a mining corporation in a city in eastern India. All of them had the same supervisor, a special officer. Each participant was requested to write the Strategic Essay. (The Matching Number test was administered following the essay writing on a subsequent day.)

The essays were scored on the Likert-type scale described later by a business school graduate and Samantaray, the researcher. The two raters then re-examined their ratings where these differed widely, and came to agree on one rating. The final rating of the essays on each scale was the consensual rating of the two raters. These were the scores that were used in the correlational analyses as reported in Table 9.1.

Table 9.1 shows the correlations among the tests including BEAF, Strategy-Essay composition, and Matching Numbers (MN). Composition scores are grouped as EOI and WM. Critical for the study is the correlation between BEAF and composition scores: EOI and BEAF have a correlation of –.514 (BEAF high score is 1 and low score is 3). The other composition score, WM, showed a negligible correlation. This provides very good evidence for establishing the validity of both BEAF and EOI as common measures of underlying Planning processes. Composition performance can be partitioned into a planning component and a writing-skill component. The correlation between the two components is substantial, and thus both measure a common writing efficiency in composition. But the planning process is relatively independent of writing efficiency.

We are again pleasantly surprised that the supervisor's rating of executive performance and EOI can be predictive of each other. The other test of Planning, MN, had no significant correlation either with BEAF or essay writing. It was a relatively simple and basic test of Planning, and, thus, did not predict complex EF/Planning processes.

Table 9.1:
Intercorrelations between essay ratings

Scale	1	2	3	4
1. EOI average	—	.565*	–.514*	.011
2. WM average	.565*	—	–.201	.113
3. BEAF	–.514*	–.201	—	.102
4. MN scaled	.011	.113	.102	—

Notes: $N = 28$. EOI—Expression, Organization, Individuality; WM—Working Memory; BEAF—Brief Evaluation of the Employee's Activity; MN—Matching Numbers.
*$p < .01$, two-tailed.

A Schematic Diagram

A partly hypothetical diagram is proposed (see Figure 9.1) considering the reported studies and their findings: (1) The study of executives in New York—their supervisors' ratings and their performance in CTC were predictive of each other; (2) Samantaray's study of executives in East India—a significant correlation is found between the supervisor's rating and the Planning component in the strategic essay; (3) the study on engineering students—CTC performance, on the one hand, and strategic essay, on the other, have been shown to have a significant correlation. Thus, we seem to have a common core of cognitive processing among the three apparently disparate tests.

Planning is the common pathway connected to biological and cultural sources. It is expressed through an executive's behavior, a supervisor's rating of an executive behavior (BEAF), essay composition, CTC. *Executive Behavior and Planning are inferred (latent)*. The Planning behavior of the subordinate executive is the target. The diagram has bidirectional arrows. Because the perception of the subordinate in regard to his/her anticipated rating of performance can influence the subordinate's behavior, ideally, the supervisor's ability for rating must also be a factor to consider.

Appendix

The Brief Evaluation of Activity Form

Instructions: When faced with many complex tasks to complete, employees can behave in various ways. This form is used to rate the individual on the following items about work performance. Please use a 3-point scale: "1" for *Always*, "2" for *Sometimes*, and "3" for *Seldom*. Rate the individual based on how often he or she acts in the ways described.

How Often Does the Employee …	Always	Sometimes	Seldom
1. Understand what is required?	1	2	3
2. Is unaware of what problems are to be avoided?	1	2	3
3. Is clearly aware of what goals are to be attained?	1	2	3

(Table Continued)

(Table Continued)

How Often Does the Employee ...	Always	Sometimes	Seldom
4. Knows what seems to be the best approach to take?	1	2	3
5. Neglects asking what previous information can be retrieved?	1	2	3
6. Knows what new information should be obtained?	1	2	3
7. Goes beyond the minimal requirement?	1	2	3
8. Ignores other alternatives?	1	2	3
9. Considers what other information might aid in the solution of the problem?	1	2	3
10. Is unaware of the pros and cons for each alternative?	1	2	3
11. Knows which alternatives appear to be the best?	1	2	3
12. Knows how to minimize risks?	1	2	3
13. Cannot develop alternative plans?	1	2	3
14. Can monitor the steps taken to solve a problem?	1	2	3
15. Thinks critically about what has been produced?	1	2	3
16. Accepts information about the drawbacks of his/her situation?	1	2	3

Source: J.P. Das and J.A. Naglieri.

10

The Influence of Emotions and Will

Decision making no longer assumes importance as a rational information processor, be it in business management or in entrepreneurship. The received view is that emotions and conation interact with cognition. Emotional learning and emotional motivation (Damasio, 1994; LeDoux, 1996) increase the salience of emotions in decision making. But what exactly are emotion and will? This chapter provides a brief introduction to emotions following Herbert Simon's suggestion of the role of synthetic, intuitive thinking. Next, we consider conscious will—Is it a force, or a feeling, or is it an illusion? Moving on, we briefly examine the complex concept of consciousness, and its role in decision making from the Euro-American and the East Indian perspectives. Is there a little man, a homunculus, who makes decisions? The context for discussion is provided by a case history of an entrepreneur. It examines and highlights the infusion of emotional determinants at each step of the decision-making process. The flawed decision in the case history is framed within PASS theory.

The final section of the chapter revisits the rational–emotional issue. Its implication for risk-taking behavior is a topic for neuroeconomics; we acknowledge that this topic, which we briefly mention, should be left for experts grounded both in economics and in neuropsychology. The concluding remarks then consider emotions and decision making, looking again at their interactions, and close with suggesting the importance of emotional intelligence, and even training to improve it in the anticipation of the next chapter.

Reason and Emotion

The thesis that decision making is not all rational, or even not at all rational, has been popular for at least the last 35 years. Perhaps Simon (1967, 1976), who has had influence in two fields—cognitive psychology and economics—is the "guru"; he provides the theoretical basis for competence in management decision making, as well as the core concepts of rationality, tacit knowledge, and intuitive thinking. Rationality is bounded by emotions, and in any case, emotions cannot be separated from rationality in either personal or business decision making. Simon's ideas are discussed in some detail in a special section. At this point, however, a general statement about the prevalence of both what are called logical–analytical thinking and synthetic thinking should be introduced.

Analytical Thinking and Synthetic Thinking

Orientation to management has been split into the analytic and the humanistic or synthetic approaches for some time now. The analytic or so-called rational approach has made the practice of management a science, often bringing in new qualifications and objectivity that were lacking in the old-style managers' hunches, gut feelings, and seat-of-the-pant decision making. Rationality itself does not seem to be appropriate in complex situations that demand innovative or creative solutions, or situations too complex to factor in all the components that demand consideration. Important issues such as the long-term goals of an organization have so many different threads that need to be synthesized, as a manager or an entrepreneur cannot contain all of this in the limited capacities of attention. Not, at least, one that is made of flesh and blood.

However, there has been powerful influence on managerial or entrepreneurial decision making from a surprisingly new source—neuropsychology. It would be best to call it cognitive neuropsychology. The limited capacity working memory system that is dependent on attention just cannot handle the complex interactions of the several components that must be taken into account in making rational decisions. Simon (1971) has alerted us to this particular difficulty that future decision makers have to deal with; it is the *economics of attention* in the context of expanding demands on information processing. Even before the contemporary craze of relating brain imaging to economics, management, and decision making, the field has been influenced by the pioneering work of Sperry in regard to split-brain research (Sperry, 1964; see, e.g., its use in Leavitt, 1975).

Sometimes, though, the extrapolation of split-brain research findings into explaining decision making has been questioned. Yet competency in decision making is no longer the sole domain of rationality—rationality that includes planning and causal thinking. At this point, then, synthetic thinking appears to be essential for the mechanism of practical decision making.

Introducing Working Memory: A Limited Capacity System

Economics of attention may be understood in the limited capacity of working memory (WM).

Imagine an executive's desk that has a limited capacity. Old files have to be pushed away to accommodate new information. However, before disposing them off, they may be stored for a little while, relevant information in them is processed, and some sort of action plans are executed as the situation may demand. Other files that may be of intrinsic importance for the executive for future use are either tagged and held for long-term WM storage if the problem is still an active one, or kept in long-term memory to be retrieved at a future time. This is a simplified account of WM found in textbooks on cognitive psychology.

Is WM simply a matter of memory, or *attention* has a central role in explaining WM? The role of attention in WM may then explain the reason behind the economy of attention. A brief review supports the pivotal role of attention in WM.

WM is an essential cognitive function that we require in Planning and decision making. WM is included frequently within the abilities that comprise executive functions (EFs). It is a short-term storage facility for information as well as a mechanism for utilizing available information for executing a plan. In earlier chapters of this book, we discussed how WM has been extensively investigated (Baddeley, 1986; Cowan, 1995) in several specific cognitive processes, including attention and its deficit, EF, and in relation to general intelligence. WM capacity is limited. Cowan (2010) explains:

> Because cognitive tasks can be completed only with sufficient ability to hold information as it is processed. The ability to repeat information depends on task demands but can be distinguished from a more constant, underlying mechanism: a central memory store limited to 3 to 5 meaningful items in young adults. (p. 51)

In WM, information must be refreshed frequently in order to be maintained for immediate access. The short-term maintenance of WM, for up to a minute or so, helps us in utilizing the information for decision making. It is logical, then, that WM is partly a function of the prefrontal area or the prefrontal cortex (PFC). The PFC is the anatomical part of the brain that is organized according to the types of cognitive operations for several important components, such as encoding information, maintaining it, and processes that are related to guiding and controlling behavior (D'Esposito, Postle, & Rypma, 2002).

We now know that decision making is not entirely a conscious activity. Especially, it is acknowledged that at least two distinct areas in the PFC are involved in decision making. The dorsolateral PFC (DLPFC) that is usually associated with making logical decisions, logical reasoning, and the orbital–frontal cortex (sometimes referred to as the ventromedial cortex) is associated with emotional and social aspects of decision making. *The analytic and synthetic, as it were, have found a local habitation in the brain*!

The Brain and Emotion

Brain imaging has been the new tool—better described as the toy—for relating neuropsychological functions to behavior, including decision-making behavior. The idea of linking emotion and cognition in an integrated framework has been legitimized by providing an anatomical location for this link in the brain. For instance, consider the paper by Gray, Braver, and Raichle (2002).

They used brain imaging (functional MRI) to test if emotional states can influence the activities of the prefrontal brain that are started by a simple cognitive task. The emotion induced by watching a video was either of happiness (pleasant mood) or of an unpleasant feeling. It was shown just before attempting to do the task. If the pleasant or unpleasant mood influenced the activities in the specific part of the brain, it would be considered to be an evidence for an integration of emotion and cognition. Indeed, the results confirmed the expectation of the researchers. Emotion and cognition could be truly integrated. It was impossible to know what brain response marked emotional response, and what was associated with pure cognition (WM).

The authors acknowledge that emotion and cognition are two major aspects of human mental life. Necessarily, therefore, decisions and problem solving are influenced by emotions. The study discussed earlier showed that the cognitive task and emotional state of the individual contribute jointly and equally to the functions of the PFC during even a simple task in WM (the task was to remember the last three digits in a continuous presentation of single digits when the examiner gives a signal and asks you to recall what the last three digits were). In a happy mood, the learner will recall more items than in an unpleasant state of feeling. Now, imagine how emotions would affect more complex mental functions, such as making decisions in a conflicting situation—making it impossible to separate the effects of emotion and of pure reasoning in decision making. Further complications in separating emotional effects from rational decision making arise because of the unconscious influences that color decisions have on even the astute managers. Unconscious inputs from the older parts of the brain play an important role in biasing decisions. We discuss it further in the next section.

Goading from the Old Brain

Significant information about both conscious and unconscious inputs in decision making has been received from brain-imaging studies, such as the aforementioned one. The surprising evidence from brain imaging concerns the fact that decision making quite often occurs when prompted by states of physiological arousal (Damasio, 1999). In other words, decisions are aided by emotions in the form of bodily states that are elicited during the deliberation of future consequences. The so-called gut feeling literally comes from the parts of the brain that are in the old brain, and drives decisions in one direction or another even before the decision maker is consciously aware of it. If I do not feel good about making a decision, my conscious feeling is really prompted by an unpleasant state that has already been initiated by these lower parts of the brain, such as the amygdala.

Those of us who have read elementary psychology struggled with the two classic theories of explaining emotion, the James–Lange theory. James and Lange, both believed that the experience of emotion causes bodily changes, but Lange went a step further. He added that the bodily changes *are* the emotions (Harlow, McGaugh, & Thompson, 1971). This old theory is revisited by Damasio (1999)—"[T]he collection of neural patterns which constitute the substrate of a feeling arise in two classes of biological changes: changes related to body state and changes related to cognitive state" (p. 29).

Somatic-marker hypothesis proposed in the early 1970s by Damasio is a neurobiological theory more in line with Lange. The hypothesis is quite relevant to decision making, as explained later. The bodily changes precede and help in making decisions under uncertain conditions, and tell us whether the different options for behavior are advantageous or disadvantageous. In fact, when specific structures in the brain are damaged, human beings take risky decisions in a gambling task, choosing high-risk behavior. Interactions between the lower structure, mainly in the amygdala and the PFC, are essential in understanding when an individual makes a high-risk decision.

So what do these brain mechanisms suggest in relation to decision making? Not only is rational analysis not entirely responsible for the decisions that we make, but conscious reasoning strategies seem to also be biased by non-conscious processes. The form of the bias could be a bodily reaction preceding decision making. What are the underlying structures for the functions of reasoning and emotion? Anatomically, the ventromedial part of the PFC is certainly the seat for emotional and social components in decision making (Damasio, 1994). Injury to this area disturbs the individual's ability for appropriate emotional responses. The individual forgets to behave in socially appropriate ways as well. However, reasoning, memory, and learning may be left intact in this brain-injured individual. Being bright is no guarantee that one will make good decisions. One has to be also contemplative and calm, and not be distracted by negative effect that poisons his or her decision making.

Another important implication emerges as well. This has to do with *agency* or authorship of one's decisions. If it is true that the subcortical structures, such as the amygdala prompt the cortical structure—the ventromedial PFC—biasing the decision that individuals will make even before they know that they are going to take that decision, then how much of their action or judgment is completely within their rational control? It is well known that the majority of neural processing and its consequences remain outside consciousness (Floresco & Ghods-Sharifi, 2007).

Emotion's Impact on Intelligence: Eastern Views

Emotions, of course, influence decision making, but what are some of the unwholesome mental states that can disturb decision making? The wisdom of the East comes into use at this point. The Buddhists (see Goleman, 1988; Guenther, 1974) specifically refer to five common negative emotions or negative effects that distract one from making good decisions: (a) passion, including desire, greed, lust; (b) aggression, including anger, hatred, resentment; (c) ignorance, which includes bewilderment, confusion, apathy; (d) pride, especially wounded pride, low self-esteem; and (e) jealousy, which includes envy and paranoia.

An executive, a manager, or an entrepreneur should be introspective and be alert to these disturbing emotions that are implicitly involved while making a decision. In fact, according to Eastern views of intelligence or *buddhi* (Radhakrishnan & Moore, 1957), we can benefit from our intelligence as long as it is not distorted by what is called egotistic attitude (*ahankara*). Literally, the term *ahankara* is translated as: "I do," a *sense of agency* that sometimes gets distorted especially when we declare that "I am right and you are wrong." It is the feeling of *ahankara*, or the egotistic feeling that distracts us from using intelligence. *Ahankara* also relates to a feeling of agency that "I am free to will this or will that." This feeling can be an illusion.

In a subsequent section, we discuss the illusion of free will, but for the present section, let it be noted that we can purify our intelligence by reducing—if not completely removing—the five disturbing emotions. No doubt, as commonsense would predict, decisions need a tranquil mind. Yoga practice aims at making the mind calm by removing the darkness and the agitation that are integral parts of the mind. An analogy explains this better: A tranquil mind is the pure and still water of a mountain lake, reflects discerning intelligence that is serene and unconcerned. In its highest level, this is pure consciousness.

The East and the West: Implications

The relation between reasoning and emotion is that they meet on a common ground. The Indian concept of intelligence (*buddhi*) embodies both reasoning and emotion (Baral & Das, 2004; Das, 1994). The relationship is interdependent, but at the same time each can be observed to have functions that are separate. This is assumed both in the Indian concept of mind and the evidence from neuropsychology that the majority of neural processing and its consequences remain outside consciousness. Unlike the Indian philosophical system of *Samkhya* that accepts the existence of self and a continuity of consciousness, Buddhism questions the very existence of consciousness (Kalupahana, 1987). Some contemporary Euro-American authorities also raise similar doubts about consciousness.

In fact, in a book summarizing work on consciousness from several contemporary sources, Blackmore (2005) comes close to the conclusion that consciousness itself is merely a concept, and likely an illusory concept. Because we cannot think of a place where consciousness resides—not certainly in the homunculus—and since it is difficult to support a *nonphysical* process that controls mental functions, we are left at an impasse. The Buddhist philosophy of the twin realities—change and nonexistence of a permanent self (*anitya, anatma*)—is in harmony with this view. The whole existence of consciousness can be questioned. Naturally, then, *will* or the conscious feeling of having willed an action must be examined. If there is no permanent self, the will may be an illusion.

Conscious Will as a Feeling

Wegner (2004) has written a much discussed book, *Illusion of Conscious Will*. The main point of the argument is that the feeling of conscious will, that is, "I will this action so I did it," is real; however, it is difficult to support that *my willing causes my behavior*. According to Wegner, when a thought appears in consciousness just before you act and it is consistent with the action, and there appears to be no other alternative causes of action, we experience conscious will. Then we ascribe authorship to ourselves for the action. In his article, "The Précis of the Book," Wegner really not only challenges conscious willing, but consciousness itself. Both are creations of our imagination, he suggests. But wait a minute, we accept that there are voluntary behaviors and then there are involuntary behaviors. The involuntary behaviors occur without conscious willing. How is that possible if all actions are willed? What is being argued is that conscious will is not a force. It does not cause an action. It is a feeling. Volition is a feeling, an emotion. We are led to consider the distinction between the experience of will (phenomenal will) and the empirical will. There is empirical will, which can be described as the causality of the person's conscious thoughts, as established by scientific analysis of their covariation with the person's behavior. Wegner does not disregard this. In contrast, phenomenal will is defined as the person's reported experience of will. He questions that it causes action.

There seems to be no quarrel, really, if Wegner (2004) accepts that a person's thinking, beliefs, intentions, or plans cause subsequent action. If I am lustful, I do lustful acts. If I have controlled my anger, I do not get angry easily. If I have planned to build a house, have got an architect, and the architect gives a plan, then I supervise the building of the house; that is empirical will. However, if I feel that my willing alone has got the house built, that my will is the cause of the house being built, then I am opening myself up to an illusion. We make the mistake that the experience of will is a causal mechanism. Why do we do that? Because we believe in causal agents—authorship, *ahankara*, or "I have done it" feelings.

In management, for example, one sets up a goal, goes ahead, and achieves it; the achiever is rewarded for having reached the goal, so the experience of conscious will feel like being a causal agent. However, when things go wrong in spite of the best-laid plans, he or she tries to blame himself/herself, feel guilty, or get depressed. Here, the feeling of conscious will is detrimental to his or her ability as a decision maker. In a complex world, there are myriad conditions; there are numerous components whose modes of action we are unaware of. So, we believe in intuition, we open ourselves to somatic responses that send affective messages to the decision-making center in the PFC. It is an adaptive behavior that has evolved.

Take a creative person, an artist. The artist creates something; he/she gets appreciation for it or gets thoroughly criticized for his or her creation. If he/she believes in the fact that his/her willing has anything to do with the praise or blame, he/she will be mistaken because what he/she has created has value only when it is judged by the public. Actually, both emotions and so-called voluntary actions have roots that are not often accessible to consciousness.

Wegner (2004) appreciatively cited T.H. Huxley's view of *volition as an emotion indicative of physical changes, but not a cause of such changes*. When discussing cause, the empiricist David Hume (Russell, 1946) rejected its existence, describing causes merely as antecedents and effects merely as consequences, there being no causal connection between them. Even if we abandon this knotty epistemological question, it still remains true that why we behave as we behave, why we engage in a specific act, and what its fruits will be are more or less an area of darkness. That is, we cannot insist that every action we engage in is completely consciously planned. So, to repeat Huxley, volition is an emotion, and conscious will/willing is a feeling; neither of the two is a cause or a force.

Indeed, this is not as harsh a conclusion for people who believe in free will. The problem is the belief in determinism that every action we do is completely determined. It cannot be so. As we discussed, the roots of action are often unconsciousness, traced to pre-existing dispositions, to habits, consequences of cultural conditioning that the Buddhists name *sanskara*, and circumstantial opportunities.

The idea that resonates with Indian philosophy (Radhakrishnan, 1993) is that of regarding action without the expectation that its fruit will be desirable. The cause of action is not to get a reward. The authority or agency we have is in planning the action as best we can, depending on our mode, emotional characteristics, and the sampling of information that we could muster to use in making a decision, being fully aware of the fact that having made the decision does not guarantee that it will pan out the way we thought it should. We may declare our intention of doing something, but the intention does not necessarily lead to action. As Wegner (2004) mentioned in his book, intentions are only signposts, declarations for oneself and others of what one would like to do. But the signposts do not make people go on the path they follow. The expression *niskaama karma* (action without craving for its fruit) might have been degraded to a cliché, but the analysis of the idea as found in various places of Bhagavad Gita (Radhakrishnan, 1948) may appear to be surprisingly profound for contemporary decision makers. Accepting partial rewards and, hence, partial satisfaction for one's action perhaps could be a compromise. The idea is taken up in the concept of satisficing.

Satisficing Will Do, Perfection Is Not Wanted

Bounded rationality is a term that Simon (1976) has coined, along with the notion of "satisficing." In view of the fact that information load is enormous, and we do not have access to how the various components in a situation we are judging are connected, we have to settle down to something that is acceptable. The manager, administrator, and entrepreneur look for a decision that is good enough and meets their minimal requirements. A satisficing decision is expected to bring about the change that will be better than the way things are now. It gathers force when compounded by the limitation of handling complex and unknown connections between components of a situation. These are the obstructions to be overcome. Additionally, emotional predispositions by way of negative and positive effects are powerful influences. Further compounding the problem is the illusion of conscious will—the sometimes unwarranted feeling of authorship or unconditional agency. Then satisficing will appear to be the best adaptive behavior.

Planning and Emotion: An Example of Entrepreneurial Decision Making That Leads to Disaster

You are a high-ranking bureaucrat in the government. You have risen to that position after working for so many years within the restricted environment of government bureaucracy, albeit in government-sponsored industries.

You are now 50 years old and have only 10 more years before retirement. You are tired of the stifling conditions, and, at the same time, you have hit the so-called middle age, and are becoming increasingly disenchanted and melancholic. You wish to break into new ventures in the private sector and decide to open a hotel in an industrial mining area in the remote part of the country. Your plan appears to be a good one. The area does not have a hotel that offers quality residential facilities. Neither does it have a reputable licensed restaurant for alcohol and food. You have easy access to loans for investment and the promise of some investors. How did you make that decision?

Start with the analysis of the *goals and objectives* and the *impact of emotion*. Your goal is to end an unpleasant condition in your current state of existence. Your objective is to make enough money so that eventually you can give up the bureaucrat's job. What you depended on are two kinds of knowledge: *tacit knowledge* and *instructed* or formally acquired knowledge about business. The knowledge you have as the *formal* knowledge, the instructed category, is quite adequate. You have an MBA. You have studied the market; you know what is needed; you have calculated the amount of investment and projected a return over the next five years. You have plans to collect enough resources for investment.

But your *tacit knowledge* is implicit; it may not depend on logic or current data that you have gathered, and you are not aware of what you know tacitly. It is not quite at the conscious level. Your tacit knowledge ultimately leads you to failure because you do not know the many uncertain components of establishing a successful hotel and restaurant in that particular region. For example, although you are aware that there would be people who are crooked and not trustworthy, you have to deal with them and you have no tacit knowledge of how to deal with such people because you have only dealt with people within the official bureaucracy. You are also unaware of the antisocial elements that would try to not only harm your business, but may also even harm you physically if you step into their territory and impede them in making illegal money.

While you are in this vulnerable position, you find that it is the restaurant licensed for alcoholic beverages that is beginning to make money. You have to decide whether or not you should focus on selling alcohol and providing a place for its consumption in the restaurant for recreational use. At this point, your *emotions* take over. You have an unconscious abhorrence associated with alcohol business. You come from a caste and a family where a business in alcohol is deprecated and is thought to be a cause for shame in your culture—a shameful business. Now you have borrowed a lot of money for investing in the hotel and the restaurant. You have to decide what to do at this point. A model of planning could help you. We present again the model of Stuss and Benson (see Chapter 1).

There are four interrelated components of planning that are quite relevant to your decision making (see a discussion of the diagram in Chapter 1, PASS theory). Your goal and objective now has changed. There is, in your mind, an overarching need to get out of the business. (1) The first thing you have to consider is *representation*. How do you represent the problem? It involves a moral repugnance toward running a licensed restaurant, although it is a "cash cow" and compensates for the loss in running the hotel. The only way, then, is to salvage whatever you can from the business, and quit it. (2) If that is how you represent the problem, what do you *anticipate*? You look for a buyer. You anticipate that the buyer who would come forward would most probably have much closer connection with the local situation, including its antisocial components. In fact, the buyer would have ways and means of handling the antisocial elements connected with doing business in that place. (3) Selection of a *strategy* is imperative. How are you going, then, to select the potential buyer? What are some of the problems that may arise when you try to disinvest? You make a plan and you are then faced with the problem of selecting the plan. What are the steps that should be taken to follow it through? (4) As you take these steps, you get continuous *feedback* in regard to how the plan in each step is working. Some of the feedback is negative and some is positive. You weigh them and organize them, and then you regulate the execution of your plans. (5) So *regulation* is the other important component in this model.

As you regulate and execute the plan and anticipate the difficulties that might arise while executing the plan, your representation of the problem keeps on getting adjusted. Instead of trying for the best outcome—maximizing—you have given up optimization. You are now in a *satisficing* mode, that is, given the circumstances—what would be the most satisfying outcome, not the best one.

The satisficing approach fits a few basic demands of the situation. One is your *limited information*, both tacit and learned information that might lead to a rational decision. Second are your *emotional predispositions* as well as your current *mood* when you are about to make a decision. You are generally depressed and, especially, in a bad mood due to a recent setback in your family. Now your objective has changed; it is to quickly end the present disastrous situation. You save face, you aim to have peace in the family, and your self-esteem needs to be restored. You have been sitting quietly thinking how you feel about what might distract you—desire, greed, lust, anger, hatred, resentment, confusion, apathy, pride, especially wounded pride, low self-esteem, and jealousy toward others who made money from a similar business. These weigh upon your decision, and you were not fully conscious of their complex interactions.

What you do next is not dependent on conscious willing. In fact, you are even reluctant to claim that you consciously took this decision and praise or blame yourself. You slip into a quasi-fatalistic attitude: "Whatever had to happen did happen, now let me get on with life. You have to begin the search again."

Concluding Remarks

Analytical and Synthetic Modes in Retrospect

Rationality is bounded by emotions, and, in any case, emotions cannot be separated from rationality in either personal or business decision making. Simon (1971) has alerted us to a particular difficulty that future decision makers have to deal with in regard to information and WM overload; it is the *economics of attention* in the context of expanding demands on information processing. Repeating these lines from the introduction to this chapter, we briefly allude to a related field of research, which is a hybrid discipline of economics and neuroscience. We are aware of its relevance to both analytic and synthetic aspects of decision making. But the current bias in neuroeconomics is toward risk-taking behavior. Risk taking is outside the focus of the present chapter. The major concepts in risk taking, such as Subjective Expected Utility theory and its broad context provided by Prospect theory (see Sanfey, 2007, for a recent statement), have not been considered here. "Neuroeconomics" may not view the individual as a single rational information processor. It admits of, at least, a dual source of decision making very much in line with the focus of the present chapter—the infusion of emotion in decision making.

What is new? Sanfey (2007) and colleagues specify brain activities during playing economic games. For example, the anterior insula is responsive to negative effect; it is more active for unfair offers, whereas the DLPFC works to maintain goal state (make money). The individual is more likely to accept unfair offer when DLPFC is more active than anterior insula. Intuitive and deliberative thinking are the two ways of thinking that are discussed throughout this chapter; one is fast, while the other is slow. Competent managers engage in both kinds of thinking.

General intelligence does not contribute significantly to excellence in executive decisions once a normal level of IQ is assured; engineering students in elite schools and executives in selected organizations have sufficient intelligence. Emotional intelligence, however, is presently considered as an important contributor to making decisions with feeling and reasoning. Reflections and mindfulness have been borrowed from the contemplative traditions of the East in contemporary styles of management. Are these amenable to training in the first place? Can these be included as part of training senior executives? The discussion continues in the next chapter.

PART V

Enhancement of Educational Achievement and Decision Making

11

Planning in Writing: Compositions and Oral Narratives

Planning is necessary for good compositions. In some of his classic studies, Luria used poor composition as an index of deficits in frontal lobe functions. Composition of an essay or a narrative requires all the major executive processes (Das, 1980; Das, Kar, & Parrila, 1996; Luria, 1970). For example, composition of essays supporting certain given strategies as a device for indicating competence among executives has been presented in some detail earlier. Evaluation of stories after viewing a picture in terms of originality and individuality of the written composition was used as one of the first measures of Planning (Das, 1980). We will continue that line of research here, and discuss first the nature of writing itself, and then the difference between composition of written and oral narratives within the broad context of planning.

Writing

We write to represent knowledge and to communicate. A broader approach to knowledge representation will include its dependence on some symbolic system, most often language. In his influential book, *The Origins of the Modern Mind*, Donald (1991) suggested that the development of language played an important role in the development of thinking. Writing, which evolved much later in phylogenesis, allowed for external memory storage of the products of that thinking that could then be engaged with both by the writers themselves to further develop the ideas and by the readers to consume, and, perhaps, to challenge. The act of writing, thus, entails choosing the thoughts to be written, translating the thoughts first into internal speech and further to grammatical expressions, and the motor acts needed to transcribe these into text (e.g., Hayes & Berninger, 2009). According to McCutchen (1995), many children have mastered the mechanics of writing by age 10, but the knowledge representation and communication remain a knotty and persistent problem.

In terms of knowledge representation in the early phase of writing acquisition, Luria (1978) and Vygotsky (1978), we believe, made a landmark contribution with their conceptualization of the "pre-history" of writing in ontogenesis. According to Luria and Vygotsky, children first resort to making marks on paper as primitive indications or signs for memory purposes. At three to four years of age, children discover that marks on paper can be used as mnemonic devices; as a result, writing obtains an auxiliary instrumental function, as external memory and drawing now turns into sign writing. When these marks evolve into letters and words, a second fundamental transformation occurs. The idiosyncratic primitive forms and procedures the child has been using up to that point transform into complex cultural forms, as the child's scribbles start to resemble the orthographic symbols— a complex cultural device, as Luria describes writing. He stated, "[T]hese devices are tried in succession and perfected and in the process transform the child as well." (Luria, 1978, p. 193) The child must make a fundamental discovery at this transition stage: One can draw not only objects, but also speech. According to Vygotsky (1978), it was this discovery in phylogenesis that led humanity to the brilliant practice of writing, using orthographic symbols. Drawing speech expands the communicative function of writing beyond that of pictorial representation in allowing intentions of the writer to become central. When writing is intentional, it is also planned.

Vygotsky (1986) indicated further that acquisition of language is critical to the development of higher level planning. He argued that the most important developmental step is when behavior becomes regulated by a symbolic language system, that is, semiotic mediation. Language is the means by which humans move from having purely sensorimotor or reflex-type responses to being reflective, purposeful actors in their environment. Planning is facilitated by acquisition of language, and, at the same time, is manifested in expressive language as a mediating variable. We will discuss the role of planning in writing, both in its early and late phases, via two very different models: Biggs' (1988) model of essay writing developed to explain university students' writing performance, and Hayes and Berninger's (2009) model of cognitive processes in writing that aims to explain writing processes of a wider variety of writers.

Biggs (1988) proposed three stages of writing: intentional, para writing, and actual writing. The intentional stage includes affective and aspirational aspects that are present prior to writing. In interviews of university students regarding their feelings about an essay assignment, Biggs found two general approaches to essay writing: a deep approach and a surface approach. The deep approach was characterized by a high degree of personal involvement, enjoyment, anticipation of a rich personally rewarding experience, and, frequently, expectation of a high grade. The surface approach, in turn, was characterized by apprehension, little personal involvement, and generally, a low expectation about the outcome. According to Biggs, these approaches exemplify two quite different orientations to essay writing. Moreover, depending on the intentional approach the students chose, the subsequent para writing and writing activities differed accordingly.

The major para writing activities in Biggs' (1988) essay writing model, all, relate to planning. Biggs suggested that when writers plan an essay, they may go through seven major steps that can be roughly summarized as follows: (1) question interpretation, (2) forming general intentions, (3) knowledge evaluation and acquisition, (4) organization of material, (5) online planning and revisions, (6) deciding on criteria for monitoring, and (7) forming specific intentions.

For Biggs (1988), writing properly begins with a transcription of focal intention into written form, followed by a review of the writing that is based on the monitoring criteria decided upon during para writing. If revisions are needed, they can either address any of the para writing activities or concentrate on the text written so far. According to Biggs, intentions and effects of writing can determine the type of review and revisions in which the writer will engage. Students with a deep approach to essay writing tend to review less often and review larger entities, whereas students with a surface approach are more concerned with reviewing individual words and sentences (similar to younger students; see, e.g., McCutchen, 1995). Revision itself is not a separate process from writing, but rather takes the writer back to planning, forming new intentions, monitoring, and so forth. Thus, writing in Biggs' terms proceeds from conceptual planning to online or opportunistic (Hayes-Roth & Hayes-Roth, 1979) planning and monitoring of a plan. His model is more consistent with cognitive planning models that regard planning as a recursive process that includes the continuous monitoring and revising of a plan than with models that emphasize planning in advance of the activity.

Hayes and Berninger (2009; see also Chenoweth & Hayes, 2001) suggest that the writers typically generate text in language bursts of six to twelve words separated by pauses that may involve planning of the next fragment or evaluation of text written so far. During the pause, the *proposer* suggests ideas for inclusion in the text and passes them to the *translator*. In generating new ideas, the proposer may have input from the *planner*, the task environment, knowledge base (long-term memory), and from the text written so far. The translator then takes the ideas and transforms them into grammatical language strings that the *transcriber* turns into written text. Throughout the process, the *evaluator* examines the outputs of other processes and passes judgment on their adequacy. This can involve judging the ideas, their translation, or the transcribed text. In this model, the *planner* is situated in the *control* level where it may negotiate with the task *initiator* (e.g., a teacher or a boss) the topic, audience, and other possible features for the text, and then sets the goals for the writing activity. Depending on the writers' skill level, goals can vary widely. From the point of view of cognitive planning, this model is clearly an advance planning model, where the *planner* possibly continues to influence the process when called for by the *proposer* and the *evaluator*.

We have used the Activity theory to bridge the two conceptualizations of planning in writing (e.g., Das & Parrila, 1995) and will review those ideas here. Figure 11.1 identifies three levels of planning (activity, action, and operation) that are derived from Leontjev's (1978, 1981) writings. At the level of *activity*, planning can be conceptualized as a method of realizing or aiming toward one's general goals and motives as a student, manager, or an employee, for example. Writers' general motivations and intentions are seldom dealt with in models of writing, yet such activities can have a significant impact on how the writer approaches the specific writing task that the models of writing then attempt to explain. Biggs' (1988) intentional stage of writing is an exception in that it nicely captures some functions of activity planning in writing. A deep approach to writing, for example, could be seen as stemming from a person's life goals (e.g., self-improvement). How these life goals are translated into the actual writing task involves activity-planning.

Figure 11.1:
Planning and knowledge base in writing

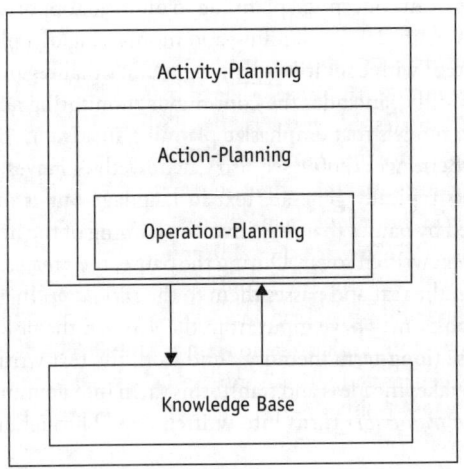

Biggs also demonstrated how deep and surface approaches to writing further affect how the writer revises the text, collects material, or decides upon style. Thus, decisions on the activity-planning level, whether conscious or not, can affect the two lower levels. This dependency is captured in Figure 11.1 by nesting the action- and operation-planning boxes in the activity box. General aspirations and conceptions of writing can also be sources of individual and developmental differences, and should certainly be targets of educational interventions.

Action planning is equivalent to problem solving. While activity planning is best understood as movement toward realizing one's general life goals, action planning aims at achieving a particular goal. An example of action-planning in writing is solving the particular problems in writing an article (or a book chapter in our present case), essay, and so forth; this is approximately equivalent to what Biggs (1988) referred to as para writing activities. The main goal at this level is to determine the specific goal of the writing task in hand, often in relation to external task demands (represented, e.g., by the initiator in Hayes and Berninger's model). Interpreting the question, choosing the audience and style, generating and organizing the content, and setting specific goals and criteria for different parts of the written work are all action-planning questions. While action-planning is logically different from text generation, it does not take place exclusively prior to text generation. Plans and goals often evolve *during* writing, as was acknowledged by Biggs. Sometimes we can begin to write out an activity plan (e.g., to promote understanding of a company's strategic goals) with a very sketchy action-plan that subsequently becomes more elaborate and inclusive as we proceed, or maybe a new plan emerges that requires a reorganization of both the already produced content and our specific goals for the writing. Moreover, each time the writer evaluates whether what is signified corresponds with the intentions, he or she engages in recursive action-planning, or online planning as discussed earlier. Thus, action-planning is a process that continues until the written product is finished and satisfies the writer's activity-planning goals and the specific goals for the current writing task, which by then may be considerably different from the goals that the writer produced prior to beginning the task.

At the levels of *operations*, plans are equivalent to strategies and tactics, and consist of working toward the solution to a problem (or a part there of) in accordance with task-imposed constraints (i.e., meeting environmental conditions). Operation-planning involves actualizing the writer's action-plans. This can entail translating and transcribing in Hayes and Berninger's (2009) model, or translating focal intentions (Biggs, 1988), or local plans (McCutchen, 1995) into written sentences that instantiate desired content and rhetorical goals. But it can also involve creating efficient cues and memory retrieval strategies for content or strategies for finding a correct spelling, as Varnhagen's (1995) work has suggested. Again, operation-planning does not end when enough text is generated or ideas are transcribed into written form. Instead, evaluation of and revisions on the word/sentence level focusing on correct spelling and grammar should also be considered as an integral part of operation-planning.

Knowledge base, both of content and of methods to locate and evaluate content, is the final component in our model and as important as the three levels of planning. According to McCutchen (1995, p. 137), the quality of children's "texts is to a large extent a function of the information retrieved from memory," partly because of their reliance on knowledge-telling strategy and still developing planning skills. What we know about the genre and the topic certainly affects the quality of our arguments and the quality of written expression as such. Knowledge base, however, is more than a stationary storage place for past experiences that are independent of planning. Both the use and the growth of the knowledge base can be directly dependent upon plans at different levels. For example, we are particularly tuned to noticing new pieces of information that seem to relate to our current goals and motives, and we actively search for examples that would allow us to make better arguments in writing. Thus, the relationship between knowledge base and planning is bidirectional.

We argue that a narrow conceptualization of planning in writing must be abandoned in favor of a broader view of planning. Planning is a recursive process that can take place simultaneously at three different levels—activity, actions, and operations—each affecting the others, and each built on the writer's knowledge base. An agenda for future research on writing must include a delineation of components of planning that children use, which in turn require us to construct models of the relationship between different levels of planning on the one hand, and the development of corresponding levels of writing skills on the other. Most reviews on children's writing suggest that they do not plan; however, this may be a reflection of the planning models assessed rather than children's actual writing processes. We will return to this topic later.

Role of Planning in Narratives

Poor writers in general and young writers in particular frequently exhibit difficulties in planning and organizing their writing tasks (e.g., McCutchen, 1995; Newcomer & Barenbaum, 1991). Ashman and Das (1980) showed that lack of planning in written compositions was related to deficiencies in simple operation-planning tasks involving visual search. Higher level planning skills may, in turn, be required for tasks such as imagining what the reader might understand from the written text (Olson, 1994). There are two questions to consider here: Is a certain degree of competency in cognitive planning required before the writer may begin to apply this skill to organize information in a composition? And do the basic writing skills need to be adequately developed before planning can influence written composition? Developmental studies suggest that very young children are capable of some planning (e.g., Wellman, Fabricius, & Sophian, 1985), but also that planning skills continue to develop into early adulthood (e.g., Dreher & Oerter, 1987). Several studies suggest that by the age of 12, children are capable of complex planning (e.g., Pea, 1982), and that their basic writing skills are sufficiently developed to allow for planning (e.g., McCutchen, 1995). According to this line of thinking, we should see planning influence composition writing by this age, if not before.

We have explored the role of planning in composing written narratives as well as in narrating an event or a story in two research studies. We present the studies in some detail here, as they have not been published in full elsewhere. The first study explored the relationship between cognitive planning (operation planning) and written composition in Grade 8 students, and the second investigated the role of action and operation planning in oral and written narratives of Grade 4, 6, and 8 students.

The purpose of the first study by Mishra and Das (1997) was to investigate: (1) If good writers are better than poor writers in cognitive tests of planning and in their use of organizational skills in written composition, and (2) Whether the relationship of planning and writing is stronger only above a certain level of competence in writing. Forty-eight boys and fifty-nine girls from regular Grade 8 (mean age close to 14 years) classes in Canada participated in the study. All participants spoke English as their first language and volunteered to participate in the study.

The writing samples were collected by the Language Arts teachers by administering the Test of Written Language-2 (TOWL-2; Hammill & Larsen, 1988) in groups. The test required the participant to write a story about a picture they were presented. The stories were then further scored using the rating scales for Planned Composition (Ashman & Das, 1980); trained graduate students scored each story separately for Expression, Organization, Wording, Mechanics, and Individuality on a 7-point scale. Three planning tests from the Planning Battery of the Cognitive Assessment System (Naglieri & Das, 1990) were also administered and the participants' scores on the Canadian Cognitive Abilities Test (CCAT) were obtained from school records.

The top and bottom 30 percent of the total sample based on the TOWL-2 scores were designated as good and poor writers respectively. According to published test norms, poor writers were found to be below the low-average range and good writers were above the mid-point for the above range in spontaneous writing. The results from the cognitive planning tasks showed that good writers performed significantly better in all the three tests (Planned Codes, Planned Connections, and Matching Numbers). The good writers were also significantly better than the poor writers in all five planned composition variables. In sum, good writers are not only better than poor writers on their use of planning and organizational skills in writing, but also on the cognitive tests of planning.

The relationship between planning and writing for good and poor writers was examined separately for children with average intelligence (90–112 on CCAT-verbal). Cognitive planning was related to writing for the good writers ($r = .40$, $p < .05$; $n = 22$), but not for the poor writers ($r = .22$, $p > .05$; $n = 24$). This supports the assumption that a certain level of competency in writing may be required before planning can influence writing. A Linear Structural Relationship model (LISREL) was then constructed to test the hypothesis that competency in cognitive planning would influence planned composition, and planned composition would influence writing performance. This meditational model (see Figure 11.2) fitted the data well, and showed that both the path from cognitive planning to planned composition (.214) and that from planned composition to writing (TOWL-2 score; .504) were significant. When the planned composition scores were limited to Expression and Organization, the two scales presumed to indicate planning in writing better than the other three scales (Wording, Mechanics, Individuality); cognitive planning to the planned composition path was significantly stronger at .538.

In conclusion, two significant findings are noted. First, in terms of the stories on TOWL-2 written by the participants, the poor writers were rated as lower on planning composition (scales were expression, organization, individuality, wording, and mechanics) than the good writers. Second, the poor writers' organization and expression difficulties, in particular, may be an extension of their difficulties in more basic planning skills. Finally, certain

Figure 11.2:
From cognitive planning to quality narratives

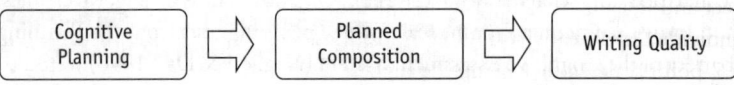

level of mastery in writing may be required before the individual can apply planning skills to writing a composition.

Oral and Written Narratives: Their Underlying Cognitive Planning Processes

Is planning necessary for good expressive language performance, both in oral and written narratives? We want to answer this within a broader perspective, and have begun to map the relationship between domain general planning skills, and written and oral narrative composition performance. The second study we report in this chapter examined just that with 154 Canadian students in Grades 4, 6, and 8 from schools in a major Canadian urban center.

Most of the planning tasks used in this study were from the Cognitive Assessment Battery: Matching Numbers, Planned Codes, Planned Connections, and Planned Search. In addition to these, a more complex Crack the Code task was administered using a desktop computer. The computer program that presented the items captured both the chronometric variables (thinking time before the first move, evaluation time at the end, and total time spent thinking about the moves in between them) for the task and number of correct items answered. On the basis of the preliminary analyses of the number of participants who answered each item correctly, we separated the Crack the Code items into Easy, Medium, and Hard, irrespective of the grades of the children.

Narrative skills were assessed using oral and written compositions. For each task, participants were given a picture from TOWL-2 and asked to either write (for written composition) or verbalize (verbal composition) a story about what is happening in the picture. Different pictures were used for the two narratives. The participants were given approximately 15 minutes to complete each task and instructed that the story must have a beginning, middle, and an ending. The verbal (transcribed) and written stories were then rated by two judges (one elementary school teacher and one university professor) on each of the five scales described earlier (and in more detail in Das et al., 1996). These scales included Expression (ability to express ideas), Organization (underlying plan and logical sequence), Wording (correct and imaginative use of words), Mechanics (grammar and syntax), and Individuality (creativity). All compositions were rated on each scale using a 7-point scale, with 1 being the highest score and 7 being the lowest. The mean of the scores from the seven scales was used as the Written and Oral composition scores.

Before examining how planning and narrative skills were associated, we examined the structure and dimensionality of the composition and planning variables. Scores for the written and oral scales were examined using exploratory factor analytic techniques. The results of this analysis are presented in Table 11.1. In each grade, there clearly were two factors—one identified with written skills and the other with oral skills. Each factor was defined by all the five composition rating scale scores, indicating unidimensionality within the domains. Further, no oral skills loaded onto the written factor and no written skills loaded onto the oral factor. It is interesting that there was no overlap between written and oral skill factors even when they were measured using the same scoring scales by the same judges. This finding suggests that there are critical differences in the skills that underlie each of these performances. We will return to this point later.

Similar exploratory factor analysis with the planning tasks also indicated two factors in all three grades. All planning tasks from the Cognitive Assessment System (CAS)—Matching Numbers, Planned Codes, Planned Connections, and Planned Search—loaded on the first factor, hypothesized to measure Operation Planning, or tactics and strategies the participants used to solve the relatively simple tasks. The second factor was mainly

Table 11.1:
Factor analysis of oral and written composition rating scale scores

	Grade 4		Grade 6		Grade 8	
	Written Skill	Oral Skill	Written Skill	Oral Skill	Written Skill	Oral Skill
Written expression	.909		.937		.919	
Written organization	.936		.935		.933	
Written wording	.842		.922		.886	
Written mechanics	.748		.845		.752	
Written individuality	.910		.903		.864	
Oral expression		.954		.960		.963
Oral organization		.960		.942		.944
Oral wording		.933		.947		.895
Oral mechanics		.812		.770		.826
Oral individuality		.945		.936		.935

defined by the total thinking time and evaluation time for the medium and hard items on the Crack the Code task. This factor seemed to capture the more reflective (consideration of moves, evaluation of their impact) aspects of task completion and was labeled Action Planning, as it was interpreted to capture both advance and online formulation of new plans. There was little overlap between the two factors, indicating that the two categories of planning are separate.

Relationship between Planning and Composition

When we examined the correlations between the four operation planning tasks and the two composition scores, no significant relationships were found in Grade 4. However, in Grade 6, the written composition score correlated significantly with Matching Numbers and Planned Codes, and in Grade 8, with all four planning tasks. Interestingly, no significant correlations were found between the four operation planning tasks and the oral composition score. In terms of the more complex action-planning measures, only performance accuracy correlated with composition scores, and only in Grade 6 (oral composition) and Grade 8 (oral and written composition). Our results in relation to age are not entirely surprising because younger and more novice writers are hypothesized to be limited in their use of planning strategies and tend to use language directly from their knowledge base (McCutchen, 1987). This pattern of results also suggests that there is a developmental component to planning. That is, the ability to plan is not fixed, but develops, and the capacity to conduct more complex planning improves between Grades 6 and 8. Finally, a further examination of these correlations reveals an interesting pattern with regard to written and oral skills. Written scores were correlated almost solely with operation planning scores; this result is similar to that found previously by Ashman and Das (1980). On the other hand, oral scores were correlated exclusively with action planning scores. This result suggests that differing levels of planning skills are necessary for writing versus oral story telling.

A cursory examination of the demands of both tasks may suggest a reason for this difference. In written composition, students are able to write, erase, rearrange, and edit as they please. They can pause for a long time while thinking. In oral production, that would seem quite odd indeed, and once the composition starts, it usually proceeds to the end on one continuous, albeit sometimes choppy flow. Oral composition requires more advance planning because there is no opportunity to edit the story. This difference would allow written skills to draw more on operation planning, and oral skills to be more reliant on action planning.

Why Do Oral and Written Narratives Not Overlap?

Even when the same scoring scales were used by the same judges to score the narratives produced by the same participants, oral and written outputs showed a complete separation. We think the explanation for this is already provided by Luria (1982) in *Language and Cognition* that has an entire chapter discussing the difference between the two types of speech ("speech" used interchangeably as "language"). First, they have different origins: "Oral speech evolves naturally in the process of social interaction between children and adults ... Written speech emerges as the result of formal learning" (Luria, 1982, p. 165). Oral speech is of two types—monologic speech and dialogic speech. The first category fits the task of telling a story from a picture, the method used to obtain narratives in our study. As Luria explained, "Oral dialogic speech may occur in the form of answers to questions or in the form of conversation, while oral monologic speech may occur in the form of a narrative" (1982, p. 160).

Although it is clear that oral narrative is identified as monologic, as it does not represent a dialogue between the narrator and the experimenter in our study, it has elements of dialogic speech simply because the narrator recognizes the presence of the other person; in our case, the experimenter who tape-recorded the narratives. Gestures, intonations, and mimicry were usual parts of oral speech during narration because of the presence of the experimenter. Had we considered these in evaluating tape-recorded speech, the difference between written and oral narratives would likely have been still wider. In spite of this, the transcribed tape-recorded narrative retained some critical features that distinguish oral from written speech.

The oral narrators did not have to produce grammatically correct syntax as in written speech, nor did they have to inhibit improvizations to expand on their thinking. They did, in contrast, witness the experimenter's immediate response to the narration, however muted it might be. Written narrative is speech without an addressee (Luria, 1982), and it is frequently addressed to an imaginary audience (Olson, 1994). Even if writers in our study may have felt that they were writing to the experimenter, they had no benefit of his response. Written speech can be examined and changed by the writer, as was in our study. Its main object and focus are the means of expression—language itself. The writer has the opportunity to conduct a conscious analysis of means of expression, thereby ensuring that individuality and originality are communicated properly. All of these must be produced according to the rules of grammar (mechanics, as in our rating scale).

Hopefully, the aforementioned comments regarding the origin of oral and written language, the emphasis on grammatical production, and the demand for creating a text that is self-sufficient and comprehensible for an imagined audience in written narratives as opposed to the presence of an actual listener for oral narrative provide some justification for anticipating the results we found in our study. We suppose there are other ways of conceptualizing the difference between writing and oral production of narratives. Furthermore, it is reasonable to conclude that written compositions produced in Grades 6 and 8, but not in Grade 4, were influenced by cognitive planning skills. This suggests that some level of writing skills are necessary before writers engage more fully in planning, which then allows for the more mature writing skills to develop in later grades.

12

Verbalization Enhances Planning: Application in Education

Verbalization boosts Planning because it allows one to formulate strategies for solving a similar problem and regulate activity through one's own overt or covert speech. We mention several experiments in support of how verbalization helps poor planners. As a theoretical context for the verbalization procedure, the method of dynamic assessment or interactive assessment is then introduced. Of special interest in these studies is the finding that the positive effect of concurrent, overt verbalization boosts problem solving, specifically for poor planners, and not for those who have adequate planning, although both groups had low performance prior to verbalization. Overt verbalization also seems to prevent quick deterioration of detailed verbal information.

Since Planning is a *metacognitive process* that utilizes information available from simultaneous and successive processing, and allocates attentional resources during problem solving (see Chapters 1 and 2), we then suggest verbalization is a part of explicit metacognition. The term *metacognition* concerns the processes that enable us to not only monitor and control our own cognitive processes, but also imagine what others are thinking during social interactions. Making it possible to share one's own experiences with others, it promotes *reflective discussion* (Frith, 2007; Frith & Frith, 2012).

We pursue this line of thinking in the next two chapters: first, presenting programs that help learn the mechanics of doing mathematics by children who need help, and second structured programs that are effective for improvement of reading and comprehension.

Verbalization Boosts Planning

Verbalizing, or talking to yourself, as you go about solving a problem has at least two beneficial effects. It influences planning as you go, and it allows yourself or an observer to record and later review the strategies you used. Ericsson and Simon (1980, 1984) have done pioneering work in this area, and, as a result, protocol analysis, or the thinking-aloud procedure, has become a reliable research method.

Verbalization after you have attempted to solve a problem allows you to formulate strategies for solving a similar problem (Ericsson & Simon, 1980, 1984). Verbalization may regulate your activity through your own overt or covert speech, as is consistent with Luria's (1961) work. If this is the intended effect of verbalization, which it is in our studies on enhancement of planning, then you are encouraged to carefully observe and explain how you did the task. Instructions to explain and describe the content of your thoughts are reliably associated with changes in your ability to solve problems correctly (Ericsson & Simon, 1993). In summary, both concurrent and retrospective verbalization show marked improvement in subsequent problem solving. We present evidence to support this as a benefit of explicit metacognition in the following studies.

How Verbalization Helps Poor Planners?

An information-processing approach to solving problems is particularly well shown in Planning—one of the PASS processes. As we wrote in an earlier article on the topic of cognitive enhancement (i.e., Cormier, Carlson, & Das, 1990), some of the most promising works in the study of individual differences in mental abilities are grounded in theoretical perspectives that are based on neuroanatomical models (Das, Kirby, & Jarman, 1979; Eysenck, 1982; Hynd & Willis, 1985; Luria, 1980). Equally promising are recently developed alternatives to traditional psychometric approaches to the assessment of mental abilities (Haywood & Tzuriel, 1992; Lidz, 1987). In the present investigation, we combine elements of these developments by applying a specific model of dynamic assessment to the measurement of mental abilities derived from a particular neuroanatomical model of cognitive functioning and information processing. We discuss the first study (i.e., Cormier et al., 1990) in some detail as it provides some sort of a template for later studies that follow.

The information-processing model employed in the early studies in verbalization as a tool for enhancing Planning was developed by Das and his associates (Das & Naglieri, 1990; Das & Varnhagen, 1986; Das et al., 1979; Naglieri & Das, 1987). This is the same model that later became the foundation for PASS theory (Das, Naglieri, & Kirby, 1994). The dynamic or interactive assessment approach is based on the work of Carlson, Wiedl, and their associates (Carlson, 1983; Carlson & Wiedl, 1976, 1979, 1992), with its broad context provided by the early work of Vygotsky (1962), and then variations of that provided by Guthke (1980, 1997), Feuerstein (Fuerstein et al., 1980), and Haywood (Haywood & Tzuriel, 1992).

The information-processing model first reviewed in Das, Kirby, and Jarman (1975), and later discussed at length in their book (1979), conforms to Luria's conception of the brain and the hypothesized three functional units that are fundamental to cognitive functioning and information processing. Since each of the three systems is interactive with the other two, the roles they play in information processing and cognitive behavior cannot be understood in isolation. The PASS theory is a more recent formulation (Das, Naglieri, & Kirby, 1994), as has been discussed in Chapters 1 and 2. Its relevance for the present chapter relates to a close connection of *planning* with the three other processes, but especially with attention–arousal.

The theory predicts that if arousal is too low or too high, the efficiency of information processing is reduced. As a consequence of low arousal, the ability of the individual to plan and execute strategies for the purpose of solving cognitive tasks may be impaired. Language, or more specifically the regulatory function of speech, helps control and optimize the level of arousal required for Planning and problem solving, as well as for Simultaneous and Successive tasks. Planning is activated by the first cognitive process—Attention–Arousal—as well as by the two other processes. Because it is located in the frontal lobes, Planning plays an important part in impulse control and allocation of attentional resources. We have discussed this at length in a previous chapter on separating Attention and Planning. We now know that besides reasoning and inferring, much of Planning involves emotional and social considerations, while the individual is engaged in problem solving and decision making. As we have described, the role of the social brain (Frith & Frith, 2012) and the orbitofrontal/ventromedial cortex in making plans and adopting strategies is now widely recognized. The planning function of the frontal lobe is thus closely associated with arousal—not only in impulse control and allocation of attentional resources, but through the regulation and control of behavior as well.

Dynamic Assessment

As a theoretical context for the verbalization procedure, the method of dynamic assessment or interactive assessment is introduced at this point. Stated generally, dynamic or interactive assessment procedures are employed to determine the extent to which cognitive performance can be modified by the activities of the examiner and the participant. Feuerstein (1980) best expounds the classic approach to dynamic assessment, while a more heterogeneous view is presented by various authors in Haywood and Tzuriel (1992). Included among these are the views of Carlson and Wiedl, and those of Das; these two have specific relevance for the discussion on verbalization in this chapter. Although presently there is no single unifying theory of dynamic assessment, and the methods used vary, we can say that practitioners share a common view: dynamic assessment provides more accurate estimates of intellectual potential than traditional psychometric methods, and it permits insight into cognitive processes during problem solving (see Grigorenko & Sternberg, 1998; Lidz, 1987 for a historical overview of dynamic assessment). How strong is the evidence that the dynamic assessment approach and its associated mechanisms for cognitive education are effective? Probably not strong enough, as Grigorenko and Sternberg (1998) mention in their review. However, the essential message in regard to the testing and intervention, common to most advocates of dynamic assessment approach, is that *learning continues to occur as the learner is engaged in solving the problem and asking questions.* New strategies are thus developed through verbalization.

Effect of Verbalization on Increasing Test Performance

Next, we present a group of studies by Carlson (2013) and his associates, including Das, in support of the improvement of planning, following verbalization during selected tasks such as Progressive Matrices. Matrices are often used as tests of intelligence. Performance increment, therefore, is key evidence for all of us who assume that children's intelligence is not really fixed, it is malleable, one of the procedures being interactive and reflective discussion.

A consistent finding in the Carlson–Wiedl research has been the positive effect which concurrent, overt verbalization has on intellectual performance. The role which verbalization plays in cognitive performance has been investigated in a number of studies by Carlson and Wiedl (1992). They precisely described a four-step procedure. The individual is required to (a) describe carefully and systematically the task at hand, (b) "think-aloud" as the problem is solved, (c) explain why the particular answer alternative chosen is correct or incorrect, and (d) explain why the non-chosen alternatives were considered to be incorrect. The tester does not provide feedback concerning the correctness of a solution. The intensity of feedback increases over the six testing conditions as follows:

1. Standard procedure for the test.
2. *Verbalization during and after solution*: This requires the child to describe the main stimulus pattern prior to searching for the correct answer, and then after a particular alternative is chosen, to explain why he/she made that choice.
3. *Verbalization after solution*: This involves the child describing the reasons for his/her choice after the choice is made.
4. *Simple feedback*: The child is informed after the choice has been made whether or not it was correct.
5. *Elaborated feedback*: This involves elaboration by the test administrator of the reasons why the chosen answer was correct or incorrect; the principles involved in the task are pointed out. A combination of (2) and (5) is recommended.
6. *Elaborated feedback plus verbalization during and after solution*: This involves informing the participant not only of the correctness of the solution, but also explaining the principles involved in the task. This last step is "problem verbalization." It is the most intensive feedback (Carlson & Wiedl, 1992). This is recommended when the other prompts are not very effective.

A study along the same line by Cormier et al. (1990) suggested that the positive effects of verbalization can be placed within the framework of Luria's model regarding the regulation of activity by internalized speech, as set forth by Das and his associates. For example, children who exhibit less than optimal arousal and are poor planners (Luria's functional unit three) would be expected to perform less well on complex cognitive tasks (functional unit two, involving simultaneous and successive information integration) than children who are good at planning and had more appropriate levels of arousal. Conversely, children who are overly aroused and/or impulsive (functional unit one) would be expected to perform less well on cognitive tasks than reflective children.

In the Cormier et al. study, the relationship between planning and performance on the Raven matrices was investigated under two conditions of test administration: the standard test administration approach outlined by Raven (1965) and the interactive approach which involves the subject's overt, concurrent verbalization. The general hypothesis guiding the study was that under the traditional, standard testing approach, children who are poor in planning would do less well on the Raven than children who are good planners. Under the verbalization condition, however, the poor planners previously determined by tests would be able to compensate and regulate their performance, and do as well on the present test as children who are good planners. Since complex tasks require substantial planning ability, it was hypothesized further that performance of the poor planners under the verbalization condition would be confined to improved performance on the cognitively complex reasoning by analogy items of the Raven.

Performance of Raven Matrices

From the groups constituted as "good" planners and "poor" planners, subjects were randomly assigned to either a standard instruction group or a verbalization group for the administration of the Raven Colored Progressive Matrices (CPM). Subjects in the standard instruction group received the instructions provided by Raven. That is, they were given a practice item and shown how only one of the answer alternatives would complete the pattern of the figure above the answer alternatives. They then proceeded through the remaining 35 items at their own pace, and without any feedback or further directions from the experimenter. Subjects in the interactive assessment—verbalization condition—were also shown the practice item. They were instructed to (a) describe the pattern in detail, (b) verbalize their thoughts as they examined the answer alternatives, (c) justify why they believed the chosen answer alternative to be the correct solution, and (d) explain why each of the non-chosen answer alternatives was incorrect. The role of the experimenter was to facilitate the child's verbalization by prompting him or her as necessary at each point of the task. The prompts took the form of phrases such as, "Now tell me what you see" or pointing to the main stimulus pattern, "How would you describe it?" The same facilitation was done with the answer alternatives with the experimenter making certain that the child explained why he or she thought the chosen answer alternative was correct. With appropriate prompting, each child was able to verbally describe each task, explain the answer alternatives, and make some statement about why the chosen alternative was correct and the others incorrect. Feedback concerning the correctness or incorrectness of the answers was not given. The final choice made by the child was scored and the experimenter turned the page to the next item of the test, whereupon the procedure began again. The findings supported the prediction—poor planners significantly improved in their performance following verbalization, whereas good planners did not gain from verbalization.

Although hypothetical and tentative, the present findings can be interpreted as supporting Luria's notion that the organization of cognitive skills with verbalization potentially activates planning activity, thereby enhancing the activity of simultaneous and successive processors. Whether or not good planners spontaneously use verbalization, it can at least be argued that verbalization provides a compensatory mechanism for poor planners. In regard to the potential neuropsychological implications of the results, our conclusions should be considered tentative until direct tests of the neural mechanisms involved in overt, concurrent verbalization, and in planning can be conducted.

In summary, the study supports and extends earlier findings that dynamic assessment enhances performance in groups defined by attribute variables referring to cognitive processes (planning, impulsivity, etc.), and not in groups defined by generic attribute variables, such as gender (see Carlson & Wiedl, 1990). The important question is whether the dynamic testing procedures then can be proved to be a better index of potential in other tasks. We think it should. The guidance function—which language provides in complex cognitive activity (Luria, 1961; Wertsch, 1985)—has been shown to be especially efficacious for individuals with performance deficiencies, a result consistent with the findings of a number of studies (e.g., Asarnow & Meichenbaum, 1979; Merz, 1969; Schunk & Cox, 1986; Wilder, Draper, & Donnelly, 1984). When performance deficiencies are related to poor planning, overt verbalization seems to be effective by making elements of planning explicit, guiding problem-solving activity, and stimulating the interaction of the three functional units described by Luria. In this sense, overt verbalization acts as a necessary prosthesis for poor planners by making the problem solver aware of the demands of the tasks, and the manner in which he or she intends to approach the problem.

We have followed this line of research in two ways. First, we have extended the benefit of verbalization in poor planners for planning tasks, rather than in solving matrices. Second, we have applied the design and verbalization procedure to help children improve in arithmetic, a series of studies by Naglieri and colleagues that we will present in a subsequent section.

Verbalization Improves Planning

The effect of verbalization on performance in Visual Search requiring planning and strategy use was investigated in two experiments by Kar, Dash, Das, and Carlson (1993). In the first experiment, we noticed that overt verbalization caused improvements in planning tasks among children. Children who were classified as poor planners because of their relatively poor performance on a Visual Search task showed more improvements in planning tasks than children classified as good planners. The second experiment involved the selection and grouping of good planners and poor planners based on the performance of planning tasks. These two groups were given different planning tasks under two separate conditions: the standard nonverbalization condition and the verbalization condition. Both groups of children showed improved performance. However, the performance of the poor planners generally improved more than that of the good planners. The results of both experiments were discussed in terms of (a) the specific benefits of dynamic assessment on planning performance and (b) the selective attention mechanisms involved in search tasks. Details of the study are presented in the next section.

The two previous studies involving verbalization that directly relate to the Kar et al. (1993) experiments are reviewed as follows. In the first study (Bethge, Carlson, & Wiedl, 1982), in examining the effect of overt verbalization on the performance of CPM, it was observed that improved performance with verbalization was also associated with systematic changes in visual scanning reflected in the eye movement patterns of the subjects. Although eye movement may not be considered as the sole index of search and planning, this study provides objective evidence of the effect of verbalization on search performance. The second study involves the compensatory effects of dynamic assessment on planning disability (Cormier et al., 1990). In this study, poor planners were found to show relatively higher positive gain on the reasoning by analogy items of the CPM than good planners.

The present research employs a variant of the Carlson and Wiedl verbalization procedure. The children in the verbalization condition were asked to verbalize the strategies they were going to use and were probed to explain why they planned to use those strategies. No attempt was made to give any feedback (e.g., "That's right, because ...." or "Next time, remember to use the same strategy if it worked."). The present research is different from the previous work by Carlson and his colleagues in as much as it examines the effect of verbalization on the performance of a planning task, rather than on g-loaded measures of mental ability. The best reference for g-loaded measures is Jensen (1998). An example of measure with high correlation with general intelligence or 'g' is Raven's Progressive Matrices. This test is used for nonverbal intelligence. It requires abstract reasoning (Jensen). However, it is a test of simultaneous processing as well (Das, Naglieri, & Kirby, 1994). The procedure for the first experiment is briefly mentioned here in order to facilitate understanding of the results and conclusions.

Experiment 1

Experiment 1 was conducted in two parts. In the first part, each subject was required to detect the target (by pointing out if it is present or by saying "not present" if the target is not found) from among the 5 numbers in each of the 50 cards. The target-present and target-absent cards were presented in a predetermined random order. A practice session with three examples of the procedure preceded the main test. Time taken by the subject to detect the target was recorded.

In part two of the experiment, subjects were randomly divided into two groups of 14 each. First group was administered the test as per the instruction and procedure in part one after a five-minute rest period during which they were engaged in conversation with the experimenter pertaining to their school activities and family. Subjects forming the second group were given an opportunity to verbalize with the following instructions in their native language, Oriya. The translated English version is: "You are already familiar with the task. I am asking you to do it again just as before. But before we start again I would like for you to tell me how you are going to proceed with searching for the target number and why you would do what you would at each step of the task. Now please tell me about it." After these instructions, the subjects verbalized for five minutes, and the experimenter probed them regarding the reasons for the strategies they said they employed. No other intervention or prompts were used. Then the subject was given 50 trials, one for each card with the same procedure of administration followed for first part of the experiment.

Strategy verbalization improved number-finding performance for the target-present series of numbers. The more competent group did not improve as much as the less competent group, regardless of verbalization.

Experiment 2

The validity of the findings from Experiment 1 was tested in a subsequent study, Experiment 2, by first identifying and classifying subjects for planning competence on a different planning task and then assessing their performance in the number-finding task with and without verbalization. Thus, good and poor planners identified by a different task were tested on the number-finding task. It was expected that the results would provide a more rigorous confirmation of the interaction between levels of planning competence and verbalization.

The results of Experiment 2 may be summarized as follows: (a) When the subjects were classified as high and low planners, high planners displayed a significantly faster rate of search in number-finding performance for both the target-present and target-absent trials; (b) Although rate of search improved as a result of verbalization for both groups, the high planners did not improve as much as the low planners; and (c) Rate of search for target-present trials decreased systematically for each serial position as a result of verbalization.

Discussion

The results of the two experiments provide further evidence for the facilitative effects of verbalization on cognitive performance corroborating and extending research by Carlson and his colleagues. While the previous work done by Carlson has shown performance improvement in nonverbal intelligence tests (Raven's matrices, Cattell's Culture Fair Test), the present research has demonstrated the efficacy of verbalization for improving performance on a search task primarily involving planning skills.

The findings in the present study are in accord with the well-known writings of Luria (1966, 1973a) and Vygotsky (1962) on the intimate participation of speech processes in the execution of plans and the role of expressive speech in the development of thought and problem solving. Verbalization helps the subjects to recognize and identify the existence of the different facets of the problem, simultaneous–successive processing as well as planning, and directs the subject's attention selectively to the properties of information. Further, it builds up expectancy and makes him or her anticipate the constraints inherent in task solution (Luria, 1966, 1973a). It also develops conscious awareness of the problem in the subject, which in turn serves to facilitate internal communication through self-instruction (Vygotsky, 1962). It is important to distinguish verbalization as social speech and thinking as inner speech, as Vygotsky did quite clearly. Ericsson and Simon (1998) discuss at length the difference between the implicit (inner speech) that characterizes thinking and verbalization (social speech), and delineate the conditions in which "verbalization of thinking can be made without reactive effects, and other circumstances where verbal descriptions and explanations of thinking serve as a tool that potentially enables changes in consciousness"(p. 178). Ericsson and Simon show when covert thinking can be externalized under certain conditions without altering it.

Our results demonstrate the compensatory effects of verbalization for poor planners, substantiating the hypothesis that the function of verbalization is to aid in the formulation of a plan. For one who does not have a plan, verbalization helps him/her generate one. This is indicated by the fact that the performance of competent planners did not improve as much as that of the less competent group. Thus, as Cormier et al. (1990) have noted,

> When performance deficiencies are related to poor planning, overt verbalization seems to be effective by making elements of planning explicit and guiding problem solving activity. In this sense, overt verbalization acts as a necessary prosthesis for poor planners making the problem solver aware of the demands of the task and of how he or she intends to approach the problem. (p. 447)

Overt verbalization also seems to prevent quick deterioration of detailed visual information (Klimesch, 1980).

Considering both Experiments 1 and 2, the findings again imply that overt verbalization aids the formulation of a scheme of action that can augment the planning process involved in the solution of a task, specifically when a planning deficiency is present. Performance deficiency, whether interpreted as a "production anomaly" or "production deficiency," may be considered as a result of strategy deficiency (Belmont & Mitchell, 1987).

To sum up, we have presented a framework for understanding verbalization and a series of experiments by our group that utilize verbalization in order to augment planning. The conceptual framework draws strength from seminal ideas of Vygotsky and Luria in regard to the role of inner speech and overt articulation in regulation of cognitive performance. A continuation of these classical concepts is seen in the distinction between implicit and explicit metacognition (Frith & Frith, 2012). Verbalization is obviously "explicit," but it may help or hinder thinking depending on certain conditions; we have mentioned this by referring to the influential work of Ericsson and Simon, but did not elaborate it. Rather we reported our experiments that show that verbalization benefits the performance of individuals only when they are relatively poor in planning strategies for problem solving. The next two chapters continue this line of thinking, first as applied to learning mathematics, and next in programs for enhancement of reading and comprehension. However, we remind ourselves that much of metacognition may be implicit, that is, not verbalized or articulated. Our job is to provide tasks and problems that will shape the development of an individual's own strategies for solving them. The learning situation should be interactive, but avoid direct instruction. The two intervention programs in the last chapter, PREP and COGENT (Das, 2009), attempt to do this; the outcome following intervention is positive presumably because the intervention did enhance the cognitive foundations of reading. We present some evidence in support.

13

Math Learning

Facilitation of Planning: Helping Children Do Mathematics

In order to approach the teaching of mathematics within the framework of Planning, there are some questions we must first ask. What cognitive processes are involved in mathematics? Can the benefits of verbalization be extended to teaching mathematics? What evidence is there to support this extension? We will attempt to answer these in the following sections.

The scope of the chapter is broader than the application of verbalization or self-talk as an aid to enhance self-reflection and promote planful behavior. Helping children to do mathematics is the general objective.

We begin then with considering math competence—what does it include? Then pass on to discuss Math Foundations that comprise the major concepts, processes, and skills that children require for learning to do math.

Finally, we devote a large part of the chapter to cognitive training to succeed in math. Included in this are, first and foremost, verbalization and self-talk; we pick up the theme of the previous chapter. The studies on planning facilitation through the verbalization technique that we discuss, however, were limited to math operations consisting of additions, multiplications, and so on. We broaden the scope to include proposals for math improvement that is specifically directed at five major concepts that are essentials for math, and specific training modules for promoting each.

Since the details cannot be accommodated within the space of this chapter, we refer then to a whole math improvement manual that has been constructed for which the present chapter serves as an introduction.

We must acknowledge at the outset the limited focus of the discussion of math cognition—which is Planning and its associated cognitive processes. We do not attempt to discuss brain localization of math abilities, tempting though it is after reading the inspiring book by Dehaene (1997), *The Number Sense*, where he explains how the very structure of our brain makes it easier to "digest" certain arithmetic concepts than others. Neither do we discuss *The Mathematical Brain* (Butterworth, 1998), a notable book whose central concept is the Number Module. The book presents a persuasive proposal on cognitive aspects of math and its basis on brain—math connection. Both books offer an extensive treatment of math cognition. We recommend instead Campbell (2005) for a recent sampler of math cognition research.

We have discussed in this chapter the cognitive foundations of math concepts, but not the specifics of measurement systems that give meaning to basic math procedures. An excellent treatment of how children should be helped to develop an understanding of simple arithmetic procedures and representation of rational numbers is found in *Children Doing Mathematics* (Nunes & Bryant, 1996). We are sympathetic to their idea that cultural tools are transmitted through formal instruction, a Vygotsky idea. To be numerate, children need to learn conventional systems. Nunes and Bryant discuss the development of math concepts from preschool through schooling, stressing the importance of building upon children's knowledge before they receive formal instruction. It is not enough to know the measurement procedures, but also to use them appropriately.

> One of the complaints of mathematics teachers is that pupils often do not know which mathematical technique to use in a new situation ... A college student may calculate the mean when the median would have been a better option. (Nunes & Bryant, 1996, p.17)

All of us who have tried our hand in helping our children and grandchildren with math have experienced how frustrating it is not to be able to use procedures out of the context that were provided by the teacher.

"No, grandpa, that's not the way *my* teacher told me how to do this."

"Tell me if in this problem, I should use subtraction or division, then I can do it."

Examples like the above illustrate the narrowness of math learning procedures without understanding.

We close this introduction to the chapter with the following quote:

> If mathematical problem-solving is always used in the class room, as a way of practicing a procedure just taught by the teacher, the social definition of mathematics becomes the use of school-taught routines. (Nunes & Bryant, 1996, p. 247)

Math Competence

Higher level math achievement requires multiple cognitive processes, including quantitative knowledge, quantitative reasoning, short-term and working memory, visual processing, and processing speed (Flanagan, Oritz, Alfonzo,

& Mascolo, 2002). Research suggests that since a multidimensional set of traits contributes to the effects of having a math disorder, tools or measures used to predict the future development of math proficiency and its disorder must also be multidimensional. The PASS theory appears to be quite useful as a tool in aiding the development of both assessment and remediation procedures that use a multidimensional approach. In fact, it is reasonable to conclude that all four PASS processes are essentially involved in math learning. Executive functions (EFs) comprising shifting and inhibition of prepotent responses as unique processes are closely connected with math operations. Problem solving in math, especially word problems, involves simultaneous processing. However, successive processing, closely associated with working memory, is obviously engaged in math problems as well (see Das, Naglieri, & Kirby, 1994).

To refresh the connection of PASS to math learning, consider the following: *planning,* including *EFs,* is responsible for controlling and organizing behavior, selecting and constructing strategies, and monitoring performance. For examples from math, consider *carry over in division, adding number of zeros to 98 when asked to multiply it by 100 or 1,000*; these require planning.

The second is the Attention process. Attention maintains arousal levels and alertness, and ensures focus on relevant stimuli. When the teacher is explaining something for too long, the child may find it boring and slip in to a state of low arousal (dosing), whereas a dynamic teacher keeps the whole class excited. Teaching is a song and a dance, as a successful teacher of a large class will tell us. Attention also comprises reception and selection. Especially important is its use for inhibition of habitual responses as in the Stroop test. Often this test is singled out as a defining exercise of executive attention.

The next two processes are ways in which we process information, sort it into groups and patterns, or into sequences—*Simultaneous and Successive processing* transform and retain information. Simultaneous processing is engaged when the relationship between different parts of a math problem need to be grouped and understood.

A 10-year-old boy's father is four times as old as he; how old is the father?

Examples of simultaneous processing also include recognizing figures, such as *a triangle within a circle versus a circle within a triangle*, or *understanding the difference between "he had $10 cash before he went shopping," and "after he went shopping he had $10." How much cash did he spend?*

Successive processing is required for organizing separate items in a sequence, such as remembering a sequence of numbers, words, or actions exactly in the order in which they had just been presented.

A friend tells you the phone number, or the sequence in which you press the numbers to open the locker.

Your teacher shows you a series of seven digits between 1 and 9 for only seconds, and asks if the year of my birth was in it (6519872); I was born in 1987.

The students have to use sequencing and review the sequence in their mind.

The PASS theory is supported by the workings of the brain (Luria, 1966, 1973a), and by studies in cognitive psychology (Das et al.,1994).

A Figure for Representing Math Competence

Figure 13.1 outlines the components of math proficiency modules. It shows the familiar division of math proficiency into computing and word problems. Planning/Executive Functioning is the predominant cognitive

Figure 13.1:
Math proficiency model

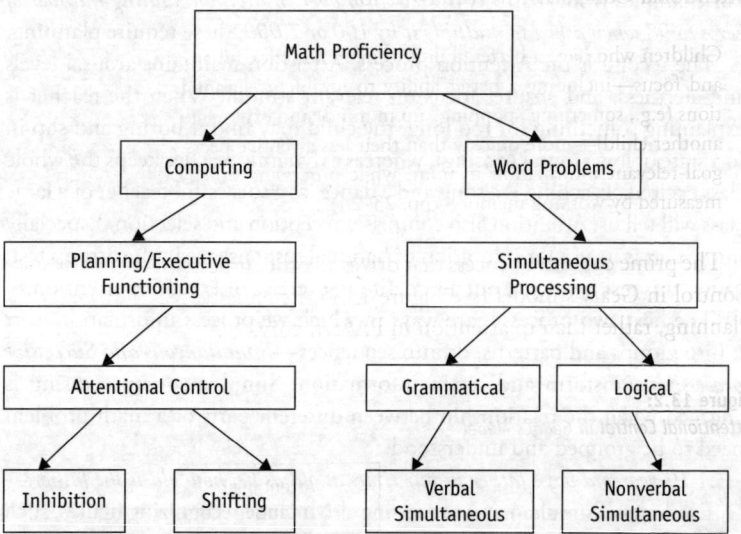

Note: The figure outlines the components of math proficiency, which is the collective aim of *Modules for Math*. It shows the familiar division of Math Proficiency into computing and word problems. Planning/Executive Functioning (EF) is the predominant cognitive process for Computing. Similarly, simultaneous processing is required for comprehension of word problems. Attentional control (Geary, 2013), we propose, is subsumed in Planning/EF, whereas simultaneous processing comprises logical–grammatical relations (following Luria, in PASS theory). The last level highlights the two components of EF, Inhibition and Shifting. For word problems, logical and grammatical divisions are to be measured by non-verbal (matrices-type tests), and verbal–simultaneous tests.

process for computations. Similarly, simultaneous processing is required for comprehension of word problems. Attentional control (Geary, 2013), we propose, is subsumed in Planning/EF. Simultaneous processing comprises logical–grammatical relations (following Luria in PASS theory). The last level highlights the two components of EF—Inhibition and Shifting. For word problems, logical and grammatical divisions are to be measured by nonverbal (matrices-type tests) and verbal simultaneous tests. Not shown as a core component is working memory; its inclusion in EF is contentious, and it can also be included in Successive processing.

More about EF and Modeling Cognition in Math

Research suggests that EF/Planning is the most important, if not the sole requirement, for learning math. Geary (2013) sums up the role of EF as Attentional Control; he explains it as follows:

> Children who have a better ability to maintain effortful attentional control and focus—including a better ability to inhibit irrelevant internal distractions (e.g., something "popping" up in mind) and external distractions (e.g., another child)—more quickly than their less attentive peers ... to maintain goal-relevant information in mind while processing other information, as measured by working memory. (pp. 23–24)

The prime cognitive process that drives all other processing is Attentional Control in Geary's model (see Figure 13.2). Essentially, it is equivalent to Planning, rather than to attention in PASS theory.

Figure 13.2:
Attentional Control in Geary's Model

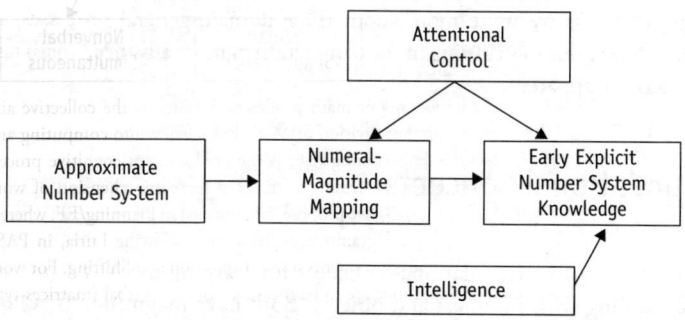

Geary's model proposes the elements that are active in the beginning of children's mathematical learning. The initial step toward learning mathematics may be based on an intuitive sense of the approximate magnitude of collections of items. The first abstract mathematical symbols that children learn are number words and Arabic numerals, which in turn acquire meaning when mapped onto this number sense. The critical next step is an explicit understanding of the relations among numerals (Geary, 2013, p. 24).

The three core elements have been discussed further in several sections of this chapter beginning with strategies and processes fundamental to math. Importantly, also as modules for improvement and cognitive training in acquiring math skills that we propose in the final section of this chapter.

Intelligence is not discussed because even Geary has sidelined its inclusion. We need to devote much more space to the unique contribution to the math proficiency model or its role in Geary's model.

Math Foundations: Strategies and Processes

Processing strategies are obviously important for competent performance in both reading and math. Specific strategies for math undergo changes as the material demands flexibility. A shift occurs from counting with fingers to conceptualizing basic operations in mental arithmetic, showing a sign of maturity in the child who is learning math. Similarly, strategies for estimating an answer in long addition, subtraction, multiplication, and division—which are used when the answer cannot be accurately given (Siegler & Booth, 2004)—may appear to be specific for math. However, both coping with reading short and long words and comprehending the meaning of a word from its context involve processes shared with math. Change in strategies or flexibility in strategy use is a central requirement of Planning. Good planning is almost synonymous with flexibility, lack of rigidity, heeding feedback, and correcting one's approach to solution. As we write more about these domain-general processes, the overarching value of Planning in the completion of more advanced math tasks will become apparent.

Foundational Concepts

What are the two foundational concepts for learning math? Let us consider dealing with numbers and objects. Both have magnitude (size) and value. Even an infant can make out a large object from a small object. At a slightly higher stage of development, children can arrange three to four objects from big to small or differentiate a densely distributed field of dots from a sparsely distributed field. At that stage, the concept of more and less may not have been clearly developed. For example, if five candies are arranged in a long row and five in a short row, and a child is asked to choose which one has more candies, he or she will choose the longer row because "longer is more." Size and weight are similarly confounded—the bigger, the heavier. Piaget's conservation tests for mass and volume are good devices for teaching the disconnection between size and volume, length, and numerosity. Seriation is a basic math requirement; however, is it simultaneous? Is it successive? Early research has shown that conservation and other concrete operation tasks are essentially examples of simultaneous processing (Das et al., 1994).

How to Help the Development of Math Abilities?

We will begin by presenting some theoretical assumptions. Learning math is concerned with the two basic concepts—magnitude or size, and value. Math also demands two processes; one is the *procedure*, which is a step-by-step thinking out of an arithmetic problem (divide 26 by 3), and the other is *conceptualizing or comprehending* the problem. We will explain each one in the following section. Besides the basics of magnitude and value, and the two processes that help math, WM is a major cognitive process that is essential for math/arithmetic. Those who are weak in WM need to be assisted. One of the procedures for boosting WM is to reduce the to-be-remembered material into smaller bits (chunks) and then remember them. The other procedure is to lighten the burden on WM by using notes or noting down the calculations as children proceed step by step when solving a division or multiplication equation (e.g., carry over).

More on Magnitude, Value, Procedure, and Conceptualization

Magnitude is size, bulk, and quantity. We express magnitude comparatively by terms such as big, medium, little, large, and small. Each of these words indicates magnitude: A big object is larger than a small object. Even an infant has a sense of magnitude, knowing that a big object can hide a small one behind it. If this is not a modular concept present at birth, there is at least a blueprint that exists to start with that is fed by experience.

A word about "magnitude" and "size": Sometimes it is easy to confuse them—magnitude refers to large or small, so does size. However in mathematics, magnitude is commonly represented by the value of a number—8 is greater than 3. Another way to represent magnitude is the distance between two digits on a number line. For example, it is easier to say that 8 > 3 than 6 > 4. Kadosh et al. (2008) clearly describe these differences as follows:

> A numerical distance effect ... it is easier to compare numbers that are quantitatively farther away from each other than numbers that are quantitatively closer to each other (e.g., people respond faster to the largest number when viewing 8 and 2, compared to when they are presented with the numbers 4 and 2). Another typical effect found when comparing numerical magnitude is the size effect, that is, comparison between numbers becomes increasingly difficult the larger the numbers are, even when the distance between them is kept constant (e.g., comparing 8 and 9 is more difficult than comparing 2 and 3). (p.133)

There is another sense in which "size" or "magnitude" is used—it is *non-numerical magnitude* (Kadosh et al., 2008). We can give the example of font size. The digit can be written in a larger font size irrespective of its value. For example, 8 can be written in a smaller font than 3; the participant may be asked to respond to the font size. The required response is "small" for 8 and "large" for 3. We have used magnitude essentially to mean non-numerical and value as a numerical representation.

Value refers to the numeric value of a number: The size of the font of a number does not necessarily correspond with its value. A number may be of the same font size as another (29 and 45), but one of them is of smaller value than the other. Value is a concept that has to be learned.

Two examples are given at the end of this chapter, each corresponding to one of two types of sub-tests, congruent and incongruent in regard to Size and Value ... incongruent task in which a relatively smaller font size was used for large value numbers where as in the congruent condition, a big font size is used large value numbers. In the other condition, a big font size is congruent when its value is also large.

The difference between magnitude and value is analogous to the distinction between speaking and reading. While speaking occurs naturally and a blueprint for it perhaps exists in human brains, reading has to be learned because reading is acquired. The question then is asked: In tracing the difficulty of a child who is beginning to do math, should we first suspect that the difficulty is related to learning value and not magnitude? Perhaps this is so.

The other aspect of math learning is related to procedure and conceptualization of the problem. Within the step-by-step procedure for working out a math problem, memory is obviously important, along with the logical sequence of the calculation. Both help the individual to plan a course of action and guide his or her actions. Planning processes, including strategies, may be as important as knowledge of the procedure and memory.

Let us reflect a bit on memory of which there are several kinds—procedural–declarative, short term–long term, episodic–semantic, and explicit–implicit. Can this kind of memory be named as procedural memory? It is tempting to name it as such in that memory of procedure is procedural memory. However, procedures have to be learnt and overlearned. They have to go through deliberation and thought many times to become automatic. Thus, the memory required in mathematical procedures passes through an explicit learning stage to become implicit, therefore, not requiring conscious effort.

We suggest that short-term memory (STM) and long-term memory (LTM) are required for successful working out of a step-by-step procedure. For example, while doing division (e.g., 26 divided by 3), the procedure involves both kinds of memory: I can keep in STM 26–24 = 2, and try to divide 2 by 3. I also use my long-term rote memory when multiplying 3 with 8 (multiplication table). The problem remains in regard to how we detect where the individual child's difficulties may lie within the operation of the procedure. Is it in STM? Is STM unusually short for his/her age? If this is the case, smaller chunks can be recommended, breaking the steps down to fit the individual's capacity. Or is it in rote memory, such as multiplication tables or in basic facts, which should have been accessed without effort as fast and automatic procedures (e.g., adding/subtracting simple one-digit numbers)? The latter is probably true given that in India and other Asian countries, generally, children have better numerical skills in early grades (Siegler, 2008). Some empirical evidence in regard to strategies and processes is discussed later in this chapter.

Recent researchers tend to not only view problem solving (conceptual) as separate from procedural operation, but also regard the two to have distinct locations in the cortex (i.e., parietal–occipital and frontal–temporal respectively). When active planning is demanded in step-by-step operations rather than accessing or reaching into LTM, then of course the frontal lobes must be involved. The above discussions should guide the teacher and the clinician in diagnosing math difficulty and in formulating a remediation program.

Math Disability: Difficulties with Magnitude, Value, Procedure, and Estimation

We now have a fairly good idea of the importance of the first three elements in programs for helping children to learn math. The fourth is *estimation*; last, but not any less important than the other three. Good teaching of math, some say, should begin with teaching children not the exact answer to a simple math question, but with teaching how to estimate the nearest approximation to the correct answer. You may ask a child in Grade 2: If we add 69 to 79, would the total be more like 89 or more like 100? Estimations can be begun even earlier in kindergarten classes: Between a car, a bus, and a train, which is the longest? Or if you put two cars end to end, would it be longer than a train? Estimates like this are useful in that, unlike the aforementioned example of addition, they do not really require number concepts and, therefore, can be used with younger children.

How we estimate is linked to the PASS process, especially to Planning.

Number Line Helps Estimation

Siegler (1988) has made a life-long study of how children learn mathematics and asked the question: What develops in development? In the development of math learning, for example, a sense of estimation develops. It is linked to an internal representation; a handy tool for this is the number line. American schools teach using a number line; if a number is to the left of a number on the number line, it is less than the other number. If it is to the right, then it is greater than that number. Siegler found that young children from kindergarten to Grade 2 could use a number line from 0 to 100. Numbers closer to the starting point of zero are estimated better than those closer to 100. For children in this age range, the distance between two or three big numbers closer to 100 is estimated to be shorter on the number line, whereas between smaller numbers, estimation is more accurate. The same inaccurate estimation is not seen for older children for numbers between 0 and 100. However, when the number line stretches to 1,000, the older children pass through the same stage of estimating distances between numbers; the numbers much farther than 0, nearer to 1,000, are estimated to have a shorter distance than numbers between 0 and 100.

Developing Automaticity

Why do some children do simple addition and multiplication equations faster than others in the same class? A major reason is how familiar the children are with numbers—the faster students can recognize the numbers almost automatically, without any effort. The same way that fast readers begin to recognize and say letters of the alphabet earlier than slow readers, familiarity with numbers helps children in their estimation—how early a word or number was learnt and used speeds up naming time for words or numbers no matter how long these may be, and how difficult it might be to read them. For example, your seven-digit telephone number is far more easily recognized than any other string of seven numbers.

Research contributions made in the mid-1980s by psychologists, such as Siegler, who were interested in children's mathematics performance, have helped to give direction to subsequent research. Siegler and his associates (Siegler, 1988; Siegler & Booth, 2004; Siegler & Opfer, 2003) have developed a model to explain one difference between students that are high math achievers and those who are low achievers. They suggested that the *strategies* that students use to answer arithmetic problems were responsible for part of the success or failure that resulted from their use. The level of understanding a child has relating to the type of math question asked determines the strategy that he or she will choose to assist in its solution. Consider addition for example. There are four general types of strategies used by children when solving basic addition problems: visibly counting fingers, representing numbers with fingers and adding without visibly counting, verbal counting, and finally retrieval of an answer from LTM. Further, research on estimation by Siegler and Booth (2004) has explored this problem.

PASS Theory's Explanation of Math Improvement through Planning: Selected Studies by Naglieri and Colleagues—Planning Facilitation and Math

How to facilitate the use of planning in math computations connects to verbalization in the previous chapter. Naglieri and colleagues (Iseman & Naglieri, 2011; Naglieri, & Gottling, 1997; Naglieri & Johnson, 2000) have extended the application of verbalization and self-reflection in a series of research studies; these provide reliable evidence (we think they do) in favor of self-talk or verbalization. The tasks are examples of schoolwork, of arithmetic operations requiring multiplication, additions, etc. The method of inserting verbalization as an intervention in between two halves of the same task followed the same principle as Carlson, Das, and colleagues had previously used (see previous chapter). However, studies by Naglieri and colleagues are important at least in two ways: First, the results showed that only those students who were relatively weak in planning as measured by the Das–Naglieri Cognitive Assessment System benefitted from verbalization; the control group who was not significantly weak in Planning scores average showed little or no improvement following intervention. Second, at least in one study on ADHD students, not only was the expected improvement demonstrated, it persisted even after a year. Additionally, the weak planning group improved in CAS scores on Planning.

The procedure for verbalization and the main findings of the ADHD studies are briefly reported below.

Each training session comprised a 10-minute math worksheet, a 10-minute planning facilitation described later, and a 10-minute math worksheet in order to check improvement in performance.

The 10-minute group discussions, known as planning facilitation, during the intervention phase were designed to encourage self-reflection.

To achieve the general goal of improved use of planning and self-reflection, teachers encouraged the children to verbalize the methods they used and be self-evaluative.

Teachers did not focus on specific mistakes of the student in the worksheet; this was in keeping with the general principle of facilitating guided discovery of strategies that the student had adopted and verbalized.

The following probes are illustrative of those used:

1. Can anyone tell me anything about these problems?
2. Let us talk about how you did the worksheet. What was same or different about the problems?
3. What could you do to make this seem easier?
4. Why did you do it that way?
5. How did you do the problems?
6. What could you have done to get more correct?
7. What did it teach you?
8. What will you do next time?

Summarizing the general findings of the studies by Naglieri and colleagues, the authors showed that there were differential effects of instruction designed to facilitate planful behavior, and that these effects were related to the Planning scores earned by the participants.

Especially, the efficacy of the planning facilitation method in those reports involving children with ADHD is particularly important (Iseman & Naglieri, 2011). These children, in general, are found to have planning deficit (see Barkley, 2006), and the facilitation procedure improved their performance in arithmetic as well as increased their Planning score (see Chapter 5 for background of ADHD).

We suggest verbalization as a mediating procedure that not only enhances local operations such as multiplication and division, but also facilitates transfer of the effect of training to improvements in basic math skills such as the recognition of differences between magnitude and value, number line, and between numerosity and WM.

MLD and Cognitive Processes: Further Elaboration of the Relationship

Mathematical Learning Difficulties (MLD) is still a relatively new area of research. Its cognitive correlates are not adequately identified. However, some conclusive evidence has emerged: (1) WM and STM have a causal influence on math competence and MLD. Planning strategies are selected and used both for solving word problems and for calculations that proceed step by step; boosting the use of such strategies is the objective of the "planning facilitation" procedure. Fluency or speed in calculations and knowledge of facts required for specific math operations, such as multiplication are a prerequisite for math learning, and a certain amount of automaticity in simple computations is a basic requirement. All of the aforementioned statements are reinforced in older studies as well as in recent ones, as evident in Mabbott and Bisanz (2008).

The cognitive correlates beyond STM and WM have not been identified adequately, as we stated before. The WM tasks used can be viewed in the context of PASS—some of them, like the Daneman–Carpenter's span task adapted for MLD (Mabbot & Bisanz, 2008), may actually have components of both Successive processing and Simultaneous processing. The other popular test of WM is Backward Digit Span. This test requires Simultaneous

Figure 13.3:
Basic math skills

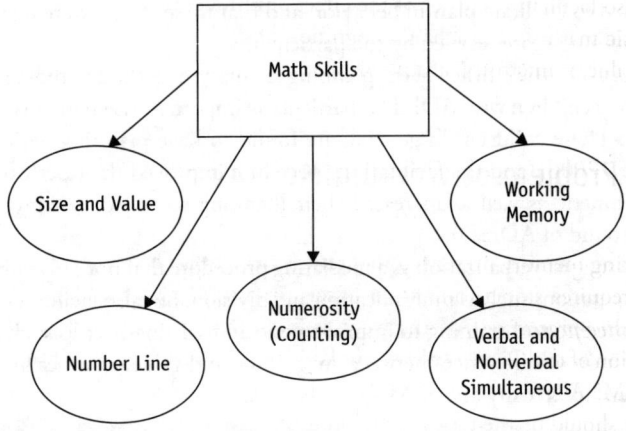

Note: This figure addresses *Math Skills* that are learned in beginning math. We have selected *five skills* that are most frequently mentioned in current literature and academia. They are presented in this figure in preparation for the specific modules that target and seek to improve different mathematical skills.

processing as reported in the book by Das, Kirby, and Jarman (1979). Step-by-step calculations use Planning (Das et al., 1994).

The discussion suggests us to include memory components such as STM, span memory (like Daneman–Carpenter) grouped within the conceptual framework of WM among skills that are essential for math learning.

A composite diagram of math skills is presented in Figure 13.3.

EF/Planning and Working Memory: A Special Note

Success in math learning relies on the ability to solve problems involving words and numbers. Comprehension of the given problem and selecting procedures for working out the solution step by step, as discussed before, are essential for math. Planning/EF, simultaneous processing, and WM have a central role in math performance. Previous chapters in this book, especially the first five chapters, discuss these domain-general processes at some length. In an earlier section, we have also presented verbalization as a technique for organizing strategies for multiplications. We suggest verbalization as a mediating procedure that not only enhances local operations as multiplication, but also facilitates transfer of the effect of training to global improvements in basic math skills, such as recognition of differences between magnitude and value, numerosity, and WM.

The Problem of Working Memory Enhancement

Working memory presents a theoretical challenge—Is it memory for order that requires storage and, to a lesser extent, "processing" represented by *Successive processing*? Alternatively, is it controlled processing, viewed as a function of the *Central executive* in Baddeley and Hitch's overarching model of WM? Alternatively, is *attention* the critical variable that defines WM? What should be the target of training?

Given that WM involves two activities that must be carried out simultaneously—storage and processing of information—it is tough to do both, especially, when we are asked to work the problem in our head that is required in mental arithmetic. A recent interpretation of how we may do it proposes that since processing and storage compete for attention, and attention is a limited resource, we cannot really attend to two things at the same time. We are obliged to switch attention from one to the other. This is possible "through the incessant and rapid switching of attention between processing and maintenance" (Barrouillet & Camos, 2012, p. 414).

How can we then improve WM? Storage suffers if processing takes more time. Compare easier and harder tasks in math even in simple additions. Ask 8-year-old children to add 1 to three numbers, and compare them with 11-year-olds in a study on WM. As we expect, older children will do better in recalling the numbers than younger ones because they can add faster, and, hence, would have more time for storage.

However, suppose we already have research to show that the speed of solving this problem becomes equal if the 11-year-olds are asked to add 2; their speed of processing is then the same as adding 1 for 8-year-olds (Barrouillet & Camos, 2012). What would we expect then? That recall will be equal, there being no difference between the older and the younger children.

As the aforementioned study reports, this indeed was confirmed.

Lesson learned: Allow more processing time as the task gets harder, then WM will not suffer.

A Manual for Cognitive Training

Cognitive training, such as in PREP and COGENT, has been shown to be effective for reading (Das, 2009). We focus now on enhancement of math performance in this additional part. The Manual comprises specific modules related to basic skills required in math, such as *Number Line,* Differentiating *Size of numbers and Value, Visual search, Selective attention* as in Stroop-like training tasks, *numerosity (counting), Simultaneous verbal and nonverbal reasoning,* and WM.

In constructing several modules for EF enhancement, we used the adaptations of tests that were presented in Chapter 6. Additionally, modules for Simultaneous processing were made of common components of tests that assess the generic process adapted specifically for arithmetic problems and appreciation of geometry.

The manual presents some 50 activities for the five modules for enhancement of each of the corresponding five basic skills.

It is available as supplementary material. In conclusion of the chapter, a diagram for the five modules is presented in Figure 13.4.

Figure 13.4:
The five modules

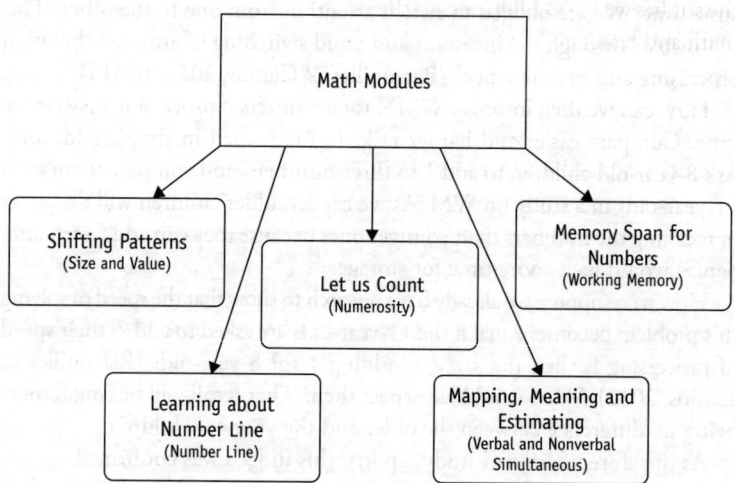

Note: This figure highlights the titles of the different modules within this manual. Each module's objective is one of the Math Skills from the previous figure. These objectives are directly beneath each module title, in brackets.

Conclusions: Helping Children Do Mathematics

This chapter has a general implication for the importance of children learning mathematics in addition to discussion of the theory and research.

Interactive assessment and cognitive intervention are constructive ways for enhancement of Planning and EF. We have shown how a dynamic approach targets the cognitive processing of the individual learner, as well as the construction of both test material and testing situation. Since processing is not like a muscle that develops through practice, how do the activities in the modules in the intervention program, such as Math Booster, get transferred to *strategies* for learning mathematics?

We suggest that the key to transfer consists of at least two mechanisms: verbalization and self-talk while learning, and exposure to different kinds of activities within a specific area of skill such as Size/Value discrimination, Number line, and WM.

Planning/EF and Simultaneous processing are suggested to be the major processes for learning math, with WM as a subset of attentional control. However, we need more empirical studies to reinforce the aforesaid observation. The efficacy of an interactive approach that promotes guided discovery is shown in test performance of students to do math, and in helping children to learn reading (as presented in the next chapter); this is the major focus of the studies we have conducted on the two important school-related subjects, math and reading.

14

Two Programs for Cognitive Strategy Training

Is verbalization the only procedure for enhancement of cognitive strategies? Although verbalization has been shown to be an effective procedure in the two preceding chapters, obviously it is not the only one.

First, we repeat that "much of metacognition may be implicit, that is, not verbalized or articulated. Our job is to provide tasks and problems that will shape the development of an individual's own strategies for solving them" (Frith & Frith, 2012).

We present two intervention programs in this chapter: PASS Remedial Program (PREP) for reading and Cognition Enhancement Training (COGENT) for getting ready for learning in school (Das, 2009). The programs, described next, have been used in several experimental and clinical studies, and have proved to be effective. Our aim in this chapter is to discuss the essential features of the tasks that are derived from the theoretical base, PASS, and especially from Vygotsky and Luria, as discussed in Chapter 12. An important feature common to both Verbalization—PREP and COGENT—is the use of an interactive or dynamic approach that facilitates reflective discussion.

Cognitive Enhancement and Training Programs: PREP and COGENT

There are several resources for applying the PASS theory to academic remediation and instruction, which we discuss briefly. We have selected two of these programs. The first is the PREP and the second, COGENT, as developed by Das (2009). Both programs enhance strategies for cognitive planning as well as the use of Executive Functions (EFs), such as control and regulation, inhibition, and shifting strategies when necessary. Both are supported by empirical studies (e.g. Das, 2001; Das, Mishra, & Pool, 1995; Das and colleagues, 2000; Hayward, Das, & Janzen, 2007), and are summarized in *Reading Difficulties and Dyslexia: An Interpretation for Teachers* (Das, 2009). The book contains several approaches to academic interventions using PASS as the interpretive framework. Two special features of instructional methods in both programs are using an inductive method and encouraging discovery learning rather than direct instruction. We present the essential features of the programs in the rest of this chapter. To reiterate, the general framework is provided by EFs and planning.

Description of the PREP and COGENT

The PREP was developed as a cognitively based remedial program derived from the PASS theory of cognitive processing (Das, Naglieri, & Kirby, 1994). It aims at improving the processing strategies—specifically, simultaneous and successive processing—that underlie reading, while at the same time avoiding the direct teaching of word-reading skills, such as phoneme segmentation or blending. PREP is also founded on the premise that the transfer of principles is best facilitated through inductive, rather than deductive, inference (see Das, 2009, for details). The program is therefore structured so that indirectly acquired strategies are likely to be used in appropriate ways.

Both of these intervention programs are in accord with the well-known writings of Luria (1966, 1973a) and Vygotsky (1962) on the intimate participation of speech processes in the execution of plans and the use of expressive speech or verbalization in problem solving.

What does Verbalization do? As discussed in the previous chapters, it helps the participating learner to recognize and identify the existence of the different facets of a problem. Along with that, it promotes the use of cognitive strategies: simultaneous–successive processing as well as planning and directing the participant's attention selectively to information available. Further, it builds up expectancy, and makes the learner anticipate the constraints inherent in task solution (Luria, 1966, 1973a).

Finally, verbalization also helps develop conscious awareness of the problem; this in turn serves to facilitate internal communication through self-instruction (Vygotsky, 1962), in essence, preparing the grounds for discovery learning.

GUIDING DISCOVERY

Allowing the child to discover the rules with the help of a teacher or an instructor is a standard procedure in our program. If the learners cannot work out those rules by themselves, they are guided for discovery by an external agent, through the mediation of the instructor. The teacher, then, becomes a facilitator. Instruction becomes a combination of the teacher's interaction with the learner and the learner's discovery of the tactics for doing the task. Vygotsky (1978) was a great advocate of guided discovery learning, where the learner is helped through prompting, but only in accordance with his or her needs.

Eventually, through the mediation of the adult, the principles of the tasks, such as sequencing or successive processing, become internalized. So, *internalization* and *mediation* become the two central activities that help children to learn, and the two modes of thinking that the teacher tries to facilitate. Obviously, one is reminded of Feuerstein's *cognitive modifiability* and its various ramifications (Feuerstein, 1980; Lidz, 1987).

Ideally, therefore, children in a good remedial program are engaged as active learners and as reflective learners. They are engaged and think about what they are doing. *A note of caution* in regard to the procedure, best named as "guided discovery." We acknowledge that facts have to be learnt through direct instruction, which is the typical style of instruction in the classroom. However, where instruction does not appear to be effective, remediation or intervention programs such as PREP and COGENT have been shown to work better. We present a few studies in support without entering into the exhaustive debates of the past on direct instruction versus guided discovery. *We repeat, allowing the child to discover the rules with the help of a teacher or an instructor is a standard procedure in our program. If the child cannot work out these rules by himself/herself, these rules are not yet internalized. So the internalization must be facilitated for the child through the mediation of the instructor.*

Planning is still a metacognitive process in the PREP and COGENT programs as it was in the Verbalization procedure in Chapter 12. Explicit and implicit metacognition as overt and internalized speech for the purpose of maintaining the goals and objectives of the task are instances of *contemplative education*. We think it is a broader approach that includes "guided discovery." Arguably, common to both is the goal to foster reflection in education, although contemplative education has an additional dimension of training in mindfulness (see the entry in Wikipedia for a quick introduction: http://en.wikipedia.org/wiki/Contemplative_education [accessed July 31, 2014]).

In the next chapter, we discuss the value of contemplation, or *reflective learning* and *metacognition* in decision making, and their connection with self-awareness and consciousness. PREP and COGENT provide an opportunity for self-awareness, and a dialogue between the teacher and the learner in addition for self-generated strategies for reading and mathematics. We suppose that the opportunity for self-awareness relieves anxiety and fear of punishment for the learners who are frustrated by difficulties they experience with reading or focusing attention. How are these programs structured, and what are the mechanisms that may enhance the learners' cognitive strategies as they go through the various tasks in the programs? What is the empirical evidence that the programs are effective?

First, we present the PREP and next the COGENT program. (See Das [2009] in the web "child learning programs" for some other details.)

Structure of the PREP Program

PREP is appropriate for poor readers in Grades 2–5 who are experiencing reading problems. Each of the 8–10 tasks in PREP involves both a cognitive processing focused-emphasis component and a curriculum-related component. The cognitive processing components, which require the application of simultaneous or successive strategies, include structured non-reading tasks.

Planning and Attention are integral parts of each of the task. Interactions between the student and the teacher, verbalization of strategies by students, and opportunities for the students to form their own strategies are included as essential parts of administering the intervention program. The PREP tasks facilitate transfer by providing the opportunity for children to develop and internalize strategies in their own way (Das et al., 1995). The curriculum-related components involve the same cognitive demands as their matched cognitive processing components. These cognitive processes have been closely linked to reading and spelling (Das et al., 1994).

Description of PREP Training Tasks

The PREP consists of four successive processing modules and four simultaneous processing modules, each involving a global and curriculum-related bridging component. The global components comprise structured nonreading tasks requiring application of successive or simultaneous strategies, while the bridging component involves the same processing and strategy used in activities linked to reading and spelling. The program provides scripted instructions for each task along with a hierarchy of scripted prompts for each global and bridging component to support and guide any child so that he/she can succeed with minimal assistance and maximal success. The first level *prompts* remain quite general, helping a student find a strategy to remember the instructions for example. The third level of prompts is much more direct; a student may be asked to watch and see how another student successfully performs the task, or the facilitator may discuss a variety of ways to successfully complete the task.

Successive Processing Tasks

Joining Shapes

Global component: Shapes (triangles, circles, squares, and hexagons) are arranged in rows on worksheets, and children must draw lines to join the shapes following a series of instructions and rules given by the facilitator.
Bridging component: Children are shown rows of letters on worksheets. Following a series of instructions and rules, children draw lines to join letters on the worksheets to make words.

Connecting Letters

Global component: Children are required to follow lines of different colors to find which letters on the left side of the page are connected to letters on the right side of the page. Each stimulus card has five letter pairs. Children write or say the letter pairs. Children repeat this procedure; however, the lines connecting letters are in black ink. At the highest level of difficulty, the stimulus cards have connecting lines in black ink and include distracter lines.
Bridging component: Stimulus cards have colored lines with letters on the left and right sides of the line and dispersed along the line to form words. Children connect the letters and say/write the word spelled by the letters.

Related Memory

Global component: Children match front and back halves of animal pictures. Each stimulus card has three front animal halves in a column; one back half is depicted on the card. Children draw a line to connect the correct front and back halves.
Bridging component: Children connect beginning and ending word parts. Beginning word parts are presented in sets of three with one word ending. Only one choice creates a real word. Children draw a line between the correct beginning and ending word parts.

Window Sequencing

Global component: Children reproduce three to six item series of colored chips shown by the facilitator and then removed from view. First, children reproduce series of different shape combinations (circles and squares), and color is held constant; next the series involve different color combinations (blue, yellow, black, and white), and shape is held constant. Finally, the series involve both color and shape variations.

2. *Bridging component:* Children are shown a series of letters that spell words (two to six letter words) shown one at a time by the facilitator. Children then reproduce the letter series they were shown.

SIMULTANEOUS PROCESSING TASKS

Tracking

Global component: Children are shown a line drawing of a village map along with a set of tracking cards, which show the road pathway to specific houses and trees in the village. Each house can be number located, while trees are letter located. Children study the tracking cards and the map to locate house numbers or tree letters.

Bridging component: There is no bridging component for this task.

Shapes and Objects

Global component: Children categorize a group of pictured common objects into one of three abstract shapes, the object most closely resembles.

Bridging component: Children read, with or without the facilitator support, a series of phrases or sentences written on stimulus cards and place the cards into one of three categories provided on written worksheets. In addition, one card in the series will not fit any category; children must also identify which card does not fit the categories.

Shape Design

Global component: Children must study a design presented for 10 seconds and reproduce the design using colored shapes. The shapes consist of large and small circles, squares, rectangles, and triangles in three different colors.

Bridging component: Children hear or read phrases that describe how to arrange two to five animals in relationships with each other. Children then complete the arrangement described in the phrase using animal pictures.

Sentence Verification

Global component: Children are shown a set of two or three scenic pictures that have similar content themes. For each picture set, there is a passage that describes only one of the pictures. Children then read the passage, with or without the facilitator support, and find the picture that best matches the passage.

Bridging component: Children view a single picture scene, and then read three to four sentences only one of which describes the picture scene. Children choose the sentence that best matches the picture.

Evidence for the PREP's Efficacy

Several studies attest to the efficacy of PREP for enhancement of reading and comprehension (Boden & Kirby, 1995; Carlson & Das,1997; Das et al., 1995; Parrila, Das, Kendrick, Papadopoulos, & Kirby, 1999).

PREP's efficacy is reported and discussed in two recent studies; we present a summary of each.

The two studies we have selected for illustration are on specially interesting populations—First Nations children in a school on the Cree nation's reserve in Canada where English is widely spoken in the community, and in the other study, the children from India in a school where English is the language of instruction, but not at home. We wish to present the efficacy of the PREP in such widely different populations (Das, Hayward, Georgiou, Janzen, & Boora, 2008) on *First Nations children*. Many of them do not have the adequately developed foundational processes. However, we show that cognitive training appears to have an advantage over direct instruction.

Effectiveness of two reading intervention programs (phonics based and the PREP) was investigated with 63 First Nations children identified as poor readers in Grades 3 and 4 in Study 1, whereas in Study 2, the efficacy of booster sessions for inductive learning or PREP was examined.

The major dependent variables in Study 1 were pretest-to-posttest changes following intervention on reading tests for word reading and pseudo-word decoding. Results of Study1 showed a significant improvement on both reading tasks following *PREP*, among children below the median in comparison with those above the median. The *phonics-based program* resulted in similar improvement in *only one* of the reading tasks—word decoding. In Study 2, the important dependent variables were word reading and word decoding, as well as passage comprehension. Results showed that PREP participants evidenced continued improvements in their reading skills following additional training in PREP, notably in comprehension.

The next study on PREP was carried out by Mahapatra, Das, Stack-Cutler, and Parrila (2011). Two groups of children, selected from two English medium schools in India, were involved. One group consisted of 15 poor readers in Grade 4 that experienced difficulty in comprehension. The other group, the comparison group, consisted of 15 normal readers in Grade 4 did not receive PREP. Performance on word reading and reading comprehension scores (Woodcock's Reading Mastery Test), and performance on tests of PASS cognitive processes were recorded pre- and post-test. Results showed a significant improvement in comprehension as well as in simultaneous processing in the treated group. Thus, PREP is effective even in children whose first language is not English. This has obvious application possibilities for all children who learn English as a second language.

COGENT

COGENT is a cognitive stimulation program that accelerates the mental development of children and the enhancement of cognition, especially linked to literacy and school learning.

The main objective of COGENT is to supplement children's literacy skills that could be acquired spontaneously at home, school, and the community. The program should benefit cognitive development of normal children as well as children with special needs. These children with special needs cover a wide range, including:

1. Children with limited exposure to literacy
2. Children with mild developmental delay
3. Children at risk for developing dyslexia and other learning difficulties

For some of these children, COGENT provides alternative routes toward the development of reading and academic skills. COGENT is based on broader developmental theories for important cognitive functions in early childhood, especially those related to language development, while using basic cognitive processes such as PASS.

Background of COGENT Modules: Regulation of Behavior through Speech

The development of speech mainly goes through two stages: first, attending to the energy value of the speech, and, secondly, to the meaning of the speech. It is the latter that is used in self-regulating the child's behavior, according to A.R. Luria. The task also allows the child to develop *internal speech*. It is obvious from the aforementioned discussion that a simple drill in phonemes or blending will not work unless these very basic developmental aspects of literacy are in place.

Instilling in the child the necessary cognitive structures of internalizing speech and orienting toward the child's inner speech lead to regulation of the child's own behavior (Luria, 1961; Vygotsky, 1962). We, therefore, designed one of the COGENT modules to do what many early literacy training programs do, that is, discrimination of phonemes, detection of rhymes, and analysis of sounds in general. These comprise the phonological coding processes that are necessary for reading acquisition (Stanovich, 1988), but there is a difference in the way we approach this. For example, the first few steps in this second task require auditory discrimination and attention, and orientation to phonemes. The phonemes are not presented for oral repetition, for example. Instead, the child is told to listen to a word that does not sound the same in a series of words, all of which involve discrimination between two phonemes contained in the two words, for example, gate and kate. The sounds "ga" and "ka" are very similar both for hearing and for speaking, as are sounds that are used in subsequent tasks—jar and char, dip and tip, tin and din, fat and pat, and finally four and pour. The design of embedding the odd sound like "kate" in a series of "gate" is taken from the basic design in orientation of response. We are not forcing the child to go through a drill. When orientation and discrimination to the relevant phoneme in the sounds gate, kate, jar, char, and so on are established, gradually the word is truncated and only the beginning sounds "ga" and "ka" are presented for discrimination.

We also wish to develop working memory in this task by giving children first two words to remember, and then three words. These words are divided into phonemically similar words, such as gate and kate or bet and vet, and phonemically dissimilar words, such as sun and book. Have we then abandoned the phonological focus of this task? No, following the development of working memory with words that rhyme or do not rhyme, the next task presents sounds without words, the sounds being similar. For example, the child is asked to say ja cha ja or ta tha ta, and so on. The procedure obviously promotes phonological awareness at the level of words, syllables, and phonemes, a core component of reading (Ziegler & Goswami, 2005).

However, in the next module entitled Funny Relatives, the training moves away from phonological aspects to focus on the use of language. The theoretical background is provided by Luria (1981), who suggested that simply naming something without formulating a thought or idea is quite artificial. Therefore, in this task the focus is on understanding sentences in the context of action. The essential nature of these actions is serial, bringing in both the importance of syntax and meaning together. Two major forms of the relationship of words in a sentence are included in this task, the syntagmatic relationship which is a function or action, and the paradigmatic relationship which is based on similarities in meaning (Das, 1999a, 1999b; Luria, 1981). Thus, we see that as early literacy researchers claim and recommend to teach comprehension, we are doing the same but in a very different way, different from simply drilling. The tasks are also highly interesting and are designed to arouse a great deal of interest in the children.

In the next module, words are analyzed into onsets and rimes (Treiman, 1985), and the task emphasizes the way in which a word may be broken apart. Here, we include the same aspects as early literacy learning, such as phonological awareness and analogies, but also globalization and short-term memory.

Finally, in Shapes, Colors, and Letters, we return to the broader issue of ecological validity of words relating to shapes, objects, colors, and the recognition of letters. The purpose is to transform a deliberate and slow recognition of shapes, objects, colors, and letters into an automatic one (Denckla & Rudel, 1979). The process of automatization ends when the recognition becomes a habit, thus releasing the cognitive resources of the child to understand the relationship between these symbols and to manipulate them for expression in speech and in writing. Automatization of letter reading occurs at the end of these training tasks, following the same procedure that was used for automatization of shapes, colors, and object naming. Rapid Automatic Naming is now routinely ensured by popular tests (e.g., Torgesen, Wagner, Comprehensive Test of Phonological Processing [CTOPP]).

It is clear then that the procedure adopted in COGENT is based on broader developmental trajectories for important cognitive functions in early childhood related to language development (Vygotsky, 1962), all the while using basic cognitive processes such as successive–simultaneous processing, and attention and planning. The learning procedure obviously reflects the recommendation that the best conditions for learning are realized when the focus is on cognition, and the motivational involvement of the child is guaranteed by structuring the task appropriately (Das, 2009).

Summary of the COGENT Modules

Module 1: Squeeze and Say

Students attend to instructions from an outside agent (i.e., a teacher or facilitator), and then internalize those instructions. The student's task is to follow an increasingly complex set of rules given by the facilitator.

Module 2: Clap and Listen

Aspects of phonological awareness and working memory are the focus of this module. The student's task is to discriminate and respond to smaller units of speech (i.e., words and syllables) presented in progressively longer and faster sequences.

Module 3: Funny Relatives

The student's task is to understand syntagmatic and then paradigmatic relationships described by the facilitator. Students demonstrate both the action and the spatial relationships expressed in each sentence and respond to questions asked by the facilitator.

Module 4: Name Game

Again, phonological awareness and working memory are the focus of this module. The student's task is to discriminate onsets and rimes.

Module 5: Shapes, Colors, and Letters

In this module, the focus is on the rapid naming of shapes, colors, objects, and letters. The student's task is to identify, and name series of shapes, colors, objects, and letters.

Evidence for the Efficacy of COGENT

Further elaboration of the COGENT program and its efficacy is provided by Das (2009). One of the studies of its efficacy is briefly described later (Hayward et al., 2007). This study is important because it suggests that COGENT and PREP were effective in samples of First Nations children. Many among those experience reading difficulties and are not ready to enter school. COGENT could show encouraging improvement in providing them with strategies for all of the basic cognitive skills as described in the five modules.

Briefly summarizing the Hayward et al. (2007) study, the research was carried out in an English medium school on First Nations Canadian children. Forty-five Grade 3 students from a reservation school in western Canada were divided into two remedial groups and a no-risk control group. One remedial group was given a COGENT program throughout the school year. The second group received COGENT for the first half of the year, followed by a pull-out cognitive-based reading enhancement program (PREP). Children were assessed for reading and some other cognitive ability at the beginning of the year, at midterm, and at the end of the school year. Results showed a significant interaction for reading measures, with students receiving classroom intervention over the school year making the greatest gains in reading. Effects of COGENT were significant improvements in word reading and comprehension measures.

Mechanisms for Cognitive Enhancement in the PREP and COGENT

When a tutor's teaching skills involve a learner-centered approach, the learners actively generate reflective comments and construct arguments. The procedure involves: (a) tutors asking questions; (b) students providing preliminary answers; (c) tutors giving positive feedback when the learners are doing the right thing or negative feedback, such as "It was a good try, but that was not exactly right"; (d) tutors prompting and engaging in scaffolding to improve students' answers or to elaborate answers; and (e) tutors estimating students' understanding of the answer.

What Is Scaffolding?

Scaffolding is defined as any guidance beyond "yes" or "no." Its essence is a dialogue between students and the teacher that actively engages the students. It is a *dialogue* going back and forth between the teacher and the learner. The type of support provided by the tutor is nondirective, for example, asking questions or making comments, such as "How will you do it?", "Try it again," and "What will you do differently?"(Brown & Campione, 1994; Campione & Brown, 1987).

Concluding Comments

The question in regard to the interactive training in contrast to direct instruction has been raised (and answered several times in different sources [see Das, 2009]). So why is it that we do not recommend direct instruction in phonemes, blending, segmentation, and even writing and spelling in PREP and COGENT?

The approach in both programs goes deep into the foundations of literacy. Rather than disseminating direct knowledge about phonemes, grammar, and vocabulary, the program builds the base of literacy. Interactions with the adult (parents, grandparents, teachers, or educational therapists) provide some fundamental elements that might be missing in home literacy, or in the community, or even in school learning. We use Vygotsky's (1962) often-cited observation that learning occurs in collaboration with others, that the source of self-awareness and control first arises externally through social interactions, and then is internalized. In this sense, one could analyze the objective of PREP and COGENT tasks. For example, in COGENT each of the five major training modules illustrates what is meant by the foundations required in literacy development.

The central purpose of both PREP and COGENT intervention programs is the same. We need to build a broad base, a pyramid of tacit learning that meets and interacts with formal learning to be successful in schools.

Appendix A: PREP

A Sample of PREP Activity: Illustration of Strategies for Cognitive Enhancement

Task: Joining shapes
Before the first session, explain the whole task. Use the Sample Item Sheet to help the students understand the task. In subsequent sessions, the explanation can be reduced once the students have become familiar with the task.

SAMPLE ITEMS

Directions
Show the Sample Item Sheet to the students and say: In this activity, you are going to join triangles, and squares to draw a pattern. There are four rules that you need to remember:

1. You must always go through a circle to join triangles and squares. (Demonstrate)
2. The line drawn must always go from left to right, as you would when you read. (Demonstrate)

3. You must remember always to continue from where you last stopped, try not to pick up your pencil. (Demonstrate)
4. Your line must go to the closest shape.

Prompting as Illustration of Scaffolding

Prompting Stage 1

After giving the instructions to the students, ask them to repeat them to make sure they understand the task. Allow the students to complete the task on their own with very minimal help. This encourages students to develop their own strategies through experience.

Direct students to the Joining Shapes—Global Worksheet in their Activity Book and say: Now follow my instructions and connect the shapes to make a pattern. Remember to follow the rules.

The facilitator says "TRIANGLE–SQUARE." When the students have finished the connection, the facilitator gives the next instruction: "SQUARE–TRIANGLE." The instructions are given one by one until the item is completed.

The students may not start working until each individual instruction has been said. (Shape names have been abbreviated to T—Triangle; S—Square; H—Hexagon on the answer keys.)

If students follow all the instructions correctly, reinforce their responses. Then ask students what strategies they used to complete the task.

If students finish all connections correctly then complete the remaining items.

If students are not able to finish all the connections correctly, go to Prompting Stage 2.

Prompting Stage 2

If the students find the task difficult in Prompting Stage I because they could not remember the instructions, suggest a way to help them remember, such as repeating the instructions to themselves. If an incorrect connection is made, review the rules with the students, and guide them to discover the rules that they did not follow.

Stop students and say: That's close, but start back here (point to the last response) and listen carefully to what I said (repeat the instruction). Allow students to correct their response.

If students are not able to make the connection, say: Do you remember the rules? Are you following the rules here? Go through the rules with students and let them correct their response.

If students finish all connections correctly, then complete the remaining items.

If students are not able to complete the item, go to Prompting Stage 3.

Prompting Stage 3

If the students have not been able to finish the task after Prompting Stage 2, using peer interaction can be effective and students can gain from cooperative learning. Ensure students learn the strategies on their own; they cannot be simply provided by the facilitator.

1. Show students the correct response. Ask the students if they can try to explain some of the strategies they used. Talk about the strategies (e.g., scanning ahead before proceeding and rehearsing the rules).
2. If students finish all connections correctly, then complete the remaining items.

Session 2 Set A—Items 5–8 (Two Instructions)

The facilitator gives two consecutive instructions at the same time, for example, by saying to the students: "TRIANGLE–SQUARE–SQUARE–SQUARE." When the students are finished with the connection, the facilitator gives the next instruction. Again, the students may not start working until sets of instructions have been said.

If a student has difficulty completing this level of the task, use Prompting Stage 1, 2, or 3 described above as needed.

Task Summary

Review the activity and discuss what strategies worked well. Ask if they liked the task. Talk about which parts were easier for the students and which were more difficult. Finally, ask how they could improve the strategies.

A page from the joining shapes task is copied as follows. Note that T—Triangle and S—Square.

Teacher/facilitator reads out "triangle to circle," but as you know it has to pass through a circle. Also look your line will move diagonally, down and up.

Joining Shapes—Global
Answer Key
Session 1—Set A

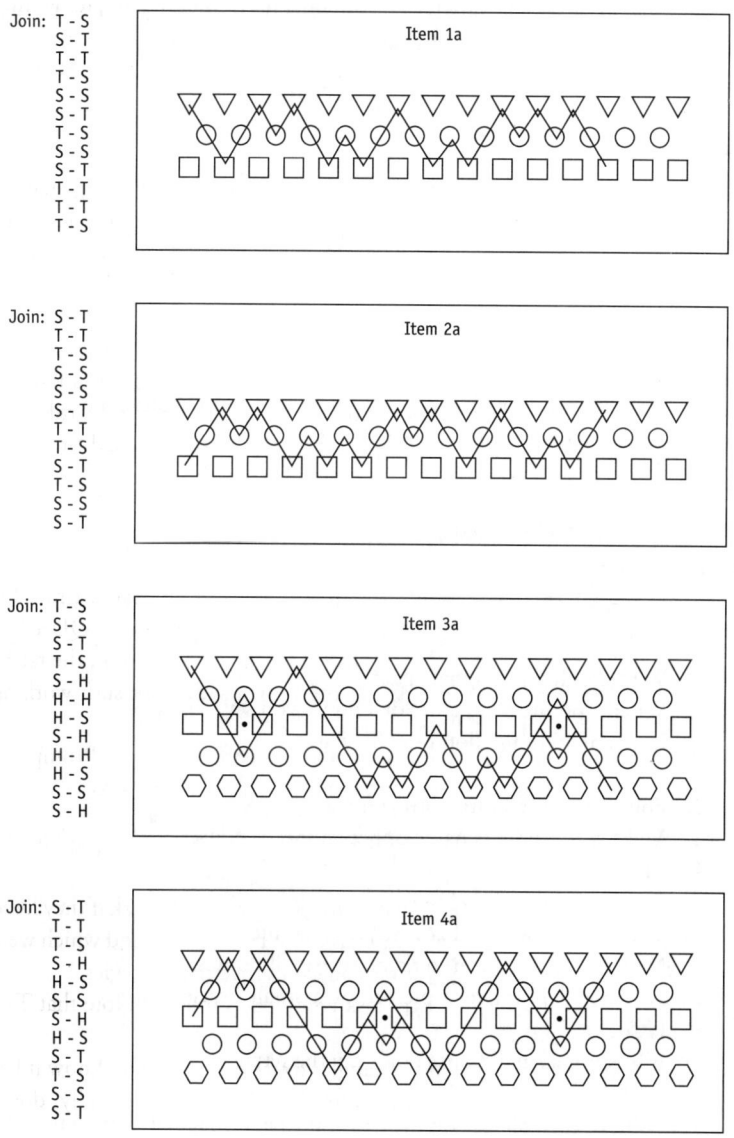

The response sheet provided to the student does not show the lines already drawn. First a sample page with a few rows is presented for practice, and then a page like the example below but without the lines is presented for the student to complete. The task becomes gradually complex by increasing the number of rows, as well as adding another shape (hexagon).

Appendix B: COGENT

Student's Workbook for Interactive Discussion Module 3 from COGENT (Note That the Task Requires Inhibition and Shifting.)

A page of pictures—small and big houses, and several other objects—is presented. A teacher/facilitator engages in the following activity with a small group of students who may be at risk for poor reading.

Activity #2
Complete as a whole class activity
Procedure:

1. Say:

    We are going to do that again.
    When I point to a picture of a house you say "HOUSE."
    If it is not a house don't say the name.

2. Point to each picture until you reach the X.
3. Make sure students name only pictures of houses.
4. Say:

    We are at an X and that means a new rule.
    Now I only want you to name the small houses.
    So when I point to a picture of a small house you say "SMALL HOUSE."
    If it is not a small house don't say the name.

5. Point to each picture on the rest of the page; make sure students only name small houses.

6. Instructor to say:

   We are going to do that again.
   Remember the first rule.
   Try to remember the two rules all by yourselves.

7. Discuss with students whether they found it easier or harder to name only the "small houses" and why.

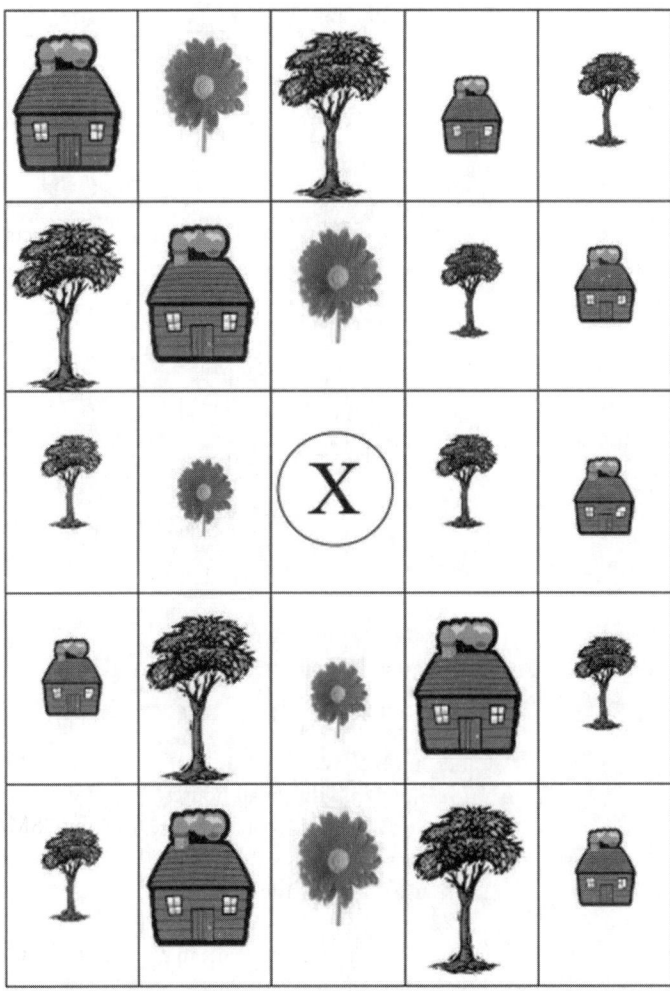

Several other instances of this task are provided by the teacher. Subsequently, touching each house is eliminated; the cross is a signal for shifting. This is followed by class activity—students in small groups are asked to devise similar tasks. (At the X sign, only touch trees; don't touch flowers or house.)

At X, only touch small flowers.

Reversal: Name the picture—Big (house), big (flower), ... At the sign of X reverse, say small when you should say big.

The central objective of this training task is to build inhibition of a prepotent response and shifting. Both are important components of EF.

15

Planning and Decision Making: Training for Enhancement

Executive Intelligence, Emotional Intelligence, and Improvement of Decision Making

Two major themes of this chapter are executive intelligence and emotional intelligence. Executives may need a special type of intelligence; we explore this concept first. Furthermore, obviously emotional intelligence is a major determinant of competence in managing an organization and working together with a team. What might be specifically a relevant combination of characteristics that constitute emotional intelligence in workplace? This is discussed at some length. We suggest that both types of "intelligence" can be regarded as components of planning and executive functions (EFs). Training for improvement of planning/EF and, particularly, decision making in management occupies a good part of this chapter.

This chapter presents training procedures for improving decision making. One of them is to present affect-laden situations for decision making. The purpose here is to test the competence of would-be executives in handling such situations. A second procedure is interactive tutoring in small group sessions. Both procedures can be integrated in a training program; practical examples and scenarios that help training are presented for discussion in this chapter.

The chapter concludes by restating the need for compassionate decision-making skills as a part of training management executives. It argues that compassion has a place along with rational analysis and intuition in contemporary styles of leadership in management. It goes on to suggest that the next step in future research would be to gather empirical research evidence that supports these approaches.

Executive Intelligence: Domain-General or Domain-Specific?

Domain-general perhaps would be the correct answer. Consider some of the recommendations mentioned by de Bono and Doerner (in Chapter 8) for executives to help them make good decisions and avoid failure of logic.

> You need to understand the matter very well.
> You need to design alternatives and possibilities.
> You need to challenge and discard existing elements.
> You need to be prepared to start over again—advises De Bono.

Doerner cautions executives in regard to avoiding failures of logic while making decisions:

> Do not lose sight of the overall goal, complex as it is, by decomposing it into partial goals.
> Do not try to reduce everything to one cause. When facts disprove your hypothesis, abandon the hypothesis; do not merely adjust it.
> Be less concerned about your self-esteem (losing face) when changing your hypothesis and decision.

There is little doubt that these generic advices will promote better decision making for administrators and managers whatever roles they may play in an organization, and help them become intelligent executives.

What Is Executive Intelligence?

Menkes (2005) defined executive intelligence as an aptitude in regard to three central contexts of work: (a) the accomplishment of tasks, (b) working with and through other people, and (c) assessing and adapting oneself. The foundation of critical thinking among business leaders is also the foundation of executive intelligence. Critical thinking essentially includes the following: how skillfully someone gathers, processes, and applies information in order to identify the best way to reach a particular goal or work through a complex situation. These criteria of critical thinking, of course, are well known in psychology. However, the major question here is this: How does critical thinking transfer itself to success in management? One has to approach it from a much broader perspective to fully understand the relationship between abilities or cognitive processes that are domain-general and domain-specific. Here are a few descriptions of what we understand these terms to mean. Do executives need to have a specific set of intellectual abilities? And if they do, what might these abilities be? Finally, how can we increase or enhance them for making better decisions? We attempt to answer these questions in this chapter.

Manager's work and roles are varied, but the cognitive skills required by them may be domain-general.

Menkes (2005) divides managerial work into three areas—accomplishing tasks, working with other people, and self-evaluation. He then identifies the cognitive skills that determine how well an executive performs in those areas listed as follows:

1. *Tasks*: To correctly define a problem, identify the highest priority issues, assess what is known, and determine what needs to be known in order to render a sound decision.
2. *Others*: To recognize underlying agendas, understand multiple perspectives, and anticipate likely emotional reactions throughout the organization.
3. *Self*: To objectively identify one's own mistakes, encourage and seek out constructive criticism, and adjust one's own behavior.

The three types of work that an executive is generally called upon to do are closer to domain-general than domain-specific categories. Menkes suggests that all of them require general information processing, and could be relatively independent of knowledge specific to the job. An able executive can operate in any of the major types of industry, such as manufacturing, production, and sales, as well as subcategories of jobs within these broad categories. He complains that employers emphasize the possession of specific knowledge that a candidate needs to have for the job rather than the possession of the aforementioned general cognitive abilities.

A useful framing for managerial work is provided by the PASS theory (see Chapters 1 and 2). To recall the essentials of the theory, four basic cognitive processes, Planning–Attention–Simultaneous–Successive, float, as it were, on knowledge base (Das, Naglieri, & Kirby, 1994). A minimum depth of knowledge is a prerequisite for any of the general cognitive processes to function effectively. This is true for both general intelligence measures and special measures such as executive intelligence.

The three "pillars" of executive intelligence proposed by Menkes are embedded in domain-specific cognitive processing as well as knowledge relevant for the industry. Another type of specificity concerns the roles that the managers have to play (briefly alluded to in Chapters 8 and 9).

The roles of managers in production are somewhat different from those in staffing or administration. An executive in senior management has at least the following major roles to play according to Mintzberg (1973).

1. A figurehead who conducts ceremonies
2. A leader who gives advice and encouragement, and provides leadership

3. A liaison who keeps channels of communication open
4. A monitor who seeks information and understands the organization
5. A disseminator who keeps everyone informed about goals and policies
6. A spokesperson
7. An entrepreneur who initiates improvement and juggles many projects
8. A disturbance handler who resolves conflicts and crises
9. A resource allocator who sets directions and allocates resources
10. A negotiator of deals and seeing them through

Perhaps all of these roles can be subsumed in the three "pillars" of executive intelligence. But do these cluster together in a few factors? We suspect that an empirical verification of the type of executive role may require specific "intelligence." Sen and Das (1990) identified three types of roles from those reported earlier. The authors used factor analysis hoping to find common factors that describe the roles in terms of distinguishable categories. These would be common to the three kinds of managers: production, staffing, and administration. The identifiable factors that emerged were as follows:

1. A busy figurehead who must also initiate changes, juggle projects, and resolve conflicts and crises
2. A planner and decision maker
3. An information generator and dispenser

Planning/executive functions may be the generic process in executive intelligence.
The PASS theory (Das et al., 1994) can frame the three role categories, mainly within planning. View the essential elements of planning as given in the figure adapted from Stuss and Benson (1986) in Chapters 1 and 10 of this book, or as in a previous book (see Das, Kar, & Parrila, 1996).

We do not know if in the scheme proposed by Menkes, which lists individual skills within each of the three categories of executive intelligence (see Menkes, 2005, p. 229), can be statistically grouped into three factors—tasks, people skills, and self—that are relatively independent of each other. Nevertheless, we will consider first the individual skills listed under each category within the broad framework of planning and EF shown in the Stuss and Benson (1986) figure. These are representation, anticipation, execution, and regulation; all the four processes are guided by an individual's over-arching goals and objectives that motivate planned behavior. We attempt to frame the basic individual skills identified by Menkes as follows:

1. Appropriately define a problem—*Representation* in the Stuss and Benson model.

2. Recognize the conclusions that can or cannot be drawn—*Anticipation.*
3. Pursue and encourage feedback, and then make appropriate adjustment (self)—*Execution* and *Regulation.*

Goals and objectives clearly guide the three components of executive intelligence—tasks, people skills, and self—and, in turn, are modified by the outcome of the planned action.

Each organization, of course, has specific domains in regard to tasks, people, and self. The generic competencies relating to representation, anticipation, evaluating the feedback following a decision, and differences in regulation and control are constrained and limited by the specific characteristics of the goals and objectives in the organization's mission statement, the appropriate time that is most favorable for the action, and the predispositions of the executive board and the CEO who make decisions. These constraints exist for an individual as well. In spite of these specific conditions, general laws of behavior can be found and tested. The relevant behavior for the present discussion concerns planning and executive functions.

Emotional Intelligence Supplements Executive Intelligence

Managers have four major roles to play as was discussed earlier.

1. Appropriately define a problem
2. Recognize the conclusions that can or cannot be drawn
3. Pursue and encourage feedback
4. Make appropriate adjustment (self)

These were then placed within the framework provided by PASS theory and Stuss and Benson's (1986) diagram.

Missing from this is the input from emotional intelligence that supplements both PASS theory and executive intelligence.

Does proficiency in emotional intelligence set the outstanding executive apart from the merely competent? If we were to select a new manager or evaluate the excellence in performance of an existing one, we should consider emotional intelligence as a requirement for competence.

Perhaps there is no longer a need to persuade a selection committee to consider emotional intelligence—the idea has been avidly advocated for a few years by Goleman (1995) and has been applied in the workplace (Cherniss & Goleman, 2001). In the latter book, an edited one, several authors have tried to answer three main questions from the perspective of workplace: What is emotional intelligence? What difference does it make? What is the best way to promote it? (see Preface to the book.)

We have selected the relevant discussion in Chapters 9 and 10, which relate to competencies, and training in emotional intelligence of managers.

Senior executives play several roles listed earlier (Mintzberg, 1973) and factor analyze these to yield three major ones: must initiate changes, juggle projects, resolve conflicts and crises; must be a planner and decision maker; and generate as well as dispense information. Emotional intelligence enters into each of these functions. It is not difficult to accept, as presented in Jacob's review in Cherniss and Goleman (2001), that there are four common competencies on which the success of the three kinds of roles can be evaluated. These are self-awareness, social awareness, self-management, and social skills.

Specifically for Managers

In Cherniss and Goleman (2001), the diagram for Emotional Intelligence is shown as a cluster of characteristics that define self-awareness. In this cluster, self-confidence becomes particularly salient for competence; it is a critical differentiator of out-standing managers.

Within the self-management cluster, trustworthiness or integrity was singled out as the differentiator along with initiative. In the social awareness cluster, it was empathy. In the social skills cluster, two characteristics may be chosen—influencing and leading others, and conflict management. The latter one is a predominant factor for senior executives for sales people. For those executives in human services, such as social workers and health professionals, the key competencies are driven by "high socialized power motive, which indicates that these people enjoy having an impact and influencing for the good of others or for the good of an organization" (McClelland cited in Jacobs' chapter, p.170, see Cherniss & Goleman, 2001). Naturally, strong social awareness and empathy go hand in hand in these executive positions. Even in the brief description above, it is clear that different types of management roles modulate the essential emotional intelligence characteristics for outstanding competence.

Back to executive intelligence, Menkes would agree with the suggestion that the salient variables for making one kind of decision rather than another depend on the type of executive position in question. Further he adds the following suggestions:

(1) The type of situation that presents itself to the management and executives should be first identified as a class of problems. Is this an emergency, or is there time for analyzing the situation?

(2) The problem situation may vary all the way from purely logical and rational to being extremely emotional.
(3) Do these types of decision making involve distinct areas of the brain?

Executive Intelligence: Need Not Look Beyond Executive Functions or Decision Making

Decision making is subsumed in planning/EF, and planning is closely associated with problem solving. All three are assumed to be within the definition and scope of EF. Chapter 1 presented this topic at some length. In Chapter 2, we wrote that planning was a broader category than problem solving. There are several ways of distinguishing between the two. First, consider planning (Stuss & Benson, 1986). Figure 2.2 relates to Luria's (1966, 1970) conceptualization of planning as an essential function of the frontal lobes. In planning for the future, we transcend or go beyond the here and the now, escape from the present problems. This, we argued, is not possible for animals other than humans. We also generate new problems and plan their solutions. We have a self-conscious mind.

Increasing Decision-Making Ability: Some Suggested Procedures

> In business, you're always in unchartered territory and must be capable of thinking for yourself. (Remarked a CEO; Menkes, 2005, p. 267)

> Beliefs that have been constructed over many years and the habits of mind that developed along with them will take multiple learning experiences, distributed over time and setting, before they will be successfully replaced with new ways of thinking and knowing about the world. (Diane Halpern, as cited in Menkes, 2005, p. 267)

Decision making in novel situations is the challenge that an executive must face. The ability to inhibit old habits or prepotent responses, "a struggle of escape from habitual modes of thought," together with an ability to shift strategies, separates the intelligent executive from the less intelligent ones. In fact, these two abilities are the core elements in EFs (Chapters 3 and 4). Training in both must be included in a program for learning executive skills.

Training for Improving Emotional Intelligence

Given that different kinds of roles that senior executives are called upon to perform in their jobs determine specific emotional competence demanded from them, there are broad and generic programs for improving emotional intelligence. This is the general assumption underlying training exercises. Another general assumption is that habits of mind cannot be changed within a short in-service training period of typically a day or two. Veterans in recommending training programs, Cherniss and Goleman (2001), accept both of these constraints and advise companies or individuals to remember this before setting up organization-wide training for their executives (Chapter 9).

Broadly speaking, training is an interventional procedure. When learning the core components that a manager has not developed, such as self-awareness, empathy, and leadership—that is, conducting oneself appropriately as a leader—training becomes necessary.

We believe that training or remedial intervention begins when learning has failed. For instance, Cherniss and Goleman mention that the dean of a major business school enthusiastically agreed with the importance of emotional intelligence at work, but when asked how his school takes steps to improve it among the MBA students, he said, "We don't do anything. I don't think that our students' emotional intelligence can be improved by the time they come here. They're already adults, and these qualities are developed early in life, primarily in the family" (p. 209).

Was the dean entirely out of step with a commonly held belief? Emotional intelligence is an instance of tacit knowledge, spontaneously acquired through experience, perhaps intuitive rather than learned deliberately. It cannot be imparted through formal teaching that lasts for a few hours. But those who have missed it need training, a sort of counterconditioning, similar to training for mindfulness or insightful meditation. Actually, Goleman considers this as one of the effective procedures for developing self-awareness and empathy.

For example, in regard to *human relations training*, Cherniss and Goleman recommend a training period of 42 hours spread over 28 weeks. It is divided into three phases: (1) The first phase was primarily cognitive learning and discussion of managerial styles for about 9 hours. Wasn't there a hands-on experience, or as we currently call it embodied cognition in psychology? (2) The second phase was primarily experiential, consisting of "numerous individual and group exercises, and corrective interview role play" for 30 hours. (3) The final phase focused on discussion and motivational theories.

No doubt, the training was rigorous, and evaluation of performance was conducted by experts—behavioral psychologists.

What is most intriguing in the study that was conducted in a steel plant was the results. Testing for the efficacy of training, its maintenance after 90 days did not show a difference between the control and the training group. However, another follow-up evaluation after 18 months showed a surprising result: "[B]y that time the trained managers had become significantly more self-aware and more sensitive to the needs of others. Their subordinates also perceived them as having improved in rapport" (p. 211).

Although the authors of the study do not mention it explicitly, we think the lasting benefits of training were mediated by practicing the elements of self-awareness and so on inadvertently during the 180 days so much so that the trained managers had developed a habit that came "naturally." Habitual practice laced with knowledge is recommended in contemplative traditions of the East.

The authors discuss two other training procedures. Behavior modeling is a separate procedure as also self-management training for problem employees. In the next section, we extend the training program for improvement of human relationship a step beyond self-awareness and empathy to include compassion. Especially in solving problems that are laden with affect, compassion should be a component of programs that encourage the application of emotional intelligence.

Special Case for Promoting Affective Decision Making: A Place for Compassion

An important part of any program for improvement of decision making focuses on mainly two types of situations—*deliberative* and *affective*. We suggested in previous chapters (see Chapters 8 and 10 of this book) that the two types of problems for the executive might be arranged in a continuum, from deliberative to affective. We discuss a few examples, and then follow by suggesting possible ways in which solutions may be found. Our purpose is to present a metacognitive framework for participating executives to improve both kinds of decision making.

COMPASSION IN MANAGEMENT

Jeff Weiner is the CEO of LinkedIn, a business-related social networking site. He started with LinkedIn in December 2008 as interim president. Prior to joining LinkedIn, he served as the executive vice president at Yahoo.

Consider the following excerpt from Jeff Weiner's writing: In reading the passage below, or others similar to it, the would-be executive's orientation will, hopefully, turn toward a more compassionate direction (https://www.linkedin.com/today/post/article/20121015034012-22330283-managing-compassionately [accessed October 15, 2012] .... Jeff Weiner Influencer)

> Of all the management principles I have adopted over the years, either through direct experience or learning from others, there is one I aspire to live by more than any other. I say "aspire" because as much as I'd like to do it consistently and without fail, I find this particular principle harder to practice consistently than others. *That principle is managing compassionately.*

There are three elements of managing compassionately I've learned through the last decade or so that have very much influenced my career path and management style. They are: (1) the meaning of compassion, and specifically how compassion differs from empathy; (2) the fact that compassion can be learned, and is not solely innate; and (3) the importance of striving to achieve both compassion and wisdom, and not one without the other.

For example, when strongly disagreeing with another, most of us have a tendency to see things solely through our own world view. In those situations, some will immediately assume that the other person is ignorant and/or has nefarious intentions. Your mind immediately turns to the thought, "How could they possibly not agree with me?"

In these circumstances, it can be constructive to take a minute to understand why the other person has reached the conclusion that they have. What in their background has led them to take that position? Do they have the appropriate experience to be making optimal decisions? Are they fearful of a particular outcome?

Asking yourself these questions, and more importantly, asking the other person these questions can take what would otherwise be a challenging situation and transform it into an occasion for learning and a collaborative experience.

COMPASSION CAN BE TAUGHT

Continuing with Jeff Weiner:

> Once I had started to fully appreciate the significance of compassion, I often times wondered whether or not it was a quality that could be taught. It turns out the answer is yes! A few weeks later, I found myself at dinner one night with my friend Fred Kofman, founder of Axialent, author of "Conscious Business," and one of the most enlightened people I've met throughout my

career. After sharing my objective with him, he said, "That's very powerful, but bear in mind, wisdom without compassion is ruthlessness, and compassion without wisdom is folly."

Expressed variously in secular and spiritual literature—this is one primary identification that can generate compassionate decision making. It provides the ground for moral and ethical judgments; it explains what has been called "cosmic piety" (Radhakrishnan, 1971). Strangely enough, *identification with all humanity* has emerged as a proper study in scientific psychology (McFarland, Brown, & Webb, 2013), strangely because it could not be considered so some 20 years ago. Given that reasoning is not infallible, and most of our spontaneous responses have their origin in the unconscious, we are persuaded to depend on an intuitive rather than a rational system for judgment, specially, affective ones.

An appeal to intuitions has been persuasively presented by Haidt (2001) by citing Hume (1777): "[T]he ultimate ends of human action can never … be accounted for by reason, but recommend themselves entirely to the sentiments and affections of mankind"(see Haidt, 2001, p. 816).

The sentiments and affections arise automatically through pre-established conditioning. These have multiple sources of origin that are interdependent. If so, then the procedure to inhibit these prepotent responses must lie in deconditioning. Buddhism suggests practicing mindfulness, a habit of mind, in order to eliminate past conditioning (Hahn, 1998). Deconditioning occurs slowly, and sets in insidiously the same way as conditioned habits. Haidt's metaphor of the emotional dog and its rational tail does not advocate irrationality. Conditioned emotional responses can be deconditioned, but neither of these can be framed within an emotional–rational dimension.

Use of Self-knowledge and Compassion: How to Deal with an Insolent Colleague

The example is a scenario that is heavy with affect. It is an abbreviated version of a case presented in Menkes (2005) that we transformed into a predicament test (Chapters 6 and 7 of this book), entitled *The Insolent Colleague*:

> You are competing for a big promotion within the company. Your main competition is a coworker named Mark, whom you have seen as a bit of a showman. You are proposing a new initiative that is based on surveys and analyses of changing customer requirements and customer satisfaction. When

you finish, and you are enjoying supportive looks from some of your colleagues, Mark blurts out, "I bet most of those surveys never even get filled out," and so on. Everyone turns back to you and waits for your response. What can you do?

Question for the participant: Do not write your name on your response sheet. Your anonymity is strictly guarded. Write down as many solutions as possible for the problem within 1 minute. Then choose the one that you think is the best and write down some justification for your choice—you have three minutes.

The response sheets are then collected. For the purpose of using the test as a training exercise, the scenario is given to participants working in small groups of five to seven. A secret code for a password of seven numbers and letters is assigned to each participant by the examiner. It appears in the back of the sheet in small print. The examiner collects the responses and makes a list of the top choice of each participant and the associated justification. Each participant is then asked to do the rating of the top choice of *other members* of the group in terms of two criteria:

1. Is it socially desirable?
2. How practical is the solution to be implemented?

Each choice is rated on a 5-point scale for each criterion. The response that gets the highest average rating on each criterion is read out.

Group discussion is the next phase. The group then discusses why a choice that received the best average on the specific criterion might be justified. In the final phase, their evaluative responses to the situation to be judged are impacted or primed by presenting them with passages that are designed to orient their decision.

In the final phase of the test and training session, each participant is asked to read two passages that should be considered in their evaluation of the group discussion. The first one is about using metacognition, and the second relates to an orientation for compassion. We may name the last two phases as *interactive tutoring* without a trainer or instructor.

Passage for Orienting Decision-makers toward Using Metacognition

Participants are asked: "To what extent do you think the overall group interactions supported the following brief?"

> The key concept in management decision making probably is sharing experience. To elaborate further, sharing experience is useful as it allows reflection

and can give us a rare glimpse into the fragility of our mental world ... From this it follows that other minds may have different representations, and even more startling, that our representations of the world might be illusory and false ... Thus reflective discussions enable us to compare our views of the world and to create improved shared views of the world.

Participants are then asked to give an answer and rate the following question on a 5-point scale:

In my opinion, group discussion on the whole was characterized by the above orientation: very much/much/neutral/a little/almost no support.

Passage for Orienting Decision-makers toward Using Compassion

Next, participants are asked to read the following passage and then asked: "To what extent do you think the overall group interaction was influenced by compassion?"

There is a place for compassion and altruism in intuitive decisions and in decisions that are laden with affect. The first step for development of compassion is empathy, not pity. We must develop our empathy or closeness to others even if the other person is suffering because he/she is unable to get rid of old habits that make him egotistic. Though he is harmful to himself, as well as to the group, the closer we are to him, the more we feel a responsibility for ending his suffering. We must reflect on the advantage of cherishing the well-being of others and observe how very much that is appreciated by the group.

Participants are asked: "Now say to what extent you think the group interactions and the majority judgment supported the sentiments expressed in the passage. Please give your rating on a 5-point scale: very much/much/neutral/a little/almost no support."

For further training purposes, the participants are presented with a few other case studies. Additional scenarios that arouse emotion/affect, as the one already mentioned, may be developed for enhancement of decision making. But this time, the participants are given a challenge: Let us try to mold our judgment in terms of adopting the same two orientations:

1. The key concept in management decision making probably is sharing experience. To elaborate further, it is useful as it "allows reflection and can give us a rare glimpse into the fragility of our mental world" (Frith, 2012).
2. There is a place for compassion and altruism in intuitive decisions and in decisions that are laden with affect.

In conclusion, the chapter discusses some esoteric concepts that have practical applications in training managers and would-be executives to develop better decision making. Self-awareness, self-knowledge, metacognition, empathy, and compassion combine with self-confidence, achievement orientation, and initiative present a consortium of characteristics that are essential for competence in decision making, both for managers of an organization and for individuals. The consortium offers alternative configurations and combinations to succeed in management. There is no best characteristic for a job.

McClelland points out "the importance of recognizing that there are alternative combinations of characteristics that lead to success in a particular job ... the same job has been performed very well by two people who appear to have quite different characteristics ... often various combinations of competencies lead to success. (McClelland cited in Cherniss & Goldman, 2001, p. 161).

Rational and intuitive decisions coexist; emotion and reason blend imperceptibly. Even in situations where the emotional dog seems to be at odds with its rational tail, decisions are not necessarily irrational.

16

Revisits and Reprise

Planning and Executive Control: The Shape of Things to Come

Is executive function (EF) identical to planning? Although we have often used planning/EF conjointly, a distinction between the two has been maintained right from the beginning of this book in the first two chapters.

Premack (2010) describes planning and problem solving as domain-general abilities, a commonly held view. Such a characterization of problem solving is consistent with the proposition that these are based on the *logical program of interconnected operations*. Luria and Tsvetkova (1990) recognize problem solving as a central purpose of human intellectual activity.

EFs, essentially, are about *execution* of plans. They are about control, control of cognition, and action. Several articles use executive control rather than function even in the title (Wiebe et al., 2011). *Executive Control Function* is also in the title of an influential report of the Committee on Research of the American Neuropsychiatric Association (Royall et al., 2007).

Thus, the distinction between broad concepts of cognitive planning, and the relatively specific ones of EF can be easily accepted in current research. Furthermore, in terms of brain regions involved in planning and executive control, there will be no compelling reason for proposing that these must be one and the same. Lastly, EF has to be defined narrowly. Consider the three components proposed by Miyake and colleagues. Each is independent, but share a common factor designated as EF. Miyake and Friedman (2012) acknowledge unity and diversity in aspects of EF. Although the tests that are used to measure each of the three core components of EF—inhibition, shifting, and updating—each cluster of tasks that measure these components is identified to share some part of the common variance of EF, and each of them also has a significant connection with other non-EFs, such as language and speed.

Imagine constraining decision making by the three core components of EF. Affect, intuitions, insights, and compassionate orientation, for instance, are rich and fuzzy concepts that would be hard to fit EF, but much easier to be included in the scope of planning, joining a cluster of even fuzzier phenomena—hopes, aspirations, and day dreams, and the need to escape from the present, as an essential characteristic of humans with intact frontal lobes according to Luria! *Executive control*, then, is a better name for EF.

Decision Making and Planning: A Second Look

This final chapter continues with the discussion of the same broad question as the previous two: How to boost decision making and planning? In the course of considering the broad objective, we find it necessary to revisit decision making and planning as the essential ingredients of "executive intelligence."

Decision making precedes an impending action, whereas planning is anticipatory to decision making. The location of decision making in the brain is the ventromedial prefrontal cortex; this is the area mostly associated with risk, fear, and the economic value of decisions. Decision making assumes self-efficacy and conscious choices. The role of an agent as the decision maker is then examined. However, the agent's judgment and knowledge may not be optimally used because affect and other unconscious conditions influence even the most rational decisions. In the preceding chapters, verbalization was discussed as a method of optimally using knowledge, and as a strategy for the enhancement of performance. We also recognize the role of unconscious and non-verbalized antecedents that influence decision making. A distinction between explicit and implicit metacognition (Frith & Frith, 2012) must be made in order to acknowledge the influence of implicit factors that contribute to decision making. This is especially relevant in affective decision making.

Elaboration of Problem Solving in Management

Executives or managers generally solve problems in contrast to others, who may engage in problem generation. They select a problem or a problem confronts them. The problem could be of two types. It either mainly requires logical deliberations or mainly relates to affect. The two kinds are often discussed within the "dual systems" variously named as rational and emotional, reason and affect, and System 1 and System 2. As we have discussed in Chapter 10, the first kind is described as deliberate, slow, and rule-bound thinking; the other laden with affect or emotion is an associative, automatic, and fast system.

A further complexity in decision making is introduced as we consider if the first one is *analytic,* and the second is *intuitive.* Intuition is defined as the recognition of patterns stored in memory, according to Simon (1987). Let us believe that intuition and non-logical thinking need not always be accessible to consciousness. Intuitive thinking, as mentioned earlier, becomes essential when the problem situation is extremely complex and quite novel. But let us here identify the two essential conditions for intuitive thinking: (a) the large number of contingencies that are associated with the problem, and (b) the interactions between the different facets of the problem situation that are complex (excerpt from Chapter 8 of this book).

Given that there are specific conditions for recommending the use of intuition, especially as advocated by Klein, a popular writer on intuitive thinking, some would nevertheless question the validity of intuitive expertise (Kahneman & Klein, 2009). Rational and intuitive knowledge are not only distinguished in their definitions and where they are processed in the brain, as we will discuss later, but also in the way one acquires each. Furthermore, the appropriate conditions that demand their use are especially important to learn for executives in management. These are the ingredients that make up "executive intelligence."

In the present chapter, therefore, we think decision making in management and its connection with planning/EF deserve a second look in order to further the discussion of executive intelligence.

Planning and Decision Making: Intuition

For one thing, decision-makers may have little time for reflection as they are under pressure for action, to act here and now. This is especially true in emergencies as faced by the team leaders in firefighting, emergency room physicians, and commanders of war. Klein (2002) gives examples like these where "intuitive" knowledge is required for use. This is in contrast to the rational method followed in decision making. We may substitute "rational planning" or "deliberate planning" in contrast to intuitive, as advocated by Kahneman (Kahneman & Klein, 2009); however, we would not mean that intuitive knowledge is "irrational." Deliberate or rational decisions require planning; however, this does not necessarily imply that action is imminent. We regard planning as anticipatory decision making, and because it is not stressed by impending action, it leaves time for evaluation. Klein's "recognition-primed decision" that has for its basis tacit experience of experts and deliberate planning share some common ground. The Klein group recommends checking out the validity of intuitive decision making by rational procedures. As Kahneman and Klein (2009) wrote, both have common concerns and similar opinions about more specific questions: "What are the activities in which skilled intuitive judgment develops with experience? What are the activities in which experience is more likely to produce overconfidence than genuine skills?"(p. 515)

We doubt that a simple distinction can be made between intuitive and rational decisions, or affective and so-called deliberate and rational decisions. Every decision-making task may be placed in a continuum of pure reasoning to pure affect (see Chapters 8 and 10). Neither can we guarantee that the expert's intuitive decisions are less likely to be wrong than the alternative, which are deliberate decisions based on analyses of facts and figures (heuristics and biases). There is no need to discuss those again. Indeed, Kahneman (2012) reports that expert opinions or insights alone are more likely to be faulty (see Chapters 8 and 10). So how should we proceed with boosting planning and decision-making competence unless we target one kind of decision making/ planning in contrast to the other?

Intuitive decision-making skills, Klein claims, are trainable. In fact, his book *Intuition at Work* (Klein, 2002) is essentially a handbook for training in intuition. Thus, he has:

> [d]evised an intuition skills training program of repeatedly practicing a series of exercises where situations are analyzed for anticipated problems and possible outcomes. A significant part of learning how to trust your instincts is evaluating information and its quality related to a certain project: is it reliable, accurate, complete or confusing? (Matson, 2002)

However, we do not think that there is conclusive scientific evidence in support of efficacy of training intuitive decision making, although we admit that under some conditions, as described in previous paragraphs, intuitive decision making should be preferred, and does occur naturally. We agree with Simon (1987; see Chapter 8) that intuition is not to be dismissed in favor of training business management executives exclusively on analytic methods.

The best conceptualization of the analytic approach, as in rational or deliberate planning, is Stuss and Benson's (1986), whose diagram we have presented in previous chapters (see Chapters 1 and 10). The diagram shows the interactive relationship among the four components of planning as an integrated mechanism comprising *representation, anticipation, execution, and regulation* (Chapter 1 of this book; Das, Kar, & Parrila, 1996). According to that scheme, we think *decision making would be characterized by execution* more accurately than the other three. The four-component interactions are fuelled by the overarching goals and objectives of the planner, and ultimately are supervised by consciousness in the hierarchy of frontal lobe according to the Stuss and Benson model. We continue to believe that cognitive planning is sufficiently broad to house most parts of executive control.

Extended Model of Frontal Lobe Functions: Self-awareness and Consciousness

The model first proposed by Stuss and Benson (1986) has been updated (Stuss & Alexander, 2000), especially in relation to the functions of the frontal lobes, in regard to a "conceptual view" of EFs.

EFs, as we have discussed earlier in this book, are associated with the same region as the broader process of planning. EF is essentially a control function. According to the revised model of Stuss and Alexander, various kinds of EFs necessarily are parts of frontal systems. In addition, Stuss and Alexander propose that "the most important role of the frontal lobes may be for affective responsiveness, social and personality development, and self-awareness and unconsciousness" (p. 289). Specifically, they add: "Self-awareness emerges from convergence of emotional states and memory... memory of abstract mental states that allow construction of expectancy and thus memory for the future" (p. 295). We postpone a discussion of the role of consciousness and self-knowledge for a later section in this chapter. For now, we revisit intuitive and deliberate thinking.

In Two Minds: Intuition and Reasoning

We wish to re-enter the System 1 versus System 2 difference that was discussed first in a previous chapter (Chapter 8). The distinction has been augmented by a hugely popular book by Kahneman (2012). In retrospect, we have more reasons to agree with Simon's original definition of intuition as recognition, a lead followed by Klein (see Kahneman & Klein, 2009). In the debate between Klein, who prefers intuition, and Kahenman, who is in favor of slow deliberate thinking, especially when intuition is likely to be faulty, we would support Kahneman especially after following his persuasive arguments in a later publication (Kahneman, 2012). Perhaps, it is relevant here to restate a *definition of intuition as recognition* that Simon (1987) had proposed, and wrote about it again (Simon, 1992):

> The situation has provided a cue; this cue has given the expert access to information stored in memory, and the information provides the answer. Intuition is nothing more and nothing less than recognition. (p. 151)

Klein's situations focused on emergencies faced by firefighters or emergency room physicians. In contrast, as Kahneman admits, his situations comprised scholars and logical thinkers, and veteran chess players who are proficient in the game. Kahneman also allows that intuitive decisions need not necessarily involve emotion-laden situations. Even entirely cognitive tasks such as adding 2 + 2 exemplify intuitive decision. The reason for failure of logic is not always emotions and egotism (Chapters 8 and 10). Add to the list provided by Doerner for failure of logic and the logic of failure discussed earlier in the present book; then Kahneman's (2012, p. 239) thoughtful observation that intuition is likely to fail when overconfidence or subjective confidence is too high and often uninformative.

Systems 1 and 2 have been revised by Stanovich (Evans & Stanovich, 2013), who created these terms, but has now replaced them with Type 1 and Type 2. Both types of performance include knowledge gained from experience; neither of them is impervious to developmental changes. However, their essential attributes, fast and spontaneous versus slow and deliberative, are retained. Importantly, Type 1 intuitive response is automatic, and does not require "controlled attention." In our previous chapters relating to EF, we regard controlled attention or attentional control (Geary, 2013) as a variation of EF. Although Stanovich (Evans & Stanovich, 2013) interprets this as: "The type 1 response does not require working memory," we do not think it is necessary to regard it as such. Neither is it necessary to agree with him that working memory is the same as fluid intelligence. However, as far as our interest is in regard to decision making is concerned, we agree with his view that intuitive decisions can be overridden by Type 2 deliberate thinking, and should be, when necessary. Kahneman uses the term *default intervention*, that is, intervention that overrides Type 1 intuitive response by Type 2 reflective thinking when intuition can go wrong due to a variety of conditions, including overconfidence, novelty of the situation, and lack of relevant experience.

We add that intuitive decisions may be harder to intervene if these are conditioned responses, specially arising from anxiety and emotion. Further, we support Kahneman in that he invokes Pavlovian conditioning, especially in situations laced with anxiety and fear—intuition to avoid certain situations or persons instantly is a form of aversive conditioning. Even one traumatic experience in the past is sufficient to evoke an aversive response and biased decision making.

A dramatic example is often cited in psychology books: One trial is enough to instantly condition the rat's aversion to radiated water—psychology texts name it as the *Garcia effect* (Garcia, Kimeldorff, & Koelling, 1955). Actually, the Garcia effect is a good example of evolution of "taste" as a powerful defense against free-ranging rats. One-trial learning may be an adaptive response, evolutionary in its origin to benefit the organism, as in the case of the rat, a free-ranging animal searching for food.

Perhaps stretching the point a bit too far, would compassion and empathy in humans be a natural and adaptive response of most of us when we witness a child in distress (a salient stimulus) and spontaneously try to help? If so, wouldn't it then be easier to enhance it through reflection and training for ameliorating the suffering of fellow human beings?

We may extend the framework of planning as a frontal lobe function engaging both the rational reflective region of the brain, dorsolateral prefrontal, and the ventromedial prefrontal region associated with emotion to cover compassionate decision making. Furthermore, one may even include metacognition, especially seeking other people's counsel while making decisions about them. We will discuss this in a subsequent section.

To conclude this section, both System 1 and System 2 (Type 1 and Type 2) mechanisms of mind can be manipulated. Aversive conditioning is open to deconditioning. Habits of mind seemingly automatic have, nevertheless, depended on their origin for a constellation of conditions. We suggest that the "dependent origination" of good and poor intuitive decisions gives us a handle for *training*. Perhaps, that would be a timely addition to Kaheneman's *Thinking, Fast and Slow*.

Compassion: An Intrusion from the East or in Step with the Times?

The Meaning of Compassion

Through the book *The Art of Happiness*—the teachings of the Dalai Lama—we learned the difference between compassion, defined as walking a mile in another person's shoes, and empathy, which is a feeling what another person feels. Though oftentimes used synonymously in western culture, the contrast between the two is an important one.

As the Dalai Lama explains, if you are walking along a trail and come along a person who is being crushed by a boulder, an empathetic reaction would result in you feeling the same sense of crushing suffocation and render you unable to help. The compassionate reaction would put you in the sufferer's shoes, thinking this person must be experiencing horrible pain, so you are going to do everything in your power to remove the boulder and alleviate his or her suffering. This idea of seeing things clearly through another person's perspective can be invaluable when it comes to relating with others, particularly in tense work situations. However, a near enemy of compassion is pity. Pity for the suffering of other person still retains a difference between yourself and the other, whereas compassion is suffering with the other, putting yourself in the other person's shoes (Kornfield, 1988). We also recommend for promoting and teaching compassionate decisions through a source book, *Tariki: Embracing Despair, Discovering Peace*, as a training material (it is a deep and persuasive book by Itsuki, 2001). An anecdote in the book illustrates the essential difference between rational and compassionate behavior.

> A young man returns home to his parents upon being released from prison after serving time for drug addiction and peddling dope. Both parents welcome him. His father then guides him to the nearest bookshelf, stacked with useful books on breaking the drug habit and self-help manuals on rehabilitation. His mother sits beside him, puts his hand in hers, and cries silently.

How Much can We Boost Compassionate Behavior? Would the Training Change the Neuralsa Interactions in the Brain?

We repeat, there is hope that we can boost compassionate behavior sufficiently by cultivating habits of mind: We still do not know how identification with all humanity develops (McFarland, Brown, & Webb, 2013). Through practice and reflection (metacognition), we can develop habits of mind conducive to development of compassionate behavior. We can train a compassionate and empathetic approach. Some would view this as a compelling need to ensure living in a civil society. Every week we get horror stories of medical negligence, of insensitive businessmen who steal from the poor and governments, who sometimes play with human lives and do whatever it takes to achieve military objectives, and so on. These are some examples of massive failure of compassionate conduct.

The brain responds positively to experience and instruction. Neuroplasticity is the technical name for this phenomenon, and scientific evidence has begun to support the idea that the brain is made to respond to change by creating new neural pathways throughout life. R. Davidson is a reputed researcher in this area. His studies include veteran meditators who have practiced "compassionate meditation" for at least 10,000 hours. They have cultivated equanimity. Their brains respond differently to conflict, aggression, and anger.

However, even short-term practice changes the brain's response. The change is best noticed in a part of the cortex, the insula that has a close connection with visceral channels (Davidson & Begley, 2012). It is the beginning, as the researchers admit; there is much more to be learned.

However, compassionate orientation cannot be achieved in one or two in-service workshops. Instead, intermittent training for boosting compassionate orientation must continue to break down old habits of thinking and replace them with a "new age" style of decision making. Research shows that there is a reason to believe that through such practice, changes occur in the workings of our brain.

Working Brain: The Self in Hot and Cold Decisions

All through the book, rational and affective decisions have been considered as relatively independent, but invariably intertwined like the strands of a rope that pulls us to bias our behavior. Affective data is "hot," unlike the "cold" logic of reasoned deliberation. Distinct areas of the brain are engaged in hot and cold decisions. However, a composite made up of both is the rule rather than an exception even in reasoning, especially motivated reasoning (see Chapters 8 and 9). It activates orbitofrontal cortex and the anterior cingulate. Mlodinow (2012), a champion of subliminal consciousness, mentions the involvement of additional regions of the brain (posterior cingulate and precueneus) when one makes moral judgments that are laden with emotions. (We wonder when moral pronouncements are made, can the moralist ever use a voice without emotion?) His main point is to focus on unconscious biases that creep into motivated reasoning, particularly when unfavorable information is dealt with. Reasoning then maintains the appearance of objectivity.

We are simply speaking two minds; Mlodinow quotes Haidt (2001): "To get at the truth, mind is in part a scientist and a lawyer. The scientist gathers information, looks for regularities to test the hypothesis. The lawyer begins with a conclusion and seeks evidence in support in order to convince others."

How common it is in management and education to seek supportive evidence that is already made? Some of the obviously faulty decisions in education may be cited—whole-language reading was imposed on primary school children who read, but need not learn to spell. Neither was phonological processing emphasized. Good readers nevertheless acquired spelling and phonological rules incidentally in a year or two, but the lower than average readers were significantly left behind. Orbitofrontal and the anterior as well as the posterior cingulate cortices overpowered the activation of the seat of cold reasoning (dorsolateral prefrontal cortex).

Although "the ghost in the machine," the limbic system, has spirited away rationality, attempts at training for compassionate decision making that Davidson and Begley (2012) advocate change both the neural activities and behavior of the trainees. Both parts of the mind, like the bird with two heads (an analogy from Hindu traditional writing, one head prevents the other from eating a poisonous fruit), obviously come together for the good of the self.

We discuss next the importance of seeing yourself as you really are.

The Importance of Self-knowledge: Seeing Yourself as You Really Are

Do they have the appropriate experience to be making optimal decisions? Are they fearful of a particular outcome?

Both of these questions are embedded in the difficulty of seeing yourself as you really are (Carlson, 2013). Remember to ask these questions when dealing with an insolent colleague. Carlson has discussed the barriers to self-knowledge at some length, along with suggesting one of the major techniques of overcoming them; it is mindfulness training. Although empirical studies might be lacking, mindfulness appears to be a reasonable enhancer of self-knowledge.

Consequently, improved self-knowledge should facilitate better decision making. Let us look at Carlson's arguments. First, the two barriers to self-knowledge: You may not have accurate information about your personality—how unusual is your behavior during social interactions? Your own personality is often hidden from conscious awareness, Carlson suggests, even though this is almost a truism for many of us.

The other barrier is motivational—you try to defend your ego. You are motivated to accept compliments, and brush off negative feedback as inaccurate. Again, not a new concept, the legendary psychoanalyst Freud focused on ego defenses as one of the dynamic unconscious mechanisms.

So, is there a technique short of embracing psychoanalysis for overcoming the barriers? Carlson advocates mindfulness training. Its twin principles are attention to your present experience, moment by moment, and a nonjudgmental observation of your current experience. Each of these promotes openness to gathering information about yourself, as well as acceptance of information without becoming defensive.

Mindfulness is an active area of consciousness studies that have their roots in the contemplative traditions of the East. Furthermore, "self-knowledge" is an objective of quest for consciousness (see Das, 2014). This is beyond the scope of the present book. However there is no denying the fact that a positive effort toward focusing on the present and lowering down your ego defenses are desirable habits of the mind. Further, it prepares the ground for compassionate decision making.

Cognitive Strategy Training: Its Implications for Education

New thinking on training strategies for improvement in reading, comprehension, and learning mathematics involves educational technologies. Computers are easily available. Programs for learning can be obtained in I-pads, podcasts, and other hand-held devices. Even in so-called emerging economies, governments, and private companies can provide such devices cheaply. Often supported by huge investments by philanthropists for entirely altruistic reasons in promoting education (and healthcare), EdTechnology offers a new stimulant for "Race to the Top" initiatives in the United States, making it possible to realize the dream of ensuring that "No child is left behind." Online learning has reduced the burden of teachers for giving lessons in a classroom and homework for pupils—a virtual classroom at home is accessible through instructional videos for students to learn at their own pace. Teachers are available for helping when the students need help, and monitor their progress. Opportunities for learning from peers have opened up through instant communication by texting and so on.

What is the role of cognitive strategy training, then, given the advancements in EdTechnology? We may suggest at least two: (1) When students do not respond to regular instructions, what needs to be done? (2) What kind of strategies should then be implemented, and tested for their efficacy?

Both of these related roles require a sound theoretical base, and programs of intervention such as PREP and COGENT, and Math Modules (discussed in previous chapters) for intensive training given individually or in small groups. Each training module in these programs allows (a) for guided discovery, and (b)delivering each tutorial session free of fear of punishment, combined with ensuring that a student experiences a success rate of 80 percent of the time on a given task before moving on to a harder level of difficulty. These are arguably the two major principles of any effective intervention program.

The goal of the three cognitive strategy programs is to help students gain a thorough understanding of the foundations of reading and mathematics, so that they are prepared to gain from classroom instruction. General cognitive strategies are framed within the broad theory of how we integrate information, and plan to solve problems as well as execute the plans—PASS theory provides the framework; however, that is not the only one. It is the reasonable one based as it is on clinical observations of how the brain works and the cognitive processes that experiments in psychological research have supported. EdTechnology would be a great help for propagating these cognitive training programs in preparation for online delivery and amplify their benefits, especially for disadvantaged children. Education has become a lucrative "business," especially in developing economies. Only the rich can have access to schools for the well-to-do. A vast number of middle class families are desperate to send their children to elitist schools. But experimenting with advanced methods of Ed-tech, even general schools in low-socioeconomic districts in the United States have succeeded in enhancing the educational achievements of their students to a level equal to private schools. Reports of even exceeding the level of achievement in high–socioeconomic-status schools are not rare.

John Danner has built seven "Rocketship" charter schools, whose model has produced results at or above average in low-income neighborhood by using technology, community engagement, and teaching coaches. Special Correspondent John Merrow profiles the California program, which aims to mass-produce quality schools.

In the present book, previous chapters on strategy training reported that students with poor reading comprehension when administered PREP could exceed the normative level following only 15 hours of one-on-one tutoring. In the words of Bill Gates, it is a special time in education. The technological co-evolution process is already happening. How this happens is a major theme of the last chapter.

Bibliography

Arbuthnott, K., & Frank, J.(2000). Trail making test, part B as a measure of executive control: validation using a set-switching paradigm. *Journal of Clinical and Experimental Neuropsychology, 22*, 518–528.
Adams, M. J. (1989). Thinking skills curricula: Their promise and progress. *Educational Psychologist, 24*, 25–77.
———. (1993). Towards making it happen. *Applied Psychology: An International Review, 42*, 214–218.
Agnoli, F., & Krantz, D. H. (1989). Suppressing natural heuristics by formal instruction: The case of the *conjunction fallacy. Cognitive Psychology, 21*, 515–550.
Agor, W. (1984). *Intuitive management*. New York: Prentice Hall.
Allyn & Bacon, & Das, J. P. (2009). *Reading difficulties and dyslexia: An interpretation for teachers*. New Delhi: SAGE Publications.
Almashat, S., Ayotte, B., Edelstein, B., & Margrett, J. (2008). Framing effect debiasing in medical *decision making. Patient Education and Counseling, 71*, 102–107.
American Psychiatric Association. (2000). *Diagnostic and Statistical Manual of Mental Disorders* (4th ed., Text Revision). Washington, DC: American Psychiatric Association.
Arkes, H., Faust, D., Guilmette, T., & Hart, K. (1988). Eliminating the hindsight bias. *Journal of Applied Psychology, 73*, 305–307.
Arkes, H. R., Christensen, C., Lai, C., & Blumer, C. (1987). Two methods of reducing overconfidence. *Organizational Behavior and Human Decision Processes, 39*, 133–144.
Aron, A. R., Fletcher, P. C., Bullmore, T., Sahakian, B. J., & Robbins, T. W. (2003). Stop-signal inhibition disrupted by damage to right inferior frontal gyrus in humans. *Nature neuroscience, 6*(2), 115–116.
Aronson, J., Fried, C., & Good, C. (2002). Reducing the effects of stereotype threat on African American college students by shaping theories of intelligence. *Journal of Experimental Social Psychology, 38*(2), 113–125.
Asarnow, J. R., & Meichenbaum, D. (1979). Verbal rehearsal and serial recall. The mediational training of kindergarten children. *Child Development, 50*, 1173–1177.
Ashman, A. F. (1978). *The relationship between planning and simultaneous and successive Synthesis*. Unpublished doctoral dissertation, University of Alberta, Edmonton, Canada.
Ashman, A. F., & Das, J. P. (1980). Relation between planning and simultaneous-successive processing. *Perception and Motor Skills, 51*, 371–382.
Audi, R. (1993). *The structure of justification*. Cambridge: Cambridge University Press.
———. (2001). The architecture of reason: The structure and substance of rationality. Oxford: Oxford University Press.
Aunola, K., Leskinen, E., Lerkkanen, M., & Nurmi, J., (2004). Developmental dynamics of math performance from preschool to grade 2. *Journal of Educational Psychology, 96*, 699–713.
Austin, W., Goble, E., Leier, B., & Byrne, P. (2009). Compassion fatigue: The experience of nurses. *Ethics and Social Welfare, 3*(2), 195–214.

Axelrod, R., & Hamilton, W. D. (1981). The evolution of cooperation. *Science, 211*, 1390–1396.
Baddeley, A. (2000). The episodic buffer: A new component of working memory? *Trends in Cognitive Science, 4*, 417–423.
Baddeley, A. D. (1986). *Working memory.* Oxford: Oxford University Press.
———. (2012). Working memory: Theories, models, and controversies. *Annual Review of Psychology, 63*, 1–29.
Baddeley, A. D., & Hitch, G. (1974). Working memory. In G. H. Bower (Ed.), *The psychology of learning and motivation: Advances in research and theory* (pp. 47–89). New York: Academic Press.
Balcetis, E., & Dunning, D. (2006). See what you want to see: Motivational influences on visual perception. *Journal of Personality and Social Psychology, 91*, 612–625.
Bandura, A. (2001). Social cognitive theory: An agentic perspective. *Annual Review of Psychology, 52*, 1–26.
Banich, M. T. (2009). Executive function: The search for an integrated account. *Current Directions in Psychological Science, 18*, 89–94.
Banks, J., & Oldfield, Z. (2007). Understanding pensions: Cognitive function, numerical ability and retirement saving. *Fiscal Studies, 28*, 143–170.
Banziger, G. (1983). Normalizing the paranormal: Short-term and long-term change in belief in the paranormal among older learners during a short course. *Teaching of Psychology, 10*, 212–214.
Baral, B. D., & Das, J. P. (2004). What is indigenous to India and what is shared? In R. J. Sternberg (Ed.), *International handbook of intelligence* (pp. 270–301). Cambridge: Cambridge University Press.
Barch, D. M., Braver, T. S., Sabb, F. W., & Noll. D. C. (2000). Anterior cingulate and the monitoring of response conflict: Evidence from an fMRI study of overt verb generation. *Journal of Cognitive Neuroscience, 12*(2), 298–309.
Barkley, R. (2006). *Attention-deficit hyperactivity disorder: A handbook for diagnosis and treatment* (3rd ed.). New York: Guilford Press.
Barkley, R. A. (1997). *ADHD and the nature of self-control.* New York: Guilford Press.
Barnard, C. (1938). *The functions of the executive.* Cambridge, Massachusetts: Harvard University Press.
Barnett, S. M., & Ceci, S. J. (2002). When and where do we apply what we learn? A taxonomy for far transfer. *Psychological Bulletin, 128*, 612–637.
Baron, J. (1981). Reflective thinking as a goal of education. *Intelligence, 5*, 291–309.
———. (1991). Beliefs about thinking. In J. Voss, D. Perkins, & J. Segal (Eds), *Informal reasoning and education* (pp. 169–186). Hillsdale, New Jersey: Erlbaum.
———. (1993). *Morality and rational choice.* Dordrecht: Kluwer.
———. (1998). Intelligent thinking and the reflective essay. In R. J. Sternberg & W. M. Williams (Eds), *Intelligence, instruction, and assessment: Theory into practice* (pp. 133–157). Mahwah, New Jersey: Lawrence Erlbaum.
———. (2008). *Thinking and deciding* (4th ed.). Cambridge, Massachusetts: Cambridge University Press.
Baron, J., Bazerman, M. H., & Shonk, K. (2006). Enlarging the societal pie through wise legislation. A psychological perspective. *Perspectives on Psychological Science, 1*, 123–132.
Baron-Cohen, S. (1989). The autistic child's theory of mind: The case of specific developmental delay. *Journal of Child Psychology and Psychiatry, 30*, 285–298.
Barrouillet, P., & Camos, V. (2012). As time goes by: Temporal constraints in working memory. *Current Directions in Psychological Science, 21*, 413–419.

Belmont, J. M., & Mitchell, D. W. (1987). The general strategy hypothesis as applied to cognitive theory in mental retardation. *Intelligence, 11*, 91–105.

Bentz, B. G., Williamson, D. A., & Franks, S. F. (2004). Debiasing of pessimistic judgments associated with anxiety. *Journal of Psychopathology and Behavioral Assessment, 26*, 173–180.

Best, J. R., Miller, P. H., & Naglieri, J. A. (2011). Relations between executive function and academic achievement from ages 5 to 17 in a large, representative national sample. *Learning and Individual Differences, 21*, 327–336.

Bethge, H. J., Carlson, J. S., & Wiedl, K. H. (1982). The effects of dynamic assessment procedures on Raven matrices performance, visual search behavior, test anxiety, and test orientation. *Intelligence, 6*, 89–97.

Bhandari, G., Hassanein, K., & Deaves, R. (2008). Debiasing investors with decision support systems: An experimental investigation. *Decision Support Systems, 46*, 399–410.

Biggs, J. (1988). Approaches to learning and to essay writing. In R. R. Schmeck (Ed.), *Learning strategies and learning styles. Perspectives on individual differences* (pp. 185–228). New York: Plenum Press.

Birnbaum, M. H. (1999). Testing critical properties of decision making on the internet. *Psychological Science, 10*, 399–407.

Blackmore, S. (2005). *Consciousness: A very short introduction.* Oxford: Oxford University Press.

Blackwell, L., Trzesniewski, K., & Dweck, C. S. (2007). Implicit theories of intelligence predict achievement across an adolescent transition: A longitudinal study and an intervention. *Child Development, 78*, 246–263.

Boden, C., & Kirby, J.R. (1995). Successive processing, phonological coding and the remediation of reading. *Journal of Cognitive Education, 4*, 19–32.

Booth, R. E., Kwiatkowski, C., Iguchi, M. Y., Pinto, F., & John, D. (1998). Facilitating treatment entry among out-of-treatment injection drug users. *Public Health Reports, 113* (Suppl. 1), 116–128.

Bowden, E. M., Jung-Beeman, M., Fleck, J., & Kounios, J. (2005). New approaches to demystifying insight. *Trends in Cognitive Sciences, 9*, 322–328.

Brailsford, A., Snart, F., & Das, J. P. (1984). Strategy training and reading comprehension. *Journal of Learning Disabilities, 17*(5), 287–290.

Brand, M., Laier, C., Pawlikowski, M., & Markowitsch, H. J. (2009). Decision making with and without feedback: The role of intelligence, strategies, executive functions, and cognitive styles. *Journal of Clinical and Experimental Neuropsychology, 31*, 984–998.

Broadbent, D. E., Fitzgerald, P., & Broadbent, M. H. (1986). Implicit and explicit knowledge in the control of complex systems. *British Journal of Psychology, 77*, 33–50.

Brooks, D. (2011). *The social animal: The hidden sources of love, character, and achievement.* New York: Random House.

Brown, A.L., & Campione, J.C. (1994). Guided discovery in a community of learners. In K. McGilly (Ed.), *Classroom lessons: Integrating cognitive theory and classroom practice* (pp. 229–270). Cambridge, Massachusetts: MIT Press.

Brown, J. M., & Miller, W. R. (1993). Impact of motivational interviewing on participation and outcome in residential alcoholism treatment. *Psychology of Addictive Behaviors, 7*, 211–218.

Bruine de Bruin, W., Parker, A. M., & Fischhoff, B. (2007). Individual differences in adult decision making competence. *Journal of Personality and Social Psychology, 92*, 938–956.

Burkett, J. P. (2006). *Microeconomics: Optimization, experiments, and behavior.* New York: Oxford University Press.

Butterworth, B. (2000). *The mathematical brain.* London: Macmillan.

Cacioppo, J. T., Petty, R. E., Feinstein, J., & Jarvis, W. (1996). Dispositional differences in cognitive motivation: The life and times of individuals varying in need for cognition. *Psychological Bulletin, 119*, 197–253.

Cahn, B. R., & Polich, J. (2006). Meditation states and traits: EEG, ERP, and neuroimaging studies. *Psychological Bulletin, 132*, 180–211.

Camerer, C. F. (2005). Three Cheers—psychological, theoretical, empirical—for loss aversion. *Journal of Marketing Research, 42*, 129–133.

Campbell, J.I.D. (Ed.) (2005). *Handbook of mathematical cognition*. New York: Psychology Press.

Campione, J. C., & Brown, A. L. (1987). Linking dynamic testing with school achievement. In C. S. Lidz (Ed.), *Dynamic assessment* (pp. 82–115). New York: Guilford Press.

Carlson, E. (2013). Overcoming barriers to self-knowledge: Mindfulness as a path to seeing yourself as you really are. *Psychological Science, 8*, 173–186.

Carlson, J., & Das, J. (1997). A process approach to remediating word-decoding deficiencies in chapter 1 children. *Learning Disability Quarterly, 20*, 93–102.

Carlson, J. S. (1983). *Dynamic assessment in relation to learning characteristics and teaching strategies for children with specific learning disability*. Final report: U. S. Department of Education, Grant No. 6008100426, CFDA, 84, 023E.

Carlson, J. S., & Wiedl, K. H. (1976). Modes of presentation of the Raven Coloured Progressive Matrices test: Toward a differential testing approach. *Trier Psychologische Berichte, 3*, 1–78.

———. (1979). Towards a differential testing approach: Testing-the-limits employing the Raven matrices. *Intelligence, 3*, 323–344.

———. (1992). Principles of dynamic assessment: The application of a specific model. *Learning and Individual Differences, 4*, 153–166.

Carroll, J.B. (1953). *The study of language*. Cambridge, Massachusetts: Harvard University Press.

———. (1993). Human cognitive abilities: A survey of factor-analytic studies. *Journal of Experimental Psychology, 47*, 763–766.

Case, D. A., Fantino, E., & Goodie, A. S. (1999). Base-rate training without case cues reduces base-rate neglect. *Psychonomic Bulletin & Review, 6*, 319–327.

Cattell, R. B. (1963). Theory for fluid and crystallized intelligence: A critical experiment.

———. (1998). Where is intelligence? Some answers from the triadic theory. In J. J. McArdle & R. W. Woodcock (Eds), *Human cognitive abilities in theory and practice* (pp. 29–38). Mahwah, New Jersey: Erlbaum.

Chan, R. C. K., Shum, D., Toulopoulou, T., & Chen, E. Y. H. (2008). Assessment of executive functions: Review of instruments and identification of critical issues. *Archives of Clinical Neuropsychology, 23*(2), 201–216.

Channon, S. (2004). Frontal lobe dysfunction and everyday problem-solving: Social and non-social contributions. *Acta Psychologica, 115*, 235–254.

Channon, S., & Crawford, S. (1999). Problem-solving in real-life-type situations: The effects of anterior and posterior lesions on performance. *Neuropsychologia, 37*, 757–770.

Cheng, P. W., Holyoak, K. J., Nisbett, R. E., & Oliver, L. M. (1986). Pragmatic versus syntactic approaches to training deductive reasoning. *Cognitive Psychology, 18*, 293–328.

Cherniss, C., & Goleman, D. (2001). *The emotionally intelligent workplace*. San Francisco, California: Jossey-Bass.

Chi, M. T. H., Siler, S. A., Jeong, H., Yamauchi, T., & Hausmann, R. G. (2001). Learning from human tutoring. *Cognitive Science, 25*, 471–533.

Chiappe, D., & MacDonald, K. (2005). The evolution of domain-general mechanisms in intelligence and learning. *Journal of General Psychology, 132*(1), 5–40.

Chomsky, N. (1957). *Syntactic structures*. The Hague: Mouton.

Christensen, A. L., Elkhonon, G., & Bougakov, D. (2009). (Eds). *Luria's legacy in the 21st century*. New York: Oxford University Press.

Cohen, M. S., Kosslyn, S.M., Breiter, H. C., DiGirola, G. J., Thompson, W. L., Anderson, A. K., Bookheimer, S. Y., Rosen, B. R., & Belliveau, J. W. (1996). Changes in cortical activity during mental rotation: A mapping study using functional magnetic resonance imaging. *Brain, 119,* 89–100.

Colom, R., Rebollo, I., Palacios, A., Juan-Espinosa, M., & Kyllonen, P. C. (2004). Working memory is (almost) perfectly predicted by g. *Intelligence, 32,* 277–296.

Connor, D. F., Edwards, G., Fletcher, K., Baird, J., Barkeley, R. A., & Steingard, R. (2003). Correlates of comorbid psychopathology in children with ADHD. *Journal of the American Academy of Child & Adolescent Psychiatry, 42,* pp. 193–200.

Corballis, M.C. (1980). Laterality and myth. *American Psychologist, 35,* 284–295.

Cormier, P., Carlson, J. S., & Das, J. P. (1990). Planning ability and cognitive performance: The compensatory effects of a dynamic assessment approach. *Learning and Individual Differences, 2,* 437–449.

Cowan, N. (1995). *Attention & memory*. Oxford: Oxford University Press.

———. (2001). The magical number 4 in short-term memory: A reconsideration of mental storage capacity. *Journal of Behavioral and Brain Science, 24,* 87–114; discussion, pp. 114–185.

———. (2010). The magical mystery four: How is working memory capacity limited, and why? *Current Directions in Psychological Science, 19,* 51–57.

Crone, E.A., Bunge, S.A., Latenstein, H., & van der Molen, M.W. (2005). Characterization of children's decision making: Sensitivity to punishment frequency, not task complexity. *Child Neuropsychology, 11,* 245–263.

Dalai Lama & Cutler, H. (1998). *The art of happiness*. Mobius: Easton Press Publication.

Dalai Lama & Vreeland, N. (2001). *An open heart*. New York: Little Brown & Co.

Damasio, A. (1999). *The feeling of what happens*. New York: Harcourt, Brace, and Company.

Damasio, A. R. (1994) *Descartes' error: Emotion, reason, and the human brain*. New York: Grosset/Putnam.

Daneman, M., & Carpenter, P. A. (1980). Individual differences in working memory and reading. *Journal of Verbal Learning and Verbal Behavior, 19,* 450–466.

Das, J., Mishra, R., & Pool, J. (1995). An experiment on cognitive remediation of word reading difficulty. *Learning disability, 2,* 66–79.

Das, J. P. (1980). Planning: Theoretical considerations and empirical evidence. *Psychological Research, 41*(Luria Memorial Issue), 141–151.

———. (1989). A system of cognitive assessment and its advantage over IQ. In D. Vickers & P. Smith (Eds), *Human information processing: Measures, mechanisms, and models* (pp. 535–546). Amsterdam: Elsevier.

———. (1994). Eastern views of intelligence. In R. J. Sternberg (Ed.), *Encyclopedia of human intelligence* (pp. 387–391). New York: Macmillan.

Das, J.P. (1999a). A neo-Lurian approach to assessment and remediation. *Neuropsychology Review, 9,* 107–115.

———. (1999b). *PASS Reading Enhancement Program (PREP)*. Edmonton, Alberta: Developmental Disabilities Centre, University of Alberta.

———. (2001). Reconceptualizing intelligence: Luria's contribution. *Psychological Studies, 46,* 1–6.

———. (2002). A better look at intelligence. *Current Directions in Psychology, 11*(1), 28–32.

———. (2003). Cognitive aging and Down Syndrome: An interpretation. *International Review of Research in Mental Retardation, 26,* 261–306.

———. (2009). *Reading difficulties and dyslexia* (rev. ed.). New Delhi: SAGE Publications.

Das, J.P. (1999a). (2010). Intelligence. In I. B. Weiner & W. E. Craigshead (Eds), *The corsini encyclopedia of psychology* (pp. 835–838). New York: Wiley.

———. (2014). *Consciousness quest where east meets west: On mind, meditation and neural correlates.* New Delhi: SAGE International publications.

Das, J. P., & Abbott, J. (1995). PASS: An alternative approach to intelligence. *Psychology and Developing Societies, 7,* 155–184.

Das, J. P., Hayward, D., Georgiou, G., Janzen, T., & Boora, N. (2008). Comparing the effectiveness of two reading intervention programs for children with reading disabilities. *Journal of Cognitive Education & Psychology, 7,* 199–222.

Das, J. P., & Heemsbergen, D. B. (1983). Planning as a factor in the assessment of cognitive processes. *Journal of Psychoeducational Assessment, 1,* 1–16.

Das, J. P., & Melnyk, L. (1989). Attention checklist: A rating scale for mildly mentally handicapped adolescents. *Psychological Reports, 64,* 1267–1274.

Das, J. P., & Misra, S. (1995). Aspects of cognitive competence and managerial behavior: *The Journal of Entrepreneurship, 4,* 145–163.

Das, J., & Naglieri, J. (1990). *Cognitive assessment system.* Itasca, Illinois: Riverside.

Das, J. P., & Naglieri, J. A. (1992). Assessment of attention, simultaneous-successive coding & planning. In H. C. Haywood & D. Tzuriel (Eds), *Interactive assessment* (pp. 207–232). New York: Springer-Verlag.

———. (2001). The Das–Naglieri cognitive assessment system in practice. In J. Andrews, D. H. Saklofske, & H. L Janzen (Eds), *Handbook of psychoeducational assessment* (pp. 33–63). San Diego, California: Academic Press.

Das, J. P., Kar, B. C., & Parrila, R. (1996). *Cognitive planning.* New Delhi: SAGE.

Das, J. P., Kirby, J. R., & Jarman R. F. (1975). Simultaneous and successive syntheses: An alternative model for cognitive abilities. *Psychological Bulletin, 82,* 87–103.

———. (1979). *Simultaneous and successive cognitive processes.* New York: Academic Press.

Das, J. P., Mensink, D., & Mishra, R. K. (1990). Cognitive processes separating good and poor readers when IQ is covaried. *Learning and Individual Differences, 2,* 423–436.

Das, J. P., Misra, S., & Mishra, R. K. (1993). Assessing ability for strategic planning. *Vikalpa, 18*(3), 29–36.

Das, J. P., Naglieri, J. A., & Kirby, J. R. (1994). *Assessment of cognitive processes: PASS theory of intelligence.* Boston, Massachusetts: Allyn & Bacon.

Das, J. P., Naglieri, J. A., & Murphy, D. (1995). Individual differences in cognitive processes of planning: A personality variable? *Psychological Records, 45,* 355–371.

Das, J. P., & Papadopoulos, T. C. (2003). Behavioral inhibition and hyperactivity: A commentary from alternative perspectives. *European Journal of Special Needs Education, 18*(2), 183–195.

Das, J. P., & Parrila, R. K. (1996). Planning in writing. *Issues in Education, 1,* 77–184.

Das, J. P., Parrila, R. K., & Papadopoulos, T. C. (2000). Cognitive education and reading disability. In A. Kozulin & Y. Rand (Eds), *Experience of mediated learning: An impact of Feuerstein's theory in education and psychology* (pp. 274–291). Oxford: Pergamon Press.

Das, J. P., Snyder, T. J., & Mishra, R. K. (1992). Assessment of attention: Teachers' rating scales and measures of selective attention. *Journal of Psychoeducational Assessment, 10,* 37–46.

Das, J. P., & Varnhagen, C. K. (1986). Neuropsychological functioning and cognitive processing. In J. E. Obzrut & G. W. Hynd (Eds), *Child neuropsychology, Vol. 1: Theory and research* (pp. 117–140). New York: Academic Press.

Davids, S. L., Schapira, M. M., McAuliffe, T. L., & Nattinger, A. B. (2004). Predictors of pessimistic breast cancer risk perceptions in a primary care population. *Journal of General Internal Medicine, 19*(4), 310–315.

Davidson, R. J., & Begley, S. (2012). *The emotional life of your brain: How its unique patterns affect the way you think, feel, and live—and how you can change them*. New York: Hudson Street Press.

Dawes, R. M. (1998). Behavioral decision making and judgment. In D. T. Gilbert, S. T. Fiske, & G. Lindzey (Eds), *The handbook of social psychology* (Vol. 1, pp. 497–548). Boston, Massachusetts: McGraw-Hill.

Dawes, R. M., van de Kragt, A. J. C., & Orbell, J. M. (1988). Not me or thee but we: The importance of group identity in eliciting cooperation in dilemma situations: Experimental manipulations. *Acta Psychologica, 68*, 83–97.

De Bono, E. (1986). *Six thinking hats*. Little Brown & Company.

———. (2009). *Simplicity*. New York: Viking.

Dehaene, S. (1997). *The number sense*. New York: Oxford University Press.

Delis, D. C., Kaplan, E., & Kramer, J. H. (2001). *The Delis–Kaplan Executive Function System: Technical manual*. San Antonio, Texas: The Psychological Corporation.

Denckla, M. (1996). A theory and model of executive function: A neuropsychological perspective. In G. Lyon & N. Krasnegor (Eds), *Attention, memory and executive function* (pp. 263–278). Baltimore, Maryland: Paul H. Brookes.

Denckla, M., & Rudel, R. (1975). Rapid 'automatized' naming (R.A.N): Dyslexia differentiated from other learning disabilities. *Neuropsychologia, 14*, 471–479.

Denes, G., & Pizzamiglio, L. (1999). *Handbook of clinical and experimental neuropsychology*, Hove, UK: Psychology Press.

D'Esposito, M., Postle, B. R., & Rypma, B. (2002). The role of lateral prefrontal cortex in working memory: Evidence from event-related FMRI studies. *International Congress Series, 1232*, 21–27.

Diamond, A. (2013). Executive Functions. *Annual Review of Psychology, 64*, 135–168.

Diamond, A., Barnett, W. S., Thomas, J., & Munro, S. (2007). Preschool program improves cognitive control. *Science, 318*, 1387–1388.

Dieckmann, N. F., Slovic, P., & Peters, E. M. (2009). The use of narrative evidence and explicit likelihood by decisionmakers varying in numeracy. *Risk Analysis, 29*, 1473–1488.

Dietrich, A. (2007). *Introduction to Consciousness*. London: Palgrave Macmillan.

Doerner, D. (1985). Thinking and organization of action. In J. Kuhl & J. Beckman (Eds), *Action control: From cognition to behaviour*. Berlin: Springer Verlag.

Doherty, M. E., Mynatt, C., Tweney, R., & Schiavo, M. (1979). Pseudodiagnositicity. *Acta Psychologica, 43*, 111–121.

Donald, M. (1991). *Origins of the modern mind*. Cambridge, Massachusetts: Harvard University Press.

Donkers, B., Melenberg, B., & van Soest, A. (2001). Estimating risk attitudes using lotteries: A large sample approach. *The Journal of Risk and Uncertainty, 22*, 165–195.

Duckworth, S., Ragland, G. G., Sommerfeld, R. E., & Wyne, M. D. (1974). Modification of conceptual impulsivity in retarded children. *American Journal of Mental Deficiency, 79*, 59–63.

Duncan, J., Seitz, R. J., Kolodny, J., Bor, D., Herzog, H., Ahmed, A., Newell, F. N., & Emsile, H. (2000). A neural basis for general intelligence. *Science, 21*, 457–460.

Echeburua, E., Baez, C., & Fernandez-Montalvo, J. (1996). Comparative effectiveness of three therapeutic modalities in the psychological treatment of pathological gambling. *Behavioral and Cognitive Psychotherapy, 24*, 51–72.

Edwards, W. (1954). The theory of decision making. *Psychological Bulletin, 51*, 380–417.

Egeland, B. (1974). Training impulsive children in the use of more efficient scanning techniques. *Child Development, 45,* 165–171.

Elliott, R., & Greenberg, L. S. (2007). The essence of process-experiential/emotion-focused therapy. *American Journal of Psychotherapy, 61,* 241–254.

Epley, N., & Gilovich, T. (2004). Are adjustments insufficient? *Personality and Social Psychology Bulletin, 30,* 447–460.

———. (2006). The anchoring-and-adjustment heuristic: Why the adjustments are insufficient. *Psychological Science, 17,* 311–318.

Ericsson, K. A., & Simon, H. A. (1980). Verbal reports as data. *Psychological Review, 87,* 215–251.

———. (1984). *Protocol Analysis. Verbal Reports as Data.* Cambridge, Massachusetts: MIT Press.

———. (1993). *Protocol analysis: Verbal reports as data* (rev. ed.). Cambridge, Massachusetts: The MIT Press.

———. (1998). How to study thinking in everyday life: Contrasting think-aloud protocols with descriptions and explanations of thinking. *Mind, culture, and activity, 5,* 178–186.

Evans, J., & Frankish, K. (Eds). (2008). *In two minds: Dual processes and beyond.* Oxford University Press.

Evans, J. St. B. T. (1998). Matching bias in conditional reasoning: Do we understand it after 25 years? *Thinking and Reasoning, 4,* 45–82.

———. (2003). In two minds: Dual-process accounts of reasoning. *Trends in Cognitive Sciences, 7*(10), 454–459.

———. (2007). *Hypothetical thinking: Dual processes in reasoning and judgment.* New York: Psychology Press.

Evans, J. St. B. T., Barston, J., & Pollard, P. (1983). On the conflict between logic and belief in *syllogistic reasoning. Memory & Cognition, 11,* 295–306.

Evans, J. St. B. T., Newstead, S., Allen, J., & Pollard, P. (1994). Debiasing by instruction: The case of belief bias. *European Journal of Cognitive Psychology, 6,* 263–285.

Evans, J. St. B. T., Newstead, S. E., & Byrne, R. M. J. (1993). *Human reasoning: The psychology of deduction.* Hove, England: Erlbaum.

Evans, J. St. B. T., & Stanovich, K. E. (2013). Dual-process theories of higher cognition: Advancing the debate. *Perspectives on Psychological Science, 8,* 223–241.

Eysenck, H. J. (1982). Introduction. In H. J. Eysenck (Ed.), *A model for intelligence* (pp. 1–10). New York: Springer-Verlag.

Facione, P. (1990). *Critical thinking: A statement of expert consensus for purposes of educational assessment and instruction (executive summary of the Delphi Report).* La Cruz, California: California Academic Press.

Fennema, M. G., & Perkins, J. D. (2008). Mental budgeting versus marginal decision making: Training, experience and justification effects on decisions involving sunk costs. *Journal of Behavioral Decision Making, 21,* 225–239.

Fenton-O'Creevy, M., Nicholson, N., Soane, E., & Willman, P. (2003). Trading on illusions: Unrealistic perceptions of control and trading performance. *Journal of Occupational and Organizational Psychology, 76,* 53–68.

Feuerstein, R. (1980). *Instrumental enrichment: An intervention program for cognitive modifiability.* Baltimore, Maryland: University Park Press.

Fischhoff, B. (1982). Debiasing. In D. Kahneman, P. Slovic, & A. Tversky (Eds), *Judgment under uncertainty: Heuristics and biases* (pp. 422–444). New York: Cambridge University Press.

———. (2002). Heuristics and biases in application. In T. Gilovich, D. Griffin & D. Kahneman (Eds), *Heuristics and biases: The psychology of intuitive judgment* (pp. 730–748). New York: Cambridge University Press.

Fishbach, A., & Trope, Y. (2005). The substitutability of external control and self-control. *Journal of Experimental Social Psychology, 41*, 256–270.

Flanagan, D., Ortiz, S., Alfonso, V., & Mascolo, J. (2002). *The achievement test desk reference (ATDR): Comprehensive assessment and learning disabilities.* Boston, Massachusetts: Allyn & Bacon.

Flanagan, D. P., & Harrison, P. L. (Eds). (2005). *Contemporary intellectual assessment: Theories, tests, and issues.* New York: The Guilford Press.

Flavell, J. (1979). Metacognition and cognitive monitoring: A new era of cognitive developmental inquiry. *American Psychologist, 34*, 906–911.

Floresco, S. B., & Ghods-Sharifi, S. (2007). Amygdala-prefrontal cortical circuitry regulates effort-based decision making. *Cerebral Cortex, 17*, 251–260.

Foley, R. (1987). *The theory of epistemic rationality.* Cambridge, Massachusetts: Harvard University Press.

Fong, G. T., Krantz, D. H., & Nisbett, R. E. (1986). The effects of statistical training on thinking about everyday problems. *Cognitive Psychology, 18*, 253–292.

Fong, G. T., & Nisbett, R. E. (1991). Immediate and delayed transfer of training effects in statistical reasoning. *Journal of Experimental Psychology: General, 120*, 34–45.

Frederick, S., Novemsky, N., Wang, J., Dhar, R., & Nowlis, S. (2009). Opportunity cost neglect. *Journal of Consumer Research, 36*, 553–561.

Frensch, P. A., & Buchner, A. (1999). Domain-generality versus domain-specificity in cognition. In R. J. Sternberg (Ed.), *The nature of cognition* (pp. 137–172). Cambridge, Massachusetts: MIT Press.

Friedman, N. P., Miyake, A., Corley, R. P., Young, S. E., DeFries, J. C., & Hewitt, J. K. (2006). Not all executive functions are related to intelligence. *Psychological Science, 17*, 172–179.

Friedman, S. L., Scholnick, E. K., & Cocking, R. R. (1987). Reflections on reflections: What planning is and how it develops. In S. L. Friedman, E. K. Scholnick, & R. R. Cocking (Eds), *Blueprints for thinking* (pp. 515–534). New York: Cambridge University Press.

Frith, C. (2007). *Making up the mind: How the brain creates our mental world.* Oxford, UK: Blackwell Publishing.

———. (2010). What is consciousness for? *Pragmatics & Cognition, 18*, 497–551.

Frith, C. D. (2012). The role of metacognition in human social interactions. *Philosophical Transactions of the Royal Society B: Biological Sciences, 367*(1599), 2213–2223.

Frith, C. D., & Frith, U. (1972). The solitaire illusion: An illusion of numerosity. *Perception & Psychophysics, 11*(6), 409–410.

———. (2012). Mechanisms of social cognition. *Annual Review of Psychology, 63*, 287–313.

Frith, U. (1989). *Autism: Explaining the enigma.* Oxford: Basil Blackwell.

———. (1997). Brain, mind and behavior in dyslexia. In C. Hulme and M. Snowling (Eds.), *Dyslexia: Biology, cognition and intervention* (pp.1–19). San Diego, California: Singular Publishing Group.

Furnham, A., & McGill, C. (2003). Medical students' attitudes about complementary and alternative medicine. *The Journal of Alternative and Complementary Medicine, 9*, 275–284.

Gailliot, M. T. (2008). Unlocking the energy dynamics of executive functioning: Linking executive functioning to brain glycogen. *Perspectives on Psychological Science, 3*(4), 245–263.

Galinsky, A. D., & Mussweiler, T. (2001). First offers as anchors: The role of perspective-taking and negotiator focus. *Journal of Personality and Social Psychology, 81*, 657–669.

Garcia, J., Kimeldorf, D. J., & Koelling, R. A. (1955). Conditioned aversion to saccharin resulting from exposure to gamma radiation. *Science, 122*, 157–158.

Garnham, A., & Oakhill, J. (1994). *Thinking and reasoning.* Wiley-Blackwell.

Garon, N., Byson, S. E., & Smith, I. M. (2008). Executive functions in preschoolers: A review using an integrative framework. *Psychological Bulletin, 134*, 31–60.

Gathercole, S. E. (2007). The concept of working memory. In Y. Dudai, R. Roediger, E. Tulving, & S. Fitzpatrick (Eds), *Science of Memory: Concepts.* NewYork: Elsevier.

Gazzaniga, M.S. (Ed.) (1979). *Neuropsychology: Handbook of Behavioral Neurobiology* (Vol. 2). New York: Plenum Press.

Geary, D. C. (1994). *Children's mathematical development: Research and practical implications.* Washington, DC: American Psychological Association.

———. (2005). *The origin of mind: Evolution of brain, cognition, and general intelligence.* Washington, DC: American Psychological Association.

———. (2013). Early foundations of mathematical learning and their relation to learning disabilities. *Current Directions in Psychological Science, 22*, 23–27.

Geary, D. C., & Brown, S. C. (1991). Cognitive addition: Strategy choice and speed-of-processing differences in gifted, normal, and mathematically disabled children. *Developmental Psychology, 27*, 398–406.

Geary, D. C., Hoard, M. K., & Hamson, C. O. (1999). Numerical and arithmetical cognition: Patterns of functions and deficits in children at risk for mathematical disability. *Journal of Experimental Child Psychology, 74*, 213–239.

Georgiou, G., Das, J.P., & Hayward, D. (2008). Comparing the contribution of two tests of working memory to reading in relation to phonological awareness and rapid naming speed. *Journal of Research in Reading, 31*, 302–318.

Gigerenzer, G., Gaissmaier, W., Kurz-Milcke, E., Schwartz, L. M., & Woloshin, S. (2007). Helping doctors and patients make sense of health statistics. *Psychological Science in the Public Interest, 8*, 53–96.

Gilovich, T., Griffin, D., & Kahneman, D. (Eds). (2002). *Heuristics and biases: The psychology of intuitive judgment.* New York: Cambridge University Press.

Goldberg, E. (2001). *The executive brain: Frontal lobes and the civilized mind.* New York: Oxford University Press.

Goleman, D. (1988). *The meditative mind.* New York: Tarcher/Putnam.

———. (1995). *Emotional intelligence.* New York: Bantam.

Gonsalves, B., & Cohen, N. (2010). Brain imaging, cognitive processes, and brain networks. *Perspectives on Psychological Science, 5*, 744–752.

Grafman, J., & Litvan, I. (1999). Importance of deficits in executive function. *Lancet, 354*, 1921–1923.

Gray, J. R., Braver, T. S., & Raichle, M. E. (2002). Integration of emotion and cognition in the lateral prefrontal cortex. *Proceedings of the National Academy of Sciences, 99*, 4115–4120.

Grigorenko, E. L., & Sternberg, R. J. (1998). Dynamic testing. *Psychological Bulletin, 124*, 75–111.

Groopman, J. (2007). *How doctors think.* Boston, Massachusetts: Houghton Mifflin.

Grossberg, S., & Seidman, D. (2006). Neural dynamics of autistic behaviors: Cognitive, emotional, and timing substrates. *Psychological Review, 113*, 483–525.

Guenther, H. V. (1974). *Philosophy and psychology in the Abhidharma.* Delhi: Motilal Banarsidas.

Guthke, J. (1980). *Ist intelligenz messbar?* Berlin: VEB.

Guthke, J., Beckman, J., & Heike, D. (1997). Dynamic testing: Problems, uses, trends, and evidence of validity. *Educational and Child Psychology, 14*, 17–32.

Gwenny et al. (2010). *International Journal of Psychology and Psychological Therapy, 10*(1), 19–40.

Haggard, P., & Tsakiris, M. (2009). The experience of agency: Feelings, judgments, and responsibility. *Current Directions in Psychological Science, 18*(4), 242–246.

Hahn, T. N. (1998). *The heart of Buddha's teaching.* New York: Broadway Books.
Haidt, J. (2001). The emotional dog and its rational tail: A social intuitionist approach to moral judgment. *Psychological review, 108,* 814–834.
Halpern, D. F. (1998). Teaching critical thinking for transfer across domains: Dispositions, skills, training, and metacognitive monitoring. *American Psychologist, 53,* 449–455.
———. (2003). Thinking critically about creative thinking. *Critical Creative Processes,* 189–207.
Hammill, D. D., & Larsen, S. C. (1988). *Test of Written Language-2.* Austin, Texas: Pro-Ed.
Harlow, H., McGaugh, J. L., & Thompson, R. F. (1971). *Psychology.* San Francisco, California: Albion Publishing Co.
Harman, G. (1995). Rationality. In E. E. Smith & D. N. Osherson (Eds), *Thinking* (Vol. 3, pp.175–211). Cambridge, Massachusetts: The MIT Press.
Hastie, R., & Dawes, R. M. (2001). *Rational choice in an uncertain world.* Thousand Oaks, California: SAGE.
Hayes, J. R., & Berninger, V. W. (2009). Relationships between idea generation and transcription: How act of writing shapes what children write. In R. K. Braverman, K. Lunsford, McLeod, S., Null, S., & A. S. P. Rogers (Eds), *Traditions of writing research* (pp. 166–180). New York: Taylorand Frances/Routledge.
Hayes-Roth, B., & Hayes-Roth, F. (1979). A cognitive model of planning. *Cognitive Science, 3,* 275–310.
Hayward, D., Das, J. P., & Janzen, T. (2007). Innovative programs for improvement in reading through cognitive enhancement: A remediation study of Canadian First Nations children. *Journal of Learning Disabilities, 40,* 443–457.
Haywood, H. C, & Tzuriel, D. (Eds). (1992). *Interactive assessment.* New York: Springer-Verlag.
Hebb, D. O. (1960). The American Revolution. *American Psychologist, 15,* 735–745.
Hill, E. (2004). Executive dysfunction in autism. *Trends in Cognitive Sciences, 8,* 26–32.
Hilton, D. J. (2003). Psychology and the financial markets: Applications to understanding and remedying irrational decision-making. In I. Brocas & J. D. Carrillo (Eds), *The psychology of economic decisions: Rationality and well-being* (Vol. 1, pp. 273–297). Oxford: Oxford University Press.
Hodgins, D. C., Currie, S. R., Currie, G., & Fick, G. H. (2009). Randomized trial of brief motivational treatments for pathological gamblers: More is not necessarily better. *Journal of Consulting and Clinical Psychology, 77,* 950–960.
Horn, J. L., & Cattell, R. B. (1967). Age differences in fluid and crystallized intelligence. *Acta Psychologica, 26,* 1–23.
Huey, E. D., Krueger, F., & Grafman, J. (2006). Representations in the human prefrontal cortex. *Current Directions in Psychological Science, 15,* 167–171.
Hynd, G. W., & Willis, G. (1985). Neurological foundations of intelligence. In B. B. Wolman (Ed.), *Handbook of intelligence: Theories, measurement, and applications* (pp. 119–157). New York: Wiley.
Janis, I. L. (1989). *Crucial decision.* New York: The Free Press.
Jarman, R. F., & Das, J. P. (1977). Simultaneous and successive synthesis and intelligence. *Intelligence, 1,* 151–169.
Jeffrey, R. C. (1983). *The logic of decision* (2nd ed.). Chicago, Illinois: University of Chicago Press.
Jensen, A. R. (1981). *Straight talk about mental tests.* New York: Free Press.
———. (1998). *The g factor: The science of mental ability.* Westport, Connecticut: Praeger.
Jensen, A. R. (2006). *Clocking the mind: Mental chronometry and individual differences.* Oxford, UK: Elsevier.

Jung, R. E., & Haier, R. J. (2007). The parieto-frontal integration theory (P-FIT) of intelligence: Converging neuroimaging evidence. *Behavioral and Brain Sciences, 30*(2), 135–154.

Iseman, J., & Naglieri, J. (2011). A cognitive strategy instruction to improve math calculation for children with ADHD and LD: A randomized controlled study. *Journal of Learning Disabilities, 44,* 184–195.

Kadosh, C., & Walsh, V. (2009) Numerical representation in the parietal lobes. *Behavioral and Brain Sciences, 32,* 313–373.

Kadosh, R.C., & Lammertyn, V. I. (2008). Are numbers special? An overview of chronometric, neuroimaging, developmental and comparative studies of magnitude representation. *Progress in Neurobiology, 84,* 132–147.

Kahneman, D. (25 October 2011). *Thinking, fast and slow.* New York: Macmillan. ISBN 978-1-4299-6935-2. Accessed April 8, 2012.

Kahneman, D., & Frederick, S. (2002). Representativeness revisited: Attribute substitution in intuitive judgment. In T. Gilovich, D. Griffin, & D. Kahneman (Eds), *Heuristics and biases: The psychology of intuitive judgment* (pp. 49–81). New York: Cambridge: University Press.

Kahneman, D., & Klein, G. (2009). Conditions for intuitive expertise: A failure to disagree. *American Psychology, 64,* 515–526.

Kahneman, D., Knetsch, J. L., & Thaler, R. H. (1990). Experimental tests of the endowment effect and the Coase theorem. *Journal of Political Economy, 98,* 1325–1348.

Kahneman, D., & Tversky, A. (Eds). *Choices, values, and frames* (pp. 288–300). Cambridge: Cambridge University Press.

Kahneman, D., & Tversky, A. (1972). Subjective probability: A judgment of representativeness. *Cognitive Psychology, 3,* 430–454.

———. (1973). On the psychology of prediction. *Psychological Review, 80,* 237–251.

———. (1979). Prospect theory: An analysis of decision under risk. *Econometrica, 47,* 263–291.

———. (1984). Choices, values, and frames. *American Psychologist, 39,* 341–350.

Kahneman, D., & Tversky, A. (Eds). (2000). *Choices, values, and frames.* Cambridge: Cambridge University Press.

Kalupahana, D. J. (1987). *The principles of Buddhist psychology.* Albany, New York: SUNY Press.

Kane, M. J., & Engle, R. W. (2002). The role of prefrontal cortex in working-memory capacity, executive attention, and general fluid intelligence: An individual-differences perspective. *Psychonomic Bulletin & Review, 9,* 637–671.

Kaplan, R., & Kaplan, S. (1989). *The experience of nature: A psychological perspective.* Cambridge University Press. ISBN 0-521-34939-7.

Kaplan, S., & Berman, M. G. (2010). Directed attention as a common resource for executive functioning and self-regulation. *Perspectives on Psychological Science, 5*(1), 43–57.

Kar, B. C., Dash, U. N., Das, J. P., & Carlson, J. (1993). Two experiments on the dynamic assessment of planning. *Learning and Individual Differences, 5,* 13–29.

Kaufman A. S., & Kaufman, N. L. (1983). *Kaufman assessment battery for children (K-ABC).* Circle Pines, Minnesota: American Guidance Service.

Kendall, P. C., Hudson, J. L., Gosch, E., Flannery-Schroeder, E., & Suveg, C. (2008). Cognitive behavioral therapy for anxiety disordered youth: A randomized clinical trial evaluating child and family modalities. *Journal of Consulting and Clinical Psychology, 76,* 282–297.

Keynes, J. M. (1936). *The general theory of employment, interest, and money.* New York: Harcourt Brace Jovanovich.

Klaczynski, P. A. (1993). Reasoning schema effects on adolescent rule acquisition and transfer. *Journal of Educational Psychology, 85*(4), 679–692.

Klaczynski, P. A. (2001). Analytic and heuristic processing influences on adolescent reasoning and decision making. *Child Development, 72*, 844–861.
Klaczynski, P. A., Gelfand, H., & Reese, H. W. (1989). Transfer of conditional reasoning: Effects of explanations and initial problem types. *Memory and Cognition, 17*(2), 208–220.
Klaczynski, P. A., & Laipple, J. (1993). Role of content domain, logic training, and IQ in rule acquisition and transfer. *Journal of Experimental Psychology: Learning, Memory, and Cognition, 19*, 653–672.
Klahr, D., & Nigam, M. (2004). The equivalence of learning paths in early science instruction: Effects of direct instruction and discovery learning. *Psychological Science, 15*, 661–667.
Klauer, K. C. (2007). Training effects in deductive reasoning: A theory-based review. In W. Schaeken, A. Vandierendonck, W. Schroyens, & G. d'Ydewalle (Eds), *The mental models theory of reasoning: Refinements and extensions*. Mahwah, New Jersey: Lawrence Erlbaum.
Klauer, K. C., Stegmaier, R., & Meiser, T. (1997). Working memory involvement in propositional and spatial reasoning. *Thinking and Reasoning, 3*, 9–47.
Klein, G. (2002). *Intuition at work: why developing your gut instincts will make you better at what you do*. New York: Currency Books.
Klemp, G. D., & McClelland, D. C. (1986). What characterizes intelligent functioning among senior managers? In R. J. Sternberg & R. K. Wagner (Eds), *Practical intelligence: Nature and origins of competence in the everyday world*. London: Cambridge University Press.
Klimesch (1980). The effect of verbalization on memory performance for complex pictures. *Zeitschrift fuĚ'r Experimentelle und Angewandte Psychologie, 27*, 225–245.
Koehler, D. J., & Harvey, N. (Eds). (2004). *Blackwell handbook of judgment and decision making*. Oxford, England: Blackwell.
Kolb, B., Gibb, R., & Robinson, T. E. (2003). Brain plasticity and behavior. *Current Directions in Psychological Science, 12*(1), 1–4.
Kolb, B., & Whishaw, I. Q. (2003). *Fundamentals of Human Neuropsychology*. New York: Feeman.
Kornfield, J. (1993). *A path with heart: A guide through the perils and promises of spiritual life*. Bantam Books.
Kosonen, P., & Winne, P. H. (1995). Effects of teaching statistical laws on reasoning about everyday problems. *Journal of Educational Psychology, 87*, 33–46.
Kowalski, P., & Taylor, A. K. (2009). The effect of refuting misconceptions in the introductory psychology class. *Teaching of Psychology, 36*, 153–159.
Kroesbergen, E. H., Johannes E. H., Luit, V., & Naglieri, J. A. (2003). Mathematical learning difficulties and PASS cognitive processes. *Journal of Learning Disabilities, 36*, 574–582.
Kuhn, D. (1989). Children and adults as intuitive scientists. *Psychological Review, 96*, 674–689.
———. (1991). *The skills of argument*. Cambridge: Cambridge University Press.
———. (1993). Connecting scientific and informal reasoning. *Merrill-Palmer Quarterly, 38*, 74–103.
———. (2001). How do people know? *Psychological Science, 12*, 1–8.
———. (2006). Do cognitive changes accompany developments in the adolescent brain? *Perspectives on Psychological Science, 1*, 5–67.
Kuhn, D., & Dean, D. J. (2005). Is developing scientific thinking all about learning to control variables? *Psychological Science, 16*, 866–870.
Kuhn, D., & Pease, M. (2008). What needs to develop in the development of inquiry skills? *Cognition and Instruction, 26*, 512–559.
Kuhn, D., & Udell, W. (2007). Coordinating own and other perspectives in argument. *Thinking & Reasoning, 13*, 90–104.

Kunda, Z. (1990). The case for motivated reasoning. *Psychological Bulletin, 108*, 480–498.
Ladouceur, R., Sylvain, C., Boutin, C., Lachance, S., Doucet, C., Leblond, J., & Christian, J. (2001). Cognitive treatment of pathological gambling. *The Journal of Nervous and Mental Disease, 189*, 774–780.
Lane, J.- E. (1986). The logic of means-end analysis. *Quality and Quantity, 20*(4), 339–356.
Larrick, R. P., Morgan, J. N., & Nisbett, R. E. (1990). Teaching the use of cost-benefit reasoning in everyday life. *Psychological Science, 1*, 362–370.
Larrick, R. P., Nisbett, R. E., & Morgan, J. N. (1993). Who uses the cost-benefit rules of choice? Implications for the normative status of microeconomic theory. *Organizational Behavior and Human Decision Processes, 56*, 331–347.
Lashley, K. S. (1929). *Brain mechanisms and intelligence: A quantitative study of injuries to the brain*. Chicago, Ilinois: University of Chicago Press.
Leavitt, H. J. (1975). Beyond the analytic manager: *California Management Review, 17*(4), 11–21.
LeBoeuf, R. A., & Shafir, E. (2005). Decision making. In K. J. Holyoak & R. G. Morrison (Eds), *The Cambridge handbook of thinking and reasoning* (pp. 243–265). New York: Cambridge University Press.
———. (2006). The long and short of it: Physical anchoring effects. *Journal of Behavioral Decision Making, 19*, 393–406.
LeDoux, J. (1996). *The emotional brain: The mysterious underpinnings of emotional life*. New York: Simon & Schuster.
Lefcourt, H. M. (1991). Locus of control. In J. P. Robinson, P. Shaver & L. S. Wrightsman (Eds), *Measures of personality and social psychological attitudes* (pp. 413–499). San Diego, California: Academic Press.
Lehman, D. R., & Nisbett, R. E. (1990). A longitudinal study of the effects of undergraduate training on reasoning. *Developmental Psychology, 26*, 952–960.
Lehman, D. R., Lempert, R. O., & Nisbett, R. E. (1988). The effect of graduate training on reasoning. *American Psychologist, 43*, 431–442.
Leontjev, A. N. (1978). *Activity, consciousness, and personality*. Englewood Cliff, New Jersey: Prentice-Hall.
———. (1979). The problem of activity in psychology. In J. V. Wertsch (Ed.), *The concepts of activity in Soviet psychology* (pp. 37–71). New York: M.E. Sharpe.
———. (1981). The problem of activity in psychology. In J. V. Wertsch (Ed.), *The concept of activity in Soviet psychology* (pp. 37–71). New York: M.E. Sharpe.
Leshowitz, B., DiCerbo, K. E., & Okun, M. A. (2002). Effects of instruction in methodological reasoning on information evaluation. *Teaching of Psychology, 29*, 5–10.
Leshowitz, B., Jenkens, K., Heaton, S., & Bough, T. L. (1993). Fostering critical thinking skills in students with learning disabilities: An instructional program. *Journal of Learning Disabilities, 26*, 483–490.
Levin, I. P., Gaeth, G. J., Schreiber, J., & Lauriola, M. (2002). A new look at framing effects: Distribution of effect sizes, individual differences, and independence of types of effects. *Organizational Behavior and Human Decision Processes, 88*, 411–429.
Levin, I. P., Schneider, S. L., & Gaeth, G. J. (1998). All frames are not created equal: A typology and critical analysis of framing effects. *Organizational Behavior and Human Decision Processes, 76*,149–188.
Lezak, M. D. (1995). *Neuropsychological assessment* (3rd ed.). New York: Oxford University Press.
Lezak, M. D. (2004). *Neuropsychological assessment* (4th ed). Oxford: Oxford University Press.
Lichtenstein, S., & Fischhoff, B. (1980). Training for calibration. *Organizational Behavior and Human Performance, 26*, 149–171.

Lidz, C. S. (1987). *Dynamic assessment*. New York: Guilford Press.
———. (1991). *Practitioner's guide to dynamic assessment*. New York: Guilford Press.
Lilienfeld, S. O., Lynn, S. J., Ruscio, J., & Beyerstein, B. L. (2010). *50 Great myths of popular psychology*. Malden, Massachusetts: Wiley-Blackwell.
Lilienfeld, S. O., Ruscio, J., & Lynn, S. J. (Eds). (2008). *Navigating the mindfield: A guide to separating science from pseudoscience in mental health*. Buffalo, New York: Prometheus Books.
Lord, C. G., Lepper, M. R., & Preston, E. (1984). Considering the opposite: A corrective strategy for social judgment. *Journal of Personality and Social Psychology, 47*, 1231–1243.
Luce, R. D., & Raiffa, H. (1957). *Games and decisions*. New York: Wiley.
Luria, A. R. (1961). *The role of speech in the regulation of normal and abnormal behavior*. Oxford: Liveright.
———. (1962). *Higher cortical functions in man*. New York: Basic Books.
———. (1963). *The mentally retarded child*. New York: MacMillan.
———. (1966). *Human brain and psychological processes*. New York: Harper and Row.
———. (1970). The functional organization of the brain. *Scientific American, 220*, 66–79.
———. (1973a). *The working brain*. New York: Basic Books.
———. (1973b). The origin and cerebral organization of man's conscious action. In S. G. Sapir & A. C. Nitzburg (Eds), *Children with learning problems* (pp. 109–130). New York: Brunner/Mazel.
———. (1978). L. S. Vygotsky and the problem of functional localization. In M. Cole (Ed.), *The selected writings of A.R.Luria* (pp. 273–281). White Plains, New York: Sharpe.
———. (1979). *The making of mind: A personal account of Soviet psychology*. In M. Cole & S. Cole (Eds), Cambridge, Massachusetts: Harvard University Press.
———. (1980). *Higher cortical functions in man* (2nd ed.). New York: Basic Books.
———. (1981). *Language and cognition*. New York: Wiley & Sons.
———. (1982). *Language and cognition*. J. V. Wertsch (Ed.). New York: John Wiley.
Luria, A.R., & Tsvetkova, L.S. (1990). *The neuropsychological analysis of problem solving*. Orlando, Florida: Paul M. Deutsch Press.
Luria, R., & Vinogradova, O. S. (1959). An objective investigation of the dynamics of semantic systems. *British Journal of Psychology, 50*, 89–105.
Mabbott, D. J., & Bisanz, J. (2008). Computational skills, working memory, and conceptual knowledge in older children with mathematics learning disabilities. *Journal of Learning Disabilities, 41*, 15–28.
MacDonald, A. W., Cohen, J. D., Stenger, V. A., & Carter, C. S. (2000). Dissociating the role of the dorsolateral prefrontal cortex and anterior cingulate cortex in cognitive control. *Science, 288*, 1835.
Mackey, L., English, M., Bisanz, J., & Kulak, A. (2002). *Executive functioning and prenatal exposure to alcohol*. Unpublished paper.
Mackintosh, N.J. (January–February 2007). Book review—Race differences in intelligence: An evolutionary hypothesis. *Intelligence, 35* (1): 94–96.
———. (2006). Response to Rushton. *Psychological Science, 17*, 919–920.
MacLeod, C. M., & McDonald, P. A. (2000). Interdimensional interference in the Stroop effect: Uncovering the cognitive and neural anatomy of attention. *Trends in Cognitive Sciences, 4*, 383–391.
Macpherson, R., & Stanovich, K. E. (2007). Cognitive ability, thinking dispositions, and instructional set as predictors of critical thinking. *Learning and Individual Differences, 17*, 115–127.
Mahapatra, S., Das, J. P., Stack-Cutler, H., & Parrila, R. (2011). Remediating reading comprehension difficulties: A cognitive processing approach. *Reading Psychology, 31*, 428–453.

Manktelow, K. I. (2004). Reasoning and rationality: The pure and the practical. In K. I. Manktelow & M. C. Chung (Eds), *Psychology of reasoning: Theoretical and historical perspectives* (pp. 157–177). Hove, England: Psychology Press.

Markovits, H., & Nantel, G. (1989). The belief-bias effect in the production and evaluation of logical conclusions. *Memory & Cognition, 17*, 11–17.

Marlatt, G. A., Baer, J. S., Kivlahan, D. R., Dimeff, L. A., Larimer, M. E., Quigley, L. A., Somers, J. M., & Williams, E. (1998). Screening and brief intervention for high-risk college student drinkers: Results from a 2-year follow-up assessment. *Journal of Consulting and Clinical Psychology, 66*, 604–615.

Mathur, P., & Das, J. P. (1997). Aspects of conceptual planning: A study on engineering students. In J. R. Isaac, S. Gupta, & M. Datta (Eds), *Cognitive systems: From intelligent systems to more human environments?* (pp. 487–492). New Delhi: Tata McGraw-Hill Publishing Company.

Matson, K. (October 2002). [Review of the book *Intuition at work: why developing your gut instincts will make you better at what you do*]. *Publisher's Weekly*. Retrieved from http://www.publishersweekly.com/978-0-385-50288-7 (accessed July 30, 2014).

Mattson, S. N., & Riley, E. P. (1998). A review of the neurobehavioral deficits in children with fetal alcohol syndrome or prenatal exposure to alcohol. *Alcoholism: Clinical and Experimental Research, 22*, 279–294.

Maurizio, C., & Shulman, G. L. (2002). Control of goal-directed and stimulus-driven attention in the brain. *Nature Reviews Neuroscience, 3*, 201–215.

McBurney, D. H. (1976). ESP in the psychology curriculum. *Teaching of Psychology, 3*(2), 66–69.

McClelland, D. C. (1973). Testing for competence rather than for "intelligence." *American Psychologist, 28*, 1–14.

McCutchen, D. (1987). Children's discourse skills: Form and modality requirements of school writing. *Discourse Processes, 10*, 267–286.

———. (1995). Cognitive processes in children's writing: Developmental and individual differences. *Issues in Education, 1*, 123–160.

McFarland, S., Brown, D. & Webb, M. (2013). Identification with all humanity as a moral construct and psychological construct. *Current Directions in Psychological Science, 22*, 194–198.

McNeel, S. P. (1973). Training cooperation in the prisoner's dilemma. *Journal of Experimental Social Psychology, 9*, 335–348.

Menkes, J. (2005). *Executive intelligence: What all great leaders have*. New York: HarperBusiness.

Mercier, H., & Sperber, D. (2011). Why do humans reason? Arguments for an argumentative theory. *Behavioral and Brain Sciences, 34*, 57–111.

Merz, F. (1969). Der einfluss des verbalisierens auf die leistung bei intelligenzaufgaben. In: Z.f.exp. u. angew. *Psychologie, 18*, S. 114–137.

Mhurchu, C. N., Margetts, B. M., & Speller, V. (1998). Randomized clinical trial comparing the effectiveness of two dietary interventions for patients with hyperlipidaemia. *Clinical Science, 95*, 479–487.

Milkman, K. L., Rogers, T., & Bazerman, M. H. (2008). Harnessing our inner angels and demons. *Perspectives on Psychological Science, 3*, 324–338.

Miller, G. A., Galanter, E. H., & Pribram, K. H. (1960). *Plans and the structure of behavior*. New York: Holt, Rinehart & Winston.

Miller, R. L., Wozniak, W. J., Rust, M. R., Miller, B. R., & Slezak, J. (1996). Counterattitudinal advocacy as a means of enhancing instructional effectiveness: How to teach students what they do not want to know. *Teaching of Psychology, 23*, 215–219.

Miller, W. R., & Rollnick, S. (2002). *Motivational interviewing: Preparing people for change* (2nd ed.). Guilford, New York: Guilford Press.
Miller, W. R., & Rose, G. S. (2009). Toward a theory of motivational interviewing. *American Psychologist, 64*, 527–537.
Mintzberg, H. (1973). *The nature of managerial work.* New York: Harper & Row.
———. (1976). Planning on the left side and managing on the right. *Harvard Business Review, 54*, 49–58.
Mishra, R. K., & Das, J .P. (1997). Unpublished technical report. Developmental disabilities Centre, University of Alberta, Edmonton.
Miyake, A., & Friedman, N. P. (2012). The nature and organization of individual differences in executive functions: Four general conclusions. *Current Directions in Psychological Science, 21*, 8–14.
Miyake, A., Friedman, N. P., Emerson, M. J., Witzki, A. H., Howerter, A., & Wager, T. D. (2000). The unity and diversity of executive functions and their contributions to complex "frontal lobe" tasks: A latent variable analysis. *Cognitive Psychology, 41*, 49–100.
Mohr, W. K. (2005). Evidence-based practice and pseudoscience. In W. K. Mohr (Ed.), *Johnson's psychiatric-mental health nursing* (6th ed., pp. 141–152). Philadelphia, Pennsylvania: Lippincott Williams & Wilkins.
Morris, M. & and Ward, G. (Eds). (2005). *The cognitive psychology of planning.* Psychology Press.
Moshman, D. (1990). Rationality as a goal of education. *Educational Psychology Review, 2*, 335–364.
———. (2004). From inference to reasoning: The construction of rationality. *Thinking and Reasoning, 10*, 221–239.
———. (2005). Commentary: The development of thinking. In J. E. Jacobs & P. A. Klaczynski (Eds), *The development of judgment and decision making in children and adolescents*.Mahwah, New Jersey: Lawrence Erlbaum.
———. (2010). The development of rationality. In H. Siegel (Ed.), *Oxford handbook of philosophy of education* (pp. 145–161). Oxford: Oxford University Press.
Moutier, S., Angeard, N., & Houdé, O. (2002). Deductive reasoning and matching-bias inhibition training: Evidence from a debiasing paradigm. *Thinking and Reasoning, 8*, 205–224.
Moutier, S., & Houdé, O. (2003). Judgement under uncertainty and conjunction fallacy inhibition training. *Thinking and Reasoning, 9*, 185–201.
Mukherjee, K. (2010). A dual system model of preferences under risk. *Psychological Review, 117*(1), 243–255. doi: 10.1037/a0017884
Mumma, G. T., & Wilson, S. B. (1995). Procedural debiasing of primacy/anchoring effects in clinical-like judgments. *Journal of Clinical Psychology, 51*, 841–853.
Murray, H. A. (1943). *Thematic Apperception Test Manual.* Cambridge, Massachusetts: Harvard University Press.
Mussweiler, T., Strack, F., & Pfeiffer, T. (2000). Overcoming the inevitable anchoring effect: Considering the opposite compensates for selective accessibility. *Personality and Social Psychology Bulletin, 26*, 1142–1150.
Muthén, B., & Muthén, L. K. (2000). Integrating person-centered and variable-centered analyses: Growth mixture modeling with latent trajectory classes. *Alcoholism: Clinical and Experimental Research, 24*, 882–891.
Nagin, D. S. (1999). Analyzing developmental trajectories: A semiparametric, group-based approach. *Psychological Methods, 4*, 139–157.
Naglieri, J., & Gottling, S. (1995). A cognitive education approach to math instruction for the learning disabled: An individual study. *Psychological Reports, 76*, 1343–1354.

Naglieri, J. A. (1999). *Essentials of CAS assessment*. New York: Wiley.

Naglieri, J. A., & Das, J. P. (1987). Construct and criterion-related validity of planning, simultaneous, and successive cognitive processing tasks. *Journal of Psychoeducational Assessment, 4*, 353–363.

———. (1988). Planning—arousal-simultaneous and-successive (PASS): A model for assessment. *Journal of School Psychology, 26*, 35–48.

———. (1990). Planning, attention, simultaneous, and successive (PASS) cognitive processes as a model for intelligence. *Journal of Psychoeducational Assessment, 8*, 303–337.

———. (1997a). *Das–Naglieri cognitive assessment system*. Itasca, Illinois: Riverside Publishing.

———. (1997b). *Cognitive assessment system interpretive handbook*. Chicago, Illinois: Riverside.

———. PASS theory and 'g'. In R. J. Sternberg & E. L. Grigorenko (Eds), *The general factor of intelligence: How general is it?* Mahwah, New Jersey: Lawrence Erlbaum Associates.

Naglieri, J. A., Goldstein, S., Iseman, J. S., & Schwebach, A. (2003). Performance of children with attention deficit hyperactivity disorder and anxiety/depression on the WISC-III and cognitive assessment system (CAS). *Journal of Psychoeducational Assessment, 21*, 32–42.

Naglieri, J., & Gottling, S. (1997). Mathematics instruction and PASS cognitive processes: An intervention study. *Journal of Learning Disabilities, 30*, 513–520.

Naglieri, J. A., & Johnson, D. (2000). Effectiveness of a cognitive strategy intervention in improving arithmetic computation based on the PASS theory. *Journal of Learning Disabilities, 33*, 591–597.

Newcomer, P. L., & Barenbaum, E. M. (1991). The written composing ability of children with learning disabilities: A re- view of the literature from 1980–1990. *Journal of Learning Disabilities, 24*, 578–593.

Newell, A., Shaw, J. C., & Simon, H. A. (1958a). Elements of a theory of human problem solving. *Psychological Review, 65*, 151–166.

———. (1958b). Chess-playing problems and the problem of complexity. *IBM Journal of Research and Development, 2*, 320–335.

———. (1959). Report on general problem-solving program. Proceedings of the International Conference on Information Processing, Paris.

———. (1972). *Human problem solving*. Englewood Cliffs, New Jersey: Prentice-Hall.

Nigg, J.T. (2010). Attention-deficit/hyperactivity disorder endophenotypes, structure, and etiological pathways. *Current Directions in Psychological Science, 19*, 24–29.

Nisbett, R. E., Fong, G. T., Lehman, D. R., & Cheng, P. W. (1987). Teaching reasoning. *Science, 238*, 625–631.

Nunes, T., & Bryant, P. (1996). *Children doing mathematics*. Oxford: Blackwell.

O'Brien, D., & Overton, W. F. (1980). Conditional reasoning following contradictory evidence: A developmental analysis. *Journal of Experimental Child Psychology, 30*, 44–61.

Odishaw, J. D. (2007). *Cognitive processing in children and adolescents with fetal alcohol spectrum disorder: Assessing alternative measures in predicting adaptive behaviour*. Unpublished doctoral dissertation, University of Alberta, Edmonton, AB.

Okuhata, S. T., Okazaki, S., & Maekawa, H. (2008). EEG coherence pattern during simultaneous and successive processing tasks. *International Journal of Psychophysiology, 72*, 89–96.

Olson, D. R. (1994). *The world on paper*. Cambridge, Massachusets: Cambridge University Press.

O'Reilly, R. C. (2010). The what and how of prefrontalcortical organization. *Trends in Neurosciences, 33*, 355–361.

Over, D. E. (2004). Rationality and the normative/descriptive distinction. In D. J. Koehler & N.Harvey (Eds), *Blackwell handbook of judgment and decision making* (pp. 3–18). Malden, Massachusetts: Blackwell Publishing.

Overton, W. F., Byrnes, J. P., & O'Brien, D. P. (1985). Developmental and individual differences in conditional reasoning: The role of contradiction training and cognitive style. *Developmental Psychology, 21*, 692–701.

Owen, A. M., Morris, R. G., Sahakian, B. J., Polkey, C. E., & Robbins, T. W. (1996). Double dissociations of memory and executive functions in working memory tasks following frontal lobe excisions, temporal lobe excisions or amygdalo-ippocampectomy in man. *Brain, 119*, 1597–1615. doi:10.1093/brain/119.5.1597. PMID 8931583.

Ozolins, D. A., & Anderson, R. P. (1980). Effects of feedback on the vigilance task performance of hyperactive and hypoactive children. *Perceptual & Motor Skills, 50*, 415–24.

Özyıldırım, I. (2009). Narrative analysis: An analysis of oral and written strategies in personal experience narratives. *Journal of Pragmatics, 41*(6), 1209–1222.

Panskepp, J. (1998). Attention deficit hyperactivity disorders, psychostimulants, and intolerance of childhood playfulness: A tragedy in the making? *Current Directions in Psychological Science, 7*, 91–98.

Papadopoulos, T. C., Das, J. P., Kodero, N. H., & Solomon, V. (2002). Assessment of attention in school children: Teachers ratings related to tests of attention. *European Journal of Special Needs Education, 17*, 1–18.

Papadopoulos, T. H., Panayiotou, G., Spanoudis, G., & Nastapoulos, D. (2005). Evidence of poor planning and children with attention deficits. *Journal of Abnormal Child Psychology, 33*, 611–623.

Parker, A. M., & Fischhoff, B. (2005). Decision-making competence: External validation through an individual differences approach. *Journal of Behavioral Decision Making, 18*, 1–27.

Parrila, R., Das, J. P., & Dash, U. N. (1996). Development of planning and its relation to other cognitive processes. *Journal of Applied Developmental Psychology, 17*, 597–624.

Parrila, R., Das, J. P., Kendrick, T. C., Papadopoulos, T. C., & Kirby, J. R. (1999). Efficacy of a cognitive reading remediation programme for At-Risk children in Grade 1. *Developmental Disabilities Bulletin*, 27, 1–31.

Parrila, R. K. (1996). *The development of planning skills in children*. Ph.D. dissertation, University of Alberta.

Pavlov, I. P. (1928). *Lectures on conditioned reflexes (Vol. I)*. (W. H. Gantt, Ed. & Trans.). New York: International Publishers.

———. (1941). *Lectures on conditioned reflexes (Vol. II): Conditioned reflexes and psychiatry*. (W. H. Gantt, Ed. & Trans.). New York: International Publishers.

Pennington, B. F., & Ozonoff, S. (1996). Executive functions and developmental psychopathology. *Journal of Child Psychology and Psychiatry, 37*, 51–87.

Peters, E., Västfjäll, D., Slovic, P., Mertz, C. K., Mazzocco, K., & Dickert, S. (2006). Numeracy and decision making. *Psychological Science, 17*, 407–413.

Petrides, M. (2005). Lateral prefrontal cortex: Architectonic and functional organization. *Philosiphical Transactions of the Royal Society London B: Biological Science, 360*(1456), 781–795.

Pinker, S. (2011). *The better angels of our nature*. New York: Viking.

Platt, R. D., & Griggs, R. A. (1993). Facilitation in the abstract selection task: The effects of attentional and instructional factors. *Quarterly Journal of Experimental Psychology, 46*(4), 591–613.

Poldrack, R. (2010). Mapping mental function to brain structure: How can cognitive neuroimaging succeed? *Perspectives on Psychological Science, 5*, 753–761.

Popper, K. (1972). *Objective knowledge: An evolutionary approach*. Cambridge: Oxford University Press.

Popper, K. R., & Eccles, J. C. (1977). *The self and its brain.* Berlin: Springer-Verlag.
Pos, A. E., Greenberg, L. S., & Warwar, S. H. (2009). Testing a model of change in the experiential treatment of depression. *Journal of Consulting and Clinical Psychology, 77*(6), 1055–1066.
Posner, M. I. (1980). Orienting of Attention. *Quarterly Journal of Experimental Psychology, 32,* 3–25.
Posner, M. I. (1993). *Foundations of cognitive science.* Cambridge, MA: MIT Press.
Posner, M. I., & Boies, S. J. (1971). Components of attention. *Psychological Review, 78*(5), 391–408.
Posner, M. I., & DiGirolamo, G. J. (2000). Cognitive neuroscience: Origins and promise. *Psychological Bulletin, 126,* 873–889.
Prabhakaran, V., & Rypma, B. (2007). P-FIT and the neuroscience of intelligence: How well does P fit? *Behavioral and Brain Sciences, 30,* 166–167.
Premack, D. (2010). Why humans are unique: Three theories. *Perspectives on Psychological Science, 5,* 22–32.
Pritchard, A. (2009). *Ways of learning: Learning theories and learning styles in the classroom.* Abingdon, UK: Routledge.
Pronin, E., & Kugler, M. B. (2007). Valuing thoughts, ignoring behavior: The introspection illusion as a source of the bias blind spot. *Journal of Experimental Social Psychology, 43,* 565–578.
Rabbitt, P. (1997). Introduction: Methodologies and models in the study of executive function. In P. Rabbitt (Ed.), *Methodology of frontal and executive function* (pp. 1–38). Hove: Psychology Press.
Radhakrishnan, S. (1948). (Ed. & Trans.). *The Bhagavadgita.* London: George Allen and Unwin. (Paperback edition 1989).
Radhakrishnan, S. (1971) *The Bhagabadgita.* Bombay: George Allen & Unwin.
Rajendran, G., & Peter, M. (2007). Cognitive theories of autism. *Developmental Review, 27,* 224–260.
———. (1993). *The Bhagavadgītā.* Canada: Harper Collins.
Radhakrishnan, S., & Moore, C.A. (1957). *A sourcebook in Indian philosophy.* Princeton, New Jersey: Princeton University Press.
Rajendran, G., & Mitchell, P. (2007). Cognitive theories of autism. *Developmental Review, 27,* 224–260.
Ratner, C. (1997). *Cultural psychology and qualitative methodology: Theoretical and empirical considerations.* New York: Plenum.
Raven, J. C. (1965). *The coloured progressive matrices test.* London: Lewis.
Rebok, G. W. (1989). Plans, actions, and transactions in solving everyday problems. In J. D. Sinnott (Ed.), *Everyday problem solving* (pp. 100–122). New York: Praeger.
Reyna, V. F. (2004). How people make decisions that involve risk. *Current Directions in Psychological Science, 13,* 60–66.
Reyna, V. F., Nelson, W. L., Han, P. K., & Dieckmann, N. F. (2009). How numeracy influences risk comprehension and medical decision making. *Psychological Bulletin, 135,* 943–973.
Richard, R., van der Plight, J., & de Vries, N. (1996). Anticipated regret and time perspective: Changing sexual risk-taking behavior. *Journal of Behavioral Decision Making, 9,* 185–199.
Robbins, T. W., James, M., Owen, A. M., Sahakian, B. J., Lawrence, A. D., McInnes, L., & Rabbitt, P. (1998). A study of performance on tests from the CANTAB battery sensitive to frontal lobe dysfunction in a large sample of normal volunteers: Implications for theories of executive functioning and cognitive aging. *Journal of the International Neuropsychological Society, 4*(5), 474–490.

Roberts, M. J. (2007). Introduction. In M. J. Roberts (Ed.), *Integration the mind: Domain general versus domain specific processes in higher cognition*. Hove, East Sussex: Psychology Press.
Rose, J. P., & Windschitl, P. D. (2008). How egocentrism and optimism change in response to feedback in repeated competitions. *Organizational Behavior and Human Decision Processes, 105*, 201–220.
Royall, D. R., Lauterbach, E. C., Kaufer, D., Malloy, P., Coburn, K. L., & Black, K. J. (2007). The cognitive correlates of functional status: A review from the committee on research of the American Neuropsychiatric Association. *The Journal of Neuropsychiatry and Clinical Neurosciences, 19*, 249–265.
Russell, B. (1946). *A history of western philosophy*. Great Britain: Allen & Unwin.
Sacerdoti, E.D. (1977). *A structure for plans and behavior*. Amsterdam: Elsevier.
Samantaray, S. (2005). Planning ability in business executives. MA thesis, Utkal University, India.
Samuels, R., & Stich, S. P. (2004). Rationality and psychology. In A. R. Mele & P. Rawling (Eds), *The Oxford handbook of rationality* (pp. 279–300). Oxford: Oxford University Press.
Sanfey, A. G. (2007). Decision neuroscience. *Current Directions in Psychological Science, 16*, 151–155.
Saunders, B., Wilkinson, C., & Phillips, M. (1995). The impact of a brief motivational intervention with opiate users attending a methadone programme. *Addiction, 90*, 415–424.
Savage, L. J. (1954). *The foundations of statistics*. New York: Wiley.
Savitsky, K., van Boven, L., Epley, N., & Wight, W. M. (2005). The unpacking effect in allocations of responsibility for group tasks. *Journal of Experimental Social Psychology, 41*, 447–457.
Schaller, M., Asp, C. H., Roseil, M. C., & Heim, S. J. (1996). Training in statistical reasoning inhibits the formation of erroneous group stereotypes. *Personality and Social Psychology Bulletin, 22*, 829–844.
Scholnick, E. K., & Friedman, S. L. (1987). The planning construct in the psychological literature. In S. L. Friedman, E. K. Scholnick, & R. R. Cocking (Eds), *Blueprints for thinking: The role of planning in cognitive development* (pp. 273–302). Cambridge, Massachusetts: Cambridge University Press.
Schommer, M. (1998). The influence of age and education on epistemological beliefs. *British Journal of Educational Psychology, 68*, 551–562.
Schunk, D. H., & Cox, P. D. (1986). Strategy training and attributional feedback with learning disabled students. *Journal of Educational Psychology, 78*, 201–209.
Schwartz, L. M., Woloshin, S., Black, W. C., & Welch, H. G. (1997). The role of numeracy in understanding the benefit of screening mammography. *Annals of Internal Medicine, 127*, 966–972.
Shafir, E., & LeBoeuf, R. A. (2002). Rationality. *Annual Review of Psychology, 53*, 491–517.
Shallice, T. (1988). *From neuropsychology to mental structure*. Cambridge: Cambridge University Press.
Shanteau, J., Grier, M., Johnson, J., & Berner, E. (1991). Teaching decision-making skills to student nurses. In J. Baron & R. V. Brown (Eds), *Teaching decision making to adolescents*. Hillsdale, New Jersey: Lawrence Erlbaum.
Shiho, T. O., Shinji, O., & Hisao, M. (2009). EEG coherence pattern during simultaneous and successive processing tasks. *International Journal of Psychophysiology, 72*, 89–96.
Shimamura, P. (2010). Hierarchical relational binding in the medial temporal lobe: The strong get stronger. *Hippocampus, 20*, 1206–1216.

Siegel, H. (1988). *Educating reason.* New York: Routledge.
Siegel, H. (1997). *Rationality redeemed? Further dialogues on an educational ideal.* New York: Routledge.
Siegler, R. S. (1988). Strategy choice procedures and the development of multiplication skill. *Journal of Experimental Psychology: General, 117,* 258–275.
Siegler, R. S., & Booth, J. L. (2004). Development of numerical estimation in young children. *Child Development, 75,* 428–444.
Siegler, R. S., & Opfer, J. (2003). The development of numerical estimation: Evidence for multiple representations of numerical quantity. *Psychological Science, 14,* 237–243.
Simon, H. (1967). Motivational and emotional controls of cognition. *Psychological Review, 74,* 29–39.
———. (1976). *Administrative behavior* (3rd ed.). New York: Free Press.
Simon, H. A. (1971). "Designing Organizations for an Information-Rich World." In M. Greenberger (Ed.), *Computers, communication, and the public interest* (pp. 40–41). Baltimore, Maryland: The Johns Hopkins Press.
———. (1978). *Rational decision-making in business organizations.* Nobel Prize in Economics documents 1978-1, Nobel Prize Committee.
———. (1987). Making management decisions: The role of intuition and emotion. *The Academy of Management Executive, 1,* 57–64.
———. (1992). Scientific discovery as problem solving. *International Studies in the Philosophy of Science, 6,* 3–14.
Simonton, D. K. (2009). Varieties of (scientific) creativity: A hierarchical model of domain-specific disposition, development, and achievement. *Perspectives on Psychological Sciences, 12,* 441–452.
Slugoski, B. R., Shields, H. A., & Dawson, K. A. (1993). Relation of conditional reasoning to heuristic processing. *Personality and Social Psychology Bulletin, 19,* 158–166.
Smith, E., & Kosslyn, S. M. (2007). *Cognitive psychology.* Upper saddle river, New Jersey: Pearson.
Sokolov, E. N. (1963). Higher nervous functions: The orienting reflex. *Annual Review of Physiology, 25,* 545–580.
Sperry, R. (1964). The great cerebral commissure. *Scientific American, 42,* 42–52.
Sperry, R. W. (1993). The impact and promise of the cognitive revolution. *American Psychologist, 48,* 878–885.
Stallard, M. J., & Worthington, D. L. (1998). Reducing the hindsight bias utilizing attorney closing arguments. *Law and Human Behavior, 22*(6), 671–683.
Stanovich, K. (1988). Explaining the differences between the dyslexic and the garden-variety poor-reader: The phonological-core variable-difference model. *Journal of Learning Disabilities, 21,* 590–604.
Stanovich, K. E. (1999). *Who is rational? Studies of individual differences in reasoning.* Mahwah, NJ: Erlbaum.
———. (2004). *The robot's rebellion: Finding meaning in the age of Darwin.* Chicago, Illinois: University of Chicago Press.
———. (2008). Higher-order preferences and the master rationality motive. *Thinking & Reasoning, 14,* 111–127.
———. (2009). *What IQ tests miss: The cognitive science of rational and irrational thinking.* New Haven, Connecticut: Yale University Press.
———. (2010a). Decision making and rationality in the modern world. New York: Oxford University Press.
———. (2010b). *How to think straight about psychology* (9th ed.). Boston, Massachusetts: Allyn & Bacon.

Stanovich, K. E., Toplak, M. E., & West, R. F. (2008). The development of rational thought: A taxonomy of heuristics and biases. *Advances in Child Development and Behavior, 36,* 251–285.

Stanovich, K. E., & West, R. F. (1998). Individual differences in rational thought. *Journal of Experimental Psychology: General, 127,* 161–188.

———. (2008). On the relative independence of thinking biases and cognitive ability. *Journal of Personality and Social Psychology, 94,* 672–695.

Stanovich, K. E., West, R. F., & Toplak, M. E. (2010). Intelligence and rationality. In R. Strenberg & S. B.Kaufman (Eds), *Cambridge handbook of intelligence* (3rd ed., pp. 726-784). Hoboken, New Jersey: Wiley

Sternberg, R. J. (2001). Why schools should teach for wisdom: The balance theory of wisdom in educational settings. *Educational Psychologist, 36,* 227–245.

———. (2002). Smart people are not stupid, but they sure can be foolish: The imbalance theory of foolishness. In R. J. Sternberg (Ed.), *Why smart people can be so stupid* (pp. 232–242). New Haven, Connecticut: Yale University Press.

———. (2003). *Wisdom, intelligence, and creativity synthesized.* Cambridge: Cambridge University Press.

Sternberg, R. J. (Ed.). (2005). *The psychology of hate.* Washington, DC: American Psychological Association.

Sternberg, R. J., & Jordan, J. (Eds). (2005). *A handbook of wisdom: Psychological perspectives.* New York: Cambridge University Press.

Stuss, D., & Alexander, M. (2000). Executive functions and the frontal lobes: A conceptual view. *Psychological Research, 63,* 289–298.

Stuss, D. T., & Alexander, M. P. (2007). Is there a dysexecutive syndrome? *Philosophical Transactions of the Royal Society B: Biological Sciences, 362,* 901–915.

Stuss, D.T., & Benson, D.F. (1984). Neuropsychological studies of frontal lobes. *Psychological Bulletin, 95,* 3–28.

———. (1986). *The frontal lobes.* New York: Raven Press.

———. (1987). The frontal lobes and control of cognition and memory. In E. Perecman (Ed.), *Frontal lobes revisited* (pp.141–158). New York: IRBN Press.

———. (1990). The frontal lobes and language. In E. Goldberg (Ed.), *Contemporary psychology and the legacy of Luria.* Hillsdale, New Jersey: Lawrence Erlbaum Associates.

Sylvester, C.-Y. C., Wager, T. D., Lacey, S. C., Hernandez, L., Nichols, T. E., Smith, E. E., & Jonides, J. (2003). Switching attention and resolving interference: fMRI measures of executive functions. *Neuropsychologia, 41,* 357–370.

Tanji, J., & Hoshi, E. (2008). Role of the lateral prefrontal cortex in executive behavioral control. *Physiological Review, 88,* 37–57.

Teuber, H.- L. (2009). The riddle of frontal lobe function in man. *Neuropsychological Review,19,* 25–46.

Thaler, R. H., & Sunstein, C. R. (2008). *Nudge: Improving decisions about health, wealth, and happiness.* New Haven, Connecticut: Yale University Press.

Thorpe, W. H. (1956). *Learning and instinct in animals.* Cambridge, Massachusetts: Harvard University Press.

Tinbergen, N. (1951). *The study of instinct.* Oxford. Oxford University Press.

Toplak, M. E., Liu, E., MacPherson, R., Toneatto, T., & Stanovich, K. E. (2007). The reasoning skills and thinking dispositions of problem gamblers: A dual-process taxonomy. *Journal of Behavioral Decision Making, 20*(2), 103–124.

Toplak, M. E., & Stanovich, K. E. (2002). The domain specificity and generality of disjunctive reasoning: Searching for a generalizable critical thinking skill. *Journal of Educational Psychology, 94,* 197–209.

Toplak, M. E., & Stanovich, K. E. (2003). Associations between myside bias on an informal reasoning task and amount of post-secondary education. *Applied Cognitive Psychology, 17*, 851–860.

Toplak, M. E., West, R. F., & Stanovich, K. E. (2012). Education for rational thought. In M. J. Lawson & J. R. Kirby (Eds), *Enhancing the quality of learning*. New York: Cambridge University Press.

Tranel, D., Anderson, S. W., & Benton, A. (1994). Development of the concept of "executive functioning" and its relation to the frontal lobes. In F. Boller, H. Spinnler, & J. A. Handler (Eds), *Handbook of neuropsychology* (pp. 125–148). Amsterdam: Elsevier.

Treiman, R. (1985). Onsets and rimes as units of spoken syllables: Evidence from children. *Journal of Experimental Child Psychology, 39*, 161–181.

Tupper, David E. (1999). Introduction: Neuropsychological assessment Après Luria *Neuropsychology Review, 9*, 57–61.

Tversky, A., & Kahneman, D. (1974). Judgment under uncertainty: Heuristics and biases. *Science, 185*, 1124–1131.

———. (1981). The framing of decisions and the psychology of choice. *Science, 211*, 453–458.

———. (1983). Extensional versus intuitive reasoning: The conjunction fallacy in probability judgment. *Psychological Review, 90*, 293–315.

———. (1986). Rational choice and the framing of decisions. *Journal of Business, 59*, 251–278.

UCSF Memory & Aging Centre. (2005). University of California, San Francisco. Retrieved from http://memory.ucsf.edu/ (accessed July 30, 2014).

Varnhagen, C. K. (1995). Children's spelling strategies. In V.W. Berninger (Ed.), *The varieties of orthographic knowledge II: Relationships to phonology, reading, and writing* (pp. 251–290). Boston, Massachusetts: Kluwer Academic Publishers.

Varnhagen, C. K., & Das, J. P. (1986). Neuropsychological functioning and cognitive processing. In J. E. Obzrut & G. W. Hynd (Eds), *Child neuropsychology, Vol. 1: Theory and research* (pp. 117–140). New York: Academic Press.

von Neumann, J., & Morgenstern, O. (1944). *The theory of games and economic behavior*. Princeton, New Jersey: Princeton University Press.

Vreeland, N. (ed.) (2002). The Dalai Lama in *An open heart*. Boston, Massachusetts: Little Brown and Company.

Vygotsky, L. (1978). *Mind in society: The development of higher psychological processes*. Cambridge, Massachusetts: Harvard University Press.

Vygotsky, L. S. (1962). *Thought and language*. Cambridge, Massachusetts: MIT Press.

———. (1986). *Thought and language*. Cambridge, Massachusetts: MIT Press.

Wade, C., & Tavris, C. (2008). *Psychology* (9th ed.). Upper Saddle River, New Jersey: Pearson Education.

Was, C. A. (2007). Further evidence that not all executive functions are equal. *Advances in Cognitive Psycholgy, 3*, 399–407.

Wegner, D. M. (2004). Précis of the illusion of conscious will. *Behavioral and Brain Sciences, 27*, 649–692.

Weiner, Jeff. *Managing compassionately*. Retrieved from http://www.linkedin.com/today/post/article/20121015034012-22330283-managing-compassionately (accessed July 30, 2014).

Wertsch, J. V. (1985). *Vygotsky and the socialfonnation of mind*. Cambridge, Massachusetts: Harvard University Press.

West, R. F., Toplak, M. E., & Stanovich, K. E. (2008). Heuristics and biases as measures of critical thinking: Associations with cognitive ability and thinking dispositions. *Journal of Educational Psychology, 100*, 930–941.

Wiebe, S. A., Sheffield, T., Nelson, J. M., Clark, C. A. C., Chevalier, N., & Kimberly, A.E. (2011). The structure of executive function in 3-year-old children. *Journal of Experimental Child Psychology, 108*(3), 436–452.

Wilder, L., Draper, T. W., & Donnelly, C. P. (1984). Overt and covert verbalization in normal and learning disabled children's problem solving. *Perceptual and Motor Skills, 58*(3), 976–978.

Wiley, J. (2005). A fair and balanced look at the news: What affects memory for controversial arguments? *Journal of Memory and Language, 53*, 95–109.

Willingham, D. T. (2007). Critical thinking: Why is it so hard to teach? *American Educator*, Summer 8–19.

Woollard, J., Beilin, L., Lord, T., Puddey, I., MacAdam, D., & Rouse, I. (1995). A controlled trial of nurse counseling on lifestyle changes for hypertensives treated in general practice: Preliminary results. *Clinical and Experimental Pharmacology and Physiology, 23*, 466–468.

Wu, G., Zhang, J., & Gonzalez, R. (2004). Decision under risk. In D. J. Koehler & N. Harvey (Eds), *Blackwell handbook of judgment and decision making* (pp. 399–423). Malden, Massachusetts: Blackwell Publishing.

Zechmeister, E. B., Rusch, K. M., & Markell, K. A. (1986). Training college-students to assess accurately what they know and don't know. *Human Learning, 5*(1), 3–19.

Zelazo, P. D., Carter, A., Reznick, J. S., & Frye, D. (1997). Early development of executive function: A problem-solving framework. *Review of General Psychology, 1*, 198–226.

Zelniker, T., Cochavi, D., & Yered, J. (1974). The relationship between speed of performance and conceptual style: The effect of imposed modification of response latency. *Child Development, 45*, 779–784.

Zelniker, T., Jeffrey, W. E., Ault, R., & Parsons, J. (1972). Analysis and modification of search strategies of impulsive and reflective children on the Matching Familiar Figures Test. *Child Development, 43*, 321–335.

Ziegler, J. C., & Goswami, U. C. (2005). Reading acquisition, developmental dyslexia and skilled reading across languages: A psycholinguistic grain size theory. *Psychological Bulletin, 131*, 3–29.

Zikmund-Fisher, B. J., Ubel, P. A., Smith, D. M., Derry, H. A., McClure, J. B., Stark, A., Pitsch, R. K., & Fagerlin, A. (2008). Communicating side effect risks in a tamoxifen prophylaxis decision aid: The debiasing influence of pictographs. *Patient Education and Counseling, 73*, 209–214.

Index

ADHD. *See* attention deficit/hyperactivity disorder
Agor, W., 164
analytical thinking, 196
Anderson, R. P., 76
Anderson, S. W., 96
Aron, A. R., 57
Ashman, A. F., 184, 216, 221
assessments
  CAS tests of planning and attention, 97–99
  Crack-the-Code test, 101–105
  executive function, 100–101
  executive function-exploratory analyses, 111–114
  history of constructs and tests, 96–97
  inhibition, 99
  shifting, 99
  working memory, 99, 105–111
attention, 92
attention deficit, 77–78
attention deficit/hyperactivity disorder
  attention, 75–79
  and autism, 89–90
  and inhibition, 86–89
  planning, 75–79
Attention Scale, 17
autism
  core components of, 81–83
  planning deficiency in, 81
Autism (Frith), 81
awareness, 92

Baddeley, A., 51
Banich, M. T., 63
Barkley, R., 75
Barnard, C., 163
BEAF. *See* Brief Evaluation of Activity Form
Begley, S., 294

Benson, D.F., 15, 19, 37, 274, 275, 288, 289
Benton, A., 96
Berman, M. G., 91
Berninger, V. W., 212
Best, J. R., 96
Biggs, J., 212, 213, 215
Bisanz, J., 247
Blackmore, S., 201
Blueprints for Thinking (Friedman), 28
Boies, S. J., 71
Booth, J. L., 245
brain and emotion, 198–199
brain maps, 64–66
Braver, T. S., 199
Brief Evaluation of Activity Form, 184
Broadbent, D. E., 178
Broadbent, M. H., 178

Campbell, J.I.D., 236
Carlson, E., 227
Carlson, J., 230
Carroll, J.B., 12
Carter, A., 44
CAS Interpretive Handbook (Naglieri and Das), 97
Channon, S., 116
Chan, R. C. K., 97
Cherniss, C., 276, 278
Cognition Enhancement Training, 252
  behavior, regulation of, 259–261
  cognitive enhancement in, 263
  description of, 253–255
  efficacy of, 262–263
  modules, 261–262, 268–270
cognitive processes, 4
cognitive training, manual for, 250
Colom, R., 52
conscious will, 202–204
Cormier, P., 228, 234

Cowan, N., 51, 73, 197
Crack-the-Code
 administration manual for, 146–159
 history and structure of, 101–103
 management executives, job performance of, 183–184
 usefulness of, 106–107
 working memory, 105–111
Crone, E.A., 59, 61
CTC. *See* Crack-the-Code

Damasio, A., 199
Dash, U. N., 230
Das–Naglieri cognitive assessment system, 5, 17
Davidson, R. J., 294
De Bono, E., 175
decision making
 ability, 277
 entrepreneurial decision making, 204–207
 executive intelligence, 277
 managerial decision making, 165–166
 and measures of planning, 182–183
 and planning, 286–289
 planning, failure of logic in, 173–175
deconstructing executive functions. *See* executive functions
Dehaene, 235
Denckla, M., 45
Diamond, A., 115
directive and selective attention, 8
Doerner, Dietrich, 165, 173
Donald, M., 211
Duncan, J., 61

Eccles, J. C., 20, 32
EFs. *See* executive functions
emotion, 195–196
 brain, 198–199
 impact on intelligence, 200–202
 planning and, 204–207
emotional intelligence
 improvement, 278–284
 training for enhancement, 271
Engle, R. W., 52
Ericsson, K. A., 224, 233
Evans, J., 169

executive attention
 of ADHD, 75–77
 attention-planning disconnection, 74–75
 measuring, 73
 orienting response, 72
 working memory, 73–75
The Executive Brain: Frontal Lobes and the Civilized Mind (Goldberg), 44
executive functions (EFs), 4
 brain for intelligence, 60–61
 brain functions for, 55–60
 deconstruction, 46–48
 definitions of, 44
 domain-general ability, 45
 and fluid intelligence, 49–50
 inhibition, 48–49
 intelligence, 45–46
 location, brain for intelligence, 60–63
 math learning, 248–249
 monitoring, 48–49
 neural correlates of executive, 63–64
 nonexecutive functions, 48–49
 planning and, 3–4, 43, 45–46, 48–49, 50–52
 shifting, 48–49
 working memory, 50–52
executive intelligence, 277
 defined, 272–275
 domain-general or domain-specific, 271–272
Executive Intelligence-What All Great Leaders Have (Menkes), 44

fetal alcohol spectrum disorder, 79–83
fetal alcohol syndrome, 78–79
Feuerstein, R., 227
Fitzgerald, P., 178
Frankish, K., 169
Friedman, N. P., 58
Frith, C., 81
frontal lobe functions, 289
Frye, D., 44
functional systems, 14

Gailliot, M. T., 91
Galanter, E. H., 181
Geary, D. C., 35, 239

general intelligence, 11
Goldberg, E., 44, 45, 115
Goleman, D., 275, 276, 278
Gray, J. R., 199
Grigorenko, E. L., 227
Guthke, 226

Haidt, J., 281, 293
Hayes, J. R., 212, 215
Hayes-Roth, B., 24, 26, 29
Hayes-Roth, F., 24, 26, 29
Hayward, D., 262
Haywood, H. C., 227
Hebb, D. O., 20
Heemsbergen, D. B., 96
Heterogeneity, 89–90
Hill, E., 82
Hoshi, E., 56
Huey, E. D., 57
hyperactive children, 76–77
hyperactivity, 93
hypoactive children, 76–77

Illusion of Conscious Will (Wegner), 202
impulsivity, 94–95
inattention, 93
intelligence, 11–12
International Congress in Psychology, 10
intuition, 287–289, 289–294
Intuition at Work (Klein), 288
IQ
  definition of, 4
  tests, 16

Janis, I. L., 179
Jarman R. F., 165, 226, 248
Jensen, A. R., 231

Kahneman, D., 288, 289
Kane, M. J., 52
Kaplan, R., 91
Kaplan, S., 91
Kar, B. C., 230
Kirby, J. R., 71, 165, 226
Klein, G., 287, 288
Klemp, G. D., 179, 180
Kolb, B., 15
Kunda, Z., 172

Leavitt, H. J., 164
Leontjev, A. N., 214
Lezak, M. D., 96
Lidz, C. S., 16
Logical program of interconnected operations, 19
Luria, A. R., 5, 8, 10, 13, 14, 15, 16, 19, 43, 72, 75, 76, 165, 211, 222, 224, 233, 253, 285
Luria's approach, 13–16

Mabbott, D. J., 247
Mahapatra, S., 258
managerial behavior
  and cognitive competence, 181–194
  crack the code and strategic essay composition, 184–185
  decision making, 164–165, 182–183
  decision making, failure of logic in, 173–175
  dissociation, 177–178
  intelligence, 170–172
  job performance of, 183–184
  managers' problems, 176–177
  motivation for reasoning, 172–173
  planning, failure of logic in, 173–175
  planning, measures of, 182–183
  quality of essay composition, 189–192
  rational decisions, 170–172
  reasoning, 168–170
  roles and activities of, 163–164
  schematic diagram, 193
  strategic essay writing, 185–189
math competence, 236–238
  EF, 239–240
  math proficiency model, 238
  modeling cognition in, 239–240
math disability, 244
The Mathematical Brain (Butterworth), 235
mathematical learning difficulties, 247–248
math foundations, 240
math learning
  conceptualization, 241–243
  foundational concepts, 240–241
  helping children, 235–236
  magnitude, 241–243
  math abilities, 241

planning facilitation, 245–247
procedure, 241–243
value, 241–243
Mathur, P., 185
McClelland, D. C., 179, 180
McCutchen, D., 211, 216
Menkes, J., 44, 272, 273, 281
mental retardation, 4
Mercier, H., 170
metacognitive process, 224
Miller, G. A., 50, 181
Miller, P. H., 96
mindfulness, 92
Mintzberg, H., 164, 273
Mishra, R. K., 217
Miyake, A., 46, 47, 58, 79, 86, 108, 285
MLD. *See* mathematical learning difficulties
Mukherjee, K., 169

Naglieri, J. A., 36, 37, 38, 77, 71, 96
The Neuropsychological Analysis of Problem Solving (Luria and Tsetkova), 19
Newell, A., 19, 25
number line helps estimation, 244
The Number Sense (Dehaene), 235
number strooptest, 122–147

Odishaw, J. D., 79
Olson, D. R., 184
oral narratives
  cognitive planning processes, 219–221
  role of planning in, 216–219
O'Reilly, R. C., 67
organ of freedom, 10
The Origins of the Modern Mind (Donald), 211
Ozolins, D. A., 76
Ozonoff, S., 89

Parrila, R., 103, 104, 258
PASS Remedial Program, 252
  cognitive enhancement in, 263, 264–268
  description of, 253–255
  evidence for, 258–259
  structure of, 255–258
PASS theory. *See* Planning–Attention–Simultaneous–Successive theory
pattern recognition, 129

Pavlov, I. P., 71, 86
Pennington, B. F., 89
Peter, M., 85
planned composition
  for children, 119–120
  instructions for, 119
  strategic essay writing, 159–160
planning
  of ADHD, 75–79
  attention-planning disconnection, 74–75
  autism, 81–83
  children with attention deficit, 77–78
  and composition, 221–222
  decision making and, 286–289
  and emotion, 204–207
  and executive functions, 3–4
  fetal alcohol spectrum disorder, 79–81
  in fetal alcohol syndrome, 78–79
  math learning, 248–249
  measuring, 73
  working memory, 73–75
  and written narratives, 222–223
Planning–Attention–Simultaneous–Successive theory
  core components of, 5–8
  executive functions, 86–90
  to intelligence, 6, 11–13
  Luria's approach, 13–16
  review by Luria, 8–11
  synopsis of, 4–5
planning models
  blueprints for thinking, 28–30
  opportunistic model, 26–28
  and problems, 30–35
  problem solving, 35–40
  problem solving heuristic, 25–26
  and structure of behavior, 20–25
Planning Scale, 17
Planning test
  cognitive decision-making, 116–118
  for executives, 116–118
Plans and Structure of Behavior (Miller), 50
Popper, K. R., 20, 32
Posner, M. I., 71, 72
prefrontal cortex (PFC), 66–68
Premack, D., 19, 285
PREP. *See* PASS Remedial Program
Pribram, K. H., 181

Rabbitt, P., 48, 71
Raichle, M. E., 199
Rajendran, G., 85
Raven, J. C., 228
Reading Difficulties and Dyslexia: An Interpretation for Teachers (Das), 252
reason and emotion, 195–196
reasoning, 289–294
Rebok, G. W., 30
reflective discussion, 224
Reznick, J. S., 44

Samantaray, S., 189
Sanfey, A. G., 169
The Self and Its Brain (Popper and Eccles), 32
self-awareness and consciousness, 289
self-knowledge, 294–296
Shaw, J. C., 19
Siegler, R. S., 244, 245
Simon, H., 165
Simon, H. A., 19, 174, 181, 182, 195, 196, 204, 207, 224, 233, 287, 288, 290
Simultaneous Scale, 17–18
Sokolov, E. N., 71
somatic-marker hypothesis, 199
Sperber, D., 170
Stack-Cutler, H., 258
Stanovich, K. E., 171
Sternberg, R. J., 227
Stuss, D.T., 15, 19, 37, 274, 275, 288, 289
Successive Scale, 18
synthetic thinking, 196

Tanji, J., 56, 60
Tariki: Embracing Despair, Discovering Peace (Itsuki, 2001), 292
test. *See* assessments
Toplak, M. E., 171
Tranel, D., 96
Tsvetkova, L.S., 285
Tzuriel, D., 227

Varnhagen, C. K., 216
verbalization
  boosts planning, 224–225
  improves planning, 230–233
  on increasing test performance, 227–229
  poor planners, 225–227
  Raven matrices, 229–230
Vygotsky, L., 16, 177, 178, 211, 212, 226, 233, 253, 254, 264

Wegner, D. M., 202, 203, 204
West, R. F., 171
Whishaw, I. Q., 15
working brain, 293–294
working memory (WM), 197–198
  enhancement, problem of, 249
  math learning, 248–249
writing
  compositions and oral narratives, 211–216
  strategic essay writing, 159–160, 188–189

Zelazo, P. D., 44

About the Authors

J.P. Das is an Indo-Canadian psychologist and an internationally recognized expert in Intelligence. Among his major contributions to psychology is the PASS (Planning, Attention, Simultaneous, and Successive) theory of intelligence. He is currently engaged in expanding planning to include executive functions. What might be the implications of these higher mental activities for education as well as management behavior is the topic of this book.

Professor Das is an Emeritus Director of the Centre on Developmental & Learning Disabilities (named after him) at the University of Alberta, Edmonton, Canada, and Emeritus Professor in Educational Psychology. He has authored and co-authored over a dozen of books and contributed more than 300 research papers to international journals and edited volumes. His earlier published titles with SAGE include *Cognitive Planning: The Psychological Basis of Intelligent Behaviour* (1996, co-authored with Binod C. Kar and Rauno K. Parrila); *The Working Mind* (1998); *Reading Difficulties and Dyslexia: An Interpretation for Teachers* (2009); and *Consciousness Quest: East Meets West* (2014).

Sasi B. Misra is Institute Professor, Entrepreneurship Development Institute of India (EDI), Gandhinagar since 2004. At EDI, he is the Editor of *The Journal of Entrepreneurship*; Chair, Centre for Research in Entrepreneurship Education and Development (CREED).

He (with Kanungo) has advanced the *Theory of Human Resourcefulness* (1992) and has published with Sherry Chand *Institution Building: An International Perspective on Management Education* (1999). He has over 50 research papers in academic and professional journals of repute.